WILLIAM AND DOROTHY
WORDSWORTH

WILLIAM AND DOROTHY WORDSWORTH

'ALL IN EACH OTHER'

LUCY NEWLYN

OXFORD

UNIVERSITY PRESS

OXFORD
UNIVERSITY PRESS

Great Clarendon Street, Oxford, OX2 6DP,
United Kingdom

Oxford University Press is a department of the University of Oxford.
It furthers the University's objective of excellence in research, scholarship,
and education by publishing worldwide. Oxford is a registered trade mark of
Oxford University Press in the UK and in certain other countries

First Edition published in 2013

Impression: 1

Published in the United States of America by Oxford University Press
198 Madison Avenue, New York, NY 10016, United States of America

British Library Cataloguing in Publication Data
Data available

ISBN 978–0–19–969639–0

Printed in Great Britain by
CPI Group (UK) Ltd, Croydon, CR0 4YY

For Pamela Woof

'Witness thou
The dear companion of my lonely walk,
My hope, my joy, my sister, and my friend,
Or something dearer still, if reason knows
A dearer thought, or in the heart of love
There be a dearer name...'

Contents

Acknowledgements

This book has been gestating for many years. I was encouraged to write it by Andrew McNeillie when he was editor at Oxford University Press. His successor, Jacqueline Baker, has been tremendously supportive—reading the book at several stages in its evolution, and giving careful, detailed feedback. A number of colleagues commented helpfully on early plans: Sharon Achinstein, John Barnard, Clare Hutton, Basil Kouvaritakis, Sally Mapstone, Seamus Perry, Steve Roberts, Fiona Stafford, Nicola Trott, Neil Vickers, and Wes Williams. I am very grateful to Stephen Gill, David Fairer, and Tim Fulford, all of whom read draft proposals and/or chapters; to the readers for the Press who made several excellent suggestions; and to Sandie Byrne, who gave up valuable time to comment on the final draft. I learnt a great deal about methods and approaches to biography from helping Hermione Lee and Roy Foster to teach an undergraduate course on Life-Writing in the English Faculty at Oxford. I am also grateful to the graduate students who have attended my course on Romantic Autobiography over the years: their interest and engagement have been perpetually stimulating.

Jeff Cowton, Curator of the Wordsworth Collection at Grasmere, has gone out of his way to help with queries; and with his inimitable patience and enthusiasm has helped me to find appropriate illustrations. Iain Bain very kindly went to the trouble of ensuring that reproductions of Bewick's woodcuts would be of the highest quality: I am very grateful to him for his guidance, as well as to Chris Verraes who undertook the scanning. Tom Clucas has been a model research assistant, photocopying vast amounts of material, patiently checking my quotations and references, and proof-reading the book in its final stages. Many thanks, also, to the team at OUP who have taken care of editing, proof-reading, marketing, and publicity. They have all been great to work with.

I am grateful to the Principal and Fellows of St Edmund Hall for a period of sabbatical leave, which enabled me to complete a first draft. Part of the book grew out of a plenary lecture delivered at the Conference on

Creativity in Leeds University in 2008. I thank the editors of *Journal for Eighteenth-Century Studies* and of *Essays in Criticism* for permission to reprint portions of arguments that have appeared in a slightly different form elsewhere. My thanks go to the Trustees of the Wordsworth Trust, Grasmere, for permission to reproduce paintings and photographs.

A more personal thank you to Martin and Emma, who have patiently put up with the making of this book since I began to write it in 2009. Last but not least, I would like to thank Pamela Woof, whose knowledge of Dorothy Wordsworth's writings is second to none. My typescript was submitted to OUP before reading her remarkable book *Dorothy Wordsworth: Wonders of the Everyday*, written to accompany the Wordsworth Trust's exhibition of March 2013–January 2014. Nonetheless, her scholarship has been an inspiration. I dedicate my book to Pamela, in friendship and with gratitude for all that she has taught me over the years in her writing and conversation.

Preface

'I have at all times a deep sympathy with those who know what fraternal affection is. It has been the building up of my being, the light of my path.'[1]

*

Separated from William and Dorothy Wordsworth in December 1798—the year of the *Lyrical Ballads*—Coleridge wrote to his friends, 'You have all in each other, but I am lonely, and want you.'[2] It was a revealing acknowledgement of the deep, almost exclusive intimacy that had by then developed between the siblings. Theirs was 'a strange love, profound, almost dumb,' wrote Virginia Woolf, 'as if brother and sister had grown together and shared not the speech but the mood, so that they hardly knew which felt, which spoke, which saw.'[3] A suspicion of something illicit in the Wordsworths' relationship began to circulate in their lifetime, and has had a habit of resurfacing.[4] In this book, however, I am interested in the siblings' cohabitation as evidence of their intense *emotional and spiritual need*, which arose out of circumstances unique to their family history.

Born in Cumberland, and parted when Dorothy was six years old by the death of their mother, the Wordsworths grew up separately—not even meeting when their father died, leaving them destitute. They were briefly reunited as adolescents, but saw each other only intermittently in the 1790s. During this time, William attended university, travelled abroad in Europe, became involved in radical politics, and fathered an illegitimate child in post-revolutionary France. He was prevented by complex circumstances from living with his new family, and turned to Dorothy for consolation and companionship. He and his sister eventually found a way to be together permanently. Preoccupied with repairing the damage caused by the trauma of early separation, their settlement in Westmorland was 'a choice of the whole heart'.[5] It helped them to recover memories associated with the lost home of their childhood, and to accumulate a store of shared associations which bonded them jointly to their local environment. In due course, their household adjusted to include William's wife Mary, later accommodating the five Wordsworth children whom Dorothy helped to raise. Although they moved several times, the Wordsworth siblings continued to live in the close vicinity of Town End, which had come to symbolize their 'home | Within a home'.[6] The long collaborative life of writing they enjoyed in Westmorland enabled them to repay their shared debt of gratitude to the Lake District for providing them with a permanent dwelling. Several tragedies beset them, but their collaborative efforts to rebuild their scattered family's regional identity proved successful. Walking, talking, remembering, and grieving were as important to their relationship as writing; and at every stage of their adult lives they drew nourishment from their immediate surroundings.

The Wordsworths' responses to each other, their local community, and the Lake District have proved of outstanding importance, shaping the observations and imaginings of generations of readers, writers, and nature-lovers. Among the thousands of people who make the pilgrimage to Dove Cottage each year, many stop to buy a copy of Dorothy's *Grasmere and Alfoxden Journals* alongside an edition of her brother's poems. Pamela Woof's edition of these two famous journals pays scrupulous attention in editorial notes to the circumstances and chronology of composition, and has made a signal contribution to our understanding of the Wordsworths' shared life. In addition, her book *Dorothy Wordsworth, Writer*, her Wordsworth Trust booklets, and a sequence of scholarly articles have deepened our understanding of Dorothy's compositional processes. However, until now there has been no comprehensive account of William's literary partnership with his 'beloved Sister', which spanned nearly fifty years—from their first reunion in 1787 until her premature decline in 1835. Biographies and critical studies have been limited by their focus on one or other side of the siblings' relationship, about which some serious misconceptions still prevail. It seems bizarre, for instance, that Dorothy is often regarded as playing an undervalued or exploited role in the household (as unpaid nanny, handmaiden to poetic genius, and supplanted companion). William's numerous acknowledgements of her importance, across the entirety of their shared life, tell us that the reality was otherwise. Looking back in his sixties, he rightly recognized her as one of 'the two Beings to whom my intellect is most indebted'.[7] Dorothy was his muse, the first reader for his poetry, his co-writer, editor, and amanuensis, his most attentive critic, and his dearest friend. She shared with her brother a vision of the 'ennobling interchange'[8] between human beings and the natural world, which found expression in her journals, poems, letters and conversation.

Dorothy's talent as a writer was fully appreciated in the family circle for whom her journals and letters were intended. But the relative scarcity of scholarly editions of her work means that the range and quality of her prose are not yet fully recognized by modern readers. Only some of her writings were designed for publication, and very small amounts appeared in print while she was still alive. With the exception of the *Grasmere and Alfoxden Journals*, her work still doesn't reach a wide popular readership, although some journals are taught in university syllabi, and a selection recently appeared in the Longman Cultural Editions (2009). Among her less well known writings, the *Journal of Days spent in Hamburgh* (1798), *Recollections of a Tour Made in Scotland* (1803), *A Narrative concerning George and Sarah Green* (1808), *Journal of a Tour on the Continent* (1820), *My Second Tour in Scotland* (1822), and *A Tour on the Isle of Man* (1828) deserve to be studied closely, both in their own right and in relation to her brother's more famous works. Dorothy's letters (some written jointly with William) are available in Ernest De Selincourt's edition, and have received serious attention. Her collected poems were first published by Susan Levin in 1987. The manuscripts of her unpublished Rydal journals—in fifteen notebooks, covering the years 1824–35—are known to only a small handful of scholars.

This book, the first literary biography of the Wordsworths' creative collaboration, brings the full range of Dorothy's prose into the foreground alongside William's poetry. It uncovers detailed interminglings in their work, analysing the part these played in their prolific output as Westmorland co-writers. My primary objectives have been to establish the equality and intrinsic value of their partnership in writing; to explore the therapeutic benefits, for both siblings, of their shared regional attachment; and to investigate their distinctively symbiotic contribution to Romantic environmentalism. My approach to their life and work is designed to tease out subtleties in their unfolding relationship, and to illuminate both writers' distinctive approaches to their chosen craft. Throughout, I offer detailed readings of their poetry and prose, emphasizing *the communal nature of their creative processes*, the complexity of which calls for close attention to

biographical circumstances as well as details of composition. The book is structured chronologically, in sixteen chapters, using Dorothy's journals to focalize
the narrative in relation to the places where she and her brother lived and wrote.
Because I share the Wordsworths' concern with homesickness—and their belief
in the healing power of nature, memory, and shared creativity—my account of
their life together has a therapeutic dimension, and is intended to be of some
practical use and inspirational value to non-specialist readers.

In writing about the Lake District, I have had in mind the many people
from all over the world who walk the mountains and valleys of Cumbria,
visiting the places William and Dorothy loved. A watercolour of Grasmere
Lake (painted from its northern side, looking south towards Loughrigg)
provides an appropriate cover for my book, which is preoccupied throughout with the nurturing influence of environment. The artist, William Green,
was an Ambleside neighbour of the Wordsworths' in 1802, later moving to
Keswick where he became Coleridge's friend. In the foreground of his
painting, two men are fishing from a boat, just as William often did with his
brother John. Absorbed in their task, the companions do not stop to point
at the view, as they would if this were a picturesque print in a guidebook.
Green shared with the Wordsworths a sense of the humanness of place,
understanding this familiar region through the lives of its local inhabitants.
To the left of the men fishing are the deciduous trees in Brothers' Wood, just
beginning to turn brown in the early autumn. When these were cut down
to make way for the new high road, William and Dorothy felt dismayed and
bereft, for they were passionately interested in the life of trees and had
precious shared memories of this particular stretch of woodland. Just
discernible in the background of Green's watercolour, threading its way
horizontally across the mountainside, is a path: one of the most important
recurring motifs (and metaphors) in the Wordsworths' collaboration. This
one is Loughrigg Terrace—a favourite place of theirs for companionable or
solitary walks. Much has changed in the local landscape since they were
there, and tourism has left its indelible mark; but walkers still find on these
and other paths the 'tranquil restoration'[9] evoked so memorably in the Wordsworths' intertwined writings.

I

Homeless

'Two of a scattered brood that could not bear
To live in loneliness'[1]

*

B iographical details are crucial if we are to understand the nature of the
Wordsworths' intense mutual attachment, their lifelong preoccupation
with the idea of home, and the importance of regional identity to their creative collaboration. Born in Cumberland eighteen months apart—William
on 7 April 1770 and Dorothy on Christmas Day 1771—they were the second
and third siblings in a sequence of five. Dorothy's name, derived from the
Greek for 'Gift of God', is evidence that her parents joyfully welcomed her
arrival on the most important date in the Christian calendar. Throughout
life, the symbolic significance of her birthday and its associations would
influence how she was perceived by William. Her baptism at All Saints'
Church took place at the same time as his, even though he was older—a
bonding ritual which prefigured their later closeness.

The children's early life together was happy and settled. Their father, John Wordsworth, worked as attorney to Sir James Lowther (the future Earl of Lonsdale), a rich landowner with huge holdings of land and coal in the North of England. Notoriously ruthless in his dealings with tenants and employees, Lowther was known locally by the nicknames 'Wicked Jimmy' and later 'The Bad Earl'.[2] He figured large in the lives and fortunes of the Wordsworth family, who lived rent-free in one of his properties in Cocker-mouth, at the northern edge of the Lake District. Memories of their family home—the grandest house on the town's main street, with a garden border-ing the river Derwent—remained with the Wordsworths all their lives. In a fragment composed in 1798–9 William recalled how the sound of the river used to reach the house, its murmurs blending with the nurse's song in the room where he lay slumbering.[3] Dorothy, as late as 1806, could picture 'as vividly as I had been there the other day' the large back garden with its terrace overlooking the river, which her parents used to keep 'in its neatness'.[4] All five children slept in the nursery at the back of the house, with a view of the garden. The house is now owned by the National Trust, and is open to visitors. One of the most touching exhibits is a line of five nightgowns in descending order of size hanging on the nursery wall—a vivid evocation of the siblings' proximity in early life.

The trouble-free childhood remembered by William and Dorothy came to an end when their mother, Ann Wordsworth, died at the age of thirty on 8 March 1778, whether of pneumonia or consumption has not been estab-lished. All five children were with her at her parents' house in Penrith dur-ing the last few weeks of her life. Three months after Ann was buried in Penrith churchyard, Dorothy went to live with a maternal cousin, Elizabeth Threlkeld, 70 miles away in the West Yorkshire town of Halifax. Separated from her father and brothers at the age of six, she never once returned home during childhood—not even on Christmas Day, a deprivation she was to recall painfully many years later.[5] The boys attended school at Hawkshead, spending their holidays either at home with their father, at Penrith with their grandparents, or with their uncle Richard on the coast at Whitehaven. Five years after their mother's death, disaster struck again. On 6 October 1783, John Wordsworth—who was riding home after conducting business in Haverigg, a village on the Duddon Estuary—lost his way in the dark and spent the night without shelter on Cold Fell, exposed to wind and rain. By the time the Christmas holidays arrived he was seriously ill; and on 30 December 1783 he died—intestate, with his financial affairs in chaos—leaving his five children orphaned and destitute. A substantial sum of money (including £5,000 arrears of John Wordsworth's salary) was owing to the family from the Lowther estate, but James Lowther proved to be an unscrupulous debtor—'the greatest of Tyrants', Dorothy once called him.[6] Despite a bitter and protracted lawsuit this sum was left unpaid in his lifetime, and it was to be nearly twenty years before the Wordsworth children came into their legal inheritance. Ousted from their Cockermouth home, the contents of which were auctioned in 1784, the boys were obliged to live during the vacations with their grandparents the Cooksons in Penrith—a strict and forbidding environment, where they were unhappy. They remained under the guardianship of their uncles, Richard Wordsworth and Christopher Cookson, until such time as they completed their education and began to earn a living. Dorothy, it was assumed, would continue as a poor relative, dependent on whichever family members could provide her with a home until she married.

The Wordsworths' lives were deeply disrupted by the tragic circumstances which beset them, but there were compensating continuities for the boys. William and Richard were already settled at Hawkshead, a small village in Northern Lancashire where they had attended the local grammar school since 1779. ('Beloved Hawkshead' is how William later referred to the place that became a second home to him during the formative years of his boyhood.)[7] The school's distinguished reputation at this time was maintained by several remarkable teachers, William Taylor in particular making a lasting impression on his pupils. Under Taylor's tutelage, William gained a solid grounding in the Classics and mathematics (which prepared him for taking up his place at Cambridge), as well as encouragement in reading and writing poetry. His landlady Ann Tyson, a childless woman in her sixties, provided him and his brothers with comfortable lodgings, kindness, and a welcome supply of local stories. In William's memories of his Hawkshead years, she occupied a position somewhere between a foster-mother, a housekeeper, and a custodian of oral traditions. Referred to affectionately in *The Prelude* as 'my Household Dame',[8] she gave him the freedom to spend many hours before and after school exploring the surrounding countryside with his friend John Fleming. Gradually the tiny Vale of Esthwaite began to work its magic on William, almost matching Cockermouth in his affections.

Dorothy's education was considerably more interrupted. In the lodgings above the haberdasher's shop in Halifax where she was sent in 1778, she found herself the youngest member of a large mixed household. Elizabeth

Threlkeld, then in her thirties, was bringing up the five orphaned children of her sister Anne Ferguson, who had died in 1773 (followed two years later by her husband). This Dissenting family—regular attenders at Northgate End Chapel—provided the security and love Dorothy needed; and she felt nothing but gratitude for the way she had been looked after. 'The loss of a Mother can only be made up by such a friend as my Dear Aunt', she once observed warmly in a letter.[9] There were, however, further upheavals. In 1781, her home life was interrupted by three years at Dr and Mrs Wilkinson's boarding school in Hipperholme, two miles away from Halifax. No sooner had she adapted to this new environment than her father died, and family resources proved insufficient to pay her school fees. Returning to her aunt's, she attended Miss Mellin's, a non-conformist co-educational day-school, between the ages of twelve and fifteen. Then, at the age of fifteen, she was once again uprooted—this time to Penrith, to live with her elderly grandparents, whose attitudes and lifestyle she found grim and constraining. 'There is so little of tenderness in her manner', she wrote of her grandmother, 'that when I am in the house I cannot at all consider myself at home. I feel like a stranger.'[10] Reduced to the status of a poor relation, she longed for the Threlkeld household in Halifax which had become her home.

It was while at Penrith, during the summer of 1787, that the Wordsworth boys were reunited with their sister after a separation lasting nine and a half years. At their first meeting, Dorothy fondly appraised their characteristics: William's and Christopher's cleverness, John's quiet practicality, Richard's diligence. She doubtless refreshed her faded memories of Cockermouth and her equally distant recollections of her father. Although the reunion was a cause for celebration, Dorothy confessed to her friend Jane Pollard that her emotions were in turmoil. As she explained, her uncle 'Kit' (Christopher Cookson) had failed to send horses to collect the boys from school for their holidays, a hurtful oversight which caused them all considerable anxiety. (Eventually, convinced after a week of waiting that someone at Penrith must be ill, William had hired a horse for himself and ridden over.) Dorothy felt a sense of grievance at the 'ill nature' of her relatives and the 'insolence' of the Cooksons' servants, who continued to treat her and her brothers with contempt:

> Many a time have Wm, J, C and myself shed tears together, tears of the bitterest sorrow, we all of us, each day, feel more sensibly the loss we sustained when we were deprived of our parents, and each day do we receive fresh insults... of the most mortifying kind.[11]

For the first time since their mother's death in 1778, all five siblings found themselves grieving together. Their collective distress brought a heightened awareness of the financial dependency and low esteem which went with their orphaned state: 'We in the same moment lost a father, a mother, a home, we have been equally deprived of our patrimony by the cruel Hand of lordly Tyranny.'[12] Dorothy's chronology is muddled, but only if we read her words literally. As an account of the feelings that overwhelmed her in 1787, the symbolic conflation of her parents' separate deaths is strikingly authentic: she was *experiencing* the deaths as if for the first time, and therefore simultaneously. 'These afflictions', she assured Jane Pollard, 'have all contributed to unite us closer by the Bonds of affection notwithstanding we have been compelled to spend our youth far asunder.'[13]

*

Bereavement, separation, and the bitterness of unfair dispossession cast their long shadows over the lives of William and Dorothy Wordsworth, just as the loss of Helpstone did over John Clare's. It would be difficult to determine at what stage memories of their lost birthplace began to shape their understanding of home as a shared source of happiness to which they would ultimately return. But it is clear that the pattern of their unfolding relationship was influenced by intense nostalgia for the house at Cockermouth where they were born. During much of their adult lives they were looking for a place that would restore them to their lost origins and compensate them for the deaths of their parents. Carrying with them the dream of repossession, they plotted their paths through experience according to archetypal patterns, measuring the quality of each temporary home against the original, which figured in their fantasies as a lost paradise. Their creative writings—deeply intertwined with their regional affiliations—were part of the joint work of rebuilding a family, a settled home, and a communal identity.

As Freud argued in 'Mourning and Melancholia', the work of grieving involves successive revisits of places and times associated with the lost object. Each of the memories revisited in the grieving process confirms the absence of the loved object; and gradually, through a 'work of severance' that is painful, as well as frequently slow, the mourner comes to terms with the absence of the deceased, and is able to return to healthy normality.[14] This kind of work is visible in the rituals of remembering and returning which the Wordsworth siblings performed throughout their lives, together and apart.

In the gradual work of coming to terms with loss, William and Dorothy developed compensatory feelings for the places they lived in or passed through, actively nurturing a language of association that bonded them jointly to each new place. Their attachment to Windy Brow in Cumberland, to Racedown and Alfoxden in the West Country, then later to Grasmere and Rydal in Westmorland, offered a form of recompense, but William spoke for them both when he wrote, in his great ode, 'There was a time':

> . . . there's a Tree, of many one,
> A single Field which I have looked upon,
> Both of them speak of something that is gone.   (ll. 51–3)

The poet is not describing, here, an attachment that can be readily trans-ferred from one object to another. He is speaking of irreplaceable feelings, whose preciousness belongs to a *particular* time, a *particular* place. He doesn't need to give us the genus of the tree, or a place name for the field, for us to know that they were actual and local before they became symbolic.

'Neither absence nor Distance nor Time can ever break the Chain', Dorothy wrote in 1793 of her bond with her brothers.[15] Gratitude for her reunion with them—and with William in particular—was to last a lifetime, but 'I cannot help heaving many a Sigh', she confessed, 'at the Reflection that I have passed one and twenty years of my Life, and the first six years only of this Time was spent in the enjoyment of the same Pleasures that were enjoyed by my Brothers, and that I was then too young to be sensible of the Blessing'.[16] Nearly a decade later she still felt her exclusion keenly: 'I have been thereby put out of the way of many recollections in common with my Brothers of that period of life which, whatever it may be actually as it goes along, generally appears more delightful than any other when it is over.'[17] Sharing memories is a fundamental activity in any family's communal identity; and special circumstances in the Wordsworths' case prompted an almost compulsive need to compensate for the past by laying up a store of memories for future years. Dorothy and William established a tradition of recording their attachment to places they had visited, whether alone or in each other's company. They saw their memories as gifts—tokens of love—to be offered to each other, in reparation for the years they had spent apart.

The anthropologist Marcel Mauss's observation that bonds are created through gifts, in a mutual interdependence of giver and receiver, is suggestive not only for the siblings' ritual exchange of memories but also for the cumulative associations which sealed and signified their reciprocity.[18] The word 'gift' occurs many times in William's poetry in the context of gratitude for Dorothy's existence. Indeed, the Greek meaning of her name came often to his mind in this context. When the siblings were parted in 1778, a gift was withdrawn and a family bond was temporarily broken; but after their reunion in 1787 each seemed like a gift to and for the other. Looking back on this reunion in *The Prelude* (1805), William gave thanks to Providence for the return of his 'sole Sister':

> Now, after separation desolate
> Restored to me, such absence that she seemed
> A gift then first bestowed.   (VI, ll. 216–18)

The little girl who was passed around among kin after her mother's death, a bit like a possession, was restored in 1787 to the status she had in her family when she was born. God-given, and associated with early memories, she became—at least in William's eyes—the bearer of gifts. In his most famous poem of gratitude, William attributed his own gift as a poet to Dorothy's influence on his sensibility, as though offering up a prayer of thanksgiving for her creative bounty. Gratitude itself becomes a gift when expressed in such eloquent and generous terms:

> She gave me eyes, she gave me ears;
> And humble cares, and delicate fears;
> A heart, the fountain of sweet tears;
> And love, and thought, and joy.
> ('The Sparrow's Nest', ll. 17–20)

William's many poetic tributes to Dorothy were part of a highly developed system of gift-exchange which began soon after they were reunited and continued throughout their shared life. In anthropological terms, the importance of these gifts was that they reinforced already existing kinship bonds, acknowledging the sister's time-honoured place at the centre of the household.

In primitive Melanesian and Polynesian societies, gifts are believed to have sacramental properties. The thing given is not inactive but invested with life; and ownership is understood as the expression of a *spiritual* bond. 'To make a gift of something to someone is to make a present of some part of oneself.'[19] In this way, the circulation of gifts can be identified with the circulation of rights and persons. 'Souls are mixed with things; things with souls. Lives are mingled together, and this is how, among persons and things so intermingled, each emerges from their own sphere and mixes together.'[20] Marcel Mauss has established that in all societies—advanced as well as primitive—gifts come with a burden attached. The receiver is obliged to reciprocate: first with expressions of gratitude, then with further gifts. In this way, the circulation of gifts through exchange produces 'an abundance of riches'.[21] Unlike commerce in a capitalist economy, however, the increase of riches produced in a gift economy is *communal*. This is especially the case in respect of creative talent. Lewis Hyde, whose classic study *The Gift* considered 'how the creative spirit transforms the world', argued that gifts of this kind nourish 'parts of our spirit that derive from nature, the group, the race, or the gods'.[22] To speak of an increase of gifts in this context is to speak of 'something simultaneously material, social, and spiritual':

> When the gift has been 'fed' with labour and a spirit of generosity, it grows and in its turn 'feeds' the giver. The gift and its bearers share a spirit which is kept alive by its motion among them, and which in turn keeps them both alive.[23]

The bonds that are established or strengthened according to the principle of 'exchange-through-gift' can be seen in contracts, covenants, and communal rituals; but they can also work *invisibly*, performing a psychological or spiritual function in the internal economy of individuals and groups. Gifts prove especially helpful when psyches are damaged and in need of integration.[24] This dimension of gift exchange—which I will refer to as *therapeutic*—was unusually strong in the Wordsworths' case. Loss of parents, of home, and of all the possessions that go with home, threatened the siblings' communal identity. In the absence of living parents or inherited property, memories—especially when made into artefacts—became 'surety' for continuing kinship bonds. Just as, in a Trobriand tribe, all precious objects are regarded as 'living beings'—magical and religious symbols of productive power—so the memories circulating between the siblings counted as 'the permanent things of the clan',[25] signifiers of the family's name, honour, standing, ancestry.

*

Until his reunion with Dorothy, William expressed his longing for home obliquely, through the strong regional attachments which helped him sublimate his grief. Very early in life, he saw the Lake District as filling the gap left by his dead parents: the bonds he formed with particular places were reparative, and his poetry was a means of returning thanks for nature's fostering him in childhood. 'The Vale of Esthwaite', his first significant gift-offering, was composed in two distinct phases. He wrote the first part while he was still at Hawkshead in 1787, never mentioning his mother's death, or separation from his sister and playmate. The poem is nonetheless steeped with a consciousness of mortality. The phrase 'Vale of Shades' connects Esthwaite with the psalm-writer's 'valley of the shadow of death', suggesting how the region is haunted by its human past. At the poem's climax, a spectre beckons the poet into 'Black Helvellyn's inmost womb', compelling him to witness a ghostly re-enactment of the battle fought at Dunmail Raise, where the last King of Cumbria was defeated by the Saxon King Edmund in the tenth century.[26] The site of Dunmail's famous last stand, marked on the hillside at the boundary between Westmorland and Cumberland by an ancient pile of stones, had given rise to numerous local stories, including the tradition that his bones were buried on that spot. It was this kind of perpetual association with the landscape which William sought to establish for the Wordsworth family, on behalf of his dead parents and his uprooted siblings. His loyal identification with the vanquished Cumbrian king was intensified by his bereavement. Orphaned and homeless, he looked for a way to commemorate his connection with the region.

The poem's second part, probably composed at Penrith during the summer vacation of 1787 as he prepared to leave for Cambridge, shows a marked development in style and preoccupation. Written after William's reunion with Dorothy, it is psychological in emphasis, revealing how communal grief has intensified his attachment to particular places: 'No spot but claims a tender tear | By Joy or grief to memory dear' (ll. 272–3). William lays claim to his family's regional identity by constructing his own kind of memorial—less heroic than tales of Cumbria's resistance to the Saxons but equally authentic. Stripping his language to its bare bones, he relates a simple domestic story of death and sorrow. On the eve of the Christmas holidays in December 1783, he had waited impatiently on High Crag, a few miles north of Hawkshead, for the horses that would take him and his brothers back to Cockermouth. Although he must already have known his father was ill, he had no way of foreseeing that he would soon die. Later, he came to understand his long solitary wait as an ironic foreshadowing of his orphaned state. The delayed consciousness of mortality gives his writing its emotional focus:

> One Evening when the wintry blast
> Through the sharp Hawthorn whistling pass'd
> And the poor flocks all pinch'd with cold

Sad drooping sought the mountain fold
Long Long upon yon steepy rock
Alone I bore the bitter shock
Long Long my swimming eyes did roam
For little Horse to bear me home   (ll. 274–81)

As if in reparation for John Wordsworth's death, William retrospectively associates his lonely vigil on High Crag with his father's fatal exposure to the elements on Cold Fell. The 'sharp hawthorn' and 'poor flocks all pinch'd with cold' are etched on his conscience by the 'bitter shock' of mortality. They become the signs and symbols of a traumatic loss to which, even as he writes, he belatedly awakens:

Flow on, in vain thou hast not flow'd
But eas'd me of a heavy load
For much it gives my soul relief
To pay the mighty debt of Grief
With sighs repeated o'er and o'er
I mourn because I mourn'd no more
For ah! The storm was soon at rest
Soon broke the Sun upon my breast
Nor did my little heart foresee
—She lost a home in losing thee   (ll. 284–93)

To understand the prominence of this moving passage within the larger structure of 'The Vale of Esthwaite', we should remember that Dorothy was the poem's first reader, and by this stage of composition its primary addressee. (Part of the concluding section is addressed to her, and she took her place alongside William's school friend, John Fleming, as the companion to whom he dedicated his memories.) The events here recalled did not directly involve her—at the time of her father's death she was nowhere near her family, nor did she accompany her brothers to his funeral at Cockermouth. But she was of course emotionally involved in the family's trauma. William genders his 'little heart' as female, so that for a moment we might read the epithet as an endearment referring to Dorothy, who also 'lost a home in losing thee'. Like her brother, she had experienced the effects of delayed mourning, and like him she would pay 'the mighty debt of grief'. Hearing William read the poem aloud in manuscript, she must have been struck by one narrative detail in particular. His account of anxiously waiting in December 1783 'for little Horse to bear me home' closely resembles their shared concern when, four years later, no horses were sent to fetch him from Hawkshead to

Penrith. Perhaps as a result of comparisons made in conversation, two timelines seem briefly to intersect in the poem's narrative.

William's poem integrates his sister into his revisiting of lonely, troubled memories, recognizing the importance of their communal grief. As the poem comes to a close, Dorothy's presence is evident in his fluid use of apostrophe. After addressing the deceased John Wordsworth as 'thee', within thirty lines he apostrophizes Fleming as 'Friend of my Soul' (l. 324). Soon after this he turns to his sister to express his devotion. As he moves from one link to the other in the 'social chain', he establishes a continuity of feeling among the people dearest to him, living and dead:

> Sister for whom I feel a love
> What warms a Brother far above
> On you as sad she marks the scene
> Why does my heart so fondly lean
> Why but because in you is giv'n
> All all my soul could wish from heav'n
> Why but because I fondly view
> All, all that heav'n has claim'd in you.   (ll. 380–6)

Brotherly affection, friendship, and even filial devotion shade into each other in these lines. The insistent use of repetition—'Why...Why...Why'—draws attention to the purity of fraternal love; while William's confession that he 'fondly leans' on Dorothy suggests that she almost fills a parental role. The pattern of pairings, 'All all...All, all', echoes an earlier moment in his narrative—'Long Long upon yon steepy rock...Long Long my swimming eyes did roam'—again linking Dorothy with his lonely vigil on the eve of the Christmas holidays. It is as if William is subliminally making reparation for the many Christmas reunions from which his sister had been excluded. Viewing 'all that heav'n has claim'd' in her, he sees his parents come alive again in her features.

*

'How we are squandered abroad', Dorothy wrote sadly to Jane Pollard in 1788.[27] She was using a phrase from *The Merchant of Venice* to describe how her family had scattered in all directions—Richard to Branthwaite, a village near Cockermouth (where he was under articles to his lawyer cousin), William to Cambridge, Christopher and John back to Hawkshead—leaving her to the stultifying atmosphere of her grandparents' house at Penrith. The quotation from Shakespeare reveals her literary sensibility. At the age of sixteen she had an extraordinary memory and a knack for literary allusions. Brought up in her 'aunt' Threlkeld's non-conformist circle, which had connections to the Warrington Academy, she had been introduced at an early age to the classics in English, Latin, and Greek. (These she supplemented with her own reading. Richardson's immensely long and sombre epistolary novel *Clarissa*, borrowed from the Old Subscription Library, was no mean feat for a fourteen-year-old girl.) As her letters show, her tastes had been formed by the Unitarian principles of plain speaking in the vernacular advocated by Joseph Priestley in his *A Course of Lectures on Oratory and Criticism* (1781). Unusually for a young provincial woman at this time, she therefore had an impressive air of critical authority. Even so, she was conscious that she had received a more haphazard and less rigorous education than her brothers at Hawkshead, a fact which held her in emulous awe of them. Intellectually stimulated by their company, she eagerly read the books they gave her: 'the Iliad, the Odyssey … Fielding's works, Hayley's poems, Gil Blas (in French) … Milton's works, Goldsmith's poems, [and] other trifling things'.[28] With William she formed a close literary bond, entering into his aspirations as a poet and finding him as charismatic as the hero of James Beattie's *The Minstrel*.[29] In turn, she proved to be more than simply a captive audience for his genius. Her presence and conversation quickened his creativity, enabling him, as we have seen, to make direct access to an elegiac voice. In the autumn, as he left for Cambridge, he found her a copy of Burns' *Poems, Chiefly in the Scottish Dialect* in the Penrith book club. Well chosen for its reader, who picked out 'To a Louse' and 'The Mountain Daisy' as her favourites, the book was a keepsake, setting a seal on their friendship and acknowledging the affinities which drew them together.

Their developing closeness was not exclusive. At least one significant other was often present alongside them in their experiences and memories. During the summer vacation of 1788, after William's first year in Cambridge, they rambled in the hills around Penrith and along the river Eamont, accompanied by Dorothy's friend Mary Hutchinson. As William remembered it in *The Prelude*, this was a time when 'love | A spirit of pleasure, and youth's golden gleam' suffused the landscape (VI, ll. 244–5). The companions climbed among the ruins of Brougham Castle (where Sir Philip Sidney had written part of his *Arcadia* for his sister) and lay 'listening to the wild flowers and the grass | As they gave out their whispers to the wind' (VI, ll. 231–2). They visited Penrith Beacon, set in a desolate spot where 'naked Pools' and 'common Crags' lay exposed to the 'bare Fell' (VI, ll. 243–4); and they wandered along their favourite path through Lowther Woods—at their best in September as the leaves turned. Walking, talking, and observing together deepened their shared attachment to this beautiful region. In some of their conversations, the three companions doubtless remembered the past. As an infant, Mary had attended Ann Birkett's school in Penrith at the same time as William. Later, she and her sister Margaret had befriended Dorothy, providing a welcome distraction from the Cooksons' depressing company. Like the Wordsworths, the Hutchinson sisters were orphans, so the two families had in common their formative experiences of bereavement and being fostered. Although these young people had reached a highly impressionable stage in their emotional development, there is little evidence that a romantic attachment formed this early between William and Mary.[30] William's affection for his sister shaped his friendship with the woman who would later become his wife. Over the years, Mary and Dorothy's love for each other proved to be so strong, and so important to his happiness, that he sometimes blurred their identities in his poetry. Domestic feelings in the Wordsworth circle were understood in a slightly amorphous way, perhaps because bonds in the family had been broken so early.

After William had returned to Cambridge, Dorothy was again uprooted, and the siblings saw each other only intermittently during the next six years. Their grandfather died in the winter of 1787. The following autumn their uncle, the Reverend William Cookson (who held a Fellowship at St John's and had served as tutor to the sons of George III), married Dorothy Cowper. On moving to a parish in Norfolk, he and his wife offered their niece a home. Willing enough to escape from her grandmother, Dorothy bade farewell to the North and departed to the handsome Georgian rectory at Forncett St Peter, near Norwich. In sharp contrast to the progressive, chapel-centred household she had known in Halifax, this one was evangelical and conservative, with strong links to public affairs through Cookson's friendship with William Wilberforce. Dorothy's time was spent in conventional ladylike activities: reading, writing, improving her French, visiting the poor. Her routine included rising at six in the morning and walking with a book till after eight. 'I have no companion', she commented in a letter,[31] but there must have been some communal reading, for she observed 'at present we are reading Hume's History of England'.[32] The devotional books she absorbed during this period in Norfolk—'a little Treatise on Re-generation' and 'the New testament with Doddridge's exposition'[33]—indicate how readily she adapted to the evangelical pursuits of the household. Her charitable work attracted the attention of Wilberforce, who gave her funds to distribute, as well as a copy of Mrs Trimmer's *Oeconomy of Charity*. She also ran a Sunday school for nine girls, taking pride as they made progress in learning the catechism. Later, as the Cooksons' children were born, she became (somewhat apprehensively) the 'head nurse, housekeeper, tutoress of the little ones or rather superintendent of the nursery'.[34] These were unpaid duties which she performed well, though regretting that they took her away from teaching. In leisure hours, she could walk from the rectory through the flat meadowlands of the Tas valley, utterly unlike the rugged Northern hills of her childhood. 'I am going to walk to Stratton three miles *alone*,' she boasted to Jane, 'am not I daring?'[35]

It was a quiet, uneventful place in which to spend the years just before and after the French Revolution. At this stage, leading a relatively sheltered life, Dorothy had little patience with 'the new-fangled Doctrine of Liberty and Equality', and her letters do not mention the Fall of the Bastille.[36] She missed her brothers, especially William, who visited her during the summer vacation of 1789. His poem 'Sweet was the walk along the narrow lane', which describes a peaceful country scene during haymaking, was probably inspired by one of their favourite evening walks near Forncett that summer. Disappointed in Cambridge life, William was indecisive about the career he should pursue. He had matriculated at St John's in the hope that one day he might fill his uncle's fellowship; but he soon lost motivation, and was not attracted to his older brother Richard's profession, the law. Homesick, he returned to Hawkshead in the summer vacation of 1788, where he was welcomed back by Ann Tyson. He stayed there again during the autumn of 1789, and kept in touch with his youngest brother Christopher, who succeeded him at Hawkshead. These revisits kept his memories of boyhood fresh, strengthening the distinctive Northern identity which marked him out from his contemporaries at Cambridge. (One of his fellow-undergraduates heard him 'speaking very highly in praise of the beauties of the North; with a warmth indeed which, at that time, appeared to me hardly short of enthusiasm'.)[37]

Rambling in his boyhood haunts provided the subject and method of William's next important poem, *An Evening Walk*, a verse epistle in couplets which he worked at intermittently throughout his undergraduate years. Material in two notebooks suggests that he may have been making drafts towards the poem, which overlaps with 'The Vale of Esthwaite' in some respects, during his Hawkshead years. There is also some evidence that it grew out of ideas he had discussed with Christopher, who showed a keen interest in poetry and some ambition to follow in his brother's footsteps. (They shared a notebook, which contains some very early lines by William, as well as detailed plans for a Latin poem 'In praise of the north', in Christopher's hand.)[38] But despite the regional pride he had in common with his brother, William addressed *An Evening Walk* to Dorothy—who had, as yet, little knowledge of the Lake District—referring to her in the opening line as 'My Dearest Friend'. As the poem develops, he speaks more intimately:

> Say, will my friend, with soft affection's ear,
> The history of a poet's ev'ning hear?   (ll. 51–2; EW, 34)

These lines imply Dorothy's listening presence, a device that serves to close the gap between the siblings, both in the present and the remembered past. The speaker guides the listener through the Lake District, following the river Derwent to Derwentwater, then walking to the Falls of Lodore and over Borrowdale Fells to Grasmere. At Rydal he stops to admire the waterfalls, then pushes on to Winander, reaching Esthwaite at night-time. Although the temporal and geographical markers imply a long walk spread over a single day, the word 'history' connotes a longer period of time—most probably the nine-year-long separation of the siblings during childhood.

An Evening Walk reaffirms William's passionate sense of belonging, not just to his native hills but to the entire region stretching from Cockermouth to Hawkshead, which he thought of as home. Confessing his devotion to a place and a time from which Dorothy had been excluded, his poem is a reparative gift, offering observations and memories as compensation for lost years. The river Derwent, a shared signifier for home, has prominence in the list of place names with which the poem opens; while the possessive pronoun 'my' is reserved for his own beloved Vale of Esthwaite. The speaker takes pride in the Lake District legends and customs he has grown up with, as well as the picturesque Northern scenes which had begun to rival their Continental counterparts in contemporary guidebooks and paintings. The notes which later accompanied the published text conveyed his authority as a native of the region, who knew that in winter nights the mountains are 'covered with immense quantities of woodcocks'; that the words 'intake' and 'gill' are local; that walls in the shape of crosses are built like that to protect the flocks—'the traveller may recollect one in Withburne, and another upon Whinlatter'; that not far from Broughton there is a Druid monument, unmentioned in any guidebooks about the region; and that 'the lily of the valley is found in great abundance in the smallest island of Winandermere [sic]'.³⁹ No one reading these details could be in any doubt that their author was intent on authenticating his distinctively regional identity.

When *An Evening Walk* was published in 1793, William dedicated it to Dorothy. The title page, identifying her discreetly, reads as follows: 'An Evening Walk. *An Epistle; in verse.* Addressed to a Young Lady, from the Lakes of the North of England.'⁴⁰ The comma between 'Young Lady' and the preposition 'from' is ambiguous, suggesting either that the young lady herself comes from the Lake District, or that the poem is written from the Lakes to a lady elsewhere. Both of these facts were true of Dorothy, whose exile—first at Halifax and later at Forncett—is thereby implied. The melancholy tone of *An Evening Walk* arises partly from William's longing to return to childhood and partly from his own exile in the south; for much of the poem was composed at Cambridge. Revisiting 'departed pleasures', he articulates his gratitude to the region which had fostered him. But the poem is much more than a form of solitary thanksgiving, for it imagines the home he and Dorothy will make together. Associating her with a moonlit night, William personifies the moon as Hope and pictures it lighting them homeward:

> Ev'n now [the moon] decks for me a distant scene,
> (For dark and broad the gulph of time between)
> Gilding that cottage with her fondest ray,
> (Sole bourn, sole wish, sole object of my way;
> How fair its lawn and silvery woods appear!
> How sweet its streamlet murmurs in mine ear!)
> Where we, my friend, to golden days shall rise,
> Till our small share of hardly-paining sighs
> (For sighs will ever trouble human breath)
> Creep hush'd into the tranquil breast of Death.   (ll. 413–22)

William consoles Dorothy for the uncertainty of their lives, vowing perpetual devotion to her and to their native region. The vision is Arcadian, but the cottage and murmuring streamlet are humble and rural, giving a local habitation to his nostalgic dream.

*

William's restlessness soon found a new outlet. In the summer of 1790, when the French were celebrating the first anniversary of the Fall of the Bastille, he sent news to Dorothy that he was on a strenuous walking tour through Europe with his friend Robert Jones. It was their last vacation

before graduating. The young men were inspired with radical fervour by the
festivities as they made their way from Calais to Lyons, at a time when
France was 'standing on the top of golden hours, | And human nature seem-
ing born again' (*Prelude*, VI, ll. 353–4). Side by side, 'each with his little knap-
sack of necessaries upon his shoulders', they walked to the Alps and the
Italian lakes.[41] From there they went to Switzerland, Rousseau's homeland
and their Romantic destination, then travelled by boat down the Rhine to
Cologne and walked through Belgium to Calais—in all, a journey of nearly
three thousand miles, which they completed in three months. From a small
village on the lake of Constance, William wrote rhapsodically to Dorothy in
September, describing the 'almost uninterrupted succession of sublime and
beautiful objects which have passed before my eyes during the course of the
last month'. In the same letter he confessed: 'I have thought of you perpetually and never have my eyes burst upon a scene of particular loveliness but
I have almost instantly wished that you could for a moment be transported
to the place where I stood to enjoy it.'[42] Energized by the excitement of
travel, William communicated his impressions enthusiastically, giving Dorothy
a vicarious taste of the wanderlust that drove him onward. As she traced
his itinerary on her map, she quoted snatches of his letter when writing to
Jane Pollard, and at one point, in a kind of ventriloquism of enjoyment,
transcribed a long passage from it almost verbatim.

William's prophecy that 'Perhaps scarce a day of my life will pass in
which I shall not derive some happiness from these images' began shortly
to come true not just for himself, but for his sister.[43] When he visited her
at Forncett for six weeks in December 1790, the tour was still fresh in his
mind. As the siblings walked together in the rectory garden that winter,
William must have reconstructed his tour in considerable detail, because
until long afterwards Dorothy associated his travels with the terrace at
Forncett. 'We used to walk every morning about two hours', she reported,
'and every evening we went into the garden at four or half past four and
used to pace backwards and forwards till six. Unless you have accustomed
yourself to this kind of walking you will have no idea that it can be pleasant, but I assure you it is most delightful.'[44] Rhythmically pacing together
to and fro was an action which later accompanied periods of intense creativity in the Wordsworth household. Although *Descriptive Sketches* was not
composed until William's return to France in 1791–2, the ideas for it were
gestating in conversation during those Forncett walks. Listening to his distinctive mixture of republican ardour and pastoral nostalgia, Dorothy

dreamed that one day she might visit Switzerland with him. Together, the siblings had evolved a form of companionable revisiting which set the pattern for their creative symbiosis.

Dorothy took pride in helping to shape William's poetry, and we know from one of her letters that he gave or sent her some early drafts of his work over the next couple of years. In May 1792, writing to Jane Pollard, she selected one of these—a sonnet, 'Sweet was the walk along the narrow lane'—and transcribed it for Jane, asking her friend to excuse its faults and not to regard it as finished work. 'It is only valuable and dear to me', she insisted, 'because the Lane which gave birth to it was a favourite Evening Walk of my dear William and me.'[45] Her interesting metaphor, 'which gave birth to it', associates the lane with procreation, suggesting her own role within a generative process. The 'narrow lane' may refer to somewhere near Forncett, or alternatively Penrith, for in both places the siblings had walked together. (Indeed, this image of walk-ing together had something of an archetypal status for the Wordsworths, as if subliminally recalling Milton's Adam and Eve, who 'hand in hand, with wan-dering steps and slow | Through Eden took their solitary way'.)[46] The phrase 'a favourite Evening Walk' may not *literally* situate the remembered walk in Cumberland, but it alludes to the landscape celebrated in William's poem of that name, suggesting that Dorothy may already have been in possession of *An Evening Walk* in manuscript. After the poem was published, she told Jane proudly that she and Christopher had sent 'a very bulky criticism' of it to William, hinting that she had become a noticeable presence in (and influence on) her brother's poetry.[47] A year later, in 1793, she was more emotionally pos-sessive, portraying their relationship as one of mutual and exclusive devotion. Fondly recalling her 'long, long conversations' with William at Forncett, she creates a touching vignette of the two of them walking together, he supporting her with his arm. As if recognizing how remote this memory now is, she refers to them both in the third person: 'he was never tired of comforting his sister, he never left her in anger, he always met her with joy, he preferred her society to every other pleasure'.[48] Dorothy's almost urgent insistence, at this later stage, on his tender solicitude is a telling symptom of increasing neediness. By 1793, the Wordsworths had undergone a rapid sequence of shocks and emotional upheavals sufficient to shake their relationship to its foundations.

*

While living in London, between January and May 1791, William associated with republicans. These included members of the Society for Constitutional

Information, such as Samuel Nicholson, and intellectuals who congregated around the radical publisher and bookseller Joseph Johnson. During this time, he read the major political documents of the day and responded with excitement to republican ideas.[49] In a spirit of political curiosity, he crossed the Channel in November 1791, leaving Dorothy to her demanding work as a nanny. His sudden departure for France initiated a separation that proved more painful for her than for him, and that had serious consequences for them both. His passionate liaison with Annette Vallon began in Orleans during the spring of 1792 and continued at Blois during the summer, by which time Annette was pregnant with his child. While abroad, he formed a close friendship with Michel Beaupuy, conversed with members of Les Amis de la Constitution, and wrote his most radical poem to date, *Descriptive Sketches*, inspired in equal measure by his walking tour of 1790 and the revolutionary sympathy which had led him back to France. Anxious for a means to support his new family, William returned to England via Paris, where he spent several dangerous and disturbing weeks, a month after the September massacres, waiting for a passport. (There followed the birth of his natural child Caroline, who was baptized at Orleans Cathedral in his absence on 15 December.) He hoped that, once safely back on home ground, his uncle would give him the financial help he needed. Penniless, and with no immediate prospects of employment, how else was he to offer Annette and Caroline a home, or to honour his equally binding responsibilities toward Dorothy?

Spurred on by a desire to prove that he could 'do something', William speedily prepared for the press his two most recent poems, *An Evening Walk* and *Descriptive Sketches*.[50] This pair of quarto volumes, published in January 1793 by Joseph Johnson, showed the importance of two different directions of travel in his life thus far. Nostalgia for childhood and pride in the Lake District permeated the first poem, symbolically dedicated to his sister. Radicalism, European consciousness, and the excitement of travel abroad characterized the second, dedicated to Robert Jones. Both poems declared a passion for the natural world; but the newly radicalized voice which had emerged during William's Continental travels marked the second out strongly from the first. His republican sympathies—reinforced by his friendship with Beaupuy and a year of living in France—sound out loud and clear as he issues a fearless rallying call to the friends of liberty: 'Lo! From th'innocuous flames, a lovely birth! | With it's own Virtues springs another earth'.[51] Among his readers, Dorothy alone is likely to have been unsurprised to find her brother's devotion to the North of England matched by his new enthusiasm for Europe. But even she must have felt a pang of jealousy when seeing in print his address to Switzerland:

> And thou! fair favoured region! which my soul
> Shall love, till Life has broke her golden bowl,
> Till Death's cold touch her cistern-wheel assail ...   (ll. 740–2)

This was a vow of fealty as devout and patriotic as if Rousseau's homeland had become the poet's. Where did it leave William's long-standing devotion to Dorothy, or his identification of a cottage in the Lake District as the 'Sole bourn, sole wish, sole object of my way'?

William's poems attracted the attention of a few discerning readers including Coleridge—'seldom, if ever, was the emergence of an original poetic genius above the literary horizon more evidently announced'[52]—as well as a number of favourable reviews, but no substantial revenue. A month after their publication, France's declaration of war on England prevented him from crossing the Channel to be with Annette and Caroline. William Cookson did not invite him to stay at Forncett, so his longing to be with Dorothy was also thwarted. Beset by uncertainties, he embarked on one of the most memorable journeys of his life, visiting the Isle of Wight for a month with his friend William Calvert before travelling alone for two days across Salisbury Plain, then up the Severn to the Wye valley and on foot to Wales. As he crossed the plain—a vast, desolate landscape without shade or habitation—he was haunted by the sacrificial history of Stonehenge, associating it with recent bloodshed in France and his inner turmoil. His later recollections in *The Prelude* transformed this solitary journey into a traumatic rite of passage. The experiences and encounters he had while on his travels prompted *Salisbury Plain*, a narrative poem in Spenserian stanzas about two homeless figures—a female vagrant and a male traveller—who meet in a ruined spital and befriend each other. William drew on his and Dorothy's experience of homelessness to flesh out the wanderers' emotions. The woman, born in Cumberland and homesick for her childhood there, relates how a greedy nobleman dispossessed her father, and how the loss of her husband and children in the American war drove her to vagrancy. The allusion to how the Wordsworth family had been treated by Lowther would have been recognized by very few of his readers; but no one could miss his outrage at social injustice. Many of William's early poems grew out of a political passion tinged with personal grievance.

Salisbury Plain concludes optimistically with a rousing command to the 'Heroes of Truth' to 'uptear | Th' Oppressor's dungeon from its deepest base' and build a new nation on the foundations of reason (ll. 541–9; SPP, 38). At a personal level, the poem has a more muted but no less hopeful message. As the two wanderers emerge at daybreak from the vast bleak plain and stand looking towards the comforting signs of human habitation, they bear a shadowy resemblance to the Wordsworth siblings, embarking on a new life:

> But now from a hill summit down they look
> Where through a narrow valley's pleasant scene
> A wreath of vapour tracked a winding brook
> Babbling through groves and lawns and meads of green.
> A smoking cottage peeped the trees between ...   (ll. 406–10)

In this scene of rural tranquillity William sketches out his vision for the future, reusing some of the images that had appeared in his address to Dorothy in *An Evening Walk*. The narrow valley, winding brook, and cottage had become recurring features in his fantasy of a life shared with his sister; here they take on a new vitality as signifiers of a pilgrimage that has reached its inevitable end. The female vagrant and her fellow traveller, walking side by side, descend from the plain. They are greeted as the sun comes up by the familiar sounds of rural life—a cock crowing, a driver whistling as he goes by on his wagon. In this way, William attempts to give his own dark narrative of dispossession and homelessness the shape of a communal homecoming.

During the long uncertainty which had followed their last meeting, Dorothy looked after her young cousins at Forncett, waited for William to return from his travels, and fantasized about a permanent life together. In December 1792 she turned twenty-one and came legally of age, an event marked by her grandmother with a gift of £100, which gave her a modicum of independence. She remained ignorant of William's recent troubles until February 1793. Her regular correspondence with Jane Pollard served as a means of exploring her thoughts and feelings. Increasingly, she wrote about her unfolding life as though seeing herself as a character in a novel. In a letter written in mid-February, she anticipated a time when she and her brother would finally be together, Jane paying them a year-long visit. She pictured all three of them in a 'little Parsonage', making home 'the central point of all our joys' just as the Swiss mountain farmers did in *Descriptive Sketches*:

> When I think of Winter I hasten to furnish our little Parlour, I close the Shutters, set out the Tea-table, brighten the Fire. When our Refreshment is

ended I produce our Work, and William brings his book to our Table and contributes at once to our Instruction and amusement, and at Intervals we lay aside the Book and each hazard our observations on what has been read without the fear of Ridicule or Censure. We talk over past days, we do not sigh for any Pleasures beyond our humble Habitation.[53]

Dorothy's confident vision of the future drew as much on her reading as on the dreams she and William had indulged together. When she imagines closing the shutters and setting out the tea-table, she alludes wittily to Cowper's famous evocation of domestic retirement in Book IV of *The Task*: 'Now stir the fire, and close the shutters fast, | Let fall the curtains, wheel the sofa round...' (ll. 36–7). Hers is an egalitarian picture of amicable sociability—reading aloud being followed by group discussion and recollection, with each member of the household contributing their part. Dorothy's longing for freedom to share ideas without fear of 'Ridicule or Censure' reflects her resentment at being treated as an inferior by her relatives at Penrith, and possibly also at Forncett. In her ideal world, there would be no room for the crying babies and household drudgery which currently filled her days.

Ironically, it was soon after writing this letter that Dorothy learnt from William of the existence of Annette Vallon and her baby Caroline, now three months old. With unhesitating loyalty to her brother, she wrote to Annette forthwith, offering affection and support. Having adjusted to the implications of William's actions, she then had to break the news to their uncle Cookson. She and her brother met with no understanding or offer of financial support from that quarter. Nonetheless Dorothy continued until the summer of 1793 to believe that somehow they would achieve their goal of 'Happiness arising from the exercise of the social Affections in Retirement and rural Quiet'.[54] This somewhat stilted formulation indicated her personal commitment not simply to William himself but also to the domestic ideology he espoused, along with numerous other writers. By June she was less concerned with such abstractions, confessing fearfully and emotionally to Jane: 'I cannot foresee the Day of my Felicity, the Day in which I am once more to find a Home under the same Roof with my Brother.'[55] The passage of time had brought her no nearer to realizing her hopes, and she became increasingly unhappy. Domestic duties at Forncett weighed her down. Her health deteriorated. Homesick, she longed to 'live over again' her childhood in the company of Jane Pollard, and began to plan a trip to Halifax: 'I look forward to meeting again the Friend of my Childhood, the companion of my pleasures "when Life reared laughing up her morning Sun".[56] Her quotation from *An Evening Walk* alludes to the happiness William had experienced when he was a boy at Hawkshead. Separated from him once again, she looked back to her Yorkshire childhood, drawing comfort from memories in which he had no part. Her letters revisited the places where she and Jane had played together, as if to consolidate the inner resilience she had developed when she was a vulnerable child:

> you remember the Enthusiasm with which we used to be fired when in the Back-Kitchen, the Croft, or in any other of our favourite Haunts we built our little Tower of Joy...Do you think you should know me in crossing the Top of the Back-lane from the shop which was formerly Leland's to your Door?...how sweetly shall we wander together along the pleasant Banks of the Calder.[57]

Dorothy's affectionate recollection of place names and quotidian activities shows how consciously she worked to retrieve a past that was sufficiently *familiar, detailed, and local* to compensate for separation from the brother she loved. Writing to Jane on 10–12 July, she was excited by the thought that her friend still had access to their 'favourite haunts' and that soon they would revisit them together: 'where are you at this moment? In Whitely wood? the old lane or Birkswood? thinking upon our past pleasures, when we used to roam in search of bilberries with our black porringers in our hands?'[58]

Nostalgia for Halifax, and for Jane's companionship, alternated in Dorothy's letters with an increasingly urgent need to be reunited with William. Conveying a hint that she was engaged in some kind of clandestine plot, she instructed Jane not to read her letters aloud. By August 1793, when she was impatiently anticipating a meeting with both her brother in Halifax, her feelings for him and Jane had become intertwined. In one of William's recent letters, she found and treasured a passionate expression of his fraternal love:

> Oh my dear dear sister *with what transport shall I again meet you*, with what rapture shall I again wear out the day in your sight...How much do I wish that each emotion of pleasure and pain that visits your heart should excite a similar pleasure or similar pain within me, by that sympathy which will almost identify us when we have stolen to our little cottage![59]

There was no reason to doubt the sincerity of William's devotion, framed here almost in terms of an imagined elopement. But with circumstances conspiring against him, Dorothy looked for proof that his determination was strong enough to secure a future by her side. Her loneliness, intensified by his continuing absence, is evident in the 'language of the heart' which she used in addressing Jane.[60] Echoing the romantic phrasing of William's letter, she wrote to her friend, 'Three months!—long, long months I measure them with a Lover's scale!'; '*Oh Jane with what Transport shall I embrace you.*'[61]

2

Windy Brow and Racedown

'Two glad Foot-travellers through sun and shower
My Love and I came hither...'[1]

*

In February 1794 Dorothy and William were at long last reunited in
Yorkshire, where they spent six weeks with their 'aunt' Elizabeth
(née Threlkeld) at her new home in Halifax. After marrying a local
merchant, William Rawson, in 1791, she had moved to Mill House on
the west bank of the river Ryburn, three miles south-west of town. It
was not the home Dorothy remembered from childhood, but she felt welcome there. The siblings' unconventional lifestyle raised no eyebrows in
the Rawsons' Unitarian household, whereas nearer blood relatives dis-
approved of William. An affectionate bond formed between Dorothy
and her uncle, a thoughtful man who later presented her with two
important volumes of poetry, both published in 1794. These were Mark

Akenside's *The Pleasures of Imagination with an essay by Mrs Barbauld* and the sixth edition of Samuel Rogers' *The Pleasures of Memory*.[2] His gift implied an interest in Dorothy's intellectual capabilities as well as knowledge of William's current poetic concerns. Rawson must have taken a liking to his nephew and niece, approving of the affinities which connected them so strongly.

While enjoying their relatives' congenial company at Mill House, the Wordsworths had a stroke of good fortune. William Calvert, a friend from William's Hawkshead days, invited them to live rent-free in Windy Brow, his family's farmhouse above Keswick. They accepted gladly. In April, brother and sister embarked on the first stage of their domestic life together. Having travelled by coach from Halifax to Kendal, they disembarked and walked 33 miles to their destination, pausing at a pub in Staveley for refreshment before continuing to Grasmere for an overnight stop. It was the first hike of this length and ardour that Dorothy had experienced. 'I walked with my brother at my side ... through the most delightful country that was ever seen', she wrote in an excited letter to Jane Pollard, relishing her 'wonderful prowess in the walking way'.[3] Ever afterwards, she and William would remember this journey as a pilgrimage. 'Two glad Foot-travellers through sun and shower', they paused near Ambleside to drink from a nearby stream, thankful for their long-anticipated happiness. Having arrived at Grasmere as the sun was setting, they spent the night at the village inn before completing the remaining 13 miles over Dunmail Raise and on to Keswick the following day.

Windy Brow, where they stayed throughout the spring, was a stone farmhouse on Latrigg Fell, a foothill of Skiddaw half a mile north-east of Keswick. Joseph Wilkinson's 1795 painting depicts the house on its steep and woody slope above the river Greta as it must have been when the Wordsworths were there. A hundred yards above the house was a terrace which gave breathtaking views south across the full length of Derwentwater to Borrowdale—then, as now, the most beautiful of all the Lakeland valleys. Out of sight beyond Bassenthwaite, the road wound north towards William and Dorothy's childhood home in Cockermouth. The spacious cultivated valley in which Keswick nestled seemed to Dorothy, as Thomas Gray had described it in his *Journal of the Lakes*, 'the Vale of Elysium'.[4] Her careful descriptive register struggled to do justice to the prospect, mixing homely metaphors with vocabulary she had learned from tour books and picturesque guides:

This vale is terminated at one end by a huge pile of grand mountains in whose lap the lovely lake of Derwent is placed, at the other end by the lake of Bassenthwaite, on one side Skiddaw towers sublime and on the other a range of mountains not of equal size but of much grandeur, and the middle part of the vale is of beautiful cultivated grounds interspersed with cottages and watered by a winding stream which runs between the lakes of Derwent and Bassenthwaite.[5]

When John Constable toured the Lake District, a decade after the Wordsworths' stay at Windy Brow, he paid tribute to 'the finest senry [sic] that ever was' in a series of pencil sketches and watercolours, many of them featuring Borrowdale and the Fells surrounding Derwentwater in autumn. He used a restricted palette (neutral washes in grey and green over pencil) to capture the gloom. Constable's home county was Suffolk, and he complained that the mountains 'oppressed his spirits'. His nature was 'particularly social and could not feel satisfied with scenery, however grand in itself, that did not abound in human associations'.[6] His marvellous watercolours depict unpeopled landscapes—the desolate emptiness of Newlands Valley and Esk Hawse in mist, the steep bare precipice of Gate Crag; the vast solitude seen from Honister Crag; Saddleback and Skiddaw stretching away into distant clouds. For the Wordsworths this terrain was equally astonishing; but very soon it became steeped in 'human associations', which they valued as highly as Constable did. Here it was that they first began to recover their joint regional identity, through walking and dwelling.

During the weeks that followed, brother and sister established a fluid daily rhythm of work and recreation. William revisited some of his earlier writing and read Italian with Dorothy; they were beginning to translate works by Ariosto and Tasso, with the help of a grammar book sent by their brother Richard. Dorothy wrote letters, cooked simple meals, and helped to make fair-copies of his poems. Together they explored the surrounding fells. When their censorious aunt Crackanthorpe wrote, criticizing their bohemian lifestyle, Dorothy replied defiantly.[7] Was she not living frugally, safe in her brother's company, improving her health and education every day? Her remarkably outspoken letter flouted convention, rejoicing openly in her new-found freedom.[8] Grateful for youth and energy, but mindful of the old and infirm, she helped William build a seat beside the steep climb from the Forge bridge over the river Greta. Here he composed his 'Inscription for a seat by the pathway side ascending to Windy Brow' to commemorate their joint attachment to this beautiful place. The gesture expressed a sense of belonging, and solidarity with future passers-by, who would pause to sit there, pondering on 'the last resting place, so near'.[9]

Just as William had responded creatively to Dorothy's presence in 1787, so now his poetry took a different shape and texture as a result of their daily interaction. When *An Evening Walk* and *Descriptive Sketches* first appeared in print, Dorothy had criticized both volumes for 'many Faults, the chief of which are Obscurity, and a too frequent use of some particular expressions and uncommon words'.[10] Taking these criticisms on board, and doubtless discussing their implications with her further, William returned to the first of the two poems, extending it to almost double its original length. He began by entering corrections and additions into a copy of the 1793 edition in May while still in Dorothy's presence. As the poem grew in length over the summer, he continued in a separate notebook (probably purchased at Kendal on their journey to Windy Brow).[11] Whereas the first version of *An Evening Walk* was too obviously indebted to loco-descriptive conventions, the revised one used a plainer lexis and a more personal register to articulate a whole new range of observations, thoughts, and feelings. Among the passages added were several descriptions of human beings, no longer seen from distance as if they were 'staffage' in a picturesque painting, but observed close up, with an intriguing element of psychological realism. The newly peopled landscape of *An Evening Walk* 1794 included a girl mourning for her lover in the quarry where he had died, shepherds responding fearfully to the imagined threat of 'civil arms', and a solitary figure toiling with 'languid steps' in the midday sun. William later requisitioned this last for 'The Ruined Cottage', its couplets turning easily into blank verse.

A deepening sense that the dead were present alongside the living pervaded much of William's new writing. When passing through Grasmere, he and Dorothy had stopped to visit the churchyard, where children from the neighbouring school sometimes played alongside the ancient gravestones:

> From seats in the rude wall the aged bend,
> And elms, above, their ragged arms extend.
> What tribes of youth their gambols there have wrought
> Nor, in their freaks and wild mirth, ever thought
> How near their warm light motion was allied
> To the dull earth that [crumbled] at their side.   (ll. 41–6; EW, 132)

The generalized moral had a personal application to the siblings now they were so close to home territory. Their mother's remains were buried in Penrith churchyard, their father's in the graveyard at Cockermouth—near enough to come to mind as they walked with 'warm light motion' under the elms at Grasmere. Dorothy's company, and their usual habit of revisiting memories connected with places, intensified William's awareness of the human history that surrounded them, and of his ambition to celebrate his regional identity in poetry—an ambition he had shared with his brother Christopher in earlier years. The details about local history which he added to *An Evening Walk* in 1794 included a description of 'a horseman skeleton of giant mould' buried beyond Penrith Beacon (l. 397f); a homage to 'the last remnant of the great and brave' who had fought to defend Cumberland against the Romans (l. 715f); a salute to the bards who had immortalized their deeds in song (ll. 730–6); and a description of the spirits of the local dead, whose 'slow-gliding forms of light' could be seen 'at the stillest watch of night' (l. 761f).

Dorothy's presence at Windy Brow transformed *An Evening Walk* from an epistle 'addressed to a young lady, from the Lakes of England' into something more closely resembling Coleridge's early Conversation Poems. William's narrative voice is quietly reflective, as it would be in his later revisit poems, 'The Ruined Cottage' and 'Tintern Abbey'. The musing tone blends easily with the direct syntax, and the demonstrative pronouns convey a sense of his thinking aloud to a nearby listener. In the first version William had asked Dorothy to attend to his 'history' of a solitary ramble. In the 1794 poem he addressed her as the beloved companion who walked at his side, quickening his joy in the natural world:

> Come with thy Poet, come, my friend, to stray,
> Where winds the road along the secret bay;
> Come, while the parting day yet serves to show
> Thy cheek that shames the water's crimson glow,
> By rills that tumble down the woody steeps,
> And run enamoured to the dimpling deeps... (ll. 414–19)

Echoing Marlowe's 'Come live with me, and be my love', William's tone is cajoling, almost seductive, as he invites Dorothy on a walk along the shores of Derwentwater, probably to the falls of Lodore. She and the landscape are described as mutually enlivening sources of energy and joy. The amatory devices are not to modern tastes, but Dorothy would have recognized and smiled at William's adaptation of the complimentary conventions of Elizabethan love poetry. Doubtless, too, she enjoyed his use of the epithet 'thy Poet', which marked a moment of bold self-definition in his life and career. Cocking a snook at the establishment relatives who disapproved of his vocation, William's phrase is a thankful reference to Dorothy's encouragement as he pursued his chosen path. Years later, in *The Prelude*, he was to acknowledge how at this time she 'preserved me still | A Poet, made me seek beneath that name | My office upon earth, and nowhere else' (X, ll. 918–20).

Dorothy's moral support was not the only thing he was grateful for during the spring of 1794. Rejoicing in the signs of nature's renewal, he found her presence life-enhancing in a deeper, spiritual sense. In an important new addition to *An Evening Walk* he introduced the idea of an active universe, animated by a mysterious 'sense' or 'being' or 'secret power'. To be fully receptive to the energy pervading natural objects, he argued, one needs a heightened sensibility:

> A heart that vibrates evermore, awake
> To feeling for all forms that Life can take;
> That wider still its sympathy extends,
> And sees not any line where being ends;
> Sees sense, through Nature's rudest forms betrayed,
> Tremble obscure in fountain, rock, and shade;
> And while a secret power these forms endears
> Their social accents never vainly hears.   (ll. 125–32)

Some scholars have commented on this passage as a surprising anticipation of the animistic beliefs which appeared in William's poetry in around 1797–8, after he had absorbed the implications of Joseph Priestley's writings through Coleridge.[12] But he and Dorothy both had access to Unitarian ideas before then: she for nine formative years of childhood (as mentioned earlier, her aunt's circle had connections with the Warrington Academy, where Priestley taught); he later, through the writers he had met in London, who were associated with Joseph Johnson, Priestley's publisher. During the six weeks immediately preceding their stay at Windy Brow, the Wordsworths had been in the company of the Rawsons' Unitarian circle in Halifax. It is entirely explicable that they were drawn to contemporary ideas about God's animating presence in the spring of 1794.

At this time of heightened emotions and responses, William began to make a distinction between 'blest' spirits, who are 'tremblingly awake' to natural beauty, and insensitive souls, 'whose languid powers unite | No interest to each rural sound or sight' (ll. 197–8). In one of the draft revisions to *An Evening Walk*, he clearly identified Dorothy as belonging to the former category:

Yes, thou art blest, my friend, with mind awake
To Nature's impulse like this living lake,
Whose mirrour makes the landscape's charms its own
With touches soft as those to Memory known;
While, exquisite of sense, the mighty mass
All vibrates to the lightest gales that pass.   (ll. 191–6)[13]

William here praises Dorothy's attentiveness to the active universe. Hers is
not just (implicitly) 'A heart that vibrates evermore, awake | To feeling for
all forms that Life can take' (ll. 125–6), but explicitly a '*mind* awake | To
Nature's impulse' (emphasis added). Comparing her with the 'living lake'
they stand admiring, William suggests that like its 'mighty mass', her mind
does not simply receive and reflect her surroundings but heightens their
beauty by adding 'touches' of its own. His simile develops John Locke's
model of the mind as a *tabula rasa* (blank slate) into a more interactive
model of mental process. Just as the lake's thin surface membrane shivers
when the breeze blows over it, causing the mountains' reflections to move,
so Dorothy's mind, in its 'exquisite' attunement to the environment, is constantly fluid, reshaping what she sees and feels. This fascinating simile reveals
William's familiarity with David Hartley's neurological approach to associationism. In his *Observations on Man* (1749) Hartley had described sensations as 'vibrations' in the nerves of the medullary substance of the
brain—associations being the result of successive and combined vibrations,
determined by each person's experience.

According to William, memory's 'soft touches' played an important role
in the mind's perpetual interaction with 'Nature's impulse'. He did not
believe that memory was a passive faculty and inferior to imagination, but
saw associative process as inherently creative. His feminization of memory
and its clear identification in 1794 with his sister emphasize his deep reverence for her intellect and sensibility. A year before his first meeting with
Coleridge, he counted Dorothy as one of

those favoured souls, who, taught
By active Fancy or by patient Thought,
See common forms prolong the endless chain
Of Joy and grief, of pleasure and of pain.   (ll. 203–6)

His 'chain' metaphor belongs partly to a traditional view of humans as com-
ponents in a Great Chain of Being; partly to the language of associationism
which had been developed by Hartley and adopted by his friend and disci-
ple Priestley.[14] In this latter context, the 'chain' connotes the emotional links

that connect human beings to each other in a continuous manifestation of sympathy, which 'wider still … extends, | And sees not any line where being ends' (ll. 127–9). For the Wordsworths, associationism was not just a reputable branch of empirical philosophy but a wholly compelling explanation of memory's communal power. They saw their own unfolding relationship as living proof of its validity. As early as 1787, William had understood the 'social accents' of this theory and its relevance to human relationships. In 'The Vale of Esthwaite', he referred to the 'social chain' linking his family and friends as well as to the 'heav'n connected chain' which joined the living members of his family with the dead. In 1793, Dorothy wrote of indissoluble bonds within the Wordsworth family: 'Neither absence nor Distance nor Time can ever break the Chain.' Since their first reunion, the affections linking the siblings had been reinforced. Together again, and briefly restored to their native environment, they saw the possibility of forging 'an endless chain' of reciprocal feelings, memories, and associations.

*

The Wordsworths were together at Windy Brow for six weeks—one of the happiest times of their lives. In his moving poem 'Septimi, Gades', almost certainly written just before they were again parted, William drew on the biblical language of the Book of Ruth to articulate a solemn and binding covenant with a female friend:

> No separate path our lives shall know
> But where thou goest I shall go
> And there my bones shall rest.[15]

In all likelihood he wrote this vow, a renewal of the one which appears at the end of *An Evening Walk,* with Dorothy in mind.[16] His poem goes on to recall a 'humble shed' in a beautiful secluded valley above the Rhone, where he had stayed while on his travels through the Alps in 1790. Remembering the tinkling stream which emerged from the woods nearby, he now identifies this spot as the unattainable object of youthful desire. Half-regretting that he cannot return there, he puts to one side his romantic dream, settling instead for 'The lone grey cots and pastoral steeps | That shine inverted on the deeps | Of Grasmere's quiet vale' (ll. 22–4). It was not the first time Grasmere had featured in his poetry as an image of tranquil domestic fulfilment, nor would it be the last. In 'The Vale of Esthwaite' and *An Evening Walk*, similarly idealized images of Grasmere vale signified his need for belonging. His great work about returning, 'Home at Grasmere', was still to come.

Whether we are considering William's vision of a 'little nest' beside Grasmere lake or the 'little Parlour' in Dorothy's fantasy of home during 1793, the archetype behind each image is the same. Homesickness—the yearning to return to their birthplace in Cockermouth—was one of the Wordsworths' most persistent shared emotions. Until long after their eventual settlement in Grasmere in 1799 they went on describing and imagining different versions of the secluded spot where they would realize (or had realized) their dream of rural happiness. Their shared objective, a Lake District cottage, preferably alongside a lake or a stream, was shaped by their particular circumstances, answering their distinctive psychological needs; while the longing itself—*heimweh*—spoke to spiritual yearnings typical of European Romanticism. Memory, dream, fantasy, object of desire, distant goal, end-point of all wandering—any and all of these words would be insufficient to do justice to the profound significance of home as they understood it.

In the seventeenth and eighteenth centuries, homesickness was considered a neurological disease with debilitating symptoms, which included persistent thoughts about home, anxiety, melancholy, insomnia, palpitations, and difficulties in breathing.[17] Its medical name, *nostalgia*, was coined by the Swiss physician Johannes Hofer from the Greek words *nostos* and *algos*, which mean, respectively, 'returning home' and 'pain, ache, or suffering'. In his 'Medical Dissertation on Nostalgia' (1688) Hofer diagnosed this condition as one to which young people exiled in foreign countries were particularly prone.[18] It arose, he observed, when these people, often soldiers, were 'sent forth to foreign lands with alien customs' and proved unable to forget the memory of their 'sweet fatherland'.[19] The disease affected the nervous system. Hofer hypothesized that the 'oval tubes of the centre of the brain' became over-stimulated by 'the uncommon and ever-present idea of the recalled native land'.[20] The 'deepest part of the brain' (the *ovale*) was, he argued, highly susceptible to 'continuous vibration of animal spirits'. If obsessional thoughts continued over an extended period of time, the *ovale* became 'afflicted constantly from the infinite nerve fibres in which the spirits continually move about in waves'.[21] Hofer's clinical case histories refer to a range of severe symptoms in patients he had treated or heard about indirectly. The symptoms included 'melancholy delirium', 'burning fever', 'stupidity of the mind', 'disturbed sleep', loss of appetite and energy, and 'morbid weakness'. In his list of the diagnostic signs of imminent nostalgia he mentions (among others) 'wandering about sad', scorning 'foreign customs', evincing a distaste of 'strange conversations', being overly sensitive to 'petty inconveniences', and making a show of 'the delights of the Fatherland'.[22]

In *Descriptive Sketches* William noted that Swiss mercenaries were forbidden to sing 'Ranz des vaches', an evocative melody about their homeland, for fear that they might fall ill with *mal de suisse*, a form of nostalgia so tenacious that it sometimes led exiled soldiers to desert the army, pine away, or die.[23] He made clear in his note that he was relaying a 'well-known' fact; so it seems unlikely that his knowledge derived from reading Hofer's erudite Latin treatise on nostalgia, either in its original form or Zwinger's later edition. The probability is that anecdotes about pining Swiss soldiers had popular currency in France. A year after *Descriptive Sketches* was published, Erasmus Darwin included the following definition of nostalgia in his medical treatise *Zoonomia* (1794), confirming that scientific interest in this iconic Swiss condition had begun to have a significant place in contemporary British medicine:

> Nostalgia. Maladie du Pais. Calenture. An unconquerable desire of returning to one's native country, frequent in long voyages, in which the patients become so insane as to throw themselves into the sea, mistaking it for green fields or meadows. The Swiss are said to be particularly liable to this disease, and when taken into foreign service frequently desert from this cause, and especially after hearing or singing a particular tune, which was used in their village dances, in their native country, on which account the playing or singing this tune was forbid by punishment of death.[24]

William wrote *Descriptive Sketches* when 'wandering about sad' (Hofer's phrase) on the banks of the Loire, and his identification with exiled Swiss soldiers may owe something to his own longing to return there while living in France. He took a special interest in the Swiss melody of 'Kuhe-Reyen' (known to the French as 'Ranz des Vaches'), which haunted him when he went back to Switzerland in 1820.[25] He also responded poetically to Darwin's explanation of 'Calenture' (heatstroke or fever) in 1800, associating it with his brother John's homesickness while at sea.[26] His poetry over the years indicated a continuing preoccupation with the pathology of nostalgia.

At a time when psychology was in its infancy, medical approaches to the nervous system were relatively unsophisticated. In the context of eighteenth-century neurology, with its strongly somatic emphasis, nostalgia was treated through the use of various remedies such as opium, leeches, and walks in the Swiss Alps.[27] Hofer himself recommended purging, 'internal hypnotic emulsions', opium, or wine. (Patients could also be helped, he said, by distractions, or the presence of sympathetic friends; although the only real cure was to return home.) By the mid-nineteenth century, however, approaches to psychosomatic illness had become more subtle. Nostalgia and homesickness were increasingly being de-synonymized. Homesickness was defined as a form of melancholia or depression; nostalgia as a longing for the past, with aesthetic and spiritual resonances. In the twentieth and twenty-first centuries, homesickness has been identified as a regressive pathology linked to loss, grief, and incomplete mourning (all significant factors in the Wordsworths' early lives).[28] Nostalgia, by contrast, is nowadays generally understood as an emotion: some recent research indicates that it may have positive benefits, such as an enhanced sense of connection with significant others, leading to altruism and empathy.[29] With these developing medical approaches in mind, we can consider homesickness as an *emotional and psychological complex*, placing the Wordsworths at a significant juncture in 'the history or science of feelings'.[30]

In early adulthood William and Dorothy were curious about modern scientific advances, especially in medicine. (It is possible that they read Erasmus Darwin's *Zoonomia* when it first appeared: William knew it well enough to want a copy of it in 1798, to check out a specific case history.)[31] Like many young people whose parents die young, they were doubtless anxious about their own life expectancy, observing each other's patterns of health, sickness, and mood variation closely. And they were keen, like many of their contemporaries, to seek out home cures and therapies for self-diagnosed ailments and diseases. Through their friendship with Coleridge, they were soon to come in contact with the Bristol physician Thomas Beddoes, whose acute understanding of 'hypochondria' as a middle class illness anticipated modern psychiatry.[32] Some aspects of the Wordsworths' approach to their nostalgia (such as vigorous walking in the countryside) were predictable in the context of 'Brunonian' medicine, which emphasized the importance of stimulants and exercise.[33] Other aspects seemed to fit in with Hofer's advice that patients seek solace in a sympathetic listener or return swiftly home. Intuitively, the siblings developed their own remedy for nostalgia through the collaborative work of jointly reattaching themselves to their regional origins. Creativity and companionship helped them to transform homesickness, with its associations of disease and melancholia, into more positive feelings of communal longing and belonging. That each sibling was essential to the other in this healing process—which continued across the entirety of their intertwined lives—is the central argument of this book.

As an adult, William always thought of creative replenishment in regional terms, tracing his well-being (physical, moral, and spiritual) back to the Lake District, away from the competitive world of publishing, reviewing, and political journalism which he associated with the stressful metropolis. His time at Cambridge, his walking tour in the Alps, his residence in post-revolutionary France and London—all of these took him away from what he saw as the fertile source of his creative life. His use of the river Derwent as an organizing metaphor for creativity in *The Prelude* is prefigured in two early poems of revisiting. Both were fragments, written in 1795–6 when the Wordsworths were living a long way from their native hills. Both speak obliquely about Dorothy's therapeutic role in William's life as he recovered his emotional equilibrium; and both take the form of apostrophes to the Derwent, the river they associated with their childhood home.

The Derwent rises at Sty-head on Scafell, running through Borrowdale to Derwentwater, then onward in a north-westerly direction to Cockermouth. While staying at Windy Brow, Dorothy and William must have been perpetually reminded of its music by the nearby sound of the tributary river Greta, which flowed into the Derwent just above Keswick. In the spring of 1794, they stopped at their birthplace en route to visit their uncle and aunt at Whitehaven, having themselves followed a north-westerly course from Keswick to Cockermouth. On arriving at their family home, they found it deserted and run down, its terrace walk, as Dorothy observed in a letter, 'buried and choked up with the old privot [*sic*] hedge which had formerly been most beautiful'.[34] Despite their disappointment at the time, both of William's later revisit poems convey the deep joy of homecoming. The first fragment, 'On returning to a cottage, a favourite residence of the author, after a long absence', suggests that travelling back to their shared origins fulfilled a need for renewal. William personifies the river, reclaiming its companionship as if recovering a buried kinship between its voice and his own:

> Derwent again I hear thy evening call
> Blend with the whispers of these elms that meet
> Round this dear lodge nor as the moon I greet
> That seems to rock as rock their summits tall
> And think how I have watched her [?trembling] face[35]

In the second fragment, he again turns to the memory of their birthplace, linking his creative powers with the river's sound:

> Yet once again, do I behold the forms
> Of these huge mountains, and yet once again,
> Standing beneath these elms, I hear thy voice,
> Beloved Derwent, that peculiar voice
> Heard in the stillness of the evening air,
> Half-heard and half-created.[36]

Inspired by the memory of his and Dorothy's return to the north, William writes these lines in the present indicative, as if in the presence of the mountains and the elms, with a palpable sense of the evening air. His use of apostrophe suggests immediacy and intimacy. But there is a wistful cadence in his repetition of 'yet once again' which calls attention to the indeterminate quality of the river's sound—somewhere between the heard and the imagined—and so to his absence from the scene he remembers.

In William's nostalgic turnings and returnings to the Derwent, there is a habitual pattern of association between his own listening as a poet, Dorothy's role as a listening sister, and the river's nurturing sound. Her distant role in his early life is perhaps suggested in the river's half-absence. There may also be a subliminal link between the names Derwent and Dorothy, suggesting that William thought of her as a *genius loci*, repeatedly embodied in the river's 'peculiar voice'. Dorothy was the first reader of William's poems, as well as frequently his amanuensis; and after 1794 there was nothing he wrote that did not imply her presence as listener, commentator, and potential contributor. The twinned and overlapping roles of the two siblings—he listening to the river's song, she to him as he composed—connote their symbiosis as well as their shared receptiveness to the spirit of place. In later poems, William was to make more explicit acknowledgements of her emotional and intellectual influence on his life. This involved further refinements in his language of implication, deepened by additional layerings of personal and topographical association.

*

During the early 1790s, the image of a shared home passed to and fro in the Wordsworths' writings like a talisman signifying their love. But their concern with belonging emerged on other levels, political and moral as well as personal. In the last decade of a century that had been marked by persistent international warfare, nostalgia had come to signify 'a disability of wartime and colonial mobility, a somatic revolt against forced travel, depopulation, emigration, and other forms of transience'.[37] Its main victims were soldiers, sailors, and expatriates compelled to live abroad; but it was also a condition experienced by the growing number of indigenous homeless people who wandered the roads of Britain looking for work and food. The Wordsworths' traumatic early experience of loss intensified their identification with the dispossessed. Like Rousseau and many other young European liberals at this time, they believed that human beings in a state of nature are free; that inequality is an intrinsic evil; and that the so-called advance of civilization brought many forms of oppression. In *An Evening Walk*, the poet's sympathy for the poor is evident in this striking vignette, which depicts a female vagrant with her children, dying of cold:

> No more her breath can thaw their fingers cold,
> Their frozen arms her neck no more can fold;
> Scarce heard, their chattering lips her shoulder chill,
> And her cold back their colder bosoms thrill.　　(ll. 281–4; EW, 64)

Redrafted over the course of several years, these lines epitomized William's encounters with human suffering while still a boy in Hawkshead. Since then, wandering through England and France in the years following the French Revolution, he had encountered many similar cases of displacement. Rootlessness and alienation were the key themes of his writing during England's war with France. Many of the poems he wrote in the 1790s depicted the plight of vagrants, whose lives on the open road pitted them against the elements, but who found greater kindness there than at the hands of exploitive landowners. Other poems focused on the domestic hardships and deprivations caused by war:

> And homeless near a thousand homes I stood,
> And near a thousand tables pined and wanted food.[38]

In the wake of the Terror, and after his first-hand experience of fathering an illegitimate child in France, William was temporarily drawn to the quietism of Godwin's *Political Justice*. The vision of perfectibility outlined in Godwin's system was grounded in reason, not the domestic affections, for a while offering respite from political and personal anxieties. But he came later to understand this Godwinian phase as a counter-intuitive detour from the main path of his life. He found his true course only when Dorothy (and the passage of time) led him back to the deeper consolations of nature, family, and home.

The Wordsworths' early attempts to build homes—first in Dorset, later in the Quantocks, and then briefly in Germany—took place in a perilous context of political unrest, when Jacobin sympathies were viewed with suspicion. William belonged to a circle of radicals whose place in public life was threatened. Many dissenters at this time (like Priestley) were driven into exile abroad. Others took refuge in obscure country retreats, like the activist John Thelwall, on the run after his trial for sedition. Throughout the dangerous years that coincided with the Wordsworths' homelessness, the memory of their birthplace played a restorative role in their emotional lives. After returning to the Lake District together in 1794, their dream of a shared future began to take shape. But although this reunion brought them personal fulfilment, it did not immediately supply the security they craved. After staying with their uncle and aunt at Whitehaven during late May 1794, they saw each other intermittently during the next month, but it was to be a further eighteen months before they lived together. Dorothy went to stay with cousins in Newcastle-upon-Tyne until the following spring, visiting the Hutchinsons at Sockburn near Darlington in April and spending the summer months of 1795 at Halifax. William returned alone to Windy Brow, where he stayed until January, giving help and comfort to his friend Raisley Calvert, who had contracted tuberculosis. Before he died, Calvert provided a bequest of £900 for William in his will, with a clause making Dorothy a co-beneficiary. This was an encouraging vote of confidence in William's creative ability, and a generous gesture toward the siblings, whose friendship had left a deep impression. The bequest, although not immediately forthcoming, gave them a modicum of security as they faced an uncertain future.

William departed from the North in early 1795 and took up residence in London, where he proposed to set up a political journal, *The Philanthropist*. ('I am of that odious class of men called democrats,' he wrote to William Mathews; 'I disapprove of monarchical and aristocratical governments, however modified.')[39] The plan for Dorothy to join him in London, earning an independent income as a translator, indicates that they envisaged a single household at the heart of the Godwinian circle in which William was then moving. As it turned out, serendipity drew them away from the capital. In September 1795, they accepted an offer from their friends John and Azariah Pinney to stay rent-free at their family home in Dorset. 'You know the pleasure which I have always attached to the idea of home, a blessing which I so early lost', Dorothy wrote excitedly to her old friend Jane Marshall (née

Pollard).[40] She and William planned to offer board, lodging, and elementary education to Basil Montagu, the child of a lawyer friend. Dorothy was well qualified as a teacher, and looking after the three-year-old Basil would bring a modest income into the household. By '*doing something*' she would be relieved of the humiliation of 'living upon the bounty of one's friends' and continuing always 'in a state of dependence, perhaps attended with poverty'.[41]

Racedown Lodge in rural west Dorset, where they moved in September 1795, was a substantial red-brick Georgian mansion in a remote spot less than 200 yards from the shore, with sea-views 'through different openings of the unequal hills'.[42] Dorothy characteristically looked for a resemblance to the Lake District in the local landscape: 'We have hills which seen from a distance almost take the character of mountains, some cultivated nearly to their summits, others in their wild state covered with furze and broom. These delight me the most as they remind me of our native wilds.'[43] For two years—long enough for them to think of the place as home—they lived there in seclusion. 'We are... both as happy as people can be who live in perfect solitude', Dorothy wrote in a letter to Jane Marshall. 'We do not see a soul.'[44] The rhythms of their domestic life together continued much as they had begun at Windy Brow, with long periods of reading and writing, interspersed with walks of 'about two hours every morning'.[45] Pilsdon Pen and Lewesdon Hill were both nearby. The post office was seven miles away at Crewkerne, and Dorothy thought nothing of walking there and back to collect letters. There was an orchard adjoining the house, and a garden where they grew vegetables. ('We plant cabbages, and... into cabbages we shall be transformed', William quipped in a letter.)[46] The Pinneys' library was well stocked, so they read widely, Dorothy's Italian greatly improving over the course of two years. Basil's education also absorbed them: they took their parental role seriously, delighting in the rapid progress he made. A servant, Peggy Marsh, helped with the housework and childcare, but they lived frugally, Dorothy having 'a good deal of employment' in repairing Basil's and William's clothes.[47] For both siblings, the two years spent in Dorset provided the foundation for lasting domestic happiness. There is no surviving evidence that Dorothy kept a journal at this time, although we know that a diary was purchased for her by Joseph Gill, overseer of Racedown Lodge, on Christmas Eve 1796.[48] Years later, showing her usual tendency to look fondly backwards, she was to remember Racedown as 'the place dearest to my recollections upon the whole surface of the island; it was the first home I had'.[49]

William had enjoyed the company of radicals while living in London, and until Coleridge's visit to Racedown in 1797 he missed the stimulation of active political engagement. But rural seclusion did nothing to soften his views. If anything, his sympathy for the poor intensified as he and Dorothy witnessed together the dreadful wartime conditions in which many rural families were living. At Windy Brow, Dorothy had observed (with more than a touch of Rousseau's romanticism) that local people were 'honest, worthy, uncorrupted', surviving on 'the bare necessaries of life';[50] but here things were otherwise. After the hard winter of 1794–5, prices had risen and the standard of living had deteriorated sharply. In November 1795, she noted with shock that 'The peasants are miserably poor; their cottages are shape-less structures... of wood and clay—indeed they are not at all beyond what might be expected in savage life.'[51] William concurred, commenting grimly that 'country people... are wretchedly poor; ignorant and overwhelmed with every vice that usually attends ignorance in that class, viz—lying and picking and stealing &c &c'.[52] As the Pitt ministry compelled public sup-port for the war, the conditions of the local poor in Dorset worsened, informing the revisions William made to *Salisbury Plain*. (Dorothy entered a fair copy of the extended poem, *Adventures on Salisbury Plain*, in a small octavo leather-bound notebook, probably in November.) In its new form, the poem protests against 'the calamities of war as they affect individuals',[53] emphasizing human suffering more clearly than the version written in 1793. A dark and haunting vision of social injustice and moral disintegration, it closes with the gruesome sacrificial image of an outlaw's body 'hung on high in iron case' (l. 820). No hope for political reform emerges; the only consolation offered is that human bonds of sympathy and love survive among the oppressed.

Despite his evident domestic happiness, William's writing indicates that throughout the Racedown years he was shaken by recent political and per-sonal events. The guilty memory of his liaison with Annette Vallon hung over him, and his faith in the cohesiveness of families was inevitably compromised by experience. Nature, during this period of disquiet, offered the consoling possibility of a benign order into which human beings could be peacefully assimilated. However, he did not subscribe to the Unitarians' faith in a system of optimism. There was always, in his thinking about nature, a combination of longing to be absorbed into oneness, and edgy, exiled consciousness. In Dorothy's company, he was able to look back on the turmoil of the previous decade and to process some of his most painful experiences. From October 1796 he was 'ardent in the composition of a tragedy', *The Borderers*, complet-ing a first draft of this five-act play by the following spring.[54] Its setting was a long way from Racedown, in the Border country between the Lake District

and Scotland which had captivated William's imagination as a child; but as
a study of betrayal, guilt, and suffering it was in keeping with his moral and
political concerns throughout 1795–7. As he took stock of the violence into
which the French Revolution had degenerated, he began to scrutinize the
motivations which drive human actions. In his anti-hero Rivers, he depicted
an amorality that was born of intellectual pride disguised as reason. It was
while writing *The Borderers* that he came to understand the insufficiency of
Godwin's system, and to reach beyond it.

When Mary Hutchinson came to stay for six months, in need of consolation after the recent death of her sister Margaret, her presence did not
disturb the quiet routine of the Wordsworths' lives. She was already accepted
almost as one of the family, and soon settled into the work of helping
Dorothy to transcribe William's poetry. Coleridge's visit in June 1797 was
more momentous, marking the beginning of a friendship which would last
many years, as well as a literary collaboration which would transform English
poetry. William had first encountered Coleridge as a radical Unitarian lec-
turer at Bristol. Their political affinities were already established; and the
two men had paid tribute to each other in poems. Coleridge greatly admired
Adventures on Salisbury Plain, a copy of which he had acquired from the
Pinneys in March 1796: it spoke directly to the concerns he himself had
been addressing in his Bristol lectures. When he turned up at Racedown—
leaping over the gate and bounding across the field to greet his new friends—
Dorothy was instantly drawn to him, mesmerized by his energy and charisma.
'He is a wonderful man', she enthused in a letter; 'His conversation teems
with soul, mind, and spirit.'[55] Friendship between the three companions
deepened during the days that followed, as they talked, exchanged memories, and read poetry.

When William read aloud 'The Ruined Cottage' and the first draft of
The Borderers, Coleridge was 'delighted' with them.[56] There was a resemblance between William's tragedy and his own, for *Osorio* too was a study of
guilt and sorrow, rich in its detailed account of psychological motivation. In
'The Ruined Cottage' (which William had also recently completed, in its
first version) he found something unique. This poem, arguably William's
greatest tragic study of the domestic affections, tells the desolating story of
a broken home. Linking the decline of an abandoned woman, Margaret,
with the disintegration of a house, it traces the gradual invasion of calm
oblivious nature into her dwelling. The poem's central arresting image of
'four ruined walls' brought into focus William's and Dorothy's preoccupa-

tions during the 1790s, working as a powerful signifier for the social conditions they had witnessed and deplored. At the same time, it spoke to their deepest personal fears, of abandonment, loneliness, and poverty on Dorothy's part; of guilt and remorse (especially in respect of Annette Vallon) on William's. Subliminally, the plot was connected at several different levels with their lives, and with their ongoing process of communal grieving. The recent death of Margaret Hutchinson may have influenced William's choice of a name for the abandoned woman. The Wordsworths' memory of losing the family home in 1783, and their experience of seeing it a decade later, deserted and run down, shaped the poem's elegiac motifs of loss and return.

No manuscript in William's hand survives of 'The Ruined Cottage' in its first form; but by the time Dorothy copied out a portion of the poem for Mary Hutchinson, in a letter dated 5 March 1798, it had grown far too long to transcribe in its entirety, so she sent only 'that part which is immediately and solely connected with the Cottage'.[57] This section of the poem, as it was 'completed' at Racedown and read to Coleridge, left the tragedy of Margaret's abandonment and death unresolved. After her death, the narrator stands looking into her overgrown garden, observing 'the secret spirit of humanity' that 'still survives' in a spot that had once been carefully tended. His need for the signs of human presence is a measure of his sympathy, quickened by the story he has heard:

> I stood, and leaning o'er the garden-gate
> Review'd that woman's suff'rings, and it seemed
> To comfort me while with a brother's love
> I bless'd her in the impotence of grief. (ll. 497–500; RCP, 73)

Dorothy, when transcribing the poem, left out a further substantial section which had been composed more recently. (This is now known as 'The Pedlar', and it concerns the narrator's relationship with Armytage, whose upbringing in the Lake District William describes in detail.) The longer version was more philosophically dense, but also more comforting, especially in its approach to death. As William extended the poem, under the influence of Coleridge's Unitarian faith, it became important to him to show that the narrator's companion, Armytage, was capable of moving beyond grief's impotence into an acceptance of mortality: 'She sleeps in the calm earth, and peace is here' (l. 512; RCP, 75). Stilled by the sight of a thistle silvered over 'By mist and silent rain-drops', Armytage understands that the recycling of human life is part of a providential pattern. Spiritual insight of this kind perhaps brought William and Dorothy comfort, not only for their own personal losses in childhood, but for the dispossession and poverty which they had witnessed, together and apart. Consolatory elements in their writings often emerged in response to each other's needs and fears, as if serving a medicinal function within the family.

*

Over the years, the Wordsworths came to believe in Nature as 'a kind of universal home'.[58] This idea would not be out of place in any of the key works of ecology published in the twentieth century: Heidegger's 'Being, Dwelling, Thinking', for instance, or Rachel Carson's *Silent Spring*, or James Lovelock's *Gaia*. The word 'ecology' derives in part from the Greek word meaning home. The perception of nature as a habitat for humans, fostering their needs and deserving care, lies at the centre of modern environmental ethics. This was not an idea that sprang out of the Wordsworths' heads fully formed. It evolved gradually through their successive attempts to make a home, strengthening with experience, the passage of time, and their interactions with other places, other minds. Coleridge's friendship and intellectual influence deepened their love of the natural world; but some of the credit must go to the beautiful environment in the West Country that surrounded the three friends during their *annus mirabilis*. An intermingling of creative voices began with Coleridge's visit to Racedown in June 1797, and continued, as we shall see in the next chapter, when he returned their hospitality in Somerset the following month. Out of this period of close companionship came Dorothy's *Alfoxden Journal*, *Lyrical Ballads*, and some blank verse poems (including, pre-eminently, 'Tintern Abbey'), which are numbered among the founding texts of Romantic environmentalism.

Much has been made of the differences (allegedly arising from gender) between William's and Dorothy's writings. But they had deep emotional and intellectual affinities which they discovered through a mutual understanding of loss, and actively sought to consolidate during their early years together. They became familiar with the ideas of Priestley, whose discovery of photosynthesis dissolved the tenuous boundary between organic and inorganic life, opening up a new world of affinities. They began to look more closely at the way that human beings can sustain a reciprocal bond with their environment through sympathy, which 'wider still...extends, | And sees not any line where being ends.'[59] Along with many of their contemporaries, they were fascinated by psychology, mental process, and the influence of environment on the emotions. Their belief in the importance of a rural upbringing for 'moral happiness' (Coleridge's phrase)[60] came partly through reading. But they also took a practical interest in education, following Rousseau's theories in *Emile*, and playing the role of foster-parents with curiosity and devotion. The idea that mattered most to them, holding their lives together and making sense of everything they did and wrote, was *association*. As an undergraduate, William had studied Locke's *Essay Concerning Human Understanding*; and from the mid-1790s he and Dorothy were familiar with the associationist psychology developed by David Hartley in *Observations on Man*. Even those who did not read this book understood its central concepts and metaphors—that the brain or *sensorium* is 'the seat of the sensitive soul'; that sensations are 'vibrations' in its 'medullary substance'; that pleasure is produced by moderate vibrations, pain by violent ones; that memories are 'traces' left by the perpetual recurrence of the same impressions or clusters of impressions; and that all the 'powers of the soul' including sympathy and the moral sense could be referred back to memory.[61] Hartley's understanding of the nervous system had an enormous impact on developments in eighteenth-century medicine (William Cullen, John Brown, and Priestley all modified his ideas); and his approach to mental process appealed to an entire generation of progressive writers, including feminists like Mary Wollstonecraft, for its egalitarianism. If as Hartley argued, the mind was shaped primarily by the environment rather than by innate characteristics, then equality was not just necessary for the progress of the human species but practical and achievable. Coleridge's assertion, for instance, that by 'beholding constantly the Best possible we at last become ourselves the best possible',[62] derived from Hartley's argument that humans were capable of perfection.

Coleridge was so devoted a Hartleyan during the 1790s that he named his first son after the philosopher. But later he came to mistrust the 'streamy' nature of associationism (its unwilled fluidity, which implied mental passivity.) In *Biographia Literaria* he was to relegate memory to the lowest and most mechanical of the mind's functions, for by that stage he believed (as Blake put it) that 'Imagination has nothing to do with memory'.[63] The Wordsworths, by contrast, kept faith with associationism throughout their lives. Hartley's account of mental process chimed with their exalted views of memory as a *creative* function, as well as reinforcing their belief in environmental influence. Their understanding of human relationships was shaped by

Hartley's ideas. When William wrote the following sentence in a letter to Dorothy in 1793, he knew he could count on her to understand the associationist context in which he was using the words 'pleasure', 'pain', and 'sympathy':

> How much do I wish that each emotion of pleasure and pain that visits your heart should excite as similar pleasure or a similar pain within me, by that sympathy which will almost identify us.[64]

William's yearning to merge his identity with his sister's, becoming almost her twin, arose from a need to heal the breach that had developed between them during childhood. If Hartley was right, even the tiniest differences in their sensibilities could be resolved in time, by companionship in the same environment. Any inequalities that might have resulted from their segregated upbringing and education could disappear altogether. For, as Hartley argued,

> If beings of the same nature, but whose affections and passions are, at present, in different proportions to each other, be exposed for an indefinite time to the same impressions and associations, all their particular differences will, at last, be overruled, and they will become perfectly similar, or even equal. They may also be made perfectly similar, in a finite time, by a proper adjustment of the impressions and associations.[65]

The meshing of associationist theory and practice provides an important key to understanding the Wordsworths' process of healing. This began in 1787 with the comparing of traumatic early memories, and continued throughout their life in joint activities: pre-eminently walking, talking, remembering, and grieving. Whether they saw things alone or together, they discussed what they wrote. As they created a common fund of memorable experiences, their use of associative language (echoes, quotations, allusions) confirmed their joint attunement to the connection between places and emotions. These rituals of communal recall were ways of mapping their unfolding lives onto their dwellings. Their function was at once elegiac, consolatory, and reparative.

3

Alfoxden

'Then it was
That the beloved Woman in whose sight
Those days were passed, now speaking in a voice
Of sudden admonition, like a brook
That does but cross a lonely road, and now
Seen, heard and felt, and caught at every turn,
Companion never lost through many a league,
Maintained for me a saving intercourse
With my true self; for, though impaired and changed
Much, as it seemed, I was no further changed
Than as a clouded, not a waning moon.'[1]

*

In the summer of 1797 the Wordsworths stayed with Coleridge at Nether
Stowey in Somerset, where he was living with his wife Sara and their
baby son Hartley. Dorothy wrote to Mary Hutchinson in July, expressing

her delight in the gently rolling downs, with views over the Bristol Channel, which they discovered in their daily walks from the tiny cottage in Lime Street. 'There is everything here; sea, woods wild as fancy ever painted, brooks clear and pebbly as in Cumberland, villages so romantic; and William and I, in a wander by ourselves, found out a sequestered waterfall in a dell.'[2] Remembering Lowther Woods near Penrith, where they had rambled together as reunited teenagers, Dorothy's letter captures some of the romantic flavour of old associations revitalized by new surroundings. Whether we call it homesickness or nostalgia, her habit of remembering the Lake District exerted a lifelong influence on how she perceived landscapes. Subliminally recalling the 'wild woods' of Milton's *Paradise Lost*, she paid Somerset her highest compliment by linking it with the lost land of her youth.[3] Adam uses this phrase (just after Eve has fallen, in Book IX) to describe the paradise he has shared with Eve, but must forego should he decide to eat the forbidden fruit. In a passionate expression of devotion, he chooses her companionship as a higher good than remaining in prelapsarian isolation:

> How can I live without thee, how forgo
> Thy sweet Converse and Love so dearly joined,
> To live again in these wild woods forlorn?
> Should God create another Eve, and I
> Another rib afford, yet loss of thee
> Would never from my heart; no no, I feel
> The link of Nature draw me: flesh of flesh,
> Bone of my bone thou art, and from thy state
> Mine never shall be parted, bliss or woe.[4]

Wandering with her brother through the Quantock woodlands, it appears that Adam's loyal and impassioned vow of fealty to Eve may have entered Dorothy's thoughts because she was imagining a paradise recovered, not lost, through human love.

The Wordsworths continued to enjoy 'sweet converse' in Somerset, but new friendships meant that they were left to their own devices less often than at Racedown. While Sara Coleridge looked after baby Hartley and attended to her guests, Dorothy helped Coleridge with last-minute corrections to *Poems* (1797), which had already been printed and bound: 'you might employ a boy for sixpence or a shilling to go thro' them & with a fine pen, and dainty ink, make the alterations in each volume', he reasoned in a letter to his Bristol publisher Joseph Cottle, enclosing a long list of errata and alterations in Dorothy's handwriting.[5] Her role as amanuensis in no way detracted from her intellectual status in Coleridge's eyes. In the same letter, he described her with the deepest respect and admiration:'Her manners are simple, ardent, impressive ... Her information various—her eye watchful in minutest observation of nature—and her taste a perfect electrometer—it bends, protrudes, and draws in, at subtlest beauties & most recondite faults.'[6] Coleridge's only sister Nancy had died in 1791, a loss which doubtless made him appreciate Dorothy all the more: he was shortly to refer to his new friend in a poem as 'My Sister'.[7] Of William he wrote absolutely, to Robert Southey:'[He] is a very great man—the only man, to whom *at all times & in all modes of excellence* I feel myself inferior.'[8] With the excitement that came from mutual admiration, the three friends shared their thoughts, feelings, memories. Among the poems they read in Coleridge's 1797 collection that summer was 'To the Rev. George Coleridge', in which the speaker wistfully recalls being 'too soon transplanted' (l. 18) from his birthplace in Devon to Christ's Hospital in London. Ideas about home, separation, exile, and familial love cannot have been very far from their thoughts whenever the companions talked.

A new arrival in the overcrowded cottage at Lime Street gave the group's psychological preoccupations a common focus. During July, Charles Lamb turned up, profoundly distressed and in need of consolation. His sister, in a fit of insanity, had killed their mother. It was a devastating tragedy, unthinkable in its violent rupture of sacred family bonds. Characteristically, both poets responded to Lamb's bereavement by offering him consolatory gifts. William, meeting him for the first time, read aloud his 'Lines left upon a seat in a yew-tree'; and Coleridge composed a new loco-descriptive poem, 'This Lime-Tree Bower my Prison'. Each poem describes a beautiful rural environment, advocating human community and celebrating nature's healing power. Wordsworth's is an inscription for a spot which had been his favourite evening walk as a boy at Hawkshead. (Drafts of it survive in a rough notebook used at Racedown, including some lines in the hand of Mary Hutchinson, which suggest early 1797 as a composition date.) It portrays a melancholy man, disenchanted with the world, who retreats to the seclusion of Esthwaite, finding some solace in its beauty but never again achieving faith in humanity. Declaring an anti-Godwinian position, William sets a higher value on love and humility than on reason or knowledge, seeking to reinforce the quasi-familial bond ('kindred loveliness') that connects human beings with the natural world. He sympathizes unequivocally with 'minds |

Warm from the labours of benevolence' (ll. 35–6) who love their fellow human beings as much as they love solitude. Drafted at Racedown, recited at Nether Stowey, and evoking the Lake District, 'Lines left upon a seat' involved a complex, layered sense of time and place.[9] There was no mistaking the environmental thrust of its moral philosophy, or its passionately regional emphasis. Lamb greatly admired the poem, which spoke implicitly to the disillusionment of a generation of radical intellectuals. Hoping for a memento of the friendships which had developed at Nether Stowey, he later wrote to Coleridge, asking for a copy of the poem: '*But above all that inscription!*—It will recall to me the tones of all your voices—and with them many a remembered kindness to one who could and can repay you all only by the silence of a grateful heart.'[10]

Inspired by William's use of inscription to evoke the healing spirit of place, Coleridge composed his poem while sitting in his neighbour Tom Poole's garden. 'This Lime-Tree Bower my Prison' commemorates a local walk taken by Lamb with the Wordsworths and Sara. The friends are described descending to the waterfall at Holford, then climbing up through the Quantock hills, returning homeward to Stowey as the sun sets. Unable to accompany them because of a recent accident, Coleridge wrote primarily to console Lamb for his tragic bereavement; but his poem shared the Wordsworths' concern with the reparative power of companionable movement through a beautiful landscape. While Lamb climbs to the hilltop with the Wordsworths, and gazes on a divinely transfigured landscape, Coleridge's solitary consciousness, embowered in Tom Poole's garden, is enlivened and soothed by tracing his friend's footsteps. Empathy with Lamb's suffering (and identification with the 'city-pent' schooldays which they had shared at Christ's Hospital), enables him to visualize this hillside walk as if he himself were there:

> So my Friend
> Struck with deep joy may stand, as I have stood,
> Silent with swimming sense; yea, gazing round
> On the wide landscape, gaze till all doth seem
> Less gross than bodily[11]

Writing from a position of exclusion (like Dorothy's during her Halifax childhood) Coleridge offers the possibility of *imagining* as a substitute for remembering. For years to come, this commemoration of walking as shared pilgrimage would be remembered in the Wordsworth circle. The pastoral meadows, rolling hills, and shorelines of Somerset continued to feature in the 'Conversation poems' of 1797–8 as the setting for real and imagined journeys towards spiritual health, each time rounding at the end to a renewed sense of belonging.

*

The daily activities that consolidated the Wordsworths' friendship with Coleridge during June and July were to continue uninterruptedly until the summer of 1798; for Dorothy and William had fallen in love with Somerset and decided to settle there. By a stroke of good fortune, shortly after Lamb's visit, Poole discovered that Alfoxden House—'a gentleman's seat, with a park & woods...in a most beautiful romantic situation by the sea-side'[12]— was currently empty. Set on the edge of the Quantocks a mile from the small village of Holford, four miles west of Nether Stowey, and available at the modest rent of £23 a year, it was ideal. They immediately signed the lease, moved in, and began to put down provisional roots. Dorothy revelled in the tremendous sense of space, unlike anywhere she had lived—'a large mansion, in a large park, with seventy head of deer around us'[13]—and the three companions soon settled into a daily routine of writing and reading, interspersed with walks to and from Stowey, through the woods of Holford Glen, and to the beaches of East Quantoxhead. They were relatively free of household cares: Peggy Marsh continued to look after their foster-child, Basil Montagu, while Sara Coleridge took care of Hartley. Visitors came to stay, bringing new creative stimuli to the neighbouring households. Coleridge's personality was like a magnet, attracting some of the foremost radical intellectuals of the age to this spot in the West Country, a region historically affiliated with dissent.[14]

The Jacobin activist John Thelwall, recently acquitted for treason but hounded from public life, became the Wordsworths' first guest at Alfoxden. 'We have been having a delightful ramble today along a wild romantic dell...through which a foaming, rushing, murmuring torrent of water winds its long artless course', he wrote to his wife Susan on 18 July.[15] Recording his impressions of this 'delightful retreat' in 'Lines written at Bridgwater' nine days later, he expressed his longing to settle permanently in the company of 'Allfoxden's musing tenant, and the maid | Of ardent eye', in an Arcadian setting where domestic bliss and 'philosophic amity' were intertwined. It would be as if a Golden Age had 'revived'.[16] Thelwall departed at the end of July, leaving a trail of damaging rumours in his wake. The local community, alerted to his presence, became convinced that this enclave of Jacobins with their strange ways was plotting sedition. At a time when fears of French invasion were intense—in February, 1,200 troops had landed near Fishguard—the alarm was raised, and the Home Office sent a special agent to make enquiries. Coleridge was later to make light of this episode in *Biographia Literaria*, remembering how the three companions were spied on while innocently rambling around the countryside talking about philosophy. But in truth the suspicions of neighbours had serious consequences, for within two months of their arrival the Wordsworths were informed that the lease on the house would not be renewed the following year.

The Godwinian philanthropist Tom Wedgwood and his brother John paid a less disruptive visit in September. They arrived with a view to persuading Coleridge and Wordsworth to run an experimental academy for young geniuses. Their objective was to encourage and systematically monitor the growth of genius from infancy, implementing the fashionable educational ideas that had developed out of Locke's associationist model of the mind. The plan appealed to the progressive idealism of the two people envisaged as superintendents; but its programmatic method was ill suited to their temperaments. As the Wedgwoods must have observed, William and Dorothy's foster-child was being raised according to principles outlined in Rousseau's *Emile*—with 'no other companions, than the flowers, the grass, the cattle, the sheep'[17]—and although Dorothy was well qualified as an infant-teacher, neither of the two men had the right credentials. The Wedgwood brothers left, disappointed; but with their admiration for Coleridge in no way diminished. A few months later, they generously provided the annuity which enabled this young man, poised on the brink of becoming a Unitarian minister, to pursue his vocation as a poet.

The Wedgwoods' visit doubtless contributed to the intellectual ferment at Alfoxden and Stowey, prompting discussions about education and further memories of childhood. William's work on 'The Pedlar' shows him thinking back to his upbringing in Cumberland, and confidently declaring that the daily presence of 'ancient mountains' and 'silent stars' was a matchless foundation for creative and moral development. In 'Frost at Midnight' Coleridge imagined Hartley's future, wandering 'like a breeze | By lakes and sandy shores' in a local landscape overlaid with Wordsworthian memories;[18] and in 'The Nightingale', a gift-poem of friendship addressed to William and Dorothy, he welcomed Hartley's pleasure in nocturnal sights and sounds as evidence that the baby (true to his name) was already learning to 'associate' the night with joy. Associationism was a philosophy that linked all three companions closely together, but in a different formation from the one proposed by the Wedgwoods. In conversation, walking, and writing, they actively explored the ways in which associations connect human beings to each other, and to a particular stretch of land. The writings produced in the Wordsworth circle during the years 1797–8 celebrated not only a place but also the bonding of three creative personalities into a community. 'I shall not preach up the idle doctrine of sympathies and instinctive attachments', Thelwall had earlier observed in *The Peripatetic*, 'but there is certainly a kind of mental attraction, by which dispositions that assimilate, like the correspondent particles of matter, have a tendency to adhere whenever they are brought within the sphere of mutual action.'[19] European ideas about friendship during the 1790s were influenced by the chemical theory of bonding to which Thelwall here alludes, and this may well have shaped how the three friends understood their intellectual and spiritual affinities in 1798.[20] The chemical meaning of 'bond' can thus be noted as one of this word's multiple meanings as we analyse the processes of exchange-through-gift which held this particular community together. A chemical analogy is also implied in the word 'amal-gamate', sometimes used in the Wordsworth circle to describe the absorp-tion of one friend's personality into another's. (Poole had 'fears about amalgamation' in respect of Coleridge's relationship with William, for instance.) Keats later observed that 'Men who live together have a silent moulding and influencing power over each other—They inter-assimilate.'[21] His model of friendship blends a vocabulary of chemical bonding with a Hartleyan approach to inter-subjectivity. The organic metaphors he uses (moulding, influencing, and inter-assimilating) are resonant in the context of many kinds of long-term relationship.

Thelwall's claim that bonding is most effective when friends are 'brought within the sphere of mutual action' is borne out by what happened to the Wordsworths and Coleridge in Somerset during 1798. The combined experi-ences of conversation, walking, and writing made this a year all three of them would treasure forever, forging powerful emotional attachments and shared memories. Energetic walking in a threesome proved extremely effective as a creative stimulus, as when 'The Ancient Mariner' emerged out of a joint tour in November to the Valley of the Rocks; 'The Thorn' out of a sight noticed with Dorothy on a Quantock ridge; and 'The Nightingale' out of a nocturnal ramble taken in the woods at Alfoxden. United in their environmental phil-osophy, the friends nonetheless had crucial differences. Initially bowled over

by his new companion's religious enthusiasm, William misguidedly succumbed
to the plan to write a philosophical epic (*The Recluse*) envisaging mankind's
progress towards enlightenment. It was a grand scheme, much better suited to
Coleridge's visionary Unitarianism than to William's meditative humanism;
and frictions would develop over the years as the poem failed to materialize.
Formal attempts at collaboration such as 'The Three Graves' and 'The Wanderings of Cain' also proved abortive, the minds of the two men pulling in opposite directions—'I soon found the style of COLERIDGE and myself would
not assimilate', William remembered many years later.[22] In collaboration on
Lyrical Ballads the fault lines of their relationship began to be clearly visible.
But work on that volume did not begin in earnest until the spring of 1798,
and in the meantime exploration of the local landscape drew the three
companions together in an intimacy they would never forget. 'Tho we were
three persons, it was but one God', Coleridge recollected.[23]

*

Dorothy's *Alfoxden Journal* was begun in January 1798 with the knowledge
that the lease on Alfoxden House would shortly run out; and the sense it
conveys of Somerset as home may have derived from her need to make a
lasting memorial of the place before leaving it. Over the course of four
months she experimented with a vivid notational prose style, catching the
transitory effects of weather and light along the woody coastline of the
Quantock hills. Keeping a journal bonded her to the surrounding countryside, just as the daily companionship of her brother and Coleridge invested
it with meaning. Precisely mapping their day-to-day movements around
Alfoxden, she recorded an intense period of collaborative activity centred on
friendship and conversation. As a repository of distilled images, precisely
located in time and place and associated with feelings, the journal may have
been treated as a kind of commonplace book, for communal use. Much of
the creative work of this year depended on three-way conversations between
William, Dorothy, and Coleridge, so at least one other person was present,
either at the scene of writing or soon after. In most journal entries it is clear
who the writing-subject is, but not always whether she is alone when observing and writing. Some are written in the present tense, suggesting they were
outdoor 'sketches'; others review the day's happenings. Personal pronouns are
often omitted, probably because the experiences described were collective.

There is no surviving manuscript of the journal, which was first published in heavily abridged form by William Knight in 1897; but its four

opening sentences appear in William's handwriting in the *Alfoxden Notebook* (DC MS 14). Because they have the appearance there of a first draft, rather than a copy, Pamela Woof has identified him as 'the base author' (p. 274). However, shared authorship is equally plausible, and Woof's hint that the Wordsworths may have talked these sentences into existence together is intriguing.[24] The celebration of fluid synergy in their syntax and imagery might indeed suggest that this is a scene of shared creativity:

> The green paths down the hill-sides are channels for streams. The young wheat is streaked by silver lines of water running between the ridges, the sheep are gathered together on the slopes. After the wet dark days, the country seems more populous. It peoples itself in the sunbeams.   (p. 141)

More formal than later entries, this one has a celebratory mood—almost psalmic—but there is nothing else to suggest that it is the first entry in a first journal. No mention of the eye that observes; no statement of intent in writing. The 'living prospect'[25] is assembled sequentially through images that are rapid and clear, like watercolour paintings, catching the vibrancy of nature through movement and relationship. The connection of each image to the next is established in a series of syntactical parallels, with metrical echoes linking them together: this gives the sense of a balanced, unified composition. The passive voice changes to the active in the third sentence, and the rhythm quickens, as if in response to the awakening countryside. The fourth sentence, a rare example of metaphor, stands out because of its brevity, and because it rethinks the sentence that comes before. With a single phrase, 'peoples itself', the journal establishes the vital link between nature and human beings which is its subject.

Over the four months in which Dorothy kept the journal, she found her own distinctive voice through the practice of writing, much as she explored the terrain she would soon be leaving behind. A clear development can be traced over the course of time. Alongside gothic touches, the opening journal-entries contain a number of fanciful metaphors, similes, and personifications, the marks of a self-conscious writer using a poetic register: the garden is a 'mimic of spring' (p. 141); moss cups are 'more proper than acorns for fairy goblins' (p. 141). As the journal progresses, so does its style. Artificial diction diminishes, giving way to straightforward syntax, clear images, and down-to-earth analogies. Dorothy's similes increasingly draw on the familiar and the homely: a labourer jumps with 'the friskiness of a cow upon a sunny day' (p. 149); the sea is 'like a basin full to the margin' (p. 147); a single

leaf dances round and round 'like a rag blown by the wind' (p. 149). She stops
naming the stars, and her interest in night skies diminishes as she becomes
more concerned with the diurnal than with the other-worldly. The *Alfoxden
Journal* enabled Dorothy to articulate her own aesthetic allegiances, while
simultaneously recording observations on behalf of the group. Even though
the personal pronoun is mostly elided, her first journal contains an embry-
onic narrative of her developing identity as a writer.

William drew on many kinds of prose, for different purposes, during
1798, but although he was creatively stimulated by guidebooks and topographical works, they didn't yield the same rich possibilities as his sister's
writing. Dorothy's journal had a combination of lyrical intensity, sentimental attachment, and grounded particularity which distinguished it
from all the other prose he was learning from at this time. Scholars have
argued that aesthetic theorists of the day, such as Uvedale Price and Richard Payne Knight, influenced how she 'stationed' herself and 'composed'
her pictures. But she was far less indebted to the picturesque tradition
than has been supposed. She mocked the local squire's efforts to shape a
fashionable garden, pointing out that 'Nature was very successfully striv-
ing to make beautiful what art had deformed' (p. 152); and she was thankful that the more permanent features of landscape could not be interfered
with: 'Happily we cannot shape the huge hills, or carve out the valleys
according to our fancy' (p. 152). In her handling of perspective, she continually broke the rules. Picturesque views are momentarily brought into
focus in one sentence, only to be dismantled in the next. Details seen at
eye level are noted, and paths draw the eye downward, enabling surfaces
to be seen in depth and detail: 'the road to the village of Holford glittered
like another stream' (p. 143). Distant prospects are displaced by objects in
the foreground, and the tiniest creatures are sometimes seen with almost
visionary clarity:

> On our return the mist still hanging over the sea, but the opposite coast clear,
> and the rocky cliffs distinguishable. In the deep Coombe, as we stood upon
> the sunless hill, we saw the hills of grass, light and glittering, and the insects
> passing.   (p. 145)

Dorothy shared with contemporary natural historians a sense of wonder at
the mysterious and beautiful intricacy of the natural world. Her absorption
in the movement of insects confirmed an instinct that was the reverse of the
picturesque. Stimulated by Erasmus Darwin, she noted botanical details with
the eye of a miniaturist: 'the purple-starred hepatica', 'the hollies capriciously

bearing berries', 'the adders tongue and the ferns' (pp. 141, 145). A questioning presence in her journal surfaced in scientific queries.

Gilbert White's *Natural History of Selborne* (1789) offered a minutely observed habitat that is comparable to Dorothy's Alfoxden. However, White's register was that of a learned scientist, cataloguing facts and weaving classical allusions into his discourse. Dorothy's language is notable for its plainness of diction, its sensual clarity, and its eye-on-the-object naturalism. It expresses her political allegiance to the Unitarian tradition of vernacular directness advocated by Priestley, inculcated at the Warrington Academy, and accepted as a norm in the progressive milieu in Halifax where she received her education. The compressed immediacy of her writing, her preference for metonymy rather than metaphor, her use of deictic syntax, enable her to celebrate her bond with nature simply by looking at what she sees in a specific place and recording one by one her impressions. Often, the omission of auxiliary verbs creates the illusion of unmediated, atemporal perception: 'The villages marked out by beautiful beds of smoke. The turf fading into the mountain road. The scarlet flowers of moss' (p. 142). Each image is a self-contained moment in time. Nothing apparently threads the images together. Taken as a sequence, the effect is as powerful as an imagist poem.

The *Alfoxden Journal* may well have sharpened William's awareness of the poetic possibilities of prose, the medium he would later put on a par with poetry in his Preface to *Lyrical Ballads*. Although it was not until 1800 that he theorized his views about the relationship between these media, 1798 was the year in which he threw off 'gaudiness and inane phraseology', experimenting instead with 'well-authenticated fact', 'personal observation', 'language [that] has been equally intelligible for these last three centuries', and 'conversation with friend[s]'.[26] Through the symbiosis of his sister's journal entries and his own writing, he realized daily that poetry and prose belong to the same family: 'They both speak by and to the same organs; the bodies in which both of them are clothed may be said to be of the same substance, their affections are kindred, and almost identical... the same human blood circulates through the veins of them both.'[27] A meeting point between poetry and prose is clearly visible in the relationship between Dorothy's journal entry for 25 January and 'A Night-Piece', both of which I quote in full below:

> The sky spread over with one continuous cloud, whitened by the light of the
> moon, which, though her dim shape was seen, did not throw forth so strong

a light as to chequer the earth with shadows. At once the clouds seemed to cleave asunder, and left her in the centre of a black-blue vault. She sailed along, followed by multitudes of stars, small, and bright, and sharp. Their brightness seemed concentrated, (half-moon).[28]

> The sky is overspread
> With a close veil of one continuous cloud
> All whitened by the moon, that just appears,
> A dim-seen orb, yet chequers not the ground
> With any shadow—plant, or tower, or tree.
> At last a pleasant instantaneous light
> Startles the musing man whose eyes are bent
> To earth. He looks around, the clouds are split
> Asunder, and above his head he views
> The clear moon and the glory of the heavens.
> There in a black-blue vault she sails along
> Followed by multitudes of stars, that small
> And bright, and sharp along the gloomy vault
> Drive as she drives. How fast they wheel away!
> Yet vanish not! The wind is in the trees;
> But they are silent. Still they roll along
> Immeasurably distant, and the vault
> Built round by those white clouds, enormous clouds,
> Still deepens its interminable depth.
> At length the vision closes, and the mind
> Not undisturbed by the deep joy it feels,
> Which slowly settles into peaceful calm,
> Is left to muse upon the solemn scene.[29]

William claimed in old age to have composed his poem 'on the road between Nether Stowey and Alfoxden, extempore'[30]—testimony which some scholars have disregarded as unreliable, preferring to approach Dorothy's prose as a source for William's poem. The bare particularity of Dorothy's style is reflected in the prosaic minimalism of William's. But whichever piece came first (and we should not rule out the possibility that the siblings were writing alongside each other), both discover a creative confluence between the resources of poetry and of prose. William's poem opens abruptly, like a journal entry, and in one or two places words and images correspond exactly ('chequer', for instance, and 'vault'). Both descriptions are shaped as epiphanies, conveying the viewer's excitement as the moon emerges clearly in the immense depth of the night sky, accompanied by stars. Both writers convey a tremendous sense of movement through paired verbs—'cleave' and 'sail' in

Dorothy's case; 'split' and 'wheel' in William's. The adjectival grouping 'small, and bright, and sharp' works in both cases to concentrate the mind on a distinct visual image. The most important difference between journal entry and poem is that Dorothy concentrates on the female moon (a traditional poetic image), staying with it till the end of her description; while William develops an analogy between the man's 'startled' consciousness and the agitated sky. To see Dorothy's journal simply as a 'source', an 'influence', or even a kind of *pre-writing* of William's verse is an over-simplification. Using exact verbal correspondences to establish priority is beside the point when we can instead think in terms of shared perceptions, shared vocabulary, even shared oral composition.

Dorothy's way of writing fed into William's creative *habits*. Its significance was as much to do with practices and processes as with subject matter and content. What he found in the *Alfoxden Journal* was nothing less than 'journal-ness' itself: the rhythms of daily experience, and local sights and sounds as the materials of poetry. This enabled him to connect vitally with nature's generative processes, drawing creative energy from his immediate environment and living mindfully in the present tense:

> The eye it cannot chuse but see,
> We cannot bid the ear be still;
> Our bodies feel, where'er they be,
> Against, or with our will.
>
> Nor less I deem that there are powers,
> Which of themselves our minds impress,
> That we can feed this mind of ours,
> In a wise passiveness.[31]

Above all, Dorothy's *Alfoxden Journal* crystallized, for William, the role played by local associations in a human sense of belonging. Its therapeutic role in freeing up his creativity was inseparable from the mnemonic function it performed in the household. The journal was a manual in the local workings of Hartleyan association which could be used as a future resource. In it, Dorothy laid the foundations for an understanding of the relation between local attachments, memory, and moral growth.[32] In consulting it, turning back to it, drawing on it, William embedded himself further in the stretch of countryside it described, much as he would later inscribe his family in the landscape round Grasmere through his 'Poems on the Naming of Places'. In this way, Dorothy's journal played its part in the sentimental afterlife of

Alfoxden as a surrogate home for the Wordsworth family: a place that almost matched Cumberland in their affections. When he came to dictate his notes to Isabella Fenwick in old age, his fullest descriptive accounts of places connected with poems were about the 'credal lyrics' of 1798.[33]

*

The Wordsworths' *annus mirabilis* in Somerset had begun at Coleridge's cottage in Nether Stowey with William reading his Esthwaite inscription to Charles Lamb. It ended with two scenes of reading in the park at Alfoxden. In 'My First Acquaintance with Poets', Hazlitt remembered how, after walking all the way from Shropshire to see Coleridge, he was entertained on two separate occasions to open-air recitals of poems later published in *Lyrical Ballads*, finding in them 'that deeper power and pathos which have been since acknowledged'.[34] This was an altogether different kind of poetry from the inscription which, the previous year, had so delighted Lamb. Many of the ballads composed in the spring of 1798 were based on West Country stories and real-life anecdotes. 'The Last of the Flock' describes how a Holford farmer is obliged to sell off his flock to feed a large family. 'The Mad Mother' drew on a story related to Coleridge by a Bristol friend. The character of Peter Bell was based on a 'wild rover' who had accompanied William on his walk from Builth to Hay-on-Wye in 1793, telling him 'strange stories'.[35] Although 'Simon Lee' names the 'sweet shire of Cardigan' as its setting, the old man portrays Christopher Trickie, a local hunstman; and the credal lyrics of this year (even those nominally set in Esthwaite) take their inspiration from the woods around Alfoxden, which also provide the setting for the child's perilous night ride under a moonlit sky in 'The Idiot Boy'. Published later the same year, the West Country provenance of many of its ballads was part of the radical volume's claim to authenticity. Hearing them read aloud, Hazlitt remembered feeling 'the sense of a new style and a new spirit in poetry'. 'It had to me', he wrote, 'something of the effect that arises from the turning up of the fresh soil, or the first welcome breath of Spring.'[36]

Hazlitt barely noticed Dorothy during his memorable visit to Alfoxden in 1798. But her influential importance, as both a sister and a writer, was acknowledged by William in two of the poems he included in *Lyrical Ballads*. The first of these, 'Lines written at a small distance from my house', was written in quatrains as a verse letter addressed to her. The tender fiction is that their young charge Basil Montagu will carry the letter into Alfoxden

House, where Dorothy sits reading, and tempt her to 'come forth' so that all three of them can join in idle enjoyment of the spring weather:

> It is the first mild day of March:
> Each minute sweeter than before,
> The red-breast sings from the tall larch
> That stands beside our door.   (ll. 1–4)

Prompted by immediate surroundings and celebrating William's newly awakened faith in nature's 'blessing', this is a quintessentially Alfoxden poem. Its domestic details—the tree by the door, the just-finished breakfast, the little boy running from the woods into the house—indicate how the local and the humdrum have begun to shape his poetry. The present tense in the quatrains, their enjoyment of immediacy, in touch with the spring, announces a fresh quality in his work:

> No joyless forms shall regulate
> Our living Calendar:
> We from to-day, my friend, will date
> The opening of the year.
>
> Love, now an universal birth,
> From heart to heart is stealing,
> From earth to man, from man to earth:
> —It is the hour of feeling.
>
> One moment now may give us more
> Than fifty years of reason:
> Our minds shall drink at every pore
> The spirit of the season.
>
> Some silent laws our hearts may make,
> Which they shall long obey:
> We for the year to come may take
> Our temper from to-day.   (ll. 17–32)

Boldly inviting Dorothy to abandon Gregorian time (as did the French Revolutionaries), William suggests that they date the year from this moment, 1 March 1798, and chronicle their future together in the 'living calendar' of feeling. His new preoccupation with diurnal time affectionately acknowledges what his sister has given him, not just emotionally, through her continuous presence, but creatively, in her journal's day-by-day celebration of their shared connection with a special place, a particular spring.

'Tintern Abbey' is the second poem in *Lyrical Ballads* to identify Dorothy's importance openly and dialogically. She features here as the friend, sister, and muse who is vital to William's spiritual and creative life. The poem was composed after the lease on Alfoxden House had come to an end, when the Wordsworths were temporarily homeless and missing Coleridge's company. On a four- or five-day tour in Monmouthshire, they crossed the Severn Ferry, walking ten miles to Tintern Abbey, where they stayed the night on 10 July. The following day they walked along the river through Monmouth to Goodrich Castle, returning to Tintern for the night of 12 July before pushing on to Chepstow and back to Bristol. As they took in the beauty of their surroundings, they were more than usually conscious of their unsettled prospects before departing for Germany. This was Dorothy's first sight of the valley, but for William the place was already overlaid with memories. On returning from France, he had wandered across Salisbury Plain, and from there to the Wye. Homeless at the time, and disturbed by his recent traumatic experiences, he drew on his encounters during that journey when writing 'A Night on Salisbury Plain' and later 'The Female Vagrant'. In 1798, as he prepared to leave England, this time with Dorothy, he reflected on his recovery from the emotional crisis of 1793, giving thanks for the years spent in his sister's company. Opening with an ellipsis, 'Tintern Abbey' is haunted by the human sense of being in time, of passing through and returning changed, of going forward into the unknown:

> Five years have passed; five summers, with the length
> Of five long winters! and again I hear
> These waters, rolling from their mountain-springs
> With a sweet inland murmur.—Once again
> Do I behold these steep and lofty cliffs,
> Which on a wild secluded scene impress
> Thoughts of more deep seclusion; and connect
> The landscape with the quiet of the sky.   (ll. 1–8)

Rooting himself in the here and now, the speaker uses immediate impressions ('these steep and lofty cliffs', 'this dark sycamore') to convey the illusion that the landscape is before him as he writes. But if his later account is to be trusted, he composed the poem in his head (probably reciting it aloud, and discussing it with Dorothy as they walked along), only to write it down on their arrival in Bristol. Her powers of recall, and the possibility that she played more than just a listening role, make it plausible that all 160 lines were composed and committed to memory during their tour.

As they walked together through the Wye Valley, either a conversation or the landscape itself must have reminded the Wordsworths of the pilgrimage to Cockermouth they had made in 1794, when they saw their childhood home deserted and run down. William had later transformed this nostalgic visit into an apostrophe to his 'Beloved Derwent', reuniting himself with his birthplace and identifying it as a creative source:

> Yet once again do I behold the forms
> Of these huge mountains, and yet once again,
> Standing beneath these elms, I hear thy voice,
> Beloved Derwent, that peculiar voice
> Heard in the stillness of the evening air,
> Half-heard and half-created.[37]

The opening lines of 'Tintern Abbey', with their mantra-like refrain—'again I hear', 'Once again | Do I behold', 'I again repose', 'Once again I see'—return to this earlier fragment, drawing on its rhythms and associations to invest the Wye with memories of home. Dorothy's presence is tacitly acknowledged through this tribute to their shared origins. Walking now beside a different river, the shadowy outline of a Cumberland landscape is clearly visible behind the 'steep and lofty cliffs' of the Wye Valley, just as the decayed family home is vestigially present in the ruined abbey a few miles downstream.

Revisiting a spot he has seen before, and conscious of the fleeting nature of his own presence in the landscape, William lays claim to the 'wild secluded scene', not as a picturesque view that can be framed or a physical possession that can be owned, but as a communal memory that can be carried everywhere:

> The day is come when I again repose
> Here, under this dark sycamore, and view
> These plots of cottage-ground, these orchard-tufts,
> Which, at this season, with their unripe fruits,
> Among the woods and copses lose themselves,
> Nor, with their green and simple hue, disturb
> The wild green landscape. Once again I see
> These hedge-rows, hardly hedge-rows, little lines
> Of sportive wood run wild; these pastoral farms
> Green to the very door; and wreathes of smoke
> Sent up, in silence, from among the trees...   (ll. 9–19)

Tacitly critiquing the tourist's craving for picturesque ruins and monuments, this description draws our attention away from the abbey itself, quietly enumerating the details of a semi-domesticated pastoral scene that would not be out of place in Dorothy's *Alfoxden Journal*.[38] The choice of register is more significant than the details selected, declaring William's allegiance to georgic, a tradition Dorothy was at home in.[39] He singles out 'unremarkable' features in the landscape, of a kind that might be found in any spot where the boundary between nature and humanity is being gradually effaced.[40] The poem allows a confluence between the prosaic and the poetic, incorporating Dorothy's detailed style of notation into the 'impassioned music' of its verse. As it progresses, the low-key descriptive register gives way to abstract religious language, affirming a 'sense sublime | Of something far more deeply interfused, | Whose dwelling is the light of setting suns' (ll. 96–8). But this impulse towards transcendence is balanced by a profound sense of embodiment, of being at home in the world: 'While with an eye made quiet by the power | Of harmony, and the deep power of joy, | We see into the life of things' (ll. 48–50).

In the benign and healing perspective 'Tintern Abbey' offers, humankind is intimately bonded to nature; not alienated from it, elevated above it, or creating dissonance within it. Nonetheless, there are disturbances in the poem's otherwise tranquil vision. The speaker touches on the presence of nearby charcoal furnaces and the conditions of life endured by 'vagrant dwellers in the houseless woods' (l. 21). He alludes to industrial pollution around the abbey with the image of 'smoke | Sent up, in silence, from among the trees' (ll. 18–19). He wards off the experience of loneliness, mid 'the din | Of towns and cities'(ll. 26–7), with the memory of beauty; and he consciously resigns political consciousness to a quietist understanding of 'the still, sad music of humanity' (l. 92). 'Tintern Abbey' is a hymn to nature, a fervent prayer that she will never betray his love, but there are moments of doubt, when the confident declarative mood modulates into the conditional and the optative: 'If this | Be but a vain belief', 'I would believe' (ll. 50–1; l. 88). The poem gives voice to wishes, hopes and needs, not to settled pieties.

Throughout, Dorothy's role as implied listener shapes this poem's wandering, exploratory methods of persuasion. She is sometimes acknowledged through echo and allusion, sometimes through hesitancies in the argument, and finally in direct address. As William builds towards his conclusion, there is a mounting urgency in his claims, and his sister begins to occupy centre stage:

> Nor, perchance,
> If I were not thus taught, should I the more
> Suffer my genial spirits to decay:

> For thou art with me, here, upon the banks
> Of this fair river; thou, my dearest Friend,
> My dear, dear Friend, and in thy voice I catch
> The language of my former heart, and read
> My former pleasures in the shooting lights
> Of thy wild eyes.   (ll. 112–20)

The solemn words 'For thou art with me' echo Psalm 23, acknowledging the deeply spiritual quality of the covenant between brother and sister: 'Yea, though I walk through the valley of the shadow of death, | I will fear no evil: *for thou art with me*'. Entrusting Dorothy with the task of sustaining the memory of this spot when he is gone, William pays tribute to her power to protect the spirit of place. His language works performatively, like a spell: 'Therefore let the moon | Shine on thee', 'Nor, perchance...wilt thou then forget' (ll. 135–6; ll. 147–50). The tone is somewhere between tender solicitation, prayer, and entreaty:

> When thy mind
> Shall be a mansion for all lovely forms,
> Thy memory be as a dwelling-place
> For all sweet sounds and harmonies; Oh! then,
> If solitude, or fear, or pain, or grief,
> Should be thy portion, with what healing thoughts
> Of tender joy wilt thou remember me.   (ll. 140–6)

Some critics have berated William for silencing his sister and co-opting her future as an extension of his own; others have accused him of infantilizing her, claiming for himself the superiority of an enhanced language and vision. None of these readings takes into account the sense of Dorothy's individual *presence*—the detail of her 'wild eyes', for instance, which connect her with the 'wild secluded scene'; or the personal history of their separation in childhood, which strengthens his gratitude for their life together. However we characterize the speaker's tone, his subject-position is one of maturity acquired through suffering.[41] Like Coleridge in 'This Lime-Tree Bower my Prison', he draws on the ancient homiletic analogy between passing through life and walking through a valley. Just as Coleridge had empathized with Lamb's experience of 'evil and pain | And strange calamity' ('This Lime-Tree Bower My Prison', ll. 31–2), so William implies that solitude, fear, pain, and grief may again be Dorothy's 'portion'. Coleridge drew on his memories to shape Lamb's imagined pilgrimage towards enlightenment: 'So my Friend | Struck with deep joy may stand, | As I have stood'.[42] In the same way,

William figures Dorothy's journey as a recapitulation of his own, but thankfully in his company: '*Together we have stood*' (emphasis added). He is in advance of his sister by virtue of age and experience, having travelled this way before and been changed in the process. Although he identifies her as a younger version of himself, now undertaking a pilgrimage by his side, he also pays tribute to her as the keeper of memories, guardian of place, and nurse of his creative spirit. The biblical echo in 'thou art with me' connotes her pastoral role as spiritual guide.

*

Lyrical Ballads (1798) was an anonymous publication—the names of Coleridge, Dorothy, and William are missing from the title page—but all three writers were involved in collaboration, and there was no competition for ownership. However, the organization of the volume is highly signifi-cant. If the 'Advertisement' is a manifesto for the poetics of familiarity which these writers shared—anti-Godwinian, boldly provincial, and centred on the domestic affections—'Tintern Abbey' is distinctively 'Wordswor-thian' in the family sense of that word. When William turns to Dorothy, identifying her first as his 'dear, dear Friend' (l. 117) and second as his 'dear, dear Sister' (l. 122), he collapses into each other the two creative identities closest to him. 'Dear Friend' is how Coleridge would later be addressed in *The Prelude*, and there were many occasions when William thought of his friend and sister in the same breath. If we take into account the position of 'Tintern Abbey' at the end of the volume, we can see that the poem fulfils an important double role. It is at once the culminating work of 1798, draw-ing the triangular conversations of the preceding year into synthesis, and the expression of a unique form of emotional and spiritual kinship. In this poem, William looks back on the years he has spent with his sister since their reunion, and folds her vision of nature into his own. He imitates the georgic realism of her journal, tacitly acknowledging her intellectual influ-ence through poetic associations and allusions. He charges her with the sacred task of preserving the valley's memory, just as she had preserved Alfoxden in her prose. In doing all this, he establishes diurnal experience and recollection as the central concerns of his writing. His blessing on her is an 'envoi' to the *Lyrical Ballads* volume. It identifies her as the *genius loci* of a specific region, but also as the guardian spirit of a particular moment in publishing history. With its elegiac echoes of Cockermouth and its moving address to Dorothy as the muse of memory, 'Tintern Abbey' remained throughout the Wordsworths' lives both a memorable credo and a touchstone for their creative collaboration.

4

Hamburg

'You can scarcely conceive how the jarring contrast between the sounds which are now for ever ringing in my ears and the sweet sounds of All-foxden makes me long for the country again. After three years residence in retirement a city in feeling, sound and prospect is hateful.'[1]

*

A 'delightful scheme' to visit Germany was hatched in Somerset during March 1798, almost as soon as it was confirmed that the lease on Alfoxden House would not be renewed. Together with the Coleridges and a few other friends, William and Dorothy would form a 'little colony' (the terms are reminiscent of Pantisocracy) 'to acquire the German language, and to furnish ourselves with a tolerable stock of information in natural science'.[2] In a letter to James Losh, inviting him to join them, William noted that they planned to live in a village, preferably 'in a pleasant, and if we can, a mountainous country'.[3] But they would also need to be near a university, because the main purpose of the visit was, as Coleridge put it, 'intellectual utility'—to which he added the experiential goals of 'moral happiness' and 'the wisdom that 3 or 4 months sojourn among a new people must give to a watchful & thinking man'.[4] Dorothy, for her part, had high hopes of the tour, which she saw as an opportunity 'to make some addition to our resources by translating from the German, the most profitable species of literary labour, and of which I can do almost as much as my Brother'.[5] However, in quitting Alfoxden—'that Dear and beautiful place'[6]—she knew she was leaving behind something very precious. From temporary lodgings on a busy street in Bristol she longed wistfully for the 'sweet sounds' of the country.[7]

Many details of the trip abroad failed to materialize, and while they were there William and Dorothy paid scant attention to the German language and writings which so fascinated Coleridge. Instead, they continued to think, talk, and write about the influence of environment on the emotions, drawing on and consolidating the distinctively English brand of nature philosophy they had evolved together at Windy Brow and in the West Country. When William began to draft *The Two-Part Prelude* (MS JJ) at Goslar, he used the notebook that already contained the last part of Dorothy's *Hamburg Journal* and his own fragment 'Essay on Morals'. The physical proximity of these three pieces of writing within a single notebook (DC MS 19) is a reminder of how closely the concerns of brother and sister interconnected. Although very different in kind, the three pieces arose out of shared circumstances, reflecting beliefs the Wordsworths had in common, which their experience of travelling and living in Germany put to the test.

The *Hamburg Journal* appears in two notebooks (DC MS 19 and DC MS 25), and records Dorothy's impressions as a tourist over a period of three to four weeks during the early autumn of 1798. It begins with a retrospective account of the journey from London to Hamburg via Cuxhaven (14–19 September) and ends with their arrival in Goslar on Saturday 6 October, after a three-day journey with an overnight stop in Brunswick. Their visit to Hamburg takes up most of the journal, with daily entries detailing observations of German manners and morals in the 'dirty ill-paved stinking streets' of a city where they felt alienated and homesick.[8] Initially, the party also included Coleridge's friend John Chester, whose activities are occasionally mentioned in passing. But during the Hamburg visit, it was decided that Coleridge would go in search of culture and sociability (first in the picturesque island resort of Ratzeburg, and later in the university town of Göttingen), while Dorothy and William went 130 miles south. They chose as their destination the medieval town of Goslar in Lower Saxony, where they hoped the wooded mountain scenery would remind them of the Lake District. The decision to go their separate ways arose from a number of practical circumstances: Coleridge's desire to acquire German quickly, and on the Wordsworths' part a shortage of money, which necessitated a more secluded, less expensive life. 'I hear that the Two noble Englishmen have parted no sooner than they set foot on german earth', Lamb observed wryly in a letter to Southey.[9] This was indeed a symbolic separation, anticipating later tensions in the three-way relationship which had thrived at Alfoxden.

The opening entry of the *Hamburg Journal* immediately establishes its stance and tone, which are markedly different from those of the *Alfoxden Journal*. Dorothy writes as a tourist embarking on her first experience of foreign travel, whose expectations of adventure are repeatedly thwarted by disappointment or discomfort. All the features of her style declare her to be a woman of sensibility, alive to her own aesthetic preferences, which are distinctly rural and romantic. She emphasizes her position as a writing-subject through retrospective narration, repeatedly using the pronoun 'I'. Adopting a mostly formal register, she remains politely silent on the matter of her seasickness during the rough two-day passage from Yarmouth to Cuxhaven: 'Before we had heaved the anchor I was consigned to the cabin' (p. 19). It is only through Coleridge's less squeamish account that we learn of the conditions that kept her and William below deck—'Wordsworth shockingly ill, his Sister worst of all—vomiting, & groaning, unspeakably!'[10] When she emerges again 'at the mouth of the Elbe on Tuesday morning', she is decorously poetic in her description of the anticlimactic and nauseating experience of voyaging on the sea: 'I was surprized to find, when I came upon deck, that we could not see the shores, though we were in the river. It was to my eyes a still sea, but oh! the gentle breezes and the gentle motion!' (p. 19).

As she remembers the boat advancing towards Cuxhaven, Dorothy's impressionistic notation conveys the sense of movement and emerging detail; but the inventory is desultory: 'the shores appeared low and flat, and thinly peopled; here and there a farmhouse, cattle feeding, hay-stacks, a cottage, a windmill' (p. 19). She briefly dismisses Cuxhaven itself as 'an ugly, black-looking place', moving on quickly to the scenery that opened around her as the boat moved up the river Elbe. Her register shifts, and the sentences are held together by a smooth, steady rhythm as she details, one by one, the poetic images she holds in her memory:

The moon shone upon the waters. The shores were visible with here and there a light from the houses. Ships lying at anchor not far from us. We drank tea upon deck by the light of the moon.   (p. 19)

The four English travelling companions—William and Dorothy, Coleridge and Chester—must have made a slightly comical grouping as they sat together on deck, drinking tea by moonlight. This scene, with its curious mix of the domestic and the romantic, belongs to a novel of sensibility, or perhaps to one of Coleridge's 'Conversation poems' written earlier in the year. Moonlight was often a feature in Dorothy's associative thinking about Coleridge, so she may be remembering 'The Foster-Mother's Tale', with its moonlight voyage up a river 'wide as any sea'. Or perhaps, sitting alongside him on deck, she caught a glimpse of the letter he wrote home that very evening: 'Over what place does the Moon hang to your eye, my dearest Sara? To me it hangs over the left bank of the Elbe; and a long trembling road of moonlight reaches from thence up to the stern of our Vessel, & there it ends.'[11] But the tranquil mood of these associations is immediately under-cut; for while she is enjoying 'solitude and quietness, and many a recollected pleasure', she is 'hearing still the unintelligible jargon of the many tongues that gabbled in the cabin' (p. 19).

In this striking opposition between quietness, pleasure, and recollection on the one hand, noise and Babel-like incoherence on the other, Dorothy takes us to the central theme of the *Hamburg Journal*. Her pairing of those two words, 'hearing' and 'still', with their half-echo of 'Tintern Abbey',[12] tell us how deeply that poem has embedded itself in her consciousness, both as a soothing memory in itself, and as a meditation on the power of memory to soothe. As the journal unfolds, it becomes apparent that she experiences Hamburg as an assault on her sensibility, threatening the creative harmony she and William had achieved at Alfoxden. The final poem of *Lyrical Ballads*, with its celebration of 'quietness and beauty' as an antidote to the 'fretful stir | Unprofitable' of the city (ll. 128, 53–4), has a symbolic relevance for the way she processes her emotional life.

Hamburg was a neutral city at this stage of the Napoleonic wars (just after Nelson's victory over the French at the Battle of the Nile), when Germany was the only European country outside Scandinavia open to trav-ellers. Kenneth Johnston has written evocatively of its atmosphere of intrigue and surveillance—'the city was teeming with agents and spies from all European governments'—suggesting that it was 'something like that of Zurich or Casablanca in the early years of World War II'.[13] Dorothy's journal, with its resolutely domestic focus, took no more notice of the world's power politics than her Alfoxden one did. Nonetheless, it conveys on almost every page her sense of disorientation and wariness in this strange city, where movements were observed and suspicions readily aroused. Some readers have compared Dorothy's impressions of Hamburg unfavourably with Coleridge's, noting that his enthusiasm in exploring the city is absent from her descriptions. But the long retrospective journal Coleridge enclosed in his letters home to Sara and Tom Poole was written in the quiet comfort of Ratzeburg, where he had the leisure to enliven and embellish his reminiscences, working from notebook entries he had made earlier. He coincided with Dorothy's view of Hamburg in many respects, remembering things they saw together, and possibly even responding to her journal. Compare, for instance, the delightful inventories of hats which appear in both journals for 19 September, from which I give excerpts below. Dorothy's entry ranges widely over all classes of women, making a quick sketch of each individual. Her metaphors are drawn mostly from a familiar, homely lexicon:

> Dutch women with immense straw bonnets, with flat crowns and rims in the shape of oyster shells...literally as large as a small-sized umbrella. Hamburgher girls with white caps, with broad overhanging borders...Hanoverians with round borders, showing all the face, and standing upright, a profusion of ribband. Fruit-women, with large straw hats in the shape of an inverted bowl, or white handkerchiefs tyed round the head like a bishop's mitre.   (p. 20)

Coleridge's descriptive method is energized by mischief, as he labours over the details of fashionable finery, decorating his sentences with alliterative clusters:

> Dutch Women with large umbrella Hats shooting out half a yard before them, and with a prodigal *plumpness* of petticoat *behind*—the Hamburghers with caps, plated on the cawl with silver or gold, or both, fringed with lace, & standing round *before* their eyes, like a canopy-veil—the Hanoverian Women with the fore-part of the Head bare, then a stiff lace standing upright like a Wall, perpendicular on the Cap; and the Cap behind *tailed* with a monstrous quantity of Ribbon which lies or tosses on the Back.[14]

Although she has none of Coleridge's cosmopolitanism, robustness, and *savoir faire* as a traveller, Dorothy does catch the continental flavour of the city, and especially its heterogeneous female community. But the pageantry happens at a distance, and her excitement with its foreignness dwindles as she fails to make a connection with the people. Neither she nor her companions could speak German. Although Coleridge made rapid progress in learning the language, the Wordsworths did not. The *Hamburg Journal* reveals none of the intimacy we see in the later *Grasmere Journal*, where observations are authentically based on habitual relationships with neighbours. Nor does it show her actively seeking out company, as she would later in her 1803 tour of Scotland, where much knowledge was gathered through conversation. Instead, she writes as an inquisitive outsider, commenting on the morals and manners of a community she has little chance of getting to know.

The Wordsworths' visit to the household of Friedrich Klopstock—'the benefactor of his country, the father of German poetry' (p. 25)—is the journal's cultural high point. Dorothy took pleasure in the animated conversation Klopstock conducted all afternoon with William in French,[15] responding with 'the most sensible emotion' to this symbolic meeting of two powerful currents in modern European poetry. But she gives more space in her journal entry to the women of the family, candidly criticizing the vanity of the poet's young wife, and signs of over-indulgence in their daughter, although noticing with pleasure the manner of a woman servant, who 'seemed more at her ease and more familiar than an English servant, and laughed and talked with the little girl' (p. 25). In its study of social formations, the *Hamburg Journal* resembles Mary Wollstonecraft's *Letters Written during a Short Residence in Sweden, Norway and Denmark*, a popular travel book during the 1790s. Dorothy's style, like Wollstonecraft's, alternates between judicious reportage and atmospheric description, showing a particular interest in domestic economy and the condition of women. She notes the 'great modesty' with which women of the lower orders dress, and the way that women sit at shop doors, knitting and sewing—'I saw one woman ironing' (p. 23). She lists the price of food at the market, the wasteful use of space in Hamburg's unusually high houses, and the relative scarcity of beggars in its streets. She shows an interest in German fashions, the furnishing of rooms, and family habits. Observing details of dress, hygiene and conduct, she sometimes achieves a tone of dispassionate objectivity reminiscent of Wollstonecraft:

> I could not but observe, notwithstanding the dirt of the houses, that the lower orders of women seemed in general much cleaner in their persons than the same rank in England. This appeared to me on the first view and all the observation I have made since has confirmed me in this opinion.   (p. 22)

But her observations are on the whole sharper and more critical, remaining with circumstantial detail rather than moving outwards into political pronouncements.

Increasingly, Dorothy's perspective was shadowed by the mood of disappointment which hung over the tour. A performance of Möller's *Count Waldon* (1770) aroused her anger: 'The piece a mixture of dull declamation and unmeaning rant. The ballet unintelligible to us' (p. 22). She repeatedly notes foul smells in the streets—'there is such a constant succession of hateful smells, that it is quite disgusting to pass near the houses' (p. 30)—and, with shocked revulsion, records that 'A little girl about 8 years old, well-dressed, took up her petticoats in full view of the crowd and upon the green where people walk, and sat undisturbed till she had finished her business' (p. 31). The journal alleges cheating on the part of shopkeepers, making generalizations about the avaricious mentality of Hamburg's citizens. Its strongly opinionated tone reflects sentiments Dorothy shared with her companions. William did not have a sense of smell, but he was if anything more acutely conscious than she was of shortage of money, and quick to accuse the Hamburgers of sharp practice. 'It is a *sad* place', he observed in a letter to Tom Poole: 'In this epithet you have the soul and essence of all the information which I have been able to gather.'[16] Coleridge was even more dismissive, referring to 'the noise and the tallow-faced roguery',[17] 'The Streets narrow and stinking, without any appropriate path for foot-passengers',[18] the 'Huddle and Ugliness, Stink and Stagnation'—'For it is a foul City!'[19]

Some readers have found the *Hamburg Journal*'s response to German life and culture insular, and even xenophobic: words that could never be applied to the cosmopolitan author of *A Vindication of the Rights of Woman*. But Wollstonecraft, who stayed there at the end of her Scandinavian tour, shared the Wordsworths' intense dislike of Hamburg, finding it 'an ill, close-built town, swarming with inhabitants'. Her sense of repugnance arose from the city's obsession with commerce and financial gain: 'the insolent vulgarity which a sudden influx of wealth usually produces in common minds, is here very conspicuous'. She used the example of Hamburg as evidence of the corrupting influence of commerce on morality, and in her bid to reform her lover, the erring Gilbert Imlay, adopted her most censorious tone when describing the Hamburgers' vices:

> An ostentatious display of wealth without elegance, and a greedy enjoyment of pleasure without sentiment, embrutes them till they term all virtue of an heroic cast romantic attempts at something above our nature; and anxiety

about the welfare of others, a search after misery, in which we have no concern.[20]

Wollstonecraft's resoundingly negative judgement on Hamburg may well have predisposed Dorothy and her fellow-travellers to a dim view of the city. The argument that 'Situation seems to be the mould in which men's characters are formed'[21] appeared bleakly despairing in so grim a 'situation'. 'To commerce everything must give way', Wollstonecraft concluded, damningly: 'profit and profit are the only speculations—double—double, toil and trouble.'[22]

Although modelled on the public epistolary style of Wollstonecraft's travel writing, the *Hamburg Journal* was intended for private circulation among family members rather than for publication. Some of the more striking incidents seem to have been recorded with *Lyrical Ballads* in mind, as if the journal served partly as a repository of poetic materials, like the *Alfoxden Journal*. The use of the pronoun 'I' usually reflects Dorothy's subject position, but the manuscript indicates that William took up his pen on 28 September to record a shocking incident witnessed by himself (but not necessarily Dorothy) in the red-light district of Altona. There is nothing noticeably different in the prose style as his narration takes over. In the context of private circulation the change in handwriting was sufficient to identify him as the author:

> Yesterday saw a man of about fifty years of age beating a woman decently dressed and about 37 years of age. He struck her on the breast several times, and beat her also with his stick. The expressions in her face were half of anger and half of a spirit of resistance. What her offence had been we could not learn. It was in the public street. He was better dressed than she was, and evidently a stranger.   (p. 27)

The distressing nature of this incident, and the sympathy with female oppression William's recording of it connotes, may indicate that he intends to make it into a poem later. His intervention in the journal is significant, especially given the issues he was thinking about as he looked back on *Lyrical Ballads* and began to plan his 'Essay on Morals'. He was increasingly dissatisfied with systems of moral philosophy, because, as he was to put it only a month later, they 'contain no picture of human life; they *describe* nothing'—their 'bald and naked reasonings are impotent over our habits'. He believed that poetry had more power to alter habits and reform society than any amount of 'such books as Mr Godwyn's, Mr Paley's, and those of the whole tribe of authors'.[23] He was, however, less interested in sensational incident than in the inner life of the emotions. If approached with subtlety, the violent abuse of a woman in a public street might provide the kind of material that could be turned into a lyrical ballad.[24] As a powerful 'tale of distress', rooted in authentic experience and conveyed accurately, it would 'melt into the affections' far more effectively than any appeal to reason.

Two days later, in Dorothy's handwriting, the journal seems to be responding to the steer William is giving, for it records a second violent incident in the streets, this time involving the persecution of a Jew.[25] The personal pronoun indicates that both siblings were present:

> When we had got nearly through the town we saw a surly-looking German driving a poor Jew forward with foul language, and making frequent use of a stick which he had in his hand. The countenance of the Jew expressed neither anger nor surprise nor agitation; he spoke, but with meekness, and unresisting pursued his way, followed by his inhuman driver, whose insolence we found was supported by law: the Jew had no right to *reign* in the city of Hamburgh, as a German told us in broken English. The soldiers who are stationed at the drawbridge looked very surly at him, and the countenances of the by-standers expressed cold unfeeling cruelty.   (p. 29)

This entry, longer and more detailed than William's, asks to be considered as its pair, continuing and amplifying his expression of sympathy for Hamburg's oppressed minorities. Dorothy captures the political relationships between all the participants in this scene, including German bystanders and English tourists. Her narrative considers the emotions of oppressor and oppressed, distinguishing her own perspective as a sympathetic witness from the 'cold unfeeling cruelty' of the Germans. There are signs of careful crafting in her narrative, suggesting that it is halfway to becoming a poetic exploration of 'man's inhumanity to man', along the lines of one of William's ballads. She draws on biblical associations to drive home the irony of this tableau, in which a Jew displays the 'meekness' traditionally associated with Christ, while the so-called Christian community scapegoats him as a foreign upstart. The trio of 'f's in the first sentence, balanced by the trio of 'c's in the last, convey the harsh repetitiveness of the bully's physical blows. The Miltonic inversion in the tetrameter, 'unresisting pursued his way', accords heroic dignity to the abused Jew; while the single italicized word in 'broken English' vividly captures the bystander's territorial resentment and hostility.

The way Dorothy embeds this episode in her journal entry for the day's events is also revealing, for it shows her hungering for the consolations offered by nature. Immediately after witnessing the Jew-baiting, she and William went on their way, along the route to Blankenese, 'passing many gentlemen's houses'. She observes that 'The buildings all seem solid and warm in themselves, but still they look cold from their nakedness of trees' (p. 29). There is a symbolic resonance in her longing for warmth, which reflects back on the previous incident. Shocked by the recent assault, she looks for reassurance in one the most ancient symbols of nature's kindness to men, the shelter provided by trees. She finds instead only further evidence of the 'coldness' she has witnessed in the cruel beating. Her critique involves class issues, as well as matters of ecology, for she implies a disturbing disconnection between the suburban 'gentlemen' of Hamburg and the ongoing processes of nature: '[The houses] are generally newly built, and placed in gardens, which are planted in front with poplars and low shrubs, but the possessors seem to have no prospective view to a shelter for their children; they do not plant behind their houses' (p. 29). Years later, in her poem 'Grasmere—A Fragment', she perhaps remembered Hamburg when describing the 'clustering trees' which sheltered the 'nest' at Town End from the north wind.

Coleridge, too, wrote about the Hamburgers' approach to gardening, but in a more complex and ambiguous way. His journal entry for 27 September records a walk from Empfelde to Hamburg, in which he sees 'light cool Country houses, *which you can look thro'*, and the gardens behind, with Trees in piazzas'. The airiness and transparency of the houses matches his mood of relaxation so closely that he almost relinquishes his prejudice as an English tourist: 'every house with neat rails before it, & green seats within the rails—everything, nature & all, neat & artificial'.[26] In the pleasure of the moment, Coleridge appears to be playing ironically with his own aesthetic and moral principles. Is he remembering the corrupt onlooker from his early poem, 'Reflections on leaving a place of Retirement'? In that poem, he aligned the gaze of 'Bristowa's citizen' with Satanic envy, and his own rural retirement with the paradisal innocence of Adam and Eve. In the journal he borrows the trope, but adjusts its moral significance. This time he is the day tripper looking in (or rather through) a summer house, and succumbing briefly to its seductive allure. Even as his stance shifts, in the next sentence, to condemnation of the vulgar Hamburgers, it is difficult to gauge his tone of voice:

if the House & Gardens & Pleasure fields had been in a better Taste...the narrow-minded, ignorant, money-loving Merchant of Hamburgh could only have *adopted*, he could not have *enjoyed*, the wild simplicity of Nature.[27]

In England at this time a tasteful commitment to picturesque principles did not necessarily coincide with a genuine love of wildness, and the Hamburgers would be no different from English gentlemen in their inability to 'enjoy' the natural scenery they 'adopted'. Coleridge's views on the picturesque were often ambivalent, and his coinage of the compound 'Pleasure fields' suggests that he is here revisiting some of the moral issues he had explored in 'Kubla Khan'. But he may also be teasing Dorothy—the woman with the 'wild eyes'—for her innocent devotion to trees.

Whether we consider the interplay between Coleridge's and Dorothy's journals as a textual dialogue, or infer they had an actual conversation about the styles of suburban gardens they each saw, it is clear that they had a mild disagreement based on different observations. Their underlying assumptions about the superiority of wildness to cultivation were identical; but Coleridge's worldly humour, his mock-cynicism, his ability to indulge, ironize, or condemn, as the whim took him, were key to his success in observing German life as a detached *flaneur*. Dorothy, by contrast, was shocked at a deep emotional level by what she saw. William took up a third position: more considered than Coleridge's, less solemn than Dorothy's, and revealing of the connections he was making at this time between poetry, environmental aesthetics, and morality. Writing to Tom Poole on 3 October, their last day in Hamburg, he looked for the positives in this 'sad City', which contained 'a world of good and honest people, if one but had the skill to find them'. On the matter of gardens, as discussed by his companions, he expressed a judgemental view which he tempered with tolerance:

> The banks of the Elbe are thickly sown with houses built by the merchants for Saturday and Sunday retirement. The English merchants have set the example, the style is in imitation of the English garden, imitated as Della Crusca might imitate Virgil. It is however something gained, the dawning of a better day.[28]

In his unflattering comparison of Hamburg's gardens to Robert Merry's sentimental verse, he takes sides in a topical literary debate, clearly priding himself on his own unfashionable tastes and allegiances. But these observations on aesthetics are subordinate to his deeper concern with moral habits. In the same letter, he tells Poole of his altercation with a German baker over the price of bread: 'he dashed the loaves from my hand in the most brutal manner...So I left the shop empty-handed.' The point of his anecdote is not, he emphasizes, to condemn brutal avarice as a national characteristic of the Germans but to reinforce his objection to the corrupting influence of commerce on human nature: 'Is there any baker in England, who would have done this to a foreigner? I am afraid we must say, yes. Money, money is here the god of universal worship.'[29]

The reality of living as strangers in a foreign city, bewildered by its currency, language, and customs, brought the Wordsworths only financial hardship and depression of spirits. Worst of all, the trip caused them to split up with their friend: for while Coleridge could afford the luxury of a German lifestyle, they could not. If we come to Dorothy's journal expecting it to show the same qualities as the *Alfoxden Journal*—an excited response to sensory and aesthetic stimuli, a celebration of creativity and friendship in a habitable place—we will be disappointed. But if we read it as a case study in alienation and emotional deprivation we will be nearer to understanding its importance. 'The view of the Elbe and the spreading country must be very interesting in a fine sunset', Dorothy wrote dutifully, after a pleasant trip to the countryside on Thursday 27th. However, 'There is a want of some atmospherical irradiation to give a richness to the scene' (p. 26). The style and content of this sentence tell us a great deal about Dorothy's understanding of the connection between physical environment and mental life. The laborious formality, the uncharacteristically scientific polysyllables, the trailing off into pictur-esque cliché—all suggest that that she chooses her words precisely, to reflect her mood of depression.[30]

During their weeks in Hamburg, the Wordsworths observed at first hand the disintegration under urban pressures of the 'moral happiness' they believed to be 'natural'. As William's subsequent writings in Goslar show, this experience confirmed and strengthened their faith in the nurturing power of a rural environment as the route to human progress. Nothing they were to see in Germany would shake the conviction they had shared with Coleridge in Somerset—that 'benevolence and quietness' grow within the individual as a response to 'fields and woods and mountains'; and that the 'bad passions' in human beings can be destroyed only 'by keeping them in inaction' through daily communion with nature.[31] Both the 'Essay on Mor-als' and the first draft of *The Prelude* are expressions of William's growing conviction that, as a poet and prophet of nature, he could do more than the Godwinian rationalists to shape moral education. His true subject was 'manners': 'not transitory manners reflecting the wearisome unintelligible obliquities of city-life, but manners connected with the permanent objects of nature and partaking of the simplicity of those objects'.[32]

In the final page of the *Hamburg Journal*, Dorothy recorded her impressions of Brunswick, 'an old, silent, dull-looking place', where they stayed overnight on the last leg of their three-day journey to Goslar. In the morning, just before taking their places on the Goslar diligence, the couple stood outside the gardens of the duke's palace, where the gates were shut. It was a scene saturated in literary and symbolic associations. The gardens 'seemed as if they would be very pleasant', but the gates denied them access, so the two of them paused, 'peeping in' from outside, 'too late to enter'. As if to underline the post-lapsarian implications, William had 'his pockets full of apples' bought from a nearby shop. 'Upon these I breakfasted', Dorothy wrote, 'and carried *Kubla* to a fountain in the neighbouring market-place, where I drank some excellent water' (p. 34). In this homely and sociable setting, Dorothy restabilized herself, and took stock of her emotions. Missing Coleridge already, she carried with her the pitcher she had punningly nicknamed 'Kubla' (alluding to the German word for a drinking-vessel, 'Kanne'). The name calls to mind his most astonishing and original poetic creation. Its subject matter? A powerful figure who creates a pleasure-house and gardens, with a river running underground and bursting forth in a fountain; and a poet who wishes to re-create them. Seated by a fountain in a foreign land, drinking the local water, and drawing nourishment from Coleridge's words about imaginative process—'a mighty fountain momently was forced'—Dorothy's identification with the language of 'Kubla Khan' is unmistakable. But did she also have an inkling of the creative torrent soon to pour forth from her brother?

The Wordsworths' retreat to Goslar expressed a longing for home which would intensify during the freezing winter that followed. Holed up in a lodging house in 'this ugly silent old desert of a City',[33] they lacked company, looked forward to letters from Coleridge, and longed for spring. 'His taking his Sister with him was a wrong Step', their friend observed with the benefit of hindsight: 'it is next to impossible for any but married women ...to be introduced to any company in Germany. Sister (here) is considered only as a name for Mistress.'[34] Coleridge, meanwhile, pursued his own very different course in Ratzeburg—assimilating the German language rapidly, spending too much money,[35] and saturating himself in Kant, but missing their company and envying them their exclusive love: 'William, my head and my heart! dear William and dear Dorothea! | You have all in each other; but I am lonely, and want you!'[36] The importance of the five months ahead lay in the extraordinary surge of creativity which the Wordsworths' shared experience of exile paradoxically released. Separation from Coleridge in Germany was as crucial to the development of all three writers as 'amalgamation' in Somerset had been. But in a sense the Wordsworths were never without Coleridge, for they carried him in their hearts and minds. They were, in the words of Browning, 'one and one with a shadowy third'.[37]

5

Goslar and Sockburn

'Was it for this
That one, the fairest of all rivers, loved
To blend his murmurs with my nurse's song,
And from his alder shades and rocky falls,
And from his fords and shallows, sent a voice
To intertwine my dreams?'[1]

*

At Goslar, during what would prove to be the coldest winter recorded
in the century, the Wordsworths missed Coleridge intensely. They
probably talked a great deal to each other; but as they had little company
and limited access to books, their expectation of learning enough German
to become translators never materialized. Though they did walk 'at least an

hour a day, often much more', they could not go very far afield.[2] It is probable that Dorothy wrote many letters during the winter months, but in the few that survive she conveys next to nothing about the city or surrounding countryside. There is no evidence that she kept a journal. The most important manuscript from this period, a self-contained poem of 150 lines, is in William's hand. Uprooted from all that was familiar and thrown back on the resources of memory, he began to apply their shared philosophy of nature to scenes from childhood:

> For this didst thou,
> O Derwent, travelling over the green plains
> Near my sweet birth-place, didst thou, beauteous stream,
> Give ceaseless music to the night and day,
> Which with its steady cadence tempering
> Our human waywardness, composed my thoughts
> To more than infant softness, giving me
> Amid the fretful tenements of man
> A knowledge, a dim earnest of the calm
> That nature breathes among her woodland haunts?[3]

As a memory of infancy, later to be incorporated into an autobiography, the passage is singular. No mother is addressed or remembered, although a maternal impulse is implied. No father is present either—although the river's voice is significantly gendered as male. There are no siblings listening to the nurse's song, and no mention of a house or garden. In a revision the poet changed 'intertwine my dreams' to 'flowed along my dreams', suggesting the seamless passage of the Derwent's voice into his unconscious.[4] Despite all this, a powerful sense of home, and indeed of family, are present in these opening lines. They are subliminally evoked by means of metaphorical transference, poetic association, and allusion, the tools of a writer addressing someone who shares his history of early bereavement and can read between the lines. Nature compensates for family members who were present in infancy and later went missing. It isn't the enfolding arms of the mother but the rhythm and sound of moving water that remind the speaker of being cradled. The river's murmur blends with the nurse's song, and both are fused in an infantile dream of warmth, safety, love. The phrase 'sweet birth-place' comes from Coleridge's 'Frost at Midnight', evoking a fireside scene where a father sits listening to his sleeping child. In Coleridge's poem, the infant's 'gentle breathings' fill up 'momentary pauses' in the father's thought.[5] This compatibility between listening father and breathing infant is transposed onto the landscape in William's memories of home. Coleridge's own memory of infancy, as a time when he and his sister were playmates, androgynously 'clothed alike', is subliminally evoked in the stream of associations called up by the quotation.[6]

Thus, although the passage seems at first sight to be tracking creativity back to a single origin, it is in fact notable for its genetic complexity, obliquely suggesting the multiple influences, or confluences, which have together 'composed' the writer's poetic identity. This fragment suggests an autobiographical subject who is permeable and mobile: acutely susceptible to impulses from outside, with a 'more than infant softness' that is akin to water. The sense of openness and fluidity in the poet's discourse is enhanced by his repeated use of questions, and by the shift in line six from narration to apostrophe. He 'turns' to the river, just as the river itself turns. The temporal sequence is momentarily disrupted, and we become conscious of overhearing a private colloquy; for as always Dorothy plays a role in William's communion with the past. Tacitly including his sister in his quest to understand the origins of creative power, William reminds her of the nurturing song they heard in infancy, and reheard when they visited their birthplace in 1794. He also alludes to the wandering spirit of the Wye, recalling its influence on him during years when they were separated, and its symbolic resonance for them both during their walking tour earlier in the year. Just as he had remembered the sound of the Derwent in the Wye Valley, so now he repeats their figurative connection the other way round. His spirit 'often turned' to the Wye 'in lonely rooms, and mid the din | Of towns and cities' (ll. 26–7). Now it turns to the Derwent's cadence 'amid the fretful tenements of man'.[7] Alienated by Goslar and composing his poem in the notebook Dorothy had earlier used for the last section of her *Hamburg Journal*, William draws on the powerful spell of the river's song to combat the 'wearisome obliquities of city life'.[8] The soothing influence ascribed to both rivers is connected with his sister through a long history of association.

All the surviving evidence of their time at Goslar (including the psychosomatic ailments that William suffered while writing) suggests that this was a period of acute homesickness for both siblings. Gaston Bachelard, who studied the symbology of home in *The Poetics of Space*, has shown how the spaces surrounding us in infancy stay with us all our lives, in memories, images, and dreams: 'Before he is "cast into the world"…man is laid in the cradle of the house. And always, in our daydreams, the house is a large cradle…Life begins well, it begins enclosed, protected, all warm in the bosom of the house.'[9] Longings for the home in Cockermouth which they had shared before being 'cast out into the world' featured strongly in the Wordsworths' vision of a future life together. 'Was it for this?' marked the beginnings of an intense process of creative restoration through remembering. Its evocation of the earliest scenes of childhood—when, 'a four year's child' William 'Made one long bathing of a summer's day' (l. 22)—is followed rapidly, with no clear chronological markers, by later memories of roving in 'high places, on the lonely peaks' (l. 34), or ranging 'half the night among the cliffs | And the smooth hollows' (ll. 79–80). The poetry is extraordinary in its sensory immediacy, bringing the Lake District vividly onto the page in a series of loosely linked, emotionally charged episodes resembling dreams. In their evocation of space, freedom, movement, and natural beauty, these lines counterbalanced the Wordsworths' culture-shock in Hamburg and their ongoing sense of exile. William's poetry may well have served as a form of highly pleasurable and spiritually uplifting therapy, enabling them to reattach themselves to the nurturing sources of their emotional life.

Writing to Coleridge in mid-December, Dorothy sent him a selection of passages from William's rapidly expanding poem, highlighting their setting in the North of England 'amongst the mountains whither we wish to decoy you'.[10] William wrote 'Skating' as a response to Coleridge's description of skating parties in Ratzeburg. When Coleridge opened Dorothy's letter, he found his own word 'tinkle' woven into William's evocation of childhood memories, like a sound they had heard together:

> Meanwhile, the precipices rang aloud,
> The leafless trees and every icy crag
> Tinkled like iron   (I, ll. 163–5)

The allusion is a poetic compliment, but also a gesture of love, and an invitation, which Dorothy follows through in her letter. She makes clear that Coleridge, in danger of being seduced by German 'high life'[11], will enjoy the delightful exercise of skating 'with every possible advantage' in the wild setting of Cumberland:

> A race with William upon his native lakes would leave to the heart and the imagination something more Dear and valuable than the gay sight of Ladies and countesses whirling along the lake of Ratzeberg.[12]

Her objective is at once moral and domestic: to remove Coleridge from a corrupting environment, restoring him to his family responsibilities and secluded rural life. The key words, 'heart' and 'imagination', are carefully chosen to appeal to her reader. She has begun to imagine a rebuilding of the intimacy that thrived in Somerset, but this time regrounded in her own native environment: 'you must come to us at the latter end of next summer', she writes enticingly: 'we will explore together every nook of that romantic country'.[13]

The Wordsworths' image of a future with Coleridge was shaped by memories of their origins, but also by the vocabulary of moral enlightenment they had evolved with him during the previous year. William's language is energized by verbs that suggest a fusion between mental and physical worlds. In sociable and boisterous activities such as skating, the poet pictures himself retiring, or leaving the 'tumultuous throng', to experience a contemplative stillness:

> and oftentimes,
> When we had given our bodies to the wind
> And all the shadowy banks on either side
> Came sweeping through the darkness, spinning still
> The rapid line of motion   (I, ll. 174–8)

The words 'given our bodies to the wind' are suggestive of a passionate abandonment to the elements, but consummation when it comes is 'tranquil', like the settling of the night sky in 'A Night-Piece',[14] or the *Alfoxden Journal's* many peaceful glimpses of the sea. This language is more physical than the 'One Life' vocabulary in which Coleridge imagines spiritual awakening. William tempts his friend north with the promise of epiphanies among the 'solitary cliffs' and 'hoary mountains'—a sustained union with the elements, of the kind Coleridge had himself envisaged for his son Hartley.[15]

As the mediator of William's memories, Dorothy selected and transcribed passages of poetry to send to Coleridge. But she also shared his role of addressee; for these memories were part of William's courtship with her: the long process of restoring her to a landscape from which she had been wrenched at the tender age of six.[16] Early separation inevitably shaped their memories of home in different ways. Dorothy could vividly picture the garden in Cockermouth, and the terrace overlooking the river Derwent, which her father and mother tended carefully ('in its neatness' is her domestic phrase).[17] But William's earlier memory of the musical rhythms of water evoked the primary sensory basis on which their developing mental lives were based. In Hartleyan terms, the opening lines of 'Was it for this?' were designed to reassure her that however separate they had been during the later part of childhood, they had a shared understanding of home.

*

Between December 1798 and February 1799, William's autobiography grew into a coherent poem of about 400 lines—effectively the first book of what is known as the *Two-Part Prelude*. Some of his memories went back to the years before his mother's death, when Dorothy was still living in Cockermouth; others belonged to his schooldays at Hawkshead. The Wordsworths had doubtless compared their childhoods often, and William had written about the region in depth already, in 'The Vale of Esthwaite' and *An Evening Walk*. In Germany, from their shared position of exile, ideas of home took on a new urgency and emotional charge. William made reparation for Dorothy's sudden removal from his life by once again inviting her to re-enter the landscape from which she had been parted after the death of their mother. Conscious that this was a place laden with poetic associations, he revisited it to bring it into line with his and Dorothy's current preoccupations. (In much the same way, he would work and rework *The Prelude* for the remainder of his life.) The inquisitive exploration of psychology and moral growth he now brought to his material derived from his ever-strengthening interest in Hartleyan associationism, his separation from the gregarious, cosmopolitan Coleridge, and Dorothy's presence beside him as he wrote.

The Wordsworths' traumatic early experiences of bereavement, parting, and dispossession intensified his idealization of Cumberland as a place that fostered creativity. He sought the 'hiding places' of creative power in a landscape saturated with memories—not of the living, but of the absent, the dead, and the soon to die. In the culminating episode of Part One, he recalled the day his father died, when he and his two brothers (without Dorothy) 'followed his body to the grave' (l. 353). There is a sombre finality in the word 'grave', morbidly reinforced by the sense that 'followed' is used metaphorically as well as literally. He dealt more obliquely with the earlier double blow of his mother's death and his sister's departure to Halifax. Instead of narrating his response to a tragic bereavement and its repercussions, he explored the ways in which his intense attachment to place compensated for their disappearance. The scene shifts from the loved, familiar landscape surrounding Cockermouth to the new region of Esthwaite, which he entered as a schoolboy soon after his mother's death. This is highlighted with a significant metaphor:

> When I was first *transplanted* to thy vale,
> Beloved Hawkshead! when thy paths, thy shores
> And brooks, were like a dream of novelty
> To my half-infant mind!   (I, ll. 260–3; my italics)

The idea of transplantation was fundamental to William's empathy with his sister, who had been more suddenly uprooted.[18] The metaphor also connotes his oblique methods of associative writing; for he understood intuitively the process which, in modern psychology, is known as displacement. The 'dream of novelty' that opened up to him as an eight year old was a sublimation of his traumatic early losses. The paths, shores, and brooks in this yet-to-be-explored place are inseparably connected with the shocked awakening that followed his bereavement. Some of the repressed material surfaces twenty lines later, spookily transmuted, in the shape of a drowned man who 'bolt upright | Rose with his ghastly face' from Esthwaite lake (I, ll. 278–9).[19]

The genius of the *Two-Part Prelude* consisted in its selection of materials that resonate with encrypted feelings. The poet explored connections he had unconsciously made between vividly remembered places and strong emotions or incidents. Some of these involved the child's sense of oneness with the elements; others focused on his crimes against nature and his acute consciousness of death: 'in my thoughts | There was a darkness, call it solitude | Or blank desertion' (I, ll. 122–4). When he later wove his memories into an autobiographical narrative, he used the phrase 'spots of time' to suggest their geographical and temporal rootedness. But even before that phrase appeared in the poem, he conveyed the sense that they were permanently embedded in his psyche. Like the enchanted places of John Clare's childhood, his 'spots' were symbolic but also localized. Sometimes his use of place names conveys a sense of regional geography; but even when the location is unspecified they are authentic in their spatial and psychic depth. The 'perilous ridge' where the boy hung alone, the hills where he heard 'low breathings' coming after him, the lake where he saw a huge cliff that 'Rose up between me and the stars', all were vividly etched on the child's imagination: haunts to which the adult compulsively returned (I, ll. 63, 47, 112).

Especially haunting were places that had witnessed his animal instincts as a child. Remembering a 'mean' and 'inglorious' occasion when he raided a raven's nest, he depicted himself perched on the cliff side,

> by knots of grass
> Or half-inch fissures in the slippery rock
> But ill sustained, and almost, as it seemed,
> Suspended by the blast which blew amain (I, ll. 58–61)

In this symbolic moment the syntax becomes ambiguous, ascribing danger and vulnerability to the nest as well as to himself. Poets have sometimes imagined the world as 'the nest of mankind', Gaston Bachelard says, and 'an immense power' holding 'the inhabitants of the world in this nest'.[20] There is something of this metaphysical sense in the terrifying line, 'suspended by the blast that blew amain'. For William, the traumatic memory of being cast out of a nest too early and too young gave him a close identification with the birds whose homes he plundered. He associated acts of 'stealth | And troubled pleasure' with the experience of dispossession, figuring his own being as, simultaneously, a guilty predator and an endangered home (I, ll. 90–1).

The nurturing role of female family members had been conspicuously missing in William's life between the ages of seven and seventeen. Dorothy's absence from this phase of William's development was an aspect of its power to 'trouble' the mature poet, who looked back on a time when his kinship with the animal world sometimes triumphed over his better instincts. The scenes of brutality he had recently witnessed in Hamburg made him curious about the respective roles of nature and nurture in 'tempering | Our human waywardness' (I, ll. 10–11). He became concerned with mapping creative development holistically, so as to understand the place of instinct and bodily experience in the complicated matrix of human emotions. In his 'Essay on Morals', written almost immediately on arrival in Goslar, he had argued that a systematic treatise on human conduct would prove inadequate because it would not be 'written with sufficient power to melt into our affections, to incorporate itself with the blood and vital juices of our minds'.[21] His emphasis on the organic nature of mind helps to explain the strongly somatic nature of his poetry while at Goslar. It also throws light on the special function he saw poetry as performing in moral enlightenment. With its pleasurable rhythmic pulse, poetic metre could 'melt into the affections' of its listener, recalling the motion of the blood and the steady beating of the heart.

Newly awakened to his responsibilities towards the natural world, William viewed his boyhood with an acute consciousness of the pleasurable arousals which accompanied crimes thoughtlessly committed. His poetry was charged with barely sublimated erotic excitement. The sexual abandonment suggested in 'given our bodies to the wind'; the 'troubled pleasure' excited by plundering nests and snaring woodcocks, were connected with his memory of the awakening sexuality of early adolescence:

> When scudding on from snare to snare I plied
> My anxious visitation, hurrying on,
> Still hurrying, hurrying onward, how my heart
> Panted; among the scattered yew-trees and the crags
> That looked upon me, how my bosom beat
> With expectation.   (I, ll. 37–42)

The confessional overtones of his writing are significant, linking him with earlier writers in this genre, such as Bunyan and Rousseau. His guilt for acts of aggression took him back to the theme of animal rights, which he and Coleridge had examined earlier in the year in 'The Ancient Mariner' and 'Peter Bell'. Tracing a fall from innocence into experience, he described his early attempts to assert mastery over nature, and nature's answering admonitions. Protected by tutelary spirits, who were at once guardians of place and guides, the Vale of Esthwaite was transformed into the theatre of his moral growth.

*

The co-presence of multiple allusions in the *Two-Part Prelude*—to aesthetics, educational theory, and poetic tradition—enabled the poet to deal obliquely with his early losses, and to construct a powerful compensatory myth of adaptation, resilience, and growth. As he worked the early drafts into a coherent autobiographical poem, he synthesized the moral and aesthetic strands of his argument. Associating some of his early memories with the terrible, awe-inspiring sublime, others with tranquillizing harmonious beauty, he set out to show how these two modes of perception became steadily intertwined in his awakening consciousness. Most of his spiritual epiphanies are structured like Coleridge's Conversation poems, with a sublime climax that falls away into a gentle, harmonized resolution. (The alternation between tumult and tranquillity is a key to the poem's compelling rhythm and pace.) This pattern suggests that he envisaged his tutelary spirits as working alongside each other to awaken his conscience through wonder. In other words, they *stood in for* his parents, leading him towards the 'moral happiness' from which, in the present, he asked his half-anxious, half-celebratory question, 'Was it for this?'. William later referred to early childhood as the 'seed-time' of his 'soul', when he grew up 'Fostered alike by beauty and by fear'.[22] The figurative role played by tutelary spirits in his poem recalls the literal foster-parents in the Wordsworths' early lives, taking us to the central experience they had in common during nine long years of separation. We can safely assume that at Goslar the process of remembering childhood involved a careful comparing of notes, with William fondly recalling Ann Tyson's kindness to him at Hawkshead and Dorothy remembering (as she did all her life) the loving care provided by her 'aunt' Threlkeld while she lived at Halifax. 'Fostered alike' was a resonant phrase, not just because of these experiences but also because of the shared responsibility of looking after Basil Montagu during the years at Racedown and Alfoxden. When planning their German trip, the Wordsworths had reluctantly decided to leave Basil behind.[23] William was anxious on many different fronts to remember with Dorothy the gifts and consolations that nature showers on her foster-children.

There are further significant patterns of displacement and compensation in the poetry he wrote while at Goslar. Two groups of lyrics—one concerning a man called Mathew, the other a girl called Lucy—dwell on childhood memories of bereavement and separation. These poems are very different in kind from his autobiography, but linked to it through their concern with fostering and death. In them, the poet transfered feelings he now associated with family members (his dead parents and sister, but also the absent Annette and Caroline Vallon) onto people who embodied the ideal qualities of father, mother, sister, friend, daughter, lover. In his 'Five Elegies', the poet honoured and celebrated the life of a village schoolmaster from his Hawkshead years. Several details connect Mathew with William Taylor, who encouraged the poet's early efforts in composition, and died at the early age of thirty-two in William's penultimate year at school. The schoolmaster's place in the hearth and home of the village, his 'mother wit', the affection owed him by women in their 'elbow chairs', all suggest that he played a feminine role in William's understanding of the domestic affections ('Elegy II', l. 22; LB, 298; 'Elegy III', l. 41; LB, 299). Filling the place of his dead mother in memories of the Hawkshead years, Mathew partly resembles Ann Tyson. But he also 'act[s] a father's part' to 'many a wanton boy';[24] and embodies the ideal moral attributes that go with the words 'father' and 'friend'.[25] In this way, he not only performs the roles of both parents as defined in a conventional nuclear family, but also binds together members of the village community in a more extended family structure.[26]

There is an intense form of compensatory myth-making in the five elegies for Mathew, powered as they are by feelings of inconsolable loss:

> Here did he sit for hours and hours,
> But then he saw the woods and plains,
> He heard the wind and saw the showers

Come streaming down the streaming panes.
But now beneath the grass-green mound
He lies a prisoner of the ground.   ('Elegy V', ll. 29–34; LB, 301)

With the repetition of 'streaming', and the wordplay in 'panes', this image of a man sitting by a window deepens into an involute signifying many kinds and levels of grief. Is the poet remembering himself as boy, watching the rain streaming down his window after one of his bereavements? Or picturing himself in the present, writing about death from his lodging in Goslar? It would be reductive to claim that the 'real' subject of these lines is William's father. But they were written in Dorothy's presence, during a period of intense creativity bound up in remembering, when the most important reference points from which to understand the finality of death were their parents.

Memories and imaginings of death came thick and fast during the winter of 1798–9. Coleridge intuitively surmised that the following 'sublime Epitaph' was written 'in some gloomier moment' when William 'fancied the moment in which his sister might die'.[27] But the poem takes on a deeper resonance if this 'fancy' about Dorothy was prompted by mourning for the death that sundered them as children—a death that William had nowhere brought himself to mention in the *Two-Part Prelude* thus far:

A slumber did my spirit seal;
I had no human fears:
She seemed a thing that could not feel
The touch of earthly years.

No motion has she now, no force;
She neither hears nor sees,
Rolled round in earth's diurnal course
With rocks and stones and trees.   (ll. 1–8)

The poet seems, here, to be recalling his first shocked awakening to the idea of what mortality entails. In the gap between first and second stanzas, he passes from wishful oblivion to blank acceptance—a passage as silent, unobtrusive, and inevitable as the death he mourns. There are no markers to suggest how long an interval elapses between life and death, or between dying and being recycled. The finality of the stanza break marks the transition as absolute, and leaves us to infer a long process of grieving.

We have no way of establishing Lucy's historical identity for certain, but of all the poems featuring her, 'Three years she grew in sun and shower' resonates most strongly with familial associations. Turning once again to the theme of fostering, William tells the story of a girl's growth towards woman-hood in the countryside, suggesting that she is singled out by Nature for special treatment, much as he is himself is in the *Two-Part Prelude*. Nature, here personified as a *genius loci* who speaks like a lover, personally vouches for the care with which she will be watched over and tended:

> Myself will to my darling be
> Both law and impulse, and with me
> The Girl in rock and plain,
> In earth and heaven, in glade and bower,
> Shall feel an overseeing power
> To kindle or restrain.   (ll. 7–12)

The lyric voice of these rhyming tetrameters is quite different in rhythm, mood, and tempo from the meditative voice of the father who speaks in 'Frost at Midnight', or the brother who speaks in 'Tintern Abbey'; but echoes from both those poems can be heard, unmistakably, in its promissory blessings: 'Thou, my babe! shalt wander like a breeze...';[28] 'And let the misty mountain winds be free | To blow against thee...'.[29]

> The floating clouds their state shall lend
> To her, for her the willow bend,
> Nor shall she fail to see
> Even in the motions of the storm
> A beauty that shall mould her form
> By silent sympathy.
>
> The stars of midnight shall be dear
> To her, and she shall lean her ear
> In many a secret place
> Where rivulets dance their wayward round,
> And beauty born of murmuring sound
> Shall pass into her face.   (ll. 19–30)

The formal grace of this poem—its gentle iambic rhythms and repeated enjambments, the delayed rhymes which give all the stanzas their closure, like musical phrases—suggests a profound attunement to natural cycles. But although the changing weather is mentioned (shower and storm), there is no reference to the passing seasons: it is as though the girl is absorbed into a perpetual, self-renewing spring. The verbs evoking nature's silent benefi-cence—'moulding', and 'passing into'—belong to a vocabulary Dorothy and William shared with Coleridge in the run-up to *Lyrical Ballads*. A number of features in the portrait are also significantly connected with Dorothy's characteristic actions of watching, listening, and feeling; and the word 'wild' suggests a link with her 'wild eyes' in 'Tintern Abbey'.[30] Furthermore, the girl's responsiveness to 'motions of the storm' and 'stars of midnight' (ll. 22, 25) is reminiscent of Dorothy's recurrent preoccupations in the *Alfoxden Journal*.

There is much to suggest, then, that this is a love poem addressed by the poet to his sister, and that although its primary subject is her growth from a small child to a young woman, the memory of her creative awakening in the 'happy dell' of Alfoxden shapes its figurative language (l. 36). The speaker's 'overseeing power | To kindle and restrain' belongs to the vocabulary of fostering which occurs elsewhere in the Goslar poetry, suggesting an elder brother's wishful compensation for absence during her formative years. But there is a darker side to the poem, which seems also to be about her imagined death, or the fear that something very precious in her has died. Its handling of chronology is ambiguous, the whole unfolding childhood happening in a suspended future tense, as if the speaker is in a trance. The sense of a promise fulfilled is countermanded by an equally strong sense of time foreshortened, life nipped in the bud. Imagining a childhood that is the mirror image of his own, William is not only remembering the lost years of Dorothy's youth— 'lost' in the sense that he did not witness them—but also prophesying the quiet passage of Caroline Vallon from infancy to womanhood. His early separation from Dorothy, and the segment of his daughter's childhood that has passed already, give a twofold poignancy to the sudden severance which brings this poem bleakly to its close:

> Thus Nature spake—The work was done—
> How soon my Lucy's race was run!
> She died and left to me
> This heath, this calm and quiet scene,
> The memory of what has been,
> And never more will be.   (ll. 37–42)

*

William's struggle to comprehend the futility of death involved, at times, an anguished admission of failure. The poems he wrote at Goslar were part of an ongoing work of reparation, establishing the deepest levels at which he and his sister were 'all in each other'. But Dorothy's voice was relatively quiet. Her depression while at Hamburg, her continuing sense of culture shock, and the absence of a journal covering their five months there, may be indications of a severe disruption to her own creativity during this period. Perhaps there remained an absolute sense in which the childhood he remembered was inaccessible to her.

Both as an offshoot of his autobiography and as a mysterious poem believed by many to be addressed to Dorothy, 'Nutting' deserves detailed attention in this context. By the poet's own account, it arose from memories of feelings he often had as a boy when gathering nuts in the coppice-wood near Esthwaite lake.[31] It has a stronger confessional tone than other episodes in the *Two-Part Prelude*, and a franker, more explicit acknowledgement of the masculine aggression that accompanies adolescent sexuality. This suggests a degree of intimacy with Dorothy in the sharing of memories—although, as we shall see, intimacy seems also to be a source of fear. The poet describes his plundering of a hazel-bower, and the feeling of self-alienation that ensued. The erotic overtones in the narrative are unmistakable. The speaker's approach towards the 'virgin scene' resembles Satan's entry into the unfallen Paradise, where the hazels tower 'Tall and erect, with milk-white clusters hung' (ll. 17–18). There is a pause in his narrative, suggestive of a kind of delayed foreplay, as he stands gazing on the scene with 'wise restraint | Voluptuous' (ll. 21–2). The pastoral interlude comes to a sudden close as he rises up and drags the laden branches to the ground, with 'crash | And merciless ravage' (ll. 42–3). He is left to ponder the vestiges of the bower, 'Deformed and sullied', and to feel a sense of pain at 'the silent trees and the intruding sky' (ll. 45, 51). The language of sexual exploitation and guilt is so powerful it hardly needs to be glossed. In the first part of his narrative, the speaker points the finger at himself for breaching a kind of unspoken covenant with nature. In its coda, he generalizes his lesson by appealing to the idea of a *genius loci*. Turning to an unnamed listener, he pleads with her to 'move along these shades' gently, for fear of disturbing a 'Spirit in the woods' (ll. 52–4). In the published version, the poem's coda is at once central to its meaning and oddly unintegrated into its narrative, for there is no prior mention of the 'dearest Maiden'. In the manuscript, however, the poem is double the length, and also addressed to 'Lucy'. In this longer version, the speaker rebukes a woman for her wilful destruction of 'two brother trees', whose stems lie 'stretch'd upon the ground'. He associates the woman's 'keen look | Half cruel in its eagerness' with the feral instincts of an animal.[32] In tones of gentle admonition, he calms the woman's turbulence:

Come rest on this light bed of purple heath
And let me see thee sink to a dream
Of gentle thoughts till once again thine eye
Be like the heart of love and happiness,
Yet still as water when the winds are gone
And no man can tell whither.[33]

There has been much speculation about the identity of the woman who features in the manuscript.[34] Unlikely though it seems that Dorothy would harm a tree, there is a strong inference that she is being upbraided for her violence and guided back towards her better nature.[35] But does the poem also point to a fantasy of forbidden incestuous desire, or even an actual scene of guilty consummation? Some readers have claimed that William here uncovers Dorothy's sexual desire for him,[36] while others have insisted the poem is primarily about a child's wilful destruction of trees, and may even have been prompted by German deforestation.[37]

As 'Nutting' progressed towards publication its meaning changed. Already, by the time Dorothy wrote it out for Coleridge in mid-December 1798, 'Lucy' had disappeared. Was this an intervention of Dorothy's, to simplify the poem's moral content? The letter in which she included it contained other passages of poetry, designed to lure Coleridge away from the temptations of Ratzeburg. We know from Coleridge's own letters that he was shocked by the loose sexual morals he witnessed in Germany; and always at the back of his mind was the memory of Sara, waiting patiently in Nether Stowey for his return. The edited poem takes on a stronger resonance if we view it as part of a triangular conversation, with Dorothy clarifying its role as a memory poem, uncluttered by whatever personal altercation prompted it. Once the central incident has been freed from its surrounding context, its conclusion becomes more reassuring. The boy's assault on the bower is implicitly contrasted with the maiden's gentleness towards its spirit. The tone of the final lines modulates from injunction to invitation. The woods are no longer connected with the Harz forest near Goslar, but revert to being firmly situated in the Vale of Esthwaite. Finally, the coda is split off from the main narrative, which gives it a disembodied quality, as if uttered by the voice of the woods themselves.[38] As the poem ends, its resemblance to an inscription intensifies the speaker's tone of protectiveness towards the hazel trees, reminding us that behind the Wordsworthian philosophy of local attachments is an ancient belief in the spirit of place:

Then, dearest Maiden! move along these shades
In gentleness of heart; with gentle hand
Touch,—for there is a Spirit in the woods. (ll. 52–4)

As we have seen, the manuscript history of 'Nutting' is complicated, raising many questions that cannot be answered. Whatever aesthetic and moral judgements were involved in the decision to shorten it, this powerfully erotic poem proved that William had found a language of 'sufficient power to melt into our affections, to incorporate itself with the blood and vital juices of our minds'. 'Nutting' simultaneously invites and resists allegory. I am tempted to read it as a poem about the sharing of private memories. If the first version explores the poet's anxieties about exposing his past to a potentially invasive reader, the second version invites her to accompany him in a benign revisiting of the past.[39] William's invitation to the maiden takes on an altogether more trusting tone in the shorter version, suggesting a gentler, more responsible attunement to the spirit of place, animated as it is by 'shades' of the dead. There is a wishfulness here which highlights the difficulties confronting the poet as he tried to diminish the gulf separating Dorothy from his Esthwaite years, and from so much else besides.

*

When William and Dorothy stopped off at Göttingen to see Coleridge in April 1799, they had just spent two months travelling in southern Germany and were on their way back to England. Their funds were depleted. All they had to show for seven months abroad was the poetry written at Goslar. While touring lower Saxony together, they kept a shared journal. Unfortunately this has not survived, so we have no knowledge of their movements between 27 February and 20 April. There is, however, one long surviving letter, written jointly from Nordhausen, which records their observations during the first week of the tour. Joint letters from the Wordsworths usually involved a division of labour, with Dorothy providing domestic details and William writing on other matters. (Each would look over what the other had written, sometimes adding comments.) In this case, William responded to a recent letter from Coleridge with reflections on contemporary German literature, going on to praise the genius of Burns and providing an update on progress with 'Peter Bell'. Dorothy's section of the letter is a 'little history of our lives since Saturday morning',[40] giving a detailed account of their journey through the Harz forest, then on to Clausthal and Osterode, arriving at Nordhausen on 27 February. As in her later travel journals, she conveys the pleasure of observations shared with her brother. Sometimes she paraphrases his words, or picks out intricate details in the landscape which she knows will appeal to Coleridge. In the Harz forest, she and William had enjoyed the 'kittenracts' (their friend's word for tiny waterfalls); and observed how the twigs hung 'like long threads of ivy in festoons' from branches. They had noticed together 'the brilliant green of the earth-moss under the trees', which 'made our eyes ache after being so long accustomed to the snow'.[41] Alive to the spring, they were clearly grateful for their release from Goslar, where they had been cooped up for far too long; but the letter also indicates that they were uncomfortable on their travels, and critical of German towns: the people seemed 'dirty, impudent, and vulgar', and Dorothy objected to being 'stared completely out of countenance' by passers-by.[42] Her 'little history' gives a sense of what a shared journal of their two-month tour might have looked like had it survived.

By the time they arrived at Göttingen on 20 April, the Wordsworths were weary and homesick. 'They burn with such impatience to return to their native Country, they who are all to each other', their friend observed in some perplexity.[43] Coleridge himself was immersed in German philosophy and (despite the recent tragic death of his child Berkeley) had no intention of joining them on their homeward trip. He was saddened to see them in low spirits—'melancholy and hypp'd' as he put it[44]—and concluded that William had 'hurtfully segregated & isolated his Being' while in Germany.[45] Without any clear idea about what to do or where to live in the long run, brother and sister took the diligence from Göttingen to Hamburg, and thence to Cuxhaven, crossing to Yarmouth at the end of April. From there they immediately went north. The only viable short-term option was to stay with the Hutchinson family—Mary, Sara, and Joanna, and their brother Tom—who were currently prospering on a farm at Sockburn-on-Tees in Yorkshire. Here they remained for the next seven months, taking stock of their financial prospects and waiting for Coleridge to join them. 'We are right glad to find ourselves in England, for we have learnt to know its value', William wrote to Joseph Cottle.[46]

With the exception of a disloyal review from Southey, the reception of Lyrical Ballads had been encouraging; but as the Wordsworths still had no regular income William began to think about publishing another volume of poems. Meanwhile, settled at Sockburn, Dorothy and Mary made fair-copies of earlier work, including The Borderers and 'The Pedlar', and he turned back to the theme of his Lake District childhood, bringing the *Two-Part Prelude* to completion before the year ended. (This, he managed to convince himself, was the necessary first stage of his ongoing work on *The Recluse*.) In 'Blest the infant babe', a key passage written for Part Two, William described a baby's earliest connection with his mother as the foundation for a healthy reciprocal relationship with the world:

> No outcast he, bewildered and depressed:
> Along his infant veins are interfused
> The gravitation and the filial bond
> Of nature that connect him with the world.
> Emphatically such a being lives
> An inmate of this *active* universe;
> From nature largely he receives, nor so
> Is satisfied but largely gives again... (II, ll. 291–8)

In this highly idealized image of the maternal bond, we can see a development of the Hartleyan and Priestleyan ideas which had emerged in his writing in 1794. The 'social chain' connecting all humans with organic nature has its origins, William suggests, in the primal connection of child and mother. The give-and-take of spiritual matter as the child feeds at his mother's breast foreshadows the adult's relationship with an active universe energized by God. Living on a farm, surrounded by four women of childbearing age, William's preoccupation with generative and nurturing processes was as much biological as spiritual. Nowadays, someone having thoughts about breastfeeding might risk being described as 'broody': is it possible that the idea of settling down with Mary and starting a family began to form at around this time? A homing instinct was implicit in William's actions soon after these lines were written, though perhaps not immediately recognizable as such.

He was ill in bed with a pain in his side (a recurring psychosomatic symptom of anxiety, overwork, or homesickness) when Coleridge eventually turned up at Sockburn with Cottle on 26 October. The following day, the three friends promptly set off on a walking tour of the Lake District, leaving Dorothy behind. Cottle dropped out of the tour very soon, but William and Coleridge were away from Sockburn for a month, John Wordsworth unexpectedly joining them for a while. Together the three companions walked many miles vigorously in the cold November weather—down to Esthwaite, then up to Keswick (stopping for a week at Grasmere), and on through Ennerdale and Borrowdale. Coleridge, overwhelmed by the beauty of Cumberland and Westmorland, found the circling 'embrace'[47] of Grasmere Vale especially beguiling. While still in Germany, Dorothy had imagined that one day she might show him 'every nook' of this romantic country. ('I long to follow at your heels and hear your dear voices again', she had written, teasing him with a slightly incongruous portrait of herself as devoted acolyte.)[48] As it turned out, she was not there to witness his first rapturous response to the Lakes, though she and Mary did receive an account of it by letter: 'Why were you not with us, Dorothy? Why were not you Mary with us?'[49]

In a notebook, Coleridge referred humorously to his holiday as a 'pikteresk tour'[50], but he knew that for his fellow walkers it was a great deal more than that. Reunited with his brother after an absence of two years, William was following his usual remedy for nostalgia by revisiting old haunts and reliving memories of boyhood. At Hawkshead, where much had changed, the brothers learnt that Ann Tyson, their much-loved foster-mother and landlady, had died three years earlier. They were doubtless glad of each other's presence as they absorbed the news. (Later, William would explore the themes of estranged homecoming and delayed realization of loss in his great eclogue, 'The Brothers'. The poem drew on his recent visit to Hawkshead as well as a tragic local accident he and Coleridge heard about shortly afterwards in Ennerdale.) The consequences of his reunion with John were understandable, even perhaps foreseeable. Soon after bidding farewell to his brother at Grisedale Tarn on 5 November, William wrote to Dorothy alerting her to a 'mad' plan he had for building or renting a house in Grasmere.[51] Thereafter, everything fell quickly into place. Coleridge returned to Sockburn, leaving his friend to sort out the domestic details. In a passage of blank verse which he later used as the opening of *The Prelude* (1805), William marvelled at the imminent prospect of realizing his long-cherished dream of home. The personal pronouns indicate his total possession of this defining moment:

> Now I am free, enfranchised and at large,
> May fix my habitation where I will.
> What dwelling shall receive me? in what Vale
> Shall be my harbour? Underneath what grove
> Shall I take up my home, and what sweet stream
> Shall with its murmurs lull me to my rest?[52]

As a rule, house-hunting is not an occupation wisely undertaken alone, but William was acting on something deeper than mere impulse. He knew he could rely on Dorothy to share his instincts. By 25 November, with extraordinary singleness of purpose, he had settled on the cottage they would live in, arranged to rent it, and returned to Sockburn to collect his sister. Winter had arrived, and the weather was bitterly cold; but the Wordsworths were about to make their way home—this time together.

6

Homecoming

'There is one Cottage in our Dale,
In naught distinguish'd from the rest
Save by a tuft of flourishing trees,
The shelter of that little nest

The publick road through Grasmere Vale
Winds close beside that Cottage small;
And there 'tis hidden by the trees
That overhang the orchard wall.

You lose it there—its serpent line
Is lost in that close household grove—
A moment lost—and then it mounts
The craggy hills above.'[1]

*

In December 1799, the Wordsworths returned to their roots, settling at Town End, a small cluster of houses near the village of Grasmere.[2] They were less than twenty miles from their birthplace and only ten miles from Hawkshead, where William had spent his schooldays. Grasmere Vale was still, as Thomas Gray had described it thirty years earlier, a 'little unsuspected paradise'.[3] The house (later known as Dove Cottage) stood directly beside the old road from Rydal, with an uninterrupted view of the lake, and was well suited to the family's needs—despite chimneys which 'smoked like a furnace' and rooms smaller than they had been used to at Racedown and Alfoxden.[4] The rent was higher than average in the region, but affordable; and there was space enough in the cottage for John, who was to join them in January for nine months. Across the road in Sykeside lived Molly Fisher, who agreed to help with the housework for two shillings a week: this released time for writing, walking, and gardening—although Dorothy had her hands full, especially when visitors came to stay. The Wordsworths were still waiting for the repayment of money owing to them by James Lowther. The legacy from Calvert made sufficient provision for them to live modestly. But, with no immediate publishing prospects, returning north was a courageous life-choice, for it removed William from the networks in London and Bristol on which his career depended. There was also a substantial risk that the Wordsworths might lose their close connection with Coleridge, who looked set to remain in the south. It was, even so, the right decision. Intuitively, they had been finding their way back home in their memories and longings for at least a year before the strenuous four-day journey (mostly on foot, and in wintry weather) from Sockburn to Grasmere.[5]

To mark the symbolic importance of their arrival, they sent an unusually long letter to Coleridge, begun on Christmas Eve and written in William's hand, as Dorothy was 'racked with the tooth-ache'.[6] Describing their journey through Yorkshire in intricate detail, the letter recalls how the valleys of Wensleydale unfolded before them, each step taking them closer to their native hills. They walked side by side, stopping to enjoy the waterfalls en route. Every word in their letter was chosen with a view to awakening Coleridge's desire to join them. It reads as a prose poem celebrating their shared love of northern landscapes, and was composed jointly. Some of Dorothy's distinctive phrases are attributed to her by William— on this occasion he was *her* amanuensis—and there are passages showing the minute attentiveness to natural beauty which is typical of her writing:

when we reached this point the valley opened out again, two rocky banks on each side, which, hung with ivy and moss and fringed luxuriantly with brush-wood, ran directly parallel to each other and then approaching with a gentle curve, at their point of union presented a lofty waterfall, the termination of the valley.[7]

At Hardraw they took a detour to admire the spectacle of Hardraw Force, 300 feet high, set in among stones of all colours and sizes 'encased in the clearest ice', and shooting from its rock face directly over their heads into a basin 'wrinkled over with masses of ice, white as snow, or rather as D says like congealed froth'. Coleridge doubtless noted with pleasure the allusion to 'Kubla Khan' in the sentence 'the stream shot from between rows of icicles in irregular fits of strength and with a body of water that *momently varied*'.[8] Recalling the mighty fountain rising 'momently' in fertile ground above caves of ice, their letter enticed him with the prospect of landscapes that would further inspire his imagination.

Written only days after arrival, their letter voices a quieter, more proprietorial pleasure in settling into Town End: 'D is much pleased with the house and *appurtenances* the orchard especially; in imagination she has already built a seat with a summer shed on the highest platform in this our little domestic slip of mountain. The spot commands a view over the roof of our house, of the lake, the church, helm cragg, and two thirds of the vale.'[9] When the word 'enclose' appears in the next sentence it carries a touch of irony, for there is a world of difference between the Wordsworths' modest plans for a front garden and the enclosure of common land by wealthy landlords:

We mean also to enclose two or three yards of ground between us and the road, this for the sake of a few flowers, and because it will make it more our own. Besides, am I fanciful when I would extend the obligation of gratitude to insensate things? May not a man have a salutary pleasure in doing something gratuitously for the sake of his house, as for an individual to which he owes so much...[10]

The question 'am I fanciful?' is hardly necessary, for Coleridge would have had no trouble in understanding William's empathy with 'mute insensate things'.[11] The key word here is 'gratitude'. It takes us to the centre of the gift economy which thrived in William and Dorothy's household throughout their lives. The idea that one might, in making a garden, be giving back to a place something that is *owing* to it suggests the depth of their thankfulness for returning to the region. From the first, they thought of Grasmere as a place that called for the unconditional gift of their love. The garden, including the 'little domestic slip of mountain' rising steeply behind the house, was dear to them both. Involving their shared creative energies (and those of their brother John) it became a symbol of the family's attunement to the region: a microcosm for the vale.

In a poem entitled 'Grasmere—a fragment', Dorothy later wrote about her feelings on first arriving in Town End on a 'lovely winter's day', after 'a night of perilous storm'. The poem is not a literal record of what happened on their first evening, but a reconstruction from memory of her symbolic journey towards happiness. In simple, lyrical quatrains she recalls her delight on seeing her 'dear abode', and how she overcame her estrangement by taking a solitary walk along a path leading eastward. In her imagination, this was probably towards Rydal, the direction of many of her favourite walks when she later got to know the region:

> A Stranger, Grasmere, in thy Vale,
> All faces then to me unknown,
> I left my sole companion-friend
> To wander out alone. (ll. 49–52)

Carefully poised between literal and figurative registers, the poem follows the track of her memory to an unnamed place, where a 'stately Rock' (l. 59), perhaps connoting the solid enduring qualities of the Westmorland landscape, is softened by richly mingled vegetation. Moss, ferns, and oak trees thrive on its surface; foxglove leaves, eglantine and rose hips hide from the wind in 'many a sheltered chink' (l. 65) on its sides. In this intricately balanced image of symbiosis, Dorothy suggests how two opposite aspects of the region—its ruggedness and its fecundity—are mingled. Her identification with a 'foaming streamlet' (l. 83) which comes 'dancing by' underlines the emotional force of her rhetorical question, 'How *could* I but rejoice?' (l. 88), celebrating a moment of glad recognition. The poem is written from a position of being no longer a 'Stranger' but an 'Inmate of this Vale'—'inmate' in this context signifying the safety of settled dwelling, as it did in 'Frost at Midnight':

> Peaceful our valley, fair and green,
> And beautiful her cottages,
> Each in its nook, its sheltered hold,
> Or underneath its tuft of trees.
>
> Many and beautiful they are;
> But there is *one* that I love best,

A lowly shed, in truth, it is,
A brother of the rest.

Yet when I sit on rock or hill,
Down looking on the valley fair,
That Cottage with its clustering trees
Summons my heart; it settles there.

Others there are whose small domain
Of fertile fields and hedgerows green
Might more seduce a wanderer's mind
To wish that *there* his home had been.

Such wish be his! I blame him not,
My fancies they perchance are wild
—I love that house because it is
The very Mountains' child.   (ll. 1–20)

Dorothy writes of her need for the 'sheltered hold' of the mountains, as if they offered a return to the primary maternal embrace. She sees a close analogy between the way the 'lowly shed' nestles into the mountainside and the way moss and lichen flourish on stone (ll. 20–4). She approaches 'insensate things'— the house, the rocks and fields—as if they too were companionable dwellers in the vale, like herself. In modern parlance, she understands Grasmere as an *eco-system*: a complex web of mutually dependent organisms, sustained by and sustaining their natural habitat. Two significant figures—'A brother of the rest' (l. 8), 'The very Mountains' child' (l. 20)—tell us how deeply this 'pastoral spot' answered to her idea of home, and how strongly she identified the place with her family.

*

It was during the first few years of settled domesticity that William established the basis for the story of his life as he would present it in *The Prelude*: the story of an earthly Paradise, lost and regained through the mediation of nature, with Dorothy/Grasmere as the recompense for bereavement and separation. Grasmere was not Cockermouth, but it stood for the Eden from which the siblings had been expelled after the death of their father, and to which they now returned: 'possession of the good | Which had been sighed for, ancient thought fulfilled | And dear Imaginations realized | Up to their highest measure, yea, and more'.[12] Milton's *Paradise Lost* and Homer's *Odyssey* helped to shape the poem's epic themes of journeying and homecoming over the next five years. Already there were Miltonic echoes in the poetry of 1800, as there would be in Dorothy's *Grasmere Journal*, begun in the early summer. Both writers had a slightly self-conscious awareness of themselves as Adam and Eve tending their garden.

'Home at Grasmere', William's great homage to the region, was mostly written during their first year there. It begins, like 'Tintern Abbey', with a train of associations set in motion by standing in a particular spot and repossessing a remembered landscape. Recalling how, as a schoolboy, he had once stopped 'on the brow of yonder hill' (Hammerscar) and looked north across the lake towards Town End, William evokes Grasmere Vale as it had seemed to him then:

> Long did I halt; I could have made it even
> My business and my errand so to halt.
> For rest of body 'twas a perfect place,
> All that luxurious nature could desire,
> But tempting to the Spirit.   (ll. 20–5)

Thomas De Quincey describes in his *Recollections of the Lakes* how, from this very spot—famous among travel writers—'the whole vale of Grasmere suddenly breaks upon the view in a style of almost theatrical surprise, with its lovely valley stretching in the distance, the lake lying immediately below, with its solemn bent-like island of five acres in size, seemingly floating on its surface'.[13] William captures the same quality of apparently endless space, but his mental prospect is teeming with organic life:

> Sunbeams, Shadows, Butterflies and Birds,
> Angels and winged Creatures that are Lords
> Without restraint of all which they behold.   (ll. 31–2)

This memory of uninhibited delight is framed as a prophetic glimpse of an earthly Paradise, which the poet has carried into adulthood, and realized. Seeing the Vale of Grasmere for the first time as a boy, bereft of his mother and sister, he had found himself thinking, 'here | Should be my home, this Valley be my World' (ll. 42–3). Returning as an adult, he lays claim to a part of himself that had always been there, waiting to be recovered: 'This solitude is mine; the distant thought | Is fetched out of the heaven in which it was. | The unappropriated bliss hath found | An owner, and that owner I am he' (ll. 83–6).

William uses the language of possession unashamedly. His is not the proprietorial consciousness of a landowner like Lowther; nor is it the colonizing wishfulness of Cowper's Selkirk, 'monarch of all I survey', 'lord of the fowl and the brute'.[14] 'Exalted with the thought | Of my possessions, of my genuine wealth | Inward and outward' (ll. 89–91), he conveys his overwhelming gratitude for metaphorical and spiritual ownership—the unworldly 'property' to which, on behalf of his wronged family, he lays claim. This poem resembles 'Tintern Abbey' and the *Two-Part Prelude* in honouring a moment of imaginative identification with a place, and memory's role in organizing spiritual growth around that moment. The child's 'spot of time' on Hammerscar has provided his lifelong connection with the vale as a surrogate home. Confirming the preciousness of the vale by returning to it, William gives thanks for Dorothy's companionship as he contemplates their joint future:

> What I keep, have gained,
> Shall gain, must gain, if sound be my belief
> From past and present, rightly understood,
> That in my day of childhood I was less
> The mind of Nature, less, take all in all,
> Whatever may be lost, than I am now.   (ll. 91–6)

Gone are the hesitations and self-questionings which at first beset him. In retrospect, the bold decision to move north has come to seem not only the natural outcome of a homing instinct but 'a choice of the whole heart' (l. 78). Following its own emotional logic, the poem offers Dorothy herself as the answer to all doubts: 'For proof, behold this Valley and behold | Yon Cottage, where with me my Emma dwells' (ll. 97–8).[15] William uses the name Emma, which derives from the German word *ermen*, meaning 'universal' or 'whole', to connote the all-embracing nature of her significance to him. (In almost all languages, Jakobson has observed, some variation of 'Mama', or its reversal, as in 'Emma', is the familiar term for 'Mother'.)[16] The verse shuttles between past and present tenses, blurring the boundary between the *idea* of Dorothy and her material presence. Always accompanying or illuminating his thoughts in the past, she is now indistinguishable from the natural home they share:

> Mine eyes did ne'er
> Rest on a lovely object, nor my mind
> Take pleasure in the midst of happy thoughts,
> But either She whom now I have, who now
> Divides with me this loved abode, was there,
> Or not far off. Where'er my footsteps turned,
> Her Voice was like a hidden Bird that sang;
> The thought of her was like a flash of light
> Or an unseen companionship, a breath
> Or fragrance independent of the wind.   (ll. 104–13)

In a touching allusion to 'Frost at Midnight', William links 'the thought of her' with the 'secret ministry' of frost, a mysterious creative power 'unhelped by any wind'.[17] Obliquely, and through a process of transference which is by now habitual, he pays tribute to her 'hidden' voice as a collaborator in his writings, her 'unseen' presence as the keeper of their shared memories.

'Home at Grasmere' can be read as an expression of the Wordsworths' hopes and longings. Like an epithalamion, it celebrates the spiritual wedding of brother and sister to each other, with Grasmere as their 'dower'.[18] At l. 143, the speaker switches from singular to plural pronouns, and backtracks to tell their moving story of separation and reunion:

> Long is it since we met to part no more,
> Since I and Emma heard each other's call
> And were Companions once again, like Birds
> Which by the intruding Fowler had been scared,
> Two of a scattered brood that could not bear
> To live in loneliness; 'tis long since we,
> Rememb'ring much and hoping more, found means
> To walk abreast, though in a narrow path,
> With undivided steps.   (ll. 171–9)

The image of a 'scattered' brood echoes Genesis 11:4: 'We are scattered abroad over the face of the whole earth.' There is a further scriptural image of brother and sister walking abreast, united in their journey along the 'narrow path' of life, like Adam and Eve after the Fall. Biblical language reinforces the sense that the Wordsworths' history follows a providential pattern. In the embedded narrative of their wintry journey to Grasmere, William draws on a long tradition of Protestant autobiography, associating the hardships of wayfaring with the trials of conscience. Instead of describing how he and Dorothy hunted for waterfalls through Wensleydale (as in the letter to Coleridge on 24 December), he pictures them embarking on a pilgrimage towards a sacred place, like Christian in *The Pilgrim's Progress*: 'Bleak season was it, turbulent and bleak, | When hitherward we journeyed, and on foot' (ll. 218–19). They undergo the rigours of journeying, are strengthened by trial, experience a vision of 'God | The Mourner, God the Sufferer' at Hart-Leap Well, and arrive at their 'little shed' in 'composing darkness' like Mary and Joseph (ll. 244–5, 264–5). Journeying towards this 'hallowed spot' fulfils a pre-destined purpose: 'grace' has been vouchsafed the poet; he has

been granted a 'boon' all the more precious for the suffering he has undergone; and he now possesses 'A portion of the blessedness' which will spread
'To all the Vales of earth and all mankind' (ll. 250–6).[19]

While much of 'Home at Grasmere' is Messianic in tone and register, the
speaker's beliefs are not easily aligned with organized religion. 'His muse riots',
Geoffrey Hartman observes, 'his creative energies almost evoke the terrestrial
paradise.'[20] The poem embodies an eccentric mix of deism, Protestant tradition,
and personal mythmaking. In returning to the Lake District with Dorothy,
William experiences anew the enfolding protection of a familiar landscape
associated with the memory of their parents:

> No where … can be found
> The one sensation that is here; 'tis here
> Here as it found its way into my heart
> In childhood, here as it abides by day,
> By night, here only.   (ll. 155–9)

Grasmere could never be his birthplace, but in this astonishingly physical
apostrophe to the landscape, he asks it to be the next best thing:

> Embrace me, then, ye Hills, and close me in,
> Now in the clear and open day I feel
> Your guardianship; I take it to my heart;
> 'Tis like the solemn shelter of the night.   (ll. 129–32)

Gaston Bachelard says of the nest-house that 'it is the natural habitat of the
function of inhabiting. For not only do we *come back* to it, but we dream of
coming back to it, the way a bird comes back to its nest, or a lamb to the fold.
This sign of *return* marks an infinite number of daydreams, for the reason that
human returning takes place in the great rhythm of human life, a rhythm that
reaches back across the years, and, through the dream, combats all absence.'[21]
The dream of home created in 'Home at Grasmere' corresponds closely to
Bachelard's 'nest', with Dorothy at its centre.

*

Settlement in Grasmere was a gradual process, and it would take a while
before the Wordsworths felt they were 'inmates' in the vale rather than newcomers. A stream of visitors came to stay, leaving memories of walks taken in
the neighbourhood: occasionally they contributed to the household's Commonplace Book. When Mary Hutchinson arrived at the end of February and
stayed for five weeks, William wrote a poem to commemorate a walk with

her and Dorothy in Rydal Upper Park. Their brother John, the 'never-resting Pilgrim of the Sea' ('Home at Grasmere', l. 866), arrived in January 1800 and stayed till September. Coleridge was with them for a month in the spring. 'I would to God I could get Wordsworth to re-take Alfoxden', he wrote to Poole, regretfully, in March: 'The society of so great a Being is of priceless value—but he will never quit the North of England.'[22] What with all the activity of settling in and looking after visitors, Dorothy did not have time to keep a journal; but William was productive throughout the winter and early spring. He worked first on 'The Brothers', a pastoral poem in which he explored the themes of exile, return, and fraternal love; then on a sequence of poems in various genres, including inscriptions and loco-descriptive verse inspired by his immediate surroundings; and finally—in the summer of 1800—on assembling the second edition of *Lyrical Ballads*, complete with its important Preface. He recollected the experience of homecoming in verse on several occasions, and his mind ran recurrently on the theme of home.

In 'When first I journeyed hither', William wrote about his brother John, honouring his important place in the household. John was an active sup-porter of William's talent, proud of his elder brother's achievements and keenly interested in the second edition of *Lyrical Ballads*. 'In time they will become popular but it will be by degrees' he observed, soon after the vol-ume's publication.[23] William's poem about his brother concerns a place which became known in the Wordsworth family as 'John's Grove'. This was a fir plantation on what is now the old road to Ambleside, opposite the Wishing Gate, and it became a favourite haunt of John's during the nine months he spent at Grasmere. Looking back on his own earliest days in the neighbourhood, the poet recalls how, during the snowbound winter of 1799/1800, one of his walks led him to this grove, where the ground was dry underfoot. Here he found an enclosed space, like a nest, in which he could observe and identify with the birds:

> The red-breast near me hopped, nor was I loth
> To sympathize with vulgar coppice birds
> That hither came.   (ll. 13–15)

This 'sequestered nook' would have been an ideal spot for al fresco composi-tion, except that the bushes had grown 'In such perplexed array' that it was difficult to move in the 'mechanic thoughtlessness' necessary for composi-tion (ll. 34–8). Abandoning the spot, he forgot about it for several months, until returning one day to discover the ground had been worn by John into a pathway 'traced around the trees' and winding in an 'easy line | Along a natural opening' by his brother (ll. 58–9).[24] The connections between path-making and versifying are literal as well as figurative, for it was William's habit to walk to and fro while composing. John's 'tracing' of a natural path round the trees, in an easy line and 'along a natural opening', embodies his attune-ment to the steady rhythm of blank verse. In suggesting that his brother has created a path for him to follow, William pays tribute to John as the 'silent poet' with whom his consciousness is twinned:

> Hither he had brought a finer eye,
> A heart more wakeful…more loth to part
> From place so lovely he had worn the track,
> One of his own deep paths! by pacing here
> With that habitual restlessness of foot
> Wherewith the Sailor measures o'er and o'er
> His short domain upon the Vessel's deck,
> While she is travelling through the dreary seas.   (ll. 67–74)

Recalling their separation as boys, their exile from Cumberland, and their eventual reunion in Grasmere, William imagines that during years of absence on 'the barren seas' (l. 47) John has carried with him 'Undying recollections' (l. 85) of home. The poem re-establishes the grounds of their intimacy, the old footing of their kinship, by revisiting shared memories of Esthwaite, Windermere and their 'native hills' (l. 46). Subsequently, the poet recalls, he visited the fir-grove regularly, continuing to define the path by walking to and fro while composing poetry. Through its associations with John, the grove became a favourite spot for contemplation of the 'solemn loveliness' of Grasmere vale, treasured now with 'a perfect love' (ll. 103, 94). Picturing his brother far out at sea, pacing to and fro on deck, 'muttering the verses which I muttered first | Among the mountains' (ll. 106–7), William suggests that they are linked across time and space by the rhythmic actions of pacing and reciting verse. Despite vast differences in their occupations and tem-peraments, their thought processes converge in a shared memory: 'Alone I tread this path, for aught I know, | Timing my steps to thine' (ll. 112–13). There is a density of associations in this poem that enables it to speak mov-ingly of all three siblings' nostalgia for their original home in Cockermouth. Rich in allegorical meaning, it plays consciously with romantic associations of sea-travel, personal memories of homeless wandering, and a long family history of separation. The poem's significance deepens if we take into account Dorothy's fondness for the fir-grove, and the fact that she often walked backwards and forwards with William while he composed his poems. The Wordsworths' affinity with place is almost indistinguishable from their affinity with each other. It is as though the action of pacing to and fro enables each of them to deepen their shared connection with Grasmere. As the ground is worn, it retains the history of their successive visits and bears the stamp of their kinship. This process resembles the gradual 'inter-assimilation' between a family and a place which usually takes place over a lifetime.[25]

It was together with John that the Wordsworths made another path, in the orchard behind Town End, and enclosed the small garden at the front of the house. During their first summer there, they began to see the fruits of their joint industry. Dorothy, writing to her friend Jane Marshall, explained that they regarded the garden with 'pride and partiality' as 'the work of our own hands'. The personal pronouns suggest that, both inside and out, the work of building their home was shared by all members of the household:

> The orchard is very small, but then it is a delightful one from its retirement, and the excessive beauty of the prospect from it. Our cottage is quite large enough for us though very small, and we have made it neat and comfortable within doors and it looks very nice on the outside, for though the roses and honeysuckles which we have planted against it are only of this year's growth yet it is covered all over with green leaves and scarlet flowers, for we have trained scarlet beans upon threads, which are not only exceedingly beautiful, but very useful, as their produce is immense.[26]

There is, perhaps, an echo of Coleridge's 'The Eolian Harp' in this arcadian image of a cottage covered in scarlet beans;[27] and the houseproud Dorothy sounds almost like a newly wedded wife, confirming that the garden is economical as well as pretty. Her letter reveals her pleasure in watching how the rough-cast and whitewashed stone walls were already being taken over by vegetation, so that, to borrow a phrase of William's, the house became 'gently incorporated with the works of nature'.[28] By 1809, it would be 'embossed—nay smothered in roses ... with as much jessamine and honeysuckle as could find room to flourish'.[29]

Coleridge, observing his friends during a three-week stay at Town End in June 1800, was half-resentful of the strength with which their new home seemed to claim and absorb them. Eventually succumbing to the pressure to live as their neighbour, he and his family moved into Greta Hall in Keswick in July; but there was a note of mischief in his remarks on their way of life. 'Wordsworth remains at Grasmere till next summer (perhaps longer)', he wrote to James Tobin, on 25 July:

His cottage is indeed in every respect so delightful a residence, the walks so
dry after the longest rains, the heath and a silky kind of fern so luxurious a
bedding on every hilltop, and the whole vicinity so tossed about on those
little hills at the feet of the majestic mountains, that he moves in an eddy; he
cannot get out of it.[30]

In this panoramic simile, the whole of Grasmere Vale is seen as if it were a tiny
boat or island, 'tossed about' below the towering crests of the mountains; and
the poet is pictured as a marooned figure, blind to the danger of being sucked
into their 'eddy'. Even on the 'little' hilltops, a 'silky kind of fern' affords William a luxurious 'bedding', sheltering him from his looming responsibilities.
Coleridge was doubtless thinking of his friend's obligation to resume work on
The Recluse, only one book of which—'Home at Grasmere'—was under way
during 1800. As Dorothy moved forward into a central position in William's
consciousness, Coleridge's pressurizing philosophical influence was gradually
sidelined, even though their friendship (and the remembrance of earlier shared
ideals and values) continued to be important. Instead of embracing his epic
task, William seemed set on a more insular course. When *Lyrical Ballads* (1800)
was published, it included three inscriptions taking island habitations as their
theme: one for Grasmere, one for Rydal, and one for Derwentwater. These
three inscriptions concern human habitations which are either incomplete or
vestigial: the spot where a hermitage once stood; the ruins of a building (itself
only a portion of a larger, unfinished set of buildings); and the remains of a
grand pleasure house, begun and thankfully abandoned. The poems partly
concern what the islands signified in the family's day-to-day life, especially
during the summer of 1800. But they also show an interest in local history,
anticipating William's much later role in *Guide to the Lakes*.

Formal inscription was a classical genre in which poets reflected on their
sacramental bond with place. In its more informal guise it became popular in
the eighteenth century as a means of commemorating domestic occasions
and feelings, however humble, in poems that were offered as gifts. William's
inscriptions, by drawing on both these traditions, ascribe a sacred significance
to local ties with the land, and cement the three-way bonds between places,
people, and history. His interest in the genre was not new. He had used it in
1797 to memorialize the Esthwaite solitary he remembered from boyhood
in his 'Lines left upon a seat in a yew-tree': a poem which Coleridge and
Lamb both admired. He had used it again in 'Tintern Abbey' to suggest the
presence of a *genius loci* in the Wye Valley. In the three island inscriptions of
1800, he calls to mind people historically associated with Grasmere, Rydal,

and Derwentwater; but simultaneously he observes how, with time, once-inhabited spots have reverted to their natural state. These poems are partly epitaphic. Written in a stoical mood, accepting human transience, they call to mind the four 'ruined walls' on which the Pedlar had mused wisely in 'The Ruined Cottage' (l. 492; RCP, 73); and behind them, the overgrown terrace at the Wordsworths' house in Cockermouth.

Of the places described in the three island poems, 'the House (an Out-House) on the Island at Grasmere' is the one most associated with William himself. A nearby spot for family outings, the island was also a perfect retreat for outdoor composition. William found there the remains of a roughly built outhouse, which he liked partly for the unnamed rustic architect it called to mind, partly for the hospitable shelter it provided:

> It is a homely pile, yet to these walls
> The heifer comes in the snow-storm, and here
> The new-dropp'd lamb finds shelter from the wind.
> And hither does one Poet sometimes row
> His Pinnace, a small vagrant barge.[31]

His imagination makes a home of this secluded spot, as if seeking intimacy with its wildlife, or identifying with the spirit of the obscure architect who planned and built its 'rude' edifice. He plays with the paradox that islands in the Lake District are far from being symbols of isolation (as in *Robinson Crusoe*, or 'The Solitude of Alexander Selkirk'), but instead are places of companionable reflection, where a poet can lie down with the sheep 'even as if they were a part | Of his own household' (ll. 24–5). The biblical touch adds solemnity to his arcadian image of restfulness, reminding one of Samuel Palmer's shepherd peacefully asleep among his flock.

We do not have to look far to find a biographical key to 'Inscription for the Spot where the hermitage stood on St Herbert's island, Derwent-Water'; for this was the lake that Coleridge looked out on, from the house in Keswick to which he and his family moved in July 1800. Of course, William identified with the reclusive impulse which drove St Herbert to retire from 'social cares' to meditate on 'everlasting things' in a recess that was guarded 'by mountains high and waters widely spread'.[32] But his inscription gives a strongly homosocial emphasis to its historical subject matter. Herbert's bond with St Cuthbert forms the poem's psychological centrepiece:

> when he pac'd
> Along the beach of this small isle and thought
> Of his Companion, he had prayed that both

> Might die in the same moment. Nor in vain
> So pray'd he: —as our Chronicles report
> Though here the Hermit number'd his last days
> Far from St Cuthbert his beloved friend,
> Those holy men both died in the same hour.   (ll. 14–21)

'Fellow-labourers' (l. 10) was a phrase William later used of his and Coleridge's joint creative endeavours; and the image of St Herbert, pacing to and fro on his island, calls to mind the twinned actions of William and John in 'When first I journeyed hither'. Like the Lucy poems, and ''Tis said that some have died for love', this poem speaks to anyone who has known affection so deep that the thought of separation can 'make the heart sink', even in happiness (l. 1). The poem draws on years of experience as a separated sibling, and its depth of feeling suggests that William's love for Coleridge is on a par with his love for Dorothy and John.

Placed directly alongside each other in *Lyrical Ballads* (1800), the Derwentwater and Grasmere inscriptions ask to be read as companion-pieces about neighbouring poets, linked metaphorically and topographically to their islands. The third inscription, 'Lines written with a Slate pencil' completes the group. Writing as an environmentalist, keen to protect natural beauty from the encroachments of nouveau riche aristocrats, William celebrates the failure of Sir William Fleming's ambition to build a grand house on one of the Rydal islands. Only a 'hillock of misshapen stones' survives to tell the tale of his abandoned plans. Of the three inscriptions, this is the one most connected with Dorothy, for it voices the Wordsworths' shared concern with protecting the Lake District's natural beauty. They were dismayed when new buildings started to appear around Grasmere, and disliked even humble buildings when whitewashed, because they stood out as eyesores against the natural stone, turf, and bracken of the fells.[33] William uses the formal device of apostrophe in the opening line, and adopts the admonitory tone that was a traditional feature of inscriptions:

> Leave
> Thy fragments to the bramble and the rose,
> There let the vernal slow-worm sun himself,
> And let the red-breast hop from stone to stone.   (ll. 32–5; LB, 210)

There is a touching recollection, here, of William's blessing on Dorothy at the end of 'Tintern Abbey': 'let the moon | Shine on thee in thy solitary walk; | And let the misty mountain winds be free | To blow against thee.' (ll. 135–8). Her affinity with wildness and freedom enters into the poet's thoughts about this solitary place as effortlessly and companionably as wild-life returns to its natural habitat.[34]

William used his island inscriptions in a number of interconnected ways: to establish his identity as a native of the Lake District, rather than an offcomer; to claim familial kinship with the region through awareness of local traditions; to renew commemorative bonds between historical people and places; and to acknowledge with humility that the Lake District had so far outlasted the vanity of human wishes. The poems were topical protests against tourism and development: their island theme had immediate local relevance. Outsiders like Thomas English and Joseph Pocklington had been indulging their deplorable tastes in the region for two decades. In 1774, English had purchased Belle Isle, an island on Windermere, and built a large circular mansion on it, which the Wordsworths despised. In 1778, Joseph Pocklington (a rich developer from Nottingham) had purchased Vicar's Island on Derwentwater, changing its name to Pocklington's Island. He had stripped it of trees, building a fake Druid circle on it to give it an air of distinguished antiquity—his model was Castlerigg Circle near Keswick—and later added Island House, a modern monstrosity designed by himself. These were the kinds of 'improvement' that threatened to spoil the Lakes' natural beauty, and in writing his inscriptions, William tried to rescue the environment from further damage.[35] His emphasis on the delights of 'rude' or 'unfinished' architecture expressed a rejection of the fashionable taste for grand designs. Just as his visual preference was for authentically local and humble dwellings, so his allegiance as a writer was to a loco-descriptive tradition, domestic in its register. The distinctive Wordsworthian aesthetic that emerged during 1800 had a bearing on how he regarded *The Recluse*, his never-to-be-completed magnum opus. Coleridge was wrong to see his friend as trapped in an inwardly spiralling 'eddy', but William was indeed moving away from the ambition to produce a philosophical epic.

One further inscription—this time for a rustic seat, not an island—belongs partly to the summer of 1800, partly to an earlier phase in the Wordsworths' life together. 'Inscription for a seat by the pathway side ascending to Windy Brow' was first composed in couplets in 1794, when William and Dorothy, newly reunited, were staying together at the Calverts' farmhouse on Latrigg Fell. The inscription (entered into MS 10 in William's hand) addresses passers-by who 'rich in vigour need not rest', urging them to be compassionate towards those less fortunate, who 'bowed by age and sickness greet | With thankfulness this timely seat', and 'ponder here | On the last resting-place, so near'.[36] A revised and extended version belonged to the summer or autumn of 1796. It was entered in the Racedown Notebook (MS 11) in Dorothy's rough handwriting, taken down while William dictated 'all too rapidly, changing his mind and trying out variants as he went along'.[37] At this stage, the poem's tight couplets had been abandoned, enabling a more relaxed blank verse inscription to emerge. Closer in its loco-descriptive texture to William's 'Lines Left upon a seat in a Yew-tree', this poem has a stronger, more inclusive message of compassion, tinged with political animus:

> Here stop and think on them
> The weary homeless vagrants of the earth
> Or that poor man the rustic artisan
> Who laden with his implements of toil
> Returns at night to his far-distant home...
> Or think on them,
> Who in the spring to meet the warmer sun
> Crawl up this steep hill side that double bends
> Their bodies bowed by age or malady   (ll. 5–9, 15–18; EPF, 754)

A further revised version was published as one of Coleridge's contributions to the *Morning Post* in 1800, the amusing Latin signature 'VENTIFRONS' (Windy Brow) setting a distinctively Coleridgean seal on its provenance. With a more generic title—'Inscription for a Seat by a road-side, half way up a steep hill, facing the south'—the poem now conveyed its message in piously Christian terms:

> And for thy future self thou shalt provide
> Through ev'ry change of various life a seat,
> Not built by hands, on which thy inner part,
> Imperishable, many a grievous hour,
> Or bleak, or sultry, may repose.'   (ll. 35–9; EPF, 756)

Appropriately, this new version draws a biblical analogy between building an actual 'seat of sods' at Windy Brow and building a place in the afterlife (l. 24). The phrase 'Not built with hands' alludes to Paul's second letter to the Corinthians, in which Paul reassured the people of Corinth of his love for them, and renewed his faith as an apostle of Christ: 'For we know that if our earthly house of this tabernacle were dissolved, we have a building of God, an house not made with hands, eternal in the heavens.'[38]

Coleridge's involvement in writing (and later publishing) the Windy Brow inscription suggests how collaborative processes in the Wordsworth circle helped to strengthen communal ties with the region. The seat at Windy

Brow was a 'threshold gift'—that is, a gift that 'attends times of passage or moments of great change'[39]—created collaboratively as an expression of community spirit. It marked two different rites of passage, combining the properties of a poem, a place, and an object commemorating feelings for a place. Symbolically associated with the Wordsworths' memories of their reunion in 1794, it had sentimental value as part of their family history. To sit together on the seat in 1794 and ponder on 'the last resting place, so near' was almost inevitably to think of their parents, both of whom had been denied old age, and one of whom was buried in the graveyard at Cockermouth. To return and rebuild the seat, six years later, was to renew their emotional ties with a dearly loved spot. In 1800, when Coleridge moved into his house at Keswick, he was closer to Windy Brow than the Wordsworths were. Participating in rebuilding the seat and rewriting the poem included him in their passionate involvement with the region. Dorothy recorded in her journal entry for 9 August that she and Coleridge walked together to Windy Brow woods, and again two days later 'Walked to windy brow'. On 13 August, she wrote, 'Made the Windy Brow seat', meaning the poem as well as the seat itself (*Grasmere Journal*, 16–17).[40] A few weeks later, as Coleridge hurried to prepare something for the *Morning Post*, he referred in his notebook to 'the sopha of sods', and also to a 'poem hid in a tin box'.[41] In all likelihood the Wordsworths' inscription was placed in a box to protect it from the weather, and buried in the earth alongside the seat. Coleridge was by this stage reckoning 'how many Lines the poem would make' in fulfilment of a contract with Daniel Stuart, his editor.[42] We can infer that the poem was understood as his and the Wordsworths' joint property, for which Coleridge would receive payment when it was published. In this way, a distinctively Wordsworthian artefact acquired an additional layer of associative history, becoming a collaborative expression of William's, Dorothy's, and Coleridge's emotional attachment to the region. With its solemn biblical reference to the 'house not made with hands', the newly published inscription was like a covenant, binding the three companions to each other.

7

Dwelling

'Look where we will, some human heart has been
Before us with its offering; not a tree
Sprinkles these little pastures, but the same
Hath furnished matter for a thought; perchance
To some one is as a familiar Friend.
Joy spreads and sorrow spreads; and this whole Vale,
Home of untutored Shepherds as it is,
Swarms with sensation, as with gleams of sunshine,
Shadows or breezes, scents or sounds.'[1]

*

Returning to the Lake District to reclaim their regional identity and re-establish their family, the Wordsworths found themselves at one remove from their childhood origins—neither insiders nor quite outsiders in Grasmere. Class-consciousness, education, and the experience of exile set them apart from the 'untutored Shepherds' whose families were long established in the vale. William and Dorothy's writings about Grasmere and its neighbourhood reflect a longing for oneness with place, intensified by early memories of dispossession. Ideas of home and of belonging permeate their language, but home is not identified exclusively with Town End by either of them. It has a more metaphorical sense, often connected with the vale's wholeness or the lake's tranquillity, as when Dorothy writes in her journal that Grasmere 'calls home the heart to quietness'.[2] In their walks, together and alone, they often imagined alternative houses in which to live. Town End was the 'home within a home' to which they always returned, but the siblings saw it as a temporary base, from which their longer-term destination would eventually be found.[3] Even in the wildest, loneliest spots, human habitation was never far from their thoughts.

'Poems on the Naming of Places' carry conviction as authentic celebrations of the Wordsworths' settlement in Grasmere, and of their identification with the vale itself as home. Forming a closely unified sequence, they are less formal than inscriptions, aligning themselves with oral, not written, traditions of remembering.[4] Like most of Dorothy's journal entries, they were shaped by walks in and around Grasmere; and although exact coordinates are not given, each is evocative of the region, describing a unique terrain in ways that make it vividly real, if not locatable. Many years after the poems were composed, when dictating his notes to Isabella Fenwick, William was able to remember their topography in detail. Yet, when asked where Joanna's rock was, while standing on Butterlip How, he is alleged to have answered 'Any place will suit; *that* as well as any other'.[5] There is some truth to this offhand remark, for the poems are evocative of feelings as much as landscapes; and in connoting attachment to a whole region, they work figuratively as well as literally.

The 'Naming of Places' poems were first published in the 1800 edition of *Lyrical Ballads*, where they occupy an important position just before the pastoral poem 'Michael'. Introduced with an advertisement and a subtitle, their coherence as a sequence is thereby highlighted. They were written 'from a wish to give some sort of record' to 'little Incidents' which have occurred in places 'unnamed or of unknown names'.[6] Each poem centres on an act of naming, connecting a loved person with a nearby place where something memorable (or worth remembering) has happened. It is consistent with *Lyrical Ballads* as a whole that the claims these poems make are low-key and unsensational: '*some sort of* record'; '*little* incidents'.[7] Dramatic events are not involved here: at issue are the psychological minutiae of a household's acceptance into the region. Occurrences which have only a 'private and peculiar' interest for family members acquire significance through acts of naming.[8] Furthermore, naming provides recognition, a bringing to consciousness, of the communal bonds that form between places and people by virtue of habitual association. Concerning the 'Significant Group'[9] of family members and friends who came and went at Town End during 1800, the poems are simultaneously gifts to people and homages to place. William and Dorothy form the nucleus of affection, with Joanna and Mary Hutchinson, Coleridge, and John Wordsworth as satellites.[10] Repeated use of the plural pronoun 'we'—unusual in the Wordsworth oeuvre—reinforces a sense that the poems are spoken by a *pair* of subjects, whose love for each other and for Grasmere spreads outwards into the group. In exploring the way that communal bonds are strengthened by shared points of environmental contact, these poems offer an intimate formulation of the Wordsworthian philosophy of local attachments. They build on a profoundly optimistic reading of Hartleyan associationism, affirming the belief that memories provide enduring foundations for community. Even when separated in time and place, individuals are linked through a chain of associations to spots which can be revisited either physically or in the memory. This philosophy is much as the poet had outlined it in the closing lines of 'Tintern Abbey', except that in Grasmere the revisiting happens daily, defining a habitual sense of dwelling.

Jonathan Bate sees something inherently literary in the act of recording names for places—an act which distinguishes the poet's self-conscious bond with the environment from that of the shepherds whose simple life he envies and admires. 'The people who know places best, who are most rooted in them, tend not to be those who give them names. They do not need to bother with maps. They are not likely to articulate, to make a meal of, their bond with the place.'[11] However, naming is not the prerogative of poets only. In any closely knit community, places become associated with the people who inhabit them; and names provide an ongoing record—often oral, rather than written—of human connections with places. John Clare observed of Langley Bush that its fame survived through the tales of 'gipsies shepherds Herdmen'[12] for more than a century after it was destroyed; and Edward Thomas wrote about how 'shovel-bearded Bob' survived through the place name 'Bob's Lane' long after the lane itself had been overgrown.[13] The Wordsworths were aware, as we see in 'Michael', 'The Brothers', and the *Grasmere Journal*, that the history of Grasmere's local farming community went back through many generations of families, and was kept alive in oral history and communal memory. On returning to the Lakes, they wanted to re-establish their regional identity by becoming part of Grasmere's. 'Poems on the Naming of Places' attempt to produce an 'inter-assimilation' of family and place, anticipating many years of settled life in the region. If we view this group of poems ethnographically, they suggest the potency of naming as a means of renewing ancient bonds of kinship with the land.

Although 'To M. H.' was probably the first poem in this sequence to be composed, it appears in print as the last. This was perhaps in recognition of Dorothy's emotional centrality for the poet at the time of publication, for he and Mary were not at this stage betrothed. 'It was an April Morning', written to and for Dorothy, appears first in the sequence. William later recalled that it was suggested on the banks of the brook that runs through Easedale, 'as wild and beautiful as brook can be. I have composed thousands of verses by the side of it.'[14] In their first week at Town End, he and Dorothy had discovered a terrace walk at Lancrigg in Easedale, 'which long remained our favourite haunt'.[15] William subsequently associated this valley with Dorothy, who often went there, alone or in his company. The poet's own presence in the scene is understated: the rivulet runs for a full seventeen lines, 'delighting in its strength' (l. 2) before the personal pronoun 'I' is introduced. However, there is a clear affinity between the brook which 'Ran with a young man's speed' (l. 3) and the poet who follows its movement upstream 'in the confusion of my heart' (l. 18). If we respond to these figurative prompts, we can read the walk along the 'continuous glen' (l. 21) as an allegory for the poet's journey through life, much as we do his and Dorothy's descent with Charles Lamb into the 'roaring dell' in Coleridge's 'This Lime-Tree Bower my Prison'. In this connection, we might note the recurring importance of rivers as similes for creative development in William's poetry, and the long-standing importance of companionable walking alongside rivers or streams in the Wordsworths' lives. When first exploring the Quantocks in 1797, Dorothy had been vividly reminded of her early childhood in Cumberland by finding pebbly brooks and 'a sequestered waterfall in a dell'.[16] It is to just such a waterfall that this poem leads.

William's topography is exact. If you wander along Easedale Beck, beginning at Goody Bridge and moving upstream, a sudden turning will indeed lead you to a small waterfall.[17] But what does the 'sudden turning' (l. 20) signify? The poet's consciousness is alive to 'The spirit of enjoyment and desire | And hopes and wishes' which 'from all living things | Went circling, like a multitude of sounds' (ll. 6–8). Arriving in a dell, he is greeted by yet more 'sallies of glad sound' (l. 23) from the waterfall, which mingle with the diurnal country sounds of birdsong, lambs bleating, a dog barking. This is poetry of glad arrival, in which the creative plenitude of Easedale seems a gift in perpetuity. The moment of wonderment recalls and resembles William's first rapturous sighting of the secluded Vale of Grasmere as a child—'Long did I halt; I could have made it even | My business and my errand so to halt' ('Home at Grasmere', ll. 20–1). Time stands still, as if to honour the poet's thankfulness for what this new turning in his life has brought; and his eye is drawn to a shepherd's hut on a nearby hill, which answers to his ideal of home:

> I gazed and gazed, and to myself I said,
> 'Our thoughts at least are ours; and this wild nook,
> My EMMA, I will dedicate to thee.'   (ll. 37–9)

The repeated verb 'gaze' conveys a deliciously protracted sense of connection with the object of his longing. The culminating dedication arises spontaneously, and shows an implicit confidence that thoughts which are 'our own' are thoughts waiting to be shared:[18]

> —Soon did the spot become my other home,
> My dwelling, and my out-of-doors abode.
> And, of the Shepherds who have seen me there,
> To whom I sometimes in our idle talk
> Have told this fancy, two or three, perhaps,
> Years after we are gone and in our graves,
> When they have cause to speak of this wild place,
> May call it by the name of EMMA'S DELL.   (ll. 40–7)

Gratitude for home is clear in the way thoughts move from the distant hut to Dorothy, then back to the dell, which is described in a linked series of near-synonyms as William's 'other home', his 'dwelling' and his 'out of doors abode'. The dell is shared with Dorothy by virtue of answering the poet's need for a 'wild place' in the landscape where he can think and write. 'Wild' is a word used three times in connection with the dell, calling to mind Dorothy's 'wild eyes' in 'Tintern Abbey'. The revelation that William has communicated his name for the dell to local shepherds suggests that he looks for trust and acceptance in the community. His long-term hopes for the place name are modest: he surmises that it may one day be remembered by 'two or three' shepherds in 'idle talk'. This wish for an afterlife in oral history is a 'fancy', offered to his sister in a spirit of devotion.

'To M. H.' is closely connected to 'It was an April Morning' in its spousal themes and images. Both poems centre on a walk that leads towards a beautiful, secluded spot, the finding of which is a source of delight. Both subliminally remember Milton's 'flowery plat, the sweet recess of Eve',[19] and recall 'Nutting' in their association of a hidden place with a beloved female. Both connect this virginal 'recess' with a nearby cottage (in one case real, in the other imagined). There is a delicate eroticism in the language of both, albeit of very different kinds, for the first is packed with tumultuous images and sounds, while the last is tranquil and resolved, leading quietly to the 'small bed of water in the woods' (l. 7), which connotes fulfilment. Much in the figurative language of these poems suggests that we should consider them as a pair, evoking complementary ideals of intimacy within paradisal seclusion. Reading the opening of 'To M. H.', one might be forgiven for assuming Mary to be the poet's only companion, but in the closing lines it becomes clear that Dorothy shares their ramble 'far among the ancient trees':

> The spot was made by Nature for herself;
> The travellers know it not, and 'twill remain
> Unknown to them; but it is beautiful,
> And if a man should plant his cottage near,
> Should sleep beneath the shelter of its trees,
> And blend its waters with his daily meal,
> He would so love it that in his death-hour
> Its image would survive among his thoughts,
> And therefore, my sweet MARY, this still nook,
> With all its beeches we have named from You.[20]

The poet finds in this 'spot' another 'home from home', to balance 'Emma's dell'. The nook's virginal self-sufficiency resembles that of Grasmere, 'A Whole without dependence or defect, | Made for itself, and happy in itself, | Perfect Contentment, Unity entire.'[21] Imagining his cottage 'planted' in these woods, his days and nights passing 'beneath the shelter of its trees', the speaker anticipates the simple life par excellence. His consciousness 'blends' with the spot, as water from its lake does with his daily meals, recalling the 'blended holiness of earth and sky' in 'Home at Grasmere' (l. 163). In his enumeration of essential needs, William conveys the pleasure of a deep absorption into the rhythms of nature. There is no mention of female companionship until the penultimate line,[22] where the tender address 'sweet MARY' and the confidently inclusive 'we' confirm that Dorothy joins in William's expression of love for the woman who will later become his wife. Like 'Tintern Abbey' and 'It was an April Morning', this poem anticipates the survival of an 'image' of domestic happiness through a whole lifetime of cohabiting.

The poem commemorating William himself is the shortest in the sequence. It concerns an unnamed 'Eminence'—'The last that parleys with the setting sun' (l. 2)—which the poet later identified as Stone-Arthur, a peak that 'rises above the road by the side of Grasmere lake, towards Keswick'.[23] Its height and heroic literary name set it apart as a symbol of aspiration, and there may be a touch of self-parody in William's identification with its towering stature. Nonetheless, the mountain is valued for sending 'its own deep quiet' to restore the heart (l. 8), a characteristic that links it with poetry's reparative influence. Although not in fact visible from the orchard above Town End, poetic licence allows it to be so (l. 3); and it can also be seen, the poet notes, from the 'public way'—the old road which ran alongside the cottage at Town End, where the Wordsworths walked together sociably at evening (ll. 4–5). Almost oxymoronically, it is 'the loneliest place *we* have among the clouds' (l. 13; emphasis added), a place that meets the need for *companionable* solitude. In revealing that Dorothy has named the peak after him, William shares with his readers a private joke at his own expense (for his lonely walks are here the object of Dorothy's affectionate teasing), and accepts the gift as an expression of their mutual dependence and love:

> She who dwells with me, whom I have loved
> With such communion, that no place on earth
> Can ever be a solitude to me,
> Hath said, this lonesome Peak shall bear my Name.   (ll. 14–17)

These lines convey the almost marital communion between brother and sister. Dorothy's naming of the 'lonesome Peak' gives it a filial relationship to the poet, the word 'bear' connoting a generative process in which she plays a maternal role. The poem offers the hope that, through permanent identification with the region, the Wordsworths will metaphorically reclaim their birthright.

*

It is hard for readers in the twenty-first century, habituated to confessional modes of address in poetry, to appreciate the experimental spirit in which the 'Poems on the Naming of Places' declared their allegiance to the domestic affections. Collectively, they reaffirm the anti-Godwinian poetics

of familiarity which had been boldly announced in the 'Advertisement' to
Lyrical Ballads (1798) and implicit in 'It is the first mild day of March' as well
as 'Tintern Abbey'. But they do so without the protection of anonymous
authorship. The identities of people are not fully disclosed by name—Emma
is a pseudonym, only Joanna's first name is given, and Mary Hutchinson is
identified by her initials—but the poems leave us in no doubt of the close
bonds of affection between the poet and his small circle of listeners. However, we should not confuse the intimacy of these poems with exclusivity.
In consolidating a network of familial relations, they express affinity with
the region and embrace the ideal of a wider community. Two poems in the
published sequence, 'To Joanna' and 'A narrow girdle of rough stones and
crags', move outside the inner circle—Dorothy, William, John, Mary—to
admit unsettling alternative perspectives. In each of these poems, the Wordsworths' sense of being at home in their environment is put to the test by a
questioning presence that draws their thoughts away from a joyful gratitude
for belonging and dwelling. In each case, an admonishment is received.
Written dialogically, 'To Joanna' overcomes a resistance to nature-worship
on the part of a family friend; while 'A narrow girdle of rough stones and
crags' reminds the poet and his companions of the poverty that can be
found just the other side of their chosen seclusion. These two poems balance each other, offering a far from complacent view of the Wordsworths'
place in their community.

'To Joanna' is addressed to Mary Hutchinson's nineteen-year-old sister.
Taking advantage of poetic licence, William describes Joanna as a city-
dweller (whereas she grew up in Penrith), and refers to a walk taken in her
company at a time when the Wordsworths were in Germany. The invented
circumstantial details provide an illusion of authenticity, signifying Joanna's
shadowy place in the Wordsworth circle. She is set a little apart from the
'significant group' of nature-worshippers, and the poet teases her affectionately, noting her scepticism toward those who 'look upon the hills with
tenderness, | And make dear friendships with the streams and groves'
(ll. 7–8). His poem attempts to win her over, using the plural pronoun 'we'
to draw her into a bond with the place and its devotees. Inventing the
memory of a walk together, he recalls how Joanna had laughed at him for
gazing with 'ravishment' at beauty:

> —When I had gazed perhaps two minutes' space,
> Joanna, looking in my eyes, beheld
> That ravishment of mine, and laughed aloud.

> The rock, like something starting from a sleep,
> Took up the Lady's voice, and laughed again:
> That ancient Woman seated on Helm-crag
> Was ready with her cavern; Hammar-scar,
> And the tall Steep of Silver-How sent forth
> A noise of laughter; southern Loughrigg heard,
> And Fairfield answered with a mountain tone...   (ll. 51–60)

The mountains spring into a strange, half-human life of their own, animated by the poet's personifications, which insistently individuate each peak by name and personality. Coleridge identified Michael Drayton's *Poly-Olbion* (1622) as the source of this passage.[24] Drayton used lists of local place names to signify national loyalty and pride, and in echoing him, William partly signals allegiance to an ancient tradition of patriotic topographical writing.[25] But in 'To Joanna' the naming of places has a subtle psychological significance too, for it connotes the poet's *need* to belong. We are left in little doubt that Joanna's laughter is a form of sacrilege against the spirit of place, equivalent to the speaker's violation of the hazel-grove in 'Nutting'. Just as the 'silent trees and the intruding sky' (l. 51) had rebuked the boy for his intrusion, so the mountains give back a distorted and magnified echo of Joanna's mockery.

Two weeks before composing 'To Joanna', Dorothy and William had heard a raven's call echoing among the mountains while rowing on Rydal. Ravens are traditionally associated with death, but although Dorothy's prose is attentive to the haunting sound of the bird, she doesn't emphasize its figurative associations. In a chain of clauses, each sliding effortlessly into the next, she captures the eeriness of the sound as it travels among the hills:

> We heard a strange sound in Bainriggs wood as we were floating on the water it *seemed* in the wood, but it must have been above it, for presently we saw a raven very high above us—it called out & the dome of the sky seemed to echoe the sound—it called again & again as it flew onwards, & the mountains gave back the sound, seeming as if from their center a musical bell-like answering to the birds hoarse voice. We heard both the call of the bird & the echoe after we could see him no longer.[26]

A clear connection can be traced between Dorothy's journal entry and 'To Joanna'; but the connection works by way of difference. There is a beautifully dreamy quality in the displaced voice of the raven, which doesn't mock the 'floating' rowers, but seems to 'call out of the dome of the sky' to something deep in the centre of the mountains. The 'musical bell-like answering' of the mountains is a giving-back, not a reproof; and whereas Joanna shelters 'from some object of her fear' (l. 76), Dorothy and William go on willingly hearing the bird and its echo long after it is lost to sight. If William remembered the raven's echo when writing 'To Joanna', he perhaps intended the contrast between these two experiences to reflect back on the sensibilities of his companions: Dorothy so attuned to the region's strange harmonies, Joanna so reactive to its discords. When he mentions the hoarse voice of a raven in 'Home at Grasmere', it is as a symbol of 'the days of love to come' (ll. 795–7). Like Coleridge's nightingale, or the 'creaking' rook in 'This Lime-Tree Bower my Prison', the Wordsworths' raven is a reminder that 'in nature there is nothing melancholy'.[27]

If 'To Joanna' shows how the poet's confidence in being at home in Grasmere could be unsettled by the presence of an outsider, the fourth poem in this sequence offers a more troubling destabilization. 'A narrow girdle of rough stones and crags' was composed in October 1800, after Dorothy had recorded in her journal a sequence of encounters with poverty-stricken people. On 26 September, she and William met 'an old man almost double' whose trade was to gather leeches: 'but now leeches are scarce and he had not strength for it—he lived by begging'.[28] On Thursday 9 October a man called at Town End: 'he was thirty years old—of Cockermouth, had lost a leg & thigh in battle…He could earn more money in travelling with his ass than at home.'[29] On 10 October, a female traveller, also from Cockermouth, arrived to sell 'thread hardware mustard etc'—'Her husband will not travel with an ass, because it is the tramper's badge—she would have one to relieve her from the weary load.'[30] It was in the context of these recent encounters that William 'sat up after me writing Point Rash Judgment' on Friday 10 October (*Grasmere Journal*, 26).

'Point Rash Judgment' was Dorothy's name for the fourth poem in the 'Naming of Places' sequence. In it, she and Coleridge are depicted strolling alongside William on the eastern shore of Grasmere, a short distance from Town End. The poem's fluid patterns of association convey the sense of a shared journey, in which thought processes branch sideways and memories of former times keep surfacing. As they saunter together, the three companions' subject-positions are included within the unifying pronoun 'we', the poet emerging as spokesman for the group.

The speaker dallies for a long time with the reader's attention, conveying the abundant leisure enjoyed by the walkers, who 'feed' their 'fancies' with

'busy' distant sounds of labourers working in the fields at harvest time
(ll. 41–5). Painstaking narration habituates us to their privileged perspective,
so that when they see 'The tall and upright figure of a Man | Attired in
peasant's garb, who stood alone | Angling beside the margin of the lake' (ll.
50–2) we are almost drawn into complicity with their hasty collective judgement: this is an 'idle man' wasting a day in mid-harvest 'when the labourer's
hire | Is ample', and he might be earning money he could save (ll. 55–60).
Nothing could be more shocking than the revelation which follows:

> Thus talking of that Peasant we approached
> Close to the spot where with his rod and line
> He stood alone; whereat he turned his head
> To greet us—and we saw a man worn down
> By sickness, gaunt and lean, with sunken cheeks
> And wasted limbs, his legs so long and lean
> That for my single self I looked at them,
> Forgetful of the body they sustained.—
> Too weak to labour in the harvest field,
> The man was using his best skill to gain
> A pittance from the dead unfeeling lake
> That knew not of his wants.   (ll. 61–72)

With its slow deliberate rhythms this long sentence conveys the gradual
advancement of the three observers towards the man, whose only movement is an equally slow deliberate turning of the head. No speech is recorded,
though the word 'greet' allows for a brief moment of recognition across an
unbridgeable gulf. As the man's head turns, William's sense of solidarity with
his companions falls away, and his consciousness is islanded: he speaks for his
'single self' in forgetting that the man's 'wasted limbs' are connected to his
body.[31] The scene has a haunting quality, reminiscent of Hamlet's meeting
with his father's ghost, or Achilles' encounter with Anchises in Virgil's under-
world. The diction is uncompromisingly spare. The paired, monosyllabic
adjectives—'gaunt and lean', 'long and lean'—convey the full shock of
delayed recognition, leaving no room for mystification or romance. The
man's body goes on haunting with its spectral thinness long after the poem
is finished, as does the speaker's shocked acknowledgement of the lake's
'dead, unfeeling' indifference to human need. If the word 'admonishment'
(l. 82) in the closing lines reminds us of the moral lessons William had been
taught by nature as a child, it also anticipates the human lesson of fortitude
taught by the leech-gatherer in his 1802 poem.[32] Coleridge recorded his

own response to the event in a notebook;[33] and all three spectators were implicated. Translating the meaning of this encounter into 'serious musing' and 'self-reproach', the name 'Point Rash-Judgment' served as a perpetual 'memorial' (a deathly word) to their shared encounter (ll. 76–83).

*

As the Wordsworths became accustomed to the neighbourhood of Grasmere, they saw more clearly what John Barrell has called 'the dark side of the landscape'.[34] During the Napoleonic wars taxes were high, and the price of food rose prohibitively. Weavers and spinners who worked from home found themselves in competition with factory labour. Farmers lost their traditional grazing rights on common land; and unemployed workers were driven onto the road in search of a livelihood. Although cases of 'extreme penury' and 'hunger's abject wretchedness' were rare among the inhabitants of Grasmere,[35] figures on the margins, who could not be incorporated into a paradisal picture, gave cause for 'serious musing' and 'self-reproach'. Dorothy's *Grasmere Journal* testified to the daily presence of pedlars, beggars, discharged soldiers and sailors, gypsies, and vagrants wandering past Town End during the war.[36] There was also evidence, in the local farming community, that the 'domestic affections' were coming under strain. Dorothy's role as journal-writer opened her eyes to poverty among her neighbours:

> John Fisher…talked much about the alteration in the times, and observed that in a short time there would be only two ranks of people, the very rich and the very poor, 'for those who have small estates', says he, 'are forced to sell, and all the land goes into one hand'.[37]

Driven by his responsibility to bear witness to the realities of rural existence, William asked 'Is there not | An art, a music, and a stream of words | That shall be life, the acknowledged voice of life?'[38] Together, the Wordsworths collected local stories of human frailty, sorrow and bereavement, reading their environment like a map on which 'some portion of its human history' was legibly marked.[39] In the second half of 'Home at Grasmere', which was written alongside Dorothy's *Grasmere Journal*, William took upon himself the role of a guide, pointing to spots in the landscape that might easily pass unnoticed, where chapters in the vale's human history were daily unfolding:

> Yon Cottage, would that it could tell a part
> Of its own story. Thousands might give ear,
> Might hear it and blush deep…

That Ridge, which elbowing from the mountain-side
Carries into the Plain its rocks and woods
Conceals a Cottage where a Father dwells
In widowhood...

From yonder grey-stone that stands alone
Close to the foaming Stream, look up and see,
Not less than half-way up the mountain-side,
A dusky Spot, a little grove of firs...   (ll. 469–71, 533–6, 607–10)

Unlike the local people whose stories Dorothy recorded, the 'untutored shepherds' in 'Home at Grasmere' remain anonymous, as do the places connected with them. But William's writing conveys how their obscure lives are inseparable from the nearby objects which serve as precise coordinates and signifiers of their emotions: 'that ridge', 'yonder grey stone'. This topographical exactitude helped him, in writing his new kind of anti-arcadian poetry, to give it the authentic grounding it needed.

The Wordsworths were not, in 1800, Burkean: their views on aristocracy, and on the inheritance of landed property, were as hostile as they had ever been. But the experience of homecoming took them close to identification with the subsistence farmers who worked the land, and who handed it down from generation to generation. In a letter to Charles James Fox, leader of the Whig opposition, William used his pastoral poems 'Michael' and 'The Brothers' to plead for the importance of the 'little tract of land' that 'serves as a kind of permanent rallying point for the domestic feelings, as a tablet upon which they are written which makes them objects of memory in a thousand instances when they would otherwise be forgotten'.[40] His domestic ideal of oneness with place is evoked through an associationist vocabulary that goes back to the 'tabula rasa' in John Locke's *Essay Concerning Human Understanding*. These terms of reference tell us as much about the Wordsworths' personal need to re-establish their regional identity as about William's grasp of agrarian economics. 'The Brothers' and 'Michael' are both concerned, like the 'Poems on the Naming of Places', with the way family identity becomes intertwined with regional identity, so that the word 'home' signifies a complex web of emotional interconnections between places and people. Reflecting different phases in the Wordsworths' life in Grasmere, these two 'pastoral' poems appear near the beginning and at the end of the 1800 edition of *Lyrical Ballads* (in the order in which they were written), framing the volume's content like bookends. Rather than claiming kinship with the vale through explicit acts of naming, they draw on local stories and communal memories to explore the psychology of homecoming and dwelling.

Dorothy recounts in one of her letters how, on first arriving in Grasmere in January 1800, John Wordsworth could not bring himself to knock on their door at Town End:

> Twice did he approach the door and lay his hand upon the latch, and stop, and turn away without the courage to enter (we had not met for several years) he then went to the Inn and sent word that he was come.[41]

The 'little incident' stayed with William as he worked on 'The Brothers', his moving study of the effects of long separation on fraternal love. The poem, first conceived in the company of Coleridge and John during their walking tour of 1799, is based on the true story of a shepherd in Ennerdale (Jerome Bowman's son), who 'broke his neck…by falling off a crag'. As Coleridge recorded in his notebook, 'He is supposed to have layed [sic] down and slept—but walked in his sleep'.[42] Coleridge's note locates the place of death precisely 'at Proud Knot on the mountain called Pillar', and provides a telling circumstantial detail: 'His pike-staff stuck midway and stayed there till it rotted away.'[43] William retains the central ingredients of this 'moving accident' but transmutes its sensational content. In the process, the tale becomes a psychological study of guilt and sorrow, with special relevance to the Wordsworths' experience of separation and exile. In reading this poem, it is worth bearing in mind that its composition coincided with John's stay at Town End, and that when William gave thanks for his brother's presence in 'Home at Grasmere', he described him as a 'Stranger of our Father's house':

> A never-resting Pilgrim of the Sea,
> Who finds at last an hour to his content
> Beneath our roof.   (ll. 866–8)

Throughout 'The Brothers', it is Leonard's estranged consciousness that holds the reader's attention. Returning from his long travels at sea, he has lost his emotional bearings in his own parish. As he wanders alone through the village graveyard, anxiously seeking reassurance that his brother James is not dead, he is observed by the parish priest, who reaches the hasty conclusion that he is a tourist—a 'moping son of Idleness' (l. 11). The dialogue between Leonard and the vicar begins as an awkward mis-meeting of minds, for the priest fails to recognize Leonard, last seen in the parish twenty years ago when he was only thirteen. The two men meet to all intents and purposes as strangers, like the Ancient Mariner and the wedding guest in

Coleridge's ballad, except that here, in an ironic reversal of roles, it is the traveller who listens spellbound to the 'plain tale' of tragic disaster at home.

Step by step, the priest takes Leonard on a journey into the past. Leonard learns about his own boyhood, his companionship with James ('the darlings of each other', l. 239), their upbringing as foster-children, their destitution when 'old Walter Ewbank' dies, Leonard's obligatory departure to sea, and James's broken heart. In relating the story of James's death, the vicar retraces his steps to the precipice where his staff was found, reconstructing his final hours as they have since been pieced together by the local community:

> we all conjectured
> That, as the day was warm, he had lain down
> Upon the grass, and, waiting for his comrades
> He there had fallen asleep, that in his sleep
> He to the margin of the precipice
> Had walked, and from the summit had fallen head-long,
> And so no doubt he perished.   (ll. 392–8)

This patient unsensational mapping of James's movements onto the landscape, together with the priest's precise identification of the scene of death, enable Leonard to refamiliarize himself with the topography of home. Even as he does so, he is adjusting to the fact that home is now an empty word, devoid of meaning: he is, to use a phrase of John Clare's, 'homeless at home'.[44] The priest has cause to retract his initial 'rash judgement' on Leonard, for he watches as his listener progresses, by slow and painful degrees, towards the recognition that his brother is buried in the graveyard where he stands. Leonard never visits the spot where James fell to his death. Leaving the village like a man adrift, and identifying himself to the priest only by letter, he is haunted by the guilt of having forsaken his brother. This poem achieves its cathartic effect partly as 'The Ruined Cottage' had, through dramatic dialogue. The priest's laconic method of narration, minimally interrupted by Leonard, enables psychological subtlety and the distillation of deep feeling. Autobiographical resonances do not obtrude. Nonetheless, the poem's graveyard setting, its emphasis on orphaned consciousness and fostering, and its concern with the belated recognition of tragic disaster, remind us how the Wordsworths' shared memories of bereavement and separation were bound up in the process of composition. There was a very real sense in which their homecoming, like Leonard's, involved a reckoning with the dead, as well as a careful negotiation of community with the living.

The tragic story told in 'Michael', of a shepherd's broken relationship with his son, was prompted partly by a nearby landmark, partly by local history. It developed out of a tale William had been told in childhood by his foster-mother Ann Tyson, relating to a sheepfold near Grasmere:

> The sheepfold, on which so much of the poem turns, remains, or rather the ruins of it. The character and circumstances of Luke were taken from a family to whom had belonged, many years before, the house we lived in at Town-End, along with some fields and woodlands on the eastern shore of Grasmere.[45]

The shepherd's connection with Town End is important, and may partly explain why the Wordsworths were so curious to follow up on his story, which had impressed itself strongly on William as a boy. In October 1800, he and Dorothy both went to look for the sheepfold in Greenhead Gill, a mountain stream to the north-east of Grasmere, where they found it on Saturday 11th, 'a fine October morning'. Dorothy describes it in her journal as 'falling away' and 'built nearly in the form of a heart unequally divided'.[46] The shape of the sheepfold, seen as if it were an inscription on the fell-side, waiting to be read by passers-by, gave William a potent emblem for the shepherd's emotional predicament. As Michael struggles to keep his land safe within his family, he is 'agitated by two of the most powerful affections of the human heart; the parental affection, and the love of property, *landed* property, including the feelings of inheritance, home, and personal and family independence'.[47] The poem traces the unequal division of his heart between these two 'powerful affections', which have become closely intertwined.

Although the tragedy of 'Michael' is not set in Town End, it resonates with a strong sense of personal identification. The linked themes of paternal love, attachment to patrimonial land, and dispossession spoke to William and Dorothy's deepest concerns. The poem celebrates the emotional bonds that develop over many generations between farmers and the land they own, seeing these bonds as tokens of a sacramental relationship with place which is intensely precious and enviable. For Michael, there is so close a connection between himself and 'his small inheritance' that they become almost indivisible:

> Fields, where with chearful spirits he had breath'd
> The common air; the hills, which he so oft
> Had climbed with vigorous steps; which had impressed

So many incidents upon his mind...
                    these fields, these hills
Which were his living Being, even more
Than his own Blood—what could they less? had laid
Strong hold on his affections, were to him
A pleasurable feeling of blind love,
The pleasure which there is in life itself.   (ll. 65–8, 74–9)

When he is persuaded by financial hardship to send his son, 'the dearest object that he knew on earth' (l. 160), away to earn a living, Michael deludes himself that 'the land | Shall not go from us, and it shall be free, | He shall possess it, free as is the wind | That passes over it' (ll. 254–7). In a moving farewell ceremony, father and son lay the foundation stone of a sheepfold, consecrating it with vows of filial loyalty and paternal love. We never learn the whereabouts of Luke after he is sent away. We learn only—and in a few brief words, shocking in their terseness—that he has gone to the bad. All our sympathy goes to the father, left with his unfinished sheepfold, the symbol of their broken covenant.

'The Brothers' and 'Michael' marked a new stage in the Wordsworth family's communal process of remembering and grieving. Honouring the dignity of humble rural lives by giving them an almost biblical stature, these poems voice the belief that 'men who do not wear fine cloaths can feel deeply'.[48] As acts of imaginative empathy, they reach across the divides created by class and education to identify with the plight of local families, scattered (as the Wordsworths themselves had been) by adverse circumstances. Along with 'Poems on the Naming of Places', they can be interpreted as 'household poems'[49]: gifts to the region, composed in a spirit of sympathy and thankfulness. If the consolation these poems offer is fellow-feeling— 'There is a comfort in the strength of love; | 'Twill make a thing endurable, which else | Would break the heart'[50]—their power to console depends on authenticity. The priest in 'The Brothers' tells Leonard that 'The thought of death sits easy on the man | Who has been born and dies among the mountains.' Dalesfolk, he says, 'have no need of names and epitaphs' on their graves, because they 'talk about the dead' by their firesides. Leonard, in response, sounds the true Wordsworthian note: 'Your dalesmen, then, do in each other's thoughts | Possess a kind of second life' (ll. 175–82). By tapping into ancient traditions of oral transmission, William gave the 'ungarnished tales' of Michael and Leonard the kind of laconic artlessness he found in fireside stories. The tale of 'Michael' is *associated*, in the full Hartleyan sense of that word, with a particular place in Greenhead Gill, where a 'straggling heap of unhewn stones' (l. 17) stands beside a path, scarcely catching the eye of anyone not closely connected with the place and its history. The narrator, as he stands beside the pile of stones to tell his tale, understands the significance of this place with an insider's local knowledge. By ensuring that the sheepfold's associative history is kept alive, he compensates for the broken bond between father and son. Aspiring to the condition of orality rather than inscription, the poem weaves a consoling web of connections between poetry and place, local history and communal memory, the teller and his tale. In handing the story of Michael down, the narrator is conscious that a 'second self' (l. 39) will prolong the story's life after he has gone, and that in this anonymous but important way, he will immortalize his own as well as Michael's connection with Greenhead Gill.

8

The Grasmere Journal

'Grasmere was very solemn in the last glimpse
of twilight it calls home the heart to quietness.'[1]

*

Dorothy kept her *Grasmere Journal* between the years 1800 and 1803, writing it in four small notebooks which had already been used by herself and/or William. Recycling partly used notebooks was a sensible and thrifty measure, especially when the price of paper was high.[2] The complex internal organization of these shared notebooks enables us to see how her experiment in life-writing took place, literally, in among William's work; and how her identity as a writer was bound up in her brother's. For instance, she used the third *Grasmere Journal* notebook (DC MS 19) to record her activities from 14 February to 2 May 1802, one of the most significant periods in her life. Both siblings had already used this notebook during 1798—William for drafts of the *Two-Part Prelude*, his 'Essay on Morals', and a record of three conversations with Klopstock; Dorothy for exercises in German grammar and the last section of her *Hamburg Journal*. Saving space by sharing notebooks brought each sibling's words into close proximity with the other's. We might see here a textual analogy for their cohabitation at Town End, or even a parallel with the behaviour of swallows. These birds build in pairs, returning after migration to refurbish nests they have built earlier.[3]

Each of the notebooks Dorothy used for her journal thus contained materials from a past she had shared with her brother. Every time she picked up her notebook in the months between 14 February and 2 May 1802, the book as physical object was a potential prompt for memories of the months they had spent together in Germany. These had been homesick months, when she had missed Coleridge's company, tried to learn German, and taken pleasure in the poetry which was pouring forth from her brother. What influence did the presence of these prior writings exert on her as she turned the pages (more or less daily, in 1802) looking for the place where she had last left off writing her journal, and would now resume? Are there connections between the 1798 materials and the 1802 ones, as there clearly are between the *Hamburg Journal*, the 'Essay on Morals', and the beginnings of the *Two-Part Prelude*? I raise these questions about their shared notebook speculatively, as a way of drawing attention to the complex, layered quality of life as it was lived and processed in the Wordsworth household. An exhaustive intertextual study of DC MS 19 lies outside the scope of this chapter, which will follow a less intricate procedure for exploring the interwoven writings of William and Dorothy during 1800–1802.

*

'Life-writing' is a vague term, encompassing a wide range of auto/biographical activities and forms; and in the case of the *Grasmere Journal* this vagueness is suggestive. Dorothy was both biographer and autobiographer—writing about her own life in notebooks she had no intention of publishing, while at the same time watching her brother's talent bear fruit in poems destined for publication. The *Grasmere Journal* appears artless—Dorothy's style has even been referred to as 'immediate'—but there is evidence from her revisions that she crafted it carefully. By the time she began keeping the journal in the summer of 1800, she had a subtle and flexible sense of what writing a 'Life' might involve, and this was not just because of William's work on *The Prelude*. The people she met in and around Grasmere exemplified the meaning and value of *obscure* lives. (A preoccupation with the importance of humble people was deeply ingrained in her character; as also in William's poetry: each one of his ballads and eclogues reads as a kind of 'Life'.) During the years covered by her journal, Dorothy also became interested in the lives of famous writers. John Wordsworth gave William a complete set of Robert Anderson's anthology *The Works of the British Poets with Prefaces, Biographical and Critical* in 1800, and Anderson is mentioned a number of times in her journal. For instance, she read his life of Ben Jonson aloud to William while he lay by the fire one winter evening in 1802; and in June of that year they read together his life of the Scottish poet John Logan—'poor Logan', Dorothy called him, with her usual quick sympathy for misfortune.[4] She also dipped into Boswell's *Life of Samuel Johnson* (1791) in September 1800, a book referred to in Anderson's anthology as 'the most copious, interesting, and finished picture of the life and opinions of an eminent man, that was ever executed'.[5] Knowledge of these famous lives, together with a consciousness of William's identity as a published poet, influenced the ways in which Dorothy observed and recorded life in the household at Town End. She was not, like Boswell, a collector of anecdotes about an already famous man; nor did she record as many of her conversations with William as biographers might wish. But her journal offers several detailed portraits of the poet in the act of creation, and provides a domestic context for reading William's work.

In the texture and tonality of her writing Dorothy found her own answer to the question, 'Is there not | An art, a music, and a stream of words | That shall be life, the acknowledged voice of life?'[6] Recording day-to-day existence, she experimented with several different kinds of narration, shifting her focus as she moved through various auto/biographical subject-positions and roles. She was clearly interested in poetry's relation to health and happiness, and concerned with her own creative processes in relation to her brother's, keeping as detailed a record of William's ailments and mood-swings as of her own. Her prose occasionally resembles a case study of the connection between health and productivity: 'William wished to break off composition, & was unable, & so did himself harm' (2 February 1802); 'William worked at the Leech gatherer almost incessantly from morning till tea-time. I copied the Leech-gatherer & other poems for Coleridge—I was oppressed and sick at heart for he wearied himself to death' (9 May 1802). The closeness with which she observed her unfolding emotions—especially in relation to William's variable moods and Coleridge's deepening unhappiness—is indicative of her interest in psychology and mental health. Every aspect of her approach to life-writing was holistic. Describing how her activities overlapped or intertwined with William's, she confirmed their mutual dependency within a shared habitat. There was also, as we shall see, an important *therapeutic* dimension to her journal, for it traced the tranquillizing influence of nature on her spirit during periods of sadness or anxiety. In this way, knowing that her prose would be read by her brother, she made it into a household gift.

Dorothy began her *Grasmere Journal* when William and John were away from home for three weeks in the early summer of 1800. (Pamela Woof has established the way in which its broken patterns of composition were dictated by William's activities, his sleep, as well as his absences, creating an opportunity for writing.)[7] She wrote it to 'give William pleasure', she says, and 'because I will not quarrel with myself'. Her entry on 16 May conveys what it meant to her to be settled in Grasmere, looking forward to his return:

> I had been very melancholy in my walk back. I had many of my saddest thoughts & I could not keep the tears within me. But when I came to Grasmere I felt that it did me good. I finished my letter to MH.—ate hasty pudding, & went to bed. As I was going out in the morning I met a half crazy old man. He showed me a pincushion, & begged a pin, afterwards a halfpenny. He began in a kind of indistinct voice in this manner 'Matthew Jobson's lost a cow. Tom Nichol has two good horses strained—Jim Jones's cow's brokken her horn, &c &c—' He went into Aggys & persuaded her to give him some whey & let him boil some porridge. She declares he ate two quarts.   (pp. 2–3)

This is a different kind of writing from the Alfoxden or Hamburg journals: more radical in its mix of registers, its counterpointing of poetic landscape description with realism. The authorial 'I' is more apparent. There is a stronger interest in narrative. Humanitarian concern for the 'half crazy old man' off-sets an inward-looking sensibility. Use of direct speech, with its jaunty, song-like rhythm and regional accent ('brokken') makes the writing vivid and immediate. And above all, there is an openly expressed concern with the idea of a secure home: the lake 'calls home the heart to quietness', as does the old man eating his two quarts of porridge in Aggy Fisher's kitchen.

Home and community are at the centre of the *Grasmere Journal*.[8] In among all the washing and drying, baking and cooking, binding carpets and mend-ing shoes, papering rooms, gathering mosses, hoeing peas, transplanting radishes, and picking and boiling gooseberries, Dorothy transcribes William's poems, writes letters, visits neighbours, and talks to beggars. When she sends the ailing Peggy Ashburner a goose, she receives in return 'some honey—with a thousand thanks' and finds herself remembering 'Simon Lee' (1798), with its humbling reflections on gratitude. As if in recognition of the role she had been given at the end of 'Tintern Abbey', Dorothy transfers its moral and political vision into a new setting. The philosophy underpinning her prose is distinctly Hartleyan, and the terms in which she develops it are those she and William had evolved together during 1798. Remaining true to the political and stylistic agenda of *Lyrical Ballads*—a book she often reread, both for pleasure and moral instruction[9]—she observes the bonds connecting human beings to each other, and the equally close bond that connects humans to the land. Her personal gratitude for belonging—which leads her to think of the Vale of Grasmere as 'a kind of universal home' (Hazlitt's phrase)—is qualified by her insight into the conditions endured by the many destitute people who wandered past Town End during the war. The depth of her sympathy for the poor is evident in every detail of her sketches: 'She searched into the lives of the poor as if they held in them the same secret as the hills', wrote Virginia Woolf.[10] Sometimes her vivid, compressed language catches the hardship of their lives in a single phrase: 'A broken soldier came to beg in the morning' (p. 52). At others, it is the painstaking, circumstantial detail that builds a credible picture:

> A young woman begged at the door—she had come from Manchester on Sunday morn with two shillings & a slip of paper which she supposed a Bank note—it was a cheat. She had buried her husband & three children within a year & a half—All in one grave—burying very dear—paupers all put in one place—20 shillings paid for as much ground as will bury a man—a grave stone to be put over it or the right will be lost—11/6 each time the ground is re-opened.   (p. 2)

Such faithful recording of the obscure lives of those around her is as radical in its implications as William's ballads, but prose enables Dorothy to stay more closely in touch with material reality than he did. When she records the words of beggars she meets on her walks, it is the rhythms of the speaking voice that strike the authentic note. Encounters with discharged soldiers, sailors, destitute mothers, are all noted down. The journal is a graphic, detailed record of destitution in wartime Grasmere.

   This telling and retelling of stories indicates Dorothy's interest in narrative, and in different *styles* of narration. Usually she gives a rapid summary of a person's life, weaving in phrases, or snippets of sentences, from their own paraphrased accounts. Increasingly she incorporates passages of direct speech, showing a sharp ear for idiomatic usages and catching idiolects precisely. She takes pleasure in observing that Molly Fisher, whom she trained in the rudiments of housekeeping, is 'happy in her work and exulting in her own importance' (p. 75); and vividly catches Molly's actual words of thanks: 'Aye mistress them 'at's Low laid would have been a proud creature could they but have [seen] where I is now fra what they thought mud be my Doom' (p. 75). She observes the way that spoken language is unobtrusively metaphorical, sometimes proverbial: 'we were all in trouble, & trouble opens folks' hearts', says Aggy Fisher (p. 113). She peppers her prose with local usages ('lass', 'bairn', 'fagging', 'auld', 'gang', 'laal'), and signals her fondness for particular phrases by repetition. On 6 February 1802, she records a phrase of Molly's: 'it snowed in the night, & was, on Saturday, as Molly expressed it, a Cauld Clash'. Two days later, she reuses it: 'we went towards Rydale for letters it was a cold "Cauld Clash"'. A paragraph later, the idiom has passed into her vocabulary: 'We walked on very wet through the clashy cold roads' (pp. 64–5). She collects local usages because, like William, she hears them as a kind of oral poetry. Noticing a ten-year-old girl, a carter's daughter, she writes, 'There was a wildness in her whole figure, not the wildness of a Mountain lass but a *Road* lass, a traveller from her Birth' (p. 69). The sentence lingers in the mind—the word 'wildness' connecting with the repetition of 'lass' to make an echoic word-cluster.

The tales of hardship and suffering that punctuate Dorothy's journal are set against her own unfolding life story. Two contrasting strands in her narrative—realistic reportage of other people's experiences, and detailed, reflective description of her own—are woven together by a persistent preoccupation with the idea of home. Her early experience of being orphaned and exiled from Cockermouth provides a powerful undercurrent of sympathy with the orphans and the homeless whose lives she tells. The intensity of happiness she feels in at last being settled in the Lake District is shadowed by an awareness of the misfortune of others, but also by fears for her future. The journal deals with a crucial turning point in her life, as she accommodates herself to William and Mary's decision to marry, and settles back into domestic happiness after a period of anxiety surrounding the marriage itself. There are two further domestic 'subplots', both involving disruptions to the steady habits of home life: the Wordsworths' highly emotional and symbolic visit to France (to see Annette Vallon and William's daughter, Caroline); and the painful dissolution of Coleridge's marriage.

The *Grasmere Journal* is not fictional, but Dorothy's awareness that, in writing down her experiences, she makes a story about herself is sometimes overtly signalled by the register she adopts. Her very first entry begins with a literary topos: the symbolic departure of the loved one, accompanied by a confession of overwhelming sadness.

> My heart was so full that I could hardly speak to W when I gave him a farewell kiss. I sate a long time upon a stone at the margin of the lake, & after a flood of tears my heart was easier. The lake looked to me I knew not why dull and melancholy, the weltering on the shores seemed a heavy sound.   (p. 1)

There could hardly be a more striking difference from her first entry in the *Alfoxden Journal*. Dorothy's self-conscious use of the pathetic fallacy, her figure of speech ('I knew not why'), and the gesture of weeping, all signal that she is writing in the style of a novel of sensibility. A combination of fidelity to the real world and heightened feeling is one of the most striking features of her style. Sometimes she draws on standard sentimental tropes, such as dissolving, melting, weeping—'my heart dissolved in what I saw' (p. 6); 'my heart was almost melted away' (p. 12)—or on well-known figures of speech: 'oppressed & sick at heart'; 'My heart fails in me' (p. 98). But more often a vivid, idiomatic phrase catches the sound of her voice, speaking directly and exactly about her feelings: 'my heart was right sad' (p. 23); 'It made my heart almost feel like a vision to me' (p. 112). The care with which she details some feelings indicates their aesthetic source or value; others she deals with more perfunctorily. Headaches, toothaches, stomach aches (all somatic indicators of heightened sensibility) are noted, but not dwelt on for longer than is necessary. Such mixing of genres and registers in the *Grasmere Journal*, along with the rapid, notational style of the entries, the shifts of mood and pace, the use of abbreviations and dashes, conveys the sense of a life being lived even as it is being processed. But of course Dorothy follows the rhythm of each day, so as to assimilate jumbled subject matter and multiple preoccupations.

It was not always possible to craft material carefully, yet even when composition was hurried, the selection of events has a discernible pattern. Dorothy's entry for Tuesday 24 November 1801 is characteristic, giving not just the highlights but the prosaic, circumstantial details. The entry is shaped by a walk with William and Mary, following an unplanned route and returning to Town End. Two key events are singled out for special attention. First, there is the shared delight of seeing a birch tree 'yielding to the gusty wind':

> It glanced in the wind like a flying sunshiny shower—it was a tree in shape with stem & branches but it was like a Spirit of water—The sun went in & it

resumed its purplish appearance the twigs still yielding to the wind but not visibly so to us. The other Birch trees that were near it looked bright & chearful—but it was a Creature by its own self among them.   (p. 40)

All three observers are linked in Dorothy's memory of the moment, which she presents as a spiritual awakening. The stationary tree is momentarily transfigured by the elements of sun and wind and rain into a moving 'spirit' or 'Creature'. Even the sun's dimming cannot take away the memory of the tree as a 'flying sunshiny shower': it goes on being a 'Creature by its own self', distinguished from all the 'other Birch trees'. (Virginia Woolf called this kind of intense vision a 'Moment of Being', while James Joyce used the word 'epiphany'.) Later that same day, Dorothy had a conversation with Peggy Ashburner, in which Peggy lamented the selling of her family's land. Dorothy records their conversation as evidence that members of the local farming community are just as susceptible as she is to the familiar beauty that surrounds them daily: 'O how pleased I used to be when they fetched [the sheep] down, & when I had been a bit poorly I would gang out upon a hill & look ower t' fields & see them & it used to do me so much good you cannot think' (p. 41). The vivid poetic phrasing of her own 'moment of being' is paralleled by the oral immediacy of Peggy's words in dialect. The pairing implies a bond of sympathy between neighbours, suggesting that their sensibilities are nurtured by the habitual impressions they share. At the end of the day, a letter from Coleridge drives William out from the fireside into the cold, where he is 'surprized & terrified by a sudden rushing of winds'. Peggy's lost land, the home Dorothy fears losing, and Coleridge's disintegrating marriage provide the day's underlying themes: they are brought into near-symbolic focus by this closing contrast between the fireside at Town End and William's exposure to the elements.

As the journal unfolds, we come to understand some of Dorothy's processes of selection, and the habits of association they entail. Over the months, among the apparently inconsequential details of daily life, she offers a chain of encounters—some with the poor and the destitute, others with the beauty of the natural world—that are analogous to William's 'spots of time'. What links them is the belief that daily contact with nature has an actively beneficial influence on moral growth. 'Forms of beauty' have a renovating power, and play their part in 'that best portion' of a good person's life: their acts of kindness, sympathy, and love.[11] Only by understanding the hold that associationism has on her thinking can we come to appreciate the analogies that link her journal entries together. Dorothy does not spell these out, because they are part of a habit of mind she takes for granted. Habit, familiar associations, and local attachments are fundamental to the way she uses figurative language as a means of reinforcing 'the curious links | With which the perishable hours of life | Are bound together'.[12] Her nature descriptions make striking use of similes: mountains give 'a musical bell-like answering' to the voice of birds (p. 14); trees give 'a sweet sea-like sound...above our heads' (p. 72); crows are 'like shapes of water passing over the green fields' (p. 87). Similes usually work by revealing an unexpected likeness between two apparently disparate things; but in Dorothy's journal they confirm an underlying relation, or unity, between phenomena that are *already* alike—alike through geographical prox-imity, and because they inhabit the same lexical field. In this way, she stays resolutely grounded in the known, familiar world: a world that is tightly bounded by habit and association, in which the same mountains are seen reflected in the same lakes, the same paths walked with the same companions, day after day. Nearly all of the journal's similes are based on natural phenom-ena that can be observed in the Vale of Grasmere, less than twenty miles away from her birthplace. The vale signified a home to which Dorothy had returned after long absence, and there is, perhaps, a connection between her distinctive use of figurative language and the vale as a home recovered. We might think of her similes as 're-familarization' rather than 'de-familiarization'.[13]

*

Poetic metre is less visible in the *Grasmere Journal* than figurative language because it came as naturally to Dorothy as walking and talking. Reading aloud and transcribing poetry were daily activities in the household, which meant that she carried poetic metres with her everywhere she went. All the evidence suggests that she had an extraordinarily powerfully oral memory. Pamela Woof has written accurately and movingly about the way that Dorothy's journal catches the changeable rhythms of life:

> It sometimes moves in little rushes when days can be noted with a staccato speed; it sometimes slows down to linger on a single figure...it sometimes slows to linger on a whole scene...It sometimes almost stops as the ear catches a ticking watch, a page being turned over, and the breathing of the silent reader by the fire; and then it starts off again at a great pace with the planting and mending and baking and washing and reading and writing and walking and talking, all the weather and the work crammed into a little space of words.[14]

It is against this background of 'real' time, with its unpredictable changes of rhythm and tempo, that Dorothy uses recurrent, metrically regular phrases to distil moments of perception, counterpointing these with their prosaic, rhythmically irregular, surroundings. Sometimes these moments of vision coincide with instances of figurative language. More often, they work as a kind of equivalent to the figurative. A typical passage from the *Grasmere Journal* gives a sequence of impressions loosely held together with dashes, containing no steady rhythm. Suddenly, a single sentence will stand clear: 'the wind was up & the waters sounding' (p. 53); 'the sykes made a sweet sound everywhere' (p. 71). Many of her sentences are written, like these, in iambic pentameters, widely held to be the most natural metre for the spoken voice, as well as for recording the steady motion of walking. Tetrameters, which convey a more lilting rhythm, and are associated with popular songs and ballads, occur less frequently: 'The corn begins to shew itself' (p. 3); 'a sweet sound of water falling' (p. 39); 'the Ash leaves lay across the Road' (p. 28). Most of her metrically regular sentences occur when she is describing nature, rather than housekeeping or beggars. But there are occasional exceptions, as in her memorable description of the tall beggar woman who called at Town End while William was away: 'She had on a very long brown cloak, & a very white cap without Bonnet—her face was excessively brown, but it had plainly once been fair' (p.9). The final clause in this sentence is a perfect iambic tetrameter, and seems to echo the opening stanza of William's ballad 'The Thorn'.

Among the varied metrical patternings of the journal, Dorothy's characteristic habits of syntax and phrasing establish her poetic voice: the habit, for instance, of using paired adjectives to close a sentence: 'snowdrops quite out, but cold and winterly' (p. 71). Or the habit of balancing a sentence (sometimes across a caesura), so that it becomes a composed unit: 'Sheep resting all things quiet' (p. 84); 'the landscape was fading, sheep & lambs quiet among the Rocks' (p. 94); 'the wind was among the light thin twigs & they yielded to it this way & that' (p. 39). Or of partially repeating a sentence, refining what comes before, as if speaking her thoughts aloud to herself: 'There was no one waterfall above another. It was a sound of waters in the air—the voice of the air' (p. 92). Repetition, or reprise, is so recurrent a feature of the journal's language that it suggests a habitual process of going over her thoughts to revise them. Looking, then looking again, Dorothy re-familiarizes herself with her impressions, instilling them more strongly in the mind.

Across the full span of the *Grasmere Journal*, Dorothy experiments with a wide range of metrical patterns, building poetic units out of more than one sentence, or breaking a single sentence down into subsidiary clauses which sound like poetic lines when they are read aloud. In the following examples, I have supplied her sentences with line breaks at points where they appear to fall naturally (where she uses punctuation marks, or a caesura) so as to show how the prose hovers on the edge of verse:

> a sweet sound of water falling
> into the quiet lake

> Helm Crag rose very bold & craggy,
> a being by itself

> the air was become still
> the lake was of a bright slate colour,
> the hills darkening.
> The Bays shot into the low fading shores.[15]

Of course, it does violence to the texture of the journal to excerpt small passages, rather than to read the whole of the journal entry in which they appear. Dorothy's handling of metre is responsive to the changing rhythms of the day, and her moments of stillness, or distilled perception, are only part of the day's happenings. To look at them in detail is to sense how they are composed to resemble pictures, and how they sound when they are read aloud. These word compositions have their own distinctive pattern, like miniature imagist poems.

On one occasion in the *Grasmere Journal*, Dorothy refers to herself as 'more than half a poet' (p. 81). Nothing can be proven about what she intended this to mean, but perhaps she observed how the recurrence of rhythmic and figurative analogies in her prose creates moments of recognition, in which the ear remembers (and the eye sees) patterns encountered before. The mnemonic function of metre makes it analogous to her use of simile: linking moments to prior moments in a web of familiarity performs something like the work of memory. 'There are no rules and structures for diary writing, as there are not for living: we take the fast and slow of it as it comes.'[16] The *Grasmere Journal* contains too many random elements, and was written in too piecemeal a fashion, to be described as 'unified'. And yet, as we have seen, its principles of organization—narrative, syntactical, figurative, and metrical—produce momentary effects of unity, as well as more extended passages that appear crafted or composed. It is the presence of these effects, across the entirety of the journal, which enables us to speak in terms of its 'poetics of prose'.

No one has written better about Dorothy's poetic qualities than Virginia Woolf, who found in her writing a vivid recognition of the way in which 'inner visions' are embedded in the texture of daily life, from where they can be 'call[ed] to mind at any time in their distinctness and in their particularity', so that they 'come back stilled and heightened' and capable of offering 'consolation and quiet'.[17] Woolf's debt to Dorothy, in formulating her idea of 'moments of being', may have been greater than the one she owed to William for his 'spots of time':

> It is only gradually that the difference between this rough notebook and others discloses itself; only by degrees that the brief notes unfurl in the mind and open a whole landscape before us, that the plain statement proves to be aimed so directly at the object that if we look exactly along the line that it points we shall see precisely what she saw. 'The moonlight lay upon the hills like snow.' 'The air was become still, the lake of a bright slate colour, the hills darkening. The bays shot into the low fading shores. Sheep resting. All things quiet.' 'There was no one waterfall above another—it was the sound of waters in the air—the voice of the air.' Even in such brief notes one feels the suggestive power which is the gift of the poet rather than of the naturalist, the power which, taking only the simplest facts, so orders them that the whole scene comes before us, heightened and composed, the lake in its quiet, the hills in their splendour.[18]

There is no intention on Woolf's part to analyse the contribution made by metre to 'the suggestive power which is the gift of the poet'. Her emphasis lies, instead, on the accuracy of Dorothy's observations. But her carefully selected trio of quotations, each resembling a line of iambic pentameter—'The moonlight lay upon the hills like snow', 'The bays shot into the low fading shores', 'It was the sound of waterfalls in the air'—conveys the sense of 'tranquil restoration'[19] she receives from Dorothy's writing. The powerful effect of these lines reminds us that it is through rhythm, above all else, that the language of the *Grasmere Journal* 'calls home the heart to quietness', knitting the poetic intensities of life into the sequential, prosaic ordinariness of living.

*

In the 'Preface' to *Lyrical Ballads* (1800) William observed, in a striking biological metaphor of kinship, that 'poetry...can boast of no celestial Ichor that distinguishes her vital juices from those of prose; the same human blood circulates through the veins of them both'.[20] It is tempting to think that the *Grasmere Journal* played an active role in sharpening his awareness of the potential confluence between two media: an awareness which had begun at Alfoxden in 1798, developing into a more clearly articulated theory of language during 1800. Coleridge is often credited with much of the original thinking that lies behind the 1800 Preface; but Dorothy also played her part, both in conversation and by example. The *Grasmere Journal* offers striking evidence of the way that prose and poetry can move alongside each other, and sometimes flow together. In placing prose on the same level as poetry, did William implicitly honour Dorothy's creative talent, acknowledging the equality of their partnership in writing?

We know for certain that the *Grasmere Journal* was sometimes read aloud by Dorothy as a prompt for poetic composition. Some of the material she collected provided the basis for poems William later wrote; and some of the poetry he had already written shaped the way she collected material. Pamela Woof has observed how much Dorothy and William talked to each other, told their experiences, and how frequently those experiences were written about in words they heard each other use.[21] The *Grasmere Journal* played an important part in their shared creativity by supplementing their recollections, providing poems with an authentic grounding in real life, and recording or initiating conversations. There is evidence to suggest that composition of prose and poetry alike was partly oral and collaborative, and that when the siblings turned back to consult the journal, they were prompted to do so by shared experiences or memories. Following a creative exchange between Dorothy and William is not simply a matter of comparing a journal 'source' with a finished poem, but of trying to understand the associations that gathered around incidents, places, and people over days, months, or sometimes years.

'Beggars', a poem written in March 1802, was based on an encounter Dorothy had two years earlier with a beggarwoman—and, later the same day, with her beautiful but deceitful sons when they were playing with butterflies near the bridge at Rydal. Circumstantial evidence for collaborative composition survives. From this it is clear that the Wordsworths turned back to the *Grasmere Journal* to supply authentic details for the poem, treating Dorothy's prose as if it were a faithful transcript of reality. William wrote the poem in three separate stages over the course of a single day:

> William finished Alice Fell, & then he wrote the Poem of the Beggar woman taken from a woman whom I had seen in May—(now nearly two years ago) when John & he were at Gallow Hill—I sate with him at Intervals all the morning, took down his stanzas &c . . . After tea I read to William that account of the little Boys belonging to the tall woman & an unlucky thing it was for he could not escape from those very words, & so he could not write the poem, he left it unfinished & went tired to Bed. In our walk from Rydale he had got warmed with the subject & had half cast the poem.   (p. 77)

William's 'writer's block' seems to have stemmed from the feeling that on this occasion Dorothy's narrative provided a *surplus* of the authenticity he was aiming for in poetry, leaving no room for his imagination. By contrast, talking as he walked enabled him to compose less self-consciously, 'casting' his poem as a sculptor might, from an existing mould.

Conversation played a crucial role in the Wordsworths' collaboration, as a catalyst for the associative processes that were vital to their creativity. We cannot recover the missing verbal exchanges that went on behind their writing; but we can reconstruct some of the associative patterns and motifs that shaped their interactions. For instance, on 14 March, immediately after composing 'The Beggars', and while the image of the two children playing with butterflies was fresh in both their minds, another poem about a butterfly came into being. The *Grasmere Journal* gives a delightfully detailed account of impromptu creativity at breakfast time in Town End:

> William had slept badly—he got up at 9 o clock, but before he rose he had finished the Beggar Boys—& while we were at Breakfast that is (for I had Breakfasted), he, with his Basin of Broth before him untouched & a little plate of Bread & butter he wrote the Poem to a Butterfly! —He ate not a morsel, nor put on his stockings but sate with his shirt neck unbuttoned, & his waist-coat open while he did it. The thought first came upon him as we were talk-ing about the pleasure we both always feel at the sight of a Butterfly. I told him that I used to chase them a little but that I was afraid of brushing the dust off their wings, & did not catch them—He told me how they used to kill all the white ones when he went to school because they were frenchmen. Mr Simpson came in just as he was finishing the Poem.   (pp. 77–8)

A poem's genesis, from the sharing of memories to completion, is here mapped out. From this detailed description, we gain an insight into the way collaborative process blurred the boundary between personal and commu-nal experience. After the Wordsworths had exchanged their different child-hood recollections, William made his poem out of the shared material. Details from Dorothy's childhood were incorporated into his early memo-ries of Cockermouth.

The poem begins with a moment of concentrated stillness: 'Stay near me—do not take thy flight! | A little longer stay in sight!' (ll. 1–2). Com-ing so soon after William's struggle to write 'Beggars', the fluid rhythms may partly stem from a sense of release.[22] As the constraining framework of Dorothy's writing fades into the background, William is able to draw freely on conversation as a creative resource: '*Much converse do I find in Thee*, | Historian of my infancy' (ll. 3–4; emphasis added). Playing with memories and allowing itself the indulgence of poetic licence, the poem reads like a prayer to the spirit of creativity in the household. In gentle, coaxing tones, the speaker entreats inspiration to stay near, stay longer, not depart, each plea sounding a note of increasing resistance to the flow of time. Dorothy's account of the poem's composition responds to William's mood of release with a tribute to his spontaneity: 'He ate not a morsel, nor put on his stockings but sate with his shirt neck unbuttoned, & his waistcoat open while he did it.' The slightly raffish, déshabillé portrait of the poet, sitting at breakfast and dashing off his poem, mirrors the mood of the moment. Arriving mysteriously, hard to pin down, inspiration for both siblings resembles a butterfly in its welcome visitations: William's 'thought for the poem', Dorothy says, '*came upon him* as we were talking'.

The contrast between William's compositional difficulty with 'Beggars' and his freedom in writing 'To a Butterfly' is suggestive. As well as indicating his preference for a creative process that was grounded in orality, the pattern of blockage on 13 March followed by release on the 14th suggests that Dorothy's *writing* (as distinct from her conversation) exerted a strong influence on William's imagination, with which he partly struggled. There may, then, have been a creative tension between the claims of prosiac 'truth' and poetic 'fiction' in the household. There are some parallels betweeen the compositional history of 'Beggars' and that of 'The Leech-Gatherer', a poem which initially drew on Dorothy's journal for its vivid circumstantial details, later toning these down to achieve an independent life. The genesis of 'The Leech-Gatherer', from journal through to published text, is a test case of what was at stake for William and Dorothy in their shared search for a language that would adequately express 'the acknowledged voice of life'.[23] There was a gap of eighteen months between the *Grasmere Journal*'s description of the Wordsworths' encounter with 'an old man almost double' on 26 September 1800 and the first version of 'The Leech-Gatherer' in 1802. Dorothy's journal entry, written a little after the event, possibly at William's prompting, dwells on the plain facts of the man's hardship as he travelled from place to place:

> he lived by begging & was making his way to Carlisle where he should buy a few godly books to sell. He said leeches were very scarce partly owing to this dry season, but many years they have been scarce...Leeches were formerly 2/6 [per] 100; they are now 30/. He had been hurt in driving a cart his leg

broke his body driven over his skull fractured—he felt no pain till he recovered from his first insensibility. It was then 'late in the evening—when the light was just going away.'   (p. 24)

Dorothy's narration is restrained. She offers no comment on the man's suffering, leaving his resilience to speak for itself. Mostly she uses paraphrase to convey her memory of the man's narrative, but she puts two of his phrases in quotation marks, perhaps moved in the first case by their dignified clarity and humility—'it pleased God to bless us'—and in the second by the naturally elegiac quality of his phrasing: 'when the light was just going away'. The power of William's poem, in its first version, is that it stays very close to the spirit of Dorothy's journal-entry. Authentic in its matter-of-factness, 'The Leech-Gatherer' catches the stoical fortitude of the old man, who does not brood self-pityingly on his troubles but simply relays the circumstances of his life. What absorbs the poet, Seamus Heaney says, 'is the equanimity with which the old man faces his crisis':[24]

> Feeble I am in health these hills to climb
> Yet I procure a living of my own
> This is my summer work in winter time
> I go with godly Books from Town to Town
> Now I am seeking Leeches up & down
> From house to house I go from Barn to Barn
> All over Cartmell Fells & up to Blellan Tarn.[25]

Local place names convey the impression of authentic reportage, much as circumstantial details do in Dorothy's journal. The *prosaic* quality of William's verse is not, I suggest, an accidental failing but a deliberately achieved effect. When Sara Hutchinson (possibly under the influence of Coleridge) objected to the poem's 'tediousness', she had in mind its thirteen stanzas of unadorned testimony. William, reproving her for insensitivity, explained that the poem's power consisted precisely in its fidelity to experience. It mattered to him, as much as it did to Dorothy, that the old man was not a fictional character but a living person; that together they had listened to his story and witnessed his strength of mind. The leech-gatherer's power to 'admonish' came from his irreducible actuality:

> I cannot conceive a figure more impressive than that of an old Man like this, the survivor of a Wife and ten children, travelling alone among the mountains and all lonely places, carrying with him his own fortitude, and the necessities which an unjust state of society has entailed upon him.[26]

This is a moving defence of the poem's subject matter and style of narration, laying its faith in the power of personal testimony to convey moral truth. Implicitly, William defends the 'ungarnished' tale ('Michael', l. 19) as it had stood in the *Grasmere Journal* shortly after he and Dorothy met the leech-gatherer in 1800: 'not stood, not sat, but *was*—the figure presented in the most naked simplicity possible'.[27] Dorothy, likewise, came stalwartly to the defence of authenticity, writing to Sara Hutchinson 'when you feel any poem of [William's] to be tedious, ask yourself in what spirit it was written'.[28] To her mind, his poem had exactly captured the spirit of their unforgettable encounter.

It appears that more was involved in the Wordsworths' collaboration than a simple division of labour, with Dorothy undertaking the documentary 'fieldwork' in her journal, and William transforming prose into poetry. The *Grasmere Journal* served not just as a reliable record but as a kind of conscience, reminding both writers of the obligations they owed to details of time, place, and circumstance. However, it was only a matter of weeks before William revised the poem, following suggestions made by the Hutchinson sisters. 'Resolution and Independence', the published text, is less prolix and more figurative than either Dorothy's journal entry or 'The Leech-Gatherer'. In its revised form, the poem demonstrates the power of imagination to shape and distil the materials it works upon. The old man takes on a mythical otherworldliness, 'Like one whom I had met with in a dream; | Or like a Man from some far region sent; | To give me human strength, and strong admonishment.' (ll. 117–19; *WW Poems*, 234) Readers rarely prefer the earlier version—'What the poet is engaged on, after all, is dream work, not documentary'[29]—and yet one senses that William had to sacrifice something important in the revisionary process. The 'matter-of-factness, or clinging to the palpable' which Coleridge detected and criticized in his friend was an important component of his levelling art.[30] To move from 'the most naked simplicity possible' into a dreamlike register was, inevitably, to lose some of the power which lodged in the original encounter.

Seamus Heaney, who comments only on the published version, observes that Dorothy's and William's accounts of the leech-gatherer 'represent not only two kinds of writing, but two orders of achievement':

> Both writings are about meeting a person at once destitute and dignified, but one is a little dossier of information about the leech gatherer as an individual broken and bent by circumstance, whilst the other is a presentation of the same man not just [as] an individual case but, in a manner of speaking, as the very measure of man.[31]

We have no record of Dorothy's contribution or response to the later version: she simply noted that William soon revised it. She was doubtless aware that her journal entry initially exerted a grounding influence on 'The Leech-Gatherer', which diminished as the poem developed. She must also have noticed that William habitually moved away from literal experience as he revised his poems ('The Sailor's Mother', for instance, loses much of its vivid realism as it progresses from manuscript to publication). Still, the Wordsworths' reverence for shared memories exerted a powerful influence on their collaborative processes. Heaney's characterization of their writing as representing 'two orders of achievement' may be a little too clear-cut; for the genesis of 'Resolution and Independence' does not suggest a strict dichotomy between prosaic journal and other-wordly poem. Rather, it points to a pattern of creative tension and development, in which there were several stages.

*

Because of the oral and collaborative nature of composition in the Wordsworth household, it is sometimes difficult to identify the 'base author' of a piece of writing. For instance, on 16 April 1802, Dorothy left William sitting by a bridge at Brothers Water. When she returned, she 'found William writing a poem descriptive of the sights & sounds we saw and heard'. Her journal entry captures her memory of the scene as they had observed it together:

> There was the gentle flowing of the stream, the glittering lively lake, green fields without a living creature to be seen on them, behind us, a flat pasture with 42 cattle feeding, to our left the road leading to the hamlet, no smoke there, the sun shone on the bare roofs. The people were at work ploughing, harrowing & sowing—Lasses spreading dung, a dogs barking now & then, cocks crowing, birds twittering, the snow in patches at the top of the highest hills, yellow palms, purple & green twigs on the Birches, ashes with their glittering spikes quite bare.   (p. 87)

In this typical piece of georgic prose, Dorothy celebrates the rhythms of daily farmwork as winter turns to spring. Her recollection is primarily visual, and she gives a full 360 degrees panorama of the landscape rather than a picturesque 'view'. She stays close to a descriptive register, retaining the exact details of the landscape, even down to the number of cattle feeding. The manuscript has several revisions, showing that her prose was carefully crafted. Her first sentence is composed in balanced clauses which capture the movement of water seen against still fields. Her second sentence is long and busy with participles, the subordinate clauses making it appear artless and jumbled, like an inventory. William picks out many of the same details, but he begins with sounds and makes a unified composition, with all the adjacent activities evoking co-operation. His poem is composed in the present continuous tense. The feminine rhymes are nonchalant, and the overall effect is like an al fresco composition:

> The cock is crowing.
> The stream is flowing,
> The small birds twitter,
> The lake doth glitter,
> The green field sleeps in the sun;
> The oldest and youngest
> Are at work with the strongest;
> The cattle are grazing,
> Their heads never raising;
> There are forty feeding like one!
>
> Like an army defeated
> The snow hath retreated,
> And now doth fare ill
> On the top of the bare hill;
> The Plough-boy is whooping—anon-anon:
> There's joy in the mountains;
> There's life in the fountains;
> Small clouds are sailing,
> Blue sky prevailing;
> The rain is over and gone!

When it appeared in print, this poem bore the title 'WRITTEN IN MARCH, While resting on the Bridge at the Foot of Brother's Water'. In some ways like an inscription, it came 'as near to extempore utterance as the written word can be',[32] and as close in spirit to Dorothy's style as William ever got. If Dorothy was partly remembering William's phrasing when she made her journal entry, she may also have helped to select details for the poem, or even 'talked it into existence' with him.[33]

Dorothy never intended her *Grasmere Journal* for publication. Its use by her brother, without acknowledgement, has engendered a great deal of speculation and commentary from critics preoccupied with issues of authorship and copyright. 'William Wordsworth is one of the most famous Romantic poets', writes Martha Woodmansee, 'Yet he relied on his sister even when writing such avowedly personal poems as "Daffodils". He was not, in fact, "wandering lonely as a cloud", but strolling with his sister. The poem deliberately presents a collective experience as a supposedly personal one.'[34] Given our knowledge of how collaborative process worked in the Wordsworth household, we might ask why 'collective' and 'personal' experience should be so sharply distinguished here. Woodmansee's insistence on this as a strict dichotomy is, on the face of it, puzzling. 'I wandered lonely as a cloud' was written at least two years after William's experience of 'strolling with his sister' by Ullswater on 15 April 1802.[35] On that windy day in April they were especially aware of each other, having recently been reunited. William had just visited Mary Hutchinson in Bishop Middleham to arrange the details of their forthcoming marriage, while Dorothy stayed with the Clarksons at Eusemere. The Wordsworths were on their way homeward to Grasmere when they saw the daffodils, and the joy of their reunion is a felt presence in Dorothy's fresh clear prose: 'When we were in the woods beyond Gowbarrow park we saw a few daffodils close to the water side', she writes, 'we fancied that the lake had floated the seeds ashore & that the little colony had so sprung up.' Pleasure gives way to wonderment as the companions realise this is not a scattering of stray daffodils, but a *substantial* colony:

> as we went along there were more & yet more & at last under the boughs of the trees, we saw that there was a long belt of them along the shore, about the breadth of a country turnpike road.   (p. 85)

In her wayfaring metaphor, Dorothy introduces a connection between the daffodils and the two companions on their journey. As her description shifts to the first person singular, she captures not just a beautiful lakeside scene in spring but a mood of excitement in herself that seems to quicken in response to the wind's movement among the daffodils. She identifies with some of the flowers that have been flattened by the wind, but equally her spirit 'dances' with the whole colony as it moves like a crowd of people, energized and unified by the wind's rhythm:

> I never saw daffodils so beautiful they grew among the mossy stones about & about them, some rested their heads upon these stones as on a pillow for weariness & the rest tossed & reeled & danced & seemed as if they verily laughed with the wind that blew upon them over the Lake, they looked so gay ever glancing ever changing. This wind blew directly over the lake to them. There was here & there a little knot & a few stragglers a few yards higher up but they were so few as not to disturb the simplicity & unity & life of that one busy highway.   (p. 85)

As a prose poem capturing the interaction of the fertile lake, the enliven-ing wind, and the dancing flowers, this epiphany has some affinities with the transfigured birch tree described by Dorothy in 1801. There is a spir-itual quality (almost biblical, in the word 'verily') which arises from her knowledge that she and William are on their journey homeward. Many of her greatest passages of prose draw on the personal associations of jour-neying. Subliminal connotations of pilgrimage are here reinforced by the road metaphor, which returns at the end in 'that one busy highway'.

Let us suppose that in 1804 William picked up Dorothy's journal, admired her carefully crafted description of the 'ever glancing ever changing' daf-fodils, and wrote 'I wandered lonely as a cloud' while he was alone—upstairs in the sitting-room at Town End, say, or out in the orchard, his favourite spot for composition. Reading the journal entry brought back his memory of their walk by Ullswater, which he then described from his *own* subject-position, supplementing her prose with emotions 'recollected in tranquillity' two years later.[36] That is one scenario, albeit a highly unlikely one. Now let us imagine an alternative scene of writing, in which William, Dorothy, and Mary are all present. Let us suppose that something prompted Dorothy to bring out her journal, to read aloud her account of the journey from Eusemere to Grasmere, including the beautiful description of the daf-fodils, and to help William create his own memory-poem by listening to him, or by suggesting ideas, metaphors, rhymes. In this family scene, the *Grasmere Journal* provides a valued record of an experience jointly remem-bered by the siblings. It gives pleasure to Mary, who was not with them on their homeward journey in April 1802; and it generates a poem. We can be fairly certain, because William let this be known in print, that Mary con-tributed 'the two best lines': 'They flash upon that inward eye | Which is the bliss of solitude' (ll. 15–16).[37] So, even without the further possibility of Dorothy's part in oral composition, it is established that two writers participated in the writing of 'I wandered lonely as a cloud'. The 'I' of the poem is not *literally* William the lonely wanderer, or William the pensive poet lying on his couch in the upstairs sitting room at Town End, but the 'I' of lyric utterance itself—an 'I' that William, Dorothy, and Mary can all identify with. Very few details in the poem, other than the metaphor of the joyous dance, correspond directly to the journal's description of the daffodils. The poem is structured around a moment of remembering, in which the speaker expresses his gratitude for a gift he received with joy at the time, but later learnt to value more consciously and fully: 'I gazed—and gazed—but little thought | What wealth the shew to me had brought' (ll. 11–12). His pleasure in the repossession of this moment is as personal as Dorothy's observation, 'I never saw daffodils so beautiful'. But William's way of articulating his pleasure makes it communal, for the phrase 'I gazed—and gazed' is a reprise of his dedicatory blessing on Dorothy in the first 'Naming of Places' poem in 1800: 'I gazed and gazed, and to myself I said, | "Our thoughts at least are ours; and this wild nook, | My EMMA, I will dedicate to thee".'[38]

William and Dorothy made an incalculable contribution to each other's writing. We should not accuse the poet of *misrepresenting* 'collective' experience as 'personal' when he transformed it into lyric poetry, for that would simply be to reprimand him for his particular choice of medium and genre. Instead, we need to observe the mnemonic function that Dorothy's journal performed in the Wordsworth household, and the crucial role that memory—especially *communal* memory—played in the family's creative activities. What is of most interest in the Wordsworths' literary partnership is their shared associative practices, their joint attachment to places, and their interdependent processes. Creativity in their household was a form of symbiosis, fostered by mutual affection and responsiveness to environment. In his wonderful book *Nature Cure*, Richard Mabey has observed that 'mind is a much broader entity than consciousness, and not necessarily confined in individual packages...It can be cultural, co-operative, perhaps even communal. And maybe in keeping with our new understanding of the unity of physical life, we could try viewing mind not as possessed by individuals, but shared between them, as a kind of field.'[39] His words resonate in the context of the Wordsworths' relationship; for they were monists at heart, seeing no 'line where being ends'.[40]

9

The Orchard at Town End

'ORCHARD PATHWAY, to and fro,
Ever with thee, did I go,
Weaving Verses, a huge store!
These, and many hundreds more.
And, in memory of the same,
This little lot shall bear Thy Name!'[1]

*

On Sunday 31 January 1802, as Dorothy and William walked round Grasmere and Rydal lakes, they talked about memories associated with the route. In the *Grasmere Journal* that evening, Dorothy recalled her own walk with William from Kendal to Windy Brow in 1794 and also Coleridge's with William on 4 November 1799. In this way she honoured the emotions linking three companions to each other and the vale. Reflecting on how Grasmere had become peopled with memories, Dorothy's thoughts moved naturally to Mary Hutchinson, a regular visitor at Town End, and soon to become a perpetual inmate of the household: 'We sate by the road-side at the foot of the Lake close to Mary's dear name which she had cut herself upon the stone. William...cut at it with his knife to make it plainer.' The Wordsworths had named a rock in Bainriggs Wood 'Mary Point' as early as August 1800; and the initials MW were carved not just on Thrang Crag at the foot of Rydal, but on the 'Rock of Names' which stood by the roadside midway between Town End and Greta Hall. William writes in 'The Waggoner' that this rock was marked by 'hands of those my soul loved best',[2] and several solemn moments were connected with it.[3] There were also memories of many walks with Mary, such as the one immortalized in William's poem 'To M. H.', and another, recorded by Dorothy on Wednes-day 18 November 1801: 'Mary and I walked as far as Saras Gate before Supper—we stood there a long time, the whole scene impressive, the moun-tains indistinct the Lake calm & partly ruffled—large Island, a sweet sound of water falling into the quiet Lake.' Visiting and revisiting favourite spots was more than a pleasurable exercise in picturesque viewing for members of the Wordsworth circle. As Dorothy's careful rhythmic sentences suggest, these moments of communion held them all together in a shared bond with the vale.

As William cut at the stone to deepen Mary's 'dear name', was he absorbed in thoughts about his future as her husband? If so, perhaps he shared them with Dorothy, just as he had shared with her the invitation he made in a letter to Mary nine months earlier:

> You will recollect that there is a gate just across the road, directly opposite the firgrove, this gate was always a favorite [sic] station of ours; we love it far more now on Sara's account. You know that it commands a beautiful prospect; Sara carved her cypher upon one of its bars and we call it her gate. We will find out another place for your cypher, but you must come and fix upon the place yourself.[4]

Much had been made 'plainer' between William and Mary since then; for although there was no formal betrothal, she had stayed at Town End for seven weeks in November 1801, and during that time they had reached a clear understanding. Early 1802 was a time of emotional upheaval as plans for their wedding crystallized. In March, when the Peace of Amiens at last made travel to France possible, William and Dorothy decided to visit Annette Vallon so that a permanent financial settlement could be made for her and Caroline. The wedding, originally planned for the spring, was postponed until the autumn, preparations for it occupying their minds over the coming months. Mary already had a secure place in both their affections, and Dorothy felt no qualms about William's future happiness: 'I have known her long, and I know her thoroughly', she wrote to her eldest brother, Richard: 'she has been a dear friend of mine, is deeply attached to William, and is disposed to feel kindly to all his family'.[5] But an era at Town End was coming to an end, and both siblings sensed an imminent change in their relationship. Dorothy's journal recorded bouts of anxiety and sleeplessness on William's part, and there was an elegiac quality in their writings as spring turned to summer.

Meanwhile, they were awaiting the settlement of their family's financial affairs. A large amount of money was still owing to them from the Lowther estate, and there was no immediately foreseeable outcome of the long legal wrangle. William worried about his insecure circumstances and his responsibilities (not just as a future husband but as an absent parent, Annette and Caroline being much on his mind). He had a clear and compelling duty to provide for all his dependents; and he fully understood the precariousness of trying to make a living from poetry. Anxious on all these fronts, he interrogated his life-choices with the kind of critical scrutiny that might come from a disapproving relative:

> My whole life I have lived in pleasant thought,
> As if life's business were a summer mood;
> As if all needful things would come unsought
> To genial faith, still rich in genial good;
> But how can He expect that others should
> Build for him, sow for him, and at his call
> Love him, who for himself will take no heed at all?
>
> ('Resolution and Independence', ll. 36–42)

The Wordsworths were also beset by worries about Coleridge. As his obsessional, unrequited love for Sara Hutchinson intensified, so his marriage and health deteriorated, and relationships all round became strained. Coleridge was painfully conscious of being a visitor rather than an insider at Town End. But was it the case that the Wordsworths had excluded him, as he now believed? Much that they wrote was for each other; but Dorothy's sympathetic identification with Coleridge's suffering is evident in the *Grasmere*

Journal, and William's poems were often in dialogue with his friend's: most notably in the 'Intimations Ode' and 'The Leech-Gatherer'. Mary and Sara were frequently present alongside William in Dorothy's thoughts; and William's feelings for his sister sometimes shaded into those for his wife-to-be. When we are listening in on a conversation between two members of the Wordsworth circle, others are often a silent but influential presence.

William marked the occasion of his informal betrothal to Mary with a poem written while travelling home on horseback after a four-day visit to see her and clarify plans for the wedding. In the poem, the speaker (who is also riding on horseback) notices a glow-worm and remembers that his lover has never seen one. He dismounts, picks the glow-worm up, and carries it to her:

> When to the dwelling of my Love I came,
> I went into the orchard quietly;
> And left the glow-worm, blessing it by name,
> Laid safely by itself, beneath a Tree.
>
> The whole next day, I hoped, and hoped with fear;
> At night the glow-worm shone beneath the tree;
> I led my Emma to the spot, 'Look here,'
> Oh! joy it was for her, and joy for me![6]

When he wrote the poem out in a letter to Coleridge, William connected it with an incident that had taken place at Racedown between himself and Dorothy.[7] Clearly the jogging motion of the horse, as he travelled homeward, had prompted an actual memory which he embedded in a chivalric context, giving his poem a slightly awkward aura of romance. Identifying Dorothy as the object of his past devotion, William seems to be offering reassurance, in the difficult run-up to his marriage, that her place at the centre of his life will continue unchanged. In the version sent to Coleridge, the lover is identified as 'Emma';[8] but when Dorothy copied the poem out to send to Mary, she revised the name to 'Mary'. In this way, a poem reassuring Dorothy of William's continuing devotion became a more tactful and timely expression of love for his bride-to-be.

Members of the Wordsworth circle were in the habit of reading associatively. They knew that poems 'carried' emotions talismanically from one place or person to another, in this way strengthening existing bonds. In 'Among all lovely things' this process occurs not only in the poem's storyline—the suitor's carrying of his gift to the lady in her bower—but in its composition and circulation. William does not record the strictly monogamous feelings that might be expected of a betrothed lover in the months leading up to his marriage. Instead, marking a significant rite of passage with the time-honoured ritual of a gift, he confirms the continuity of pre-existing family bonds within a newly defined household. If we feel a sense of discomfort in observing the switch from one addressee to the other, we should remember that the triangular relationship between William, Dorothy and Mary had very solid foundations, dating back to 1788. Moreover, this kind of family structure was less unusual in the nineteenth century than it would be now. With the rise of individualism, traditional ties of blood, honour, and social identity would eventually give way to the more strictly defined 'nuclear family' structure which nowadays we take to be the norm. (Wives became gradually more and more important as the nineteenth century progressed, with sisters occupying an increasingly dependent role.) But at the turn of the eighteenth century, the old system of consanguinity was still strong in many families, ensuring that sisters, equally with their brothers, were seen as 'keepers of the family honour, bearers of the family name'.[9] As she prepared herself for William's wedding, Dorothy was fearful that she might be displaced. Her brother's poems reveal his loyalty to ancient ties of kinship, and his continuing devotion to the woman whom he loved as much as his future wife. Looking after blood relations was 'the heart and soul of proper feeling'.[10]

*

As William's marriage to Mary approached, the Wordsworths expressed their gratitude for each other's presence more and more clearly. Some of the lyrics William wrote in 1802 were explicitly homages to Dorothy; several have the quality of love poems; and many can be considered as threshold gifts. Focusing on butterflies, wild flowers, birds who built their nests in the orchard, some were inspired by Burns, others by seventeenth-century poems of devotion and praise. Intricately constructed, but often adopting a childlike voice, they celebrated a natural world in which the smallest living creatures could awaken wonderment and joy. The concluding stanza of 'To the Small Celandine' reads like a manifesto, defiant in tone, for a new kind of poetry:

> Prophet of delight and mirth,
> Scorn'd and slighted upon earth!
> Herald of a mighty band,
> Of a joyous train ensuing,
> Singing at my heart's command,

> In the lanes my thoughts pursuing,
> I will sing, as doth behove,
> Hymns in praise of what I love!   (ll. 57–64; PTV, 81)

William's attentiveness to the awakening spring, and to thoughts and memories arising from day-to-day life in Town End, drew his writing very close to his sister's. Her beautifully crafted entries in the *Grasmere Journal* showed how diurnal experience could be distilled, and how days could be 'Bound each to each by natural piety'.[11] The similarity and interconnectedness of the Wordsworths' writing at this time indicate the depth of their intimacy.

The orchard behind Town End proved the perfect environment for creativity during spring and early summer, featuring on numerous occasions in William's poems as a paradisal retreat. Here it was that he heard the cuckoo's 'hollow shout' as it passed from hill to hill, and was transported back to the lost land of his childhood:

> Thrice welcome, Darling of the Spring!
> Even yet thou art to me
> No Bird; but an invisible Thing,
> A voice, a mystery.   ('To the Cuckoo', ll. 13–16)

The entire garden, steeped with associations, was a collaborative tribute from the Wordsworths to the vale—a kind of thanksgiving for the family's restoration to the Lake District. John had planted trees in the orchard; Dorothy and William had ritually collected and transplanted wild flowers, ferns, and mosses from the fells; Coleridge found a seat under the trees and cleared it of brambles; William set to work rebuilding the seat, and with Dorothy's help brought it to completion. There was also a terrace walk under the apple trees: the *Grasmere Journal* mentions that Dorothy often walked to and fro with William there while he composed out loud.[12] In 'The Orchard Pathway' he expressed his thanks for the creative companionship associated with the place. Composed in trochaic rhyming couplets, this lyric could almost belong to the 'Naming of Places' sequence, for the path receives the poet's blessing, just as its associated poems do. Dorothy is not mentioned, but her presence is implied in the line 'Ever with thee did I go', with its subtle echo of 'Septimi Gades', written at Windy Brow in 1794: 'No separate path our lives shall know | But where thou goest I will go'.[13] She is both a companion on the path and *identified with* the path's companionship. The idiomatic phrase 'This little lot' ('The Orchard Pathway', l. 6; PTV, 63) puns nicely on the plot/allotment of land behind the house. Although the poem did not, as it transpired, appear as a dedication to *Poems, in Two Volumes* in 1807, it caught the spirit of the volume.

In the group of poems William eventually collected under the title 'Moods of my own Mind', the orchard's paradisal associations accompany the recurring theme of childhood innnocence, with subliminal suggestions of an imminent fall. William composed two poems called 'To a Butterfly' in the spring of 1802, both remembering Dorothy as a child. The first butterfly poem (discussed in chapter 8) was a quintessentially Grasmere lyric, treasuring the quality of shared happiness and deepening with the 'solemn image' of a vanished past, before the siblings were separated by their mother's death.[14] Dorothy's hesitant, loving relationship with the natural world formed the centrepiece of William's imaginative reconstruction of their early childhood. William completed his second butterfly poem on 20 April. On this occasion, the orchard is explicitly present as a setting, and the poem gives a more developed sense of the connection between the Wordsworths' garden at Town End in 1802 and the garden at Cockermouth where they played as children. The speaker holds himself and his sister close in the orchard's seclusion, possessing the moment as if it were a place: 'This plot of Orchard-ground is ours; | My trees they are, my Sister's flowers.'[15] Dorothy is included in his intimacy with the butterfly, the personal pronoun shifting from 'I' to 'we' as it does in 'Home at Grasmere', to signal reciprocity. The second stanza's expected nine lines stretch to ten, suggesting how the days of childhood are prolonged in the speaker's memory. Even present happiness is as nothing compared to the endless summers in Cockermouth, evoked nostalgically as signifiers of a lost paradise:

> We'll talk of sunshine and of song;
> And summer days, when we were young,
> Sweet childish days, that were as long
> As twenty days are now!   (ll. 16–19)

A double timeline ran through the Wordsworths' writings about Town End. Through its associations with Cockermouth, the orchard came to signify an Eden that had been regained during the last few months of William's unmarried life. But even as the siblings recovered early memories, their happiness was shadowed by a sense of imminent loss. Elegiac tones and allusions are discernible even in William's most joyous poems, and the 'Immortality Ode' voices an underlying sense of sadness: 'But there's a Tree, of many one, | A single Field which I have looked upon, | Both of them speak of something that is gone' (ll. 51–3).

The story of the Fall, and its retelling in *Paradise Lost,* came often into the Wordsworths' minds during 1802. As the garden took centre stage in their writings, they played with various post-lapsarian motifs. On 17 April Dorothy wrote, 'I saw a Robin chacing [*sic*] a scarlet butterfly this morning', but her journal gives no description of what she saw. On the following day she noted, 'William wrote the poem on the Robin and the Butterfly.' Later that day, 'he met me with the conclusion of the poem of the robin. I read it to him in Bed. We left out some lines.' Dorothy's account of the poem's genesis suggests that William and she collaborated on it, and that it arose out of conversation.[16] In 'The Redbreast and the Butterfly', the speaker upbraids the robin for its predatory instincts in a tone that moves from gentle remonstrance to protective entreaty. The proto-Darwinian theme of 'nature red in tooth and claw' is handled with a light touch. Lamenting the animal world's cruelty, William connects the scene Dorothy has witnessed with a postlapsarian consciousness of strife: 'Could Father Adam open his eyes, | And see this sight beneath the skies, | He'd wish to close them again.'[17] In his acerbic review of *Poems* (1807), Francis Jeffrey later dismissed these lines as 'downright raving', but their sense is clear enough: the paradisal orchard at Town End has been darkened by knowledge of evil.[18] In observing the robin's destructive behaviour in the orchard, and passing the knowledge of it on to William, Dorothy had given him a storyline resonant with symbolic implications.

'Foresight', another springtime orchard poem connected with *Paradise Lost*, was composed on 28 April. 'I happened to say that when I was a Child I would not have pulled a strawberry blossom', Dorothy wrote in her journal that day: 'At dinner time [William] came in with the poem of "Children gathering flowers"'. Her description conjures the image of William composing in the orchard, then bearing his poem as a gift to her—an image subtly reinforced by her improvised title. In the poem, retitled 'Foresight' for publication in 1807, an older sibling remonstrates with a younger one:

> Strawberry-blossoms, one and all,
> We must spare them—here are many:
> Look at it—the Flower is small,
> Small and low, though fair as any:
> > Do not touch it!   (ll. 3–7; PTV, 251–2)

There is a subliminal echo, here, of the closing lines of 'Nutting'—'with gentle hand | Touch,—for there is a spirit in the woods' (ll. 53–4)—as well as an ominous allusion to the tree of temptation in Eden: 'Do not touch it!' The poem may also draw on the memory of a 'little incident' recorded by Dorothy on 31 January when she was walking by Grasmere lake:

> I found a strawberry blossom in a rock, the little slender flower had more courage than the green leaves, for *they* were but half expanded & half grown, but the blossom was spread full out. I uprooted it rashly, & I felt as if I had been committing an outrage, so I planted it again—it will have but a stormy life of it, but let it live if it can.   (p. 61)

There is no evidence that William consulted this journal entry before writing 'Foresight', but he was with Dorothy by the lake on 31 January, so it seems probable that she communicated her anxiety for the blossom. The metaphor of uprooting applies to her experience as a child, abruptly severed from her birthplace and family at the age of six. Guiltily rerooting the plant, Dorothy fears for its future, as for her own, now resettled in the Lake District. Implicitly, William's poem pays tribute to the natural piety she has taught her brothers— 'do as Charles and I are doing!' (l. 2)—while also offering sympathy to the damaged child still vulnerably alive in the fully grown woman.

'Foresight' leads naturally into the most famous of William's tributes to his sister, 'The Sparrow's Nest'. This poem was inspired partly by a real sparrow building its nest in the orchard;[19] partly by memories of the Wordsworths' garden overlooking the Derwent. In the notes he dictated to Isabella Fenwick in old age, William gave more contextual detail about it than about any of his other lyrics of 1802: 'At the end of the garden of my Father's house at Cockermouth was a high terrace that commanded a fine view of the River Derwent and Cockermouth Castle. This was our favourite play-ground. The terrace wall, a low one, was covered with closely-clipt privet, and roses which gave an almost impervious shelter to birds that built their nests there. The latter of these Stanzas alludes to one of the nests.'[20] The poem begins in the present tense with a moment of excited discovery: 'Look, five blue eggs are gleaming there! | Few visions have I seen more fair!' The five gleaming eggs awaken so fresh a memory of childhood that the speaker is startled:

> Nor many prospects of delight
> More pleasing than that simple sight!
> I started, seeming to espy
> The home and sheltered bed,

> The Sparrow's dwelling, which, hard by
> My Father's House, in wet and dry
> My Sister Emmeline and I
>   Together visited.   (ll. 3–10)

Composed in the same stanza form as both the poems titled 'To a Butterfly', 'The Sparrow's Nest' calls them to mind, suggesting that even in infancy William learned from Dorothy's gentleness. His plundering instincts as a boy (vividly captured in the birds-nesting episode in the *Two-Part Prelude*) are here suppressed to make way for an expression of gratitude for all that Dorothy has taught him:

> She looked at it as if she feared it;
> Still wishing, dreading to be near it:
> Such heart was in her, being then
> A little Prattler among men.
> The Blessing of my later years
> Was with me when a Boy;
> She gave me eyes, she gave me ears;
> And humble cares, and delicate fears;
> A heart, the fountain of sweet tears;
> And love, and thought, and joy.   (ll. 11–20)

There is a shadowy Miltonic subtext in this poem, as there was in others composed in the orchard that spring. As the two children hover temptingly near the nest, the four verbs—looking, fearing, wishing, dreading—convey Dorothy's anxieties in anticipating what is forbidden. In William's imagination, she is the unfallen Eve, whose 'heart' keeps her safe, even despite her precocity as 'a little Prattler among men'. The phrase 'sheltered bed' connotes both the sparrow's nest itself and the nursery at the back of the house in Cockermouth, overlooking the terrace garden. Here all five children slept in the same room: significantly, the same number of sleeping children in the nursery as there are eggs in the sparrow's nest of William's poem. There is no mention of a mother in the speaker's memory of home, which is evoked as a masculine place, with Dorothy as the single female sibling. The sense of a supervening authority is succinctly conveyed in the phrase 'My Father's House', with its echo of St John's Gospel: 'In my Father's house are many mansions.'[21] William had echoed this verse before, in the closing lines of 'Tintern Abbey', where it connoted both the afterlife and a distant memory of Cockermouth associated with the ruined abbey. Its recurrence in 1802 is significant. It calls to mind the homeless wanderings

of the Wordsworth siblings, and their now tantalising closeness to the parental nest, twenty miles away from Grasmere.

*

William and Dorothy played interestingly fluid roles in each other's lives
and writing. Because of the interweaving of biographical and autobiographical elements in the work of both siblings, interpreting their creative collaboration calls for a kind of mythography. If we are inclined to read the
Grasmere Journal as more faithful to real life than William's poems, we should
remember that Dorothy began writing it to give pleasure to him, and that
her prose played both a personal and a communal role in the creative economy of the household. Threading its way through the journal there is the
shadowy plot line for a novel, in which William is the hero and she his
devoted, soon-to-be-displaced lover. To argue that the journal's resemblance
to a love story is coincidental—Dorothy is doing no more than telling
things as they happened—would be to miss the way her awareness of genre
shapes her experience and perception of reality. She selects incidents so as
to heighten their narrative significance as stages in her own emotional life.
For instance, when she records that she has picked an apple for William (or
that she has found and treasured one he has half-eaten) she writes with a
playful consciousness of the paradisal associations of the garden, and of their
roles as Adam and Eve.

If the journal at times resembles a love story, nowhere is it more intense
than in the spring and summer months of 1802. Dorothy's register shifts
subtly to reflect a range of moods and emotions, shading from sexual to
tenderly maternal. We need to backtrack a little to see how her feelings
changed between March and July. On 4 March, soon after William had
departed on a trip to see Coleridge in Keswick, she writes like a fond
mother doting on an absent child: 'Now for my walk...I *will* look well &
be well when he comes back to me. O the Darling! here is one of his bitten
apples! I can hardly find in my heart to throw it into the fire.' On Wednesday
17th she enjoys the tenderness of physical contact: 'we made a pillow of my
shoulder, I read to him & my Beloved slept' (p. 79). Six days later, on
23 March, she records a day in which they quietly carried out their work
alongside each other, like a married couple:

> A mild morning William worked at the Cuckow poem. I sewed beside him.
> After dinner he slept I read German, & at the closing in of day went to sit in
> the Orchard—he came to me, & walked backwards & forwards, we talked

about C—Wm repeated the poem to me—I left him there & in 20 minutes
he came in rather tired with attempting to write.　(p. 82)

At the end of the day, the tense alters. Dorothy captures a peaceful fireside
scene, reminiscent of the cottage at Nether Stowey in Coleridge's 'Frost at
Midnight'. The surrounding silence is so profound at Town End that
Dorothy can hear William's breathing:

> he is now reading Ben Jonson I am going to read German it is about 10 o
> clock, a quiet night. The fire flutters & the watch ticks I hear nothing else save
> the Breathings of my Beloved & he now & then pushes his book forward &
> turns over a leaf.　(p. 82)

In several highly charged symbolic entries such as this, the *Grasmere Journal*
memorialized the last months of Dorothy's life alone with William through
framed moments of gesture, stillness, and meaningful silence signifying
reciprocal love.

On 29 April, there is a hint of primitive nature-worship in the Wordsworths' intimacy: 'William lay, & I lay in the trench under the fence—he
with his eyes shut & listening to the waterfalls & the Birds.' Enclosed alongside him, in a space that has the properties of a nest, a bed, and a grave,
Dorothy is aware of how deeply he is absorbed in the sounds going on
around them. Their bodies and identities are separate—'William lay, & I
lay'—but the sound of nearby waterfalls suggests their spiritual union, and
even the thought of death is companionable:

> There was no one waterfall above another—it was a sound of waters in the
> air—the voice of the air. William heard me breathing & rustling now & then
> but we both lay still, & unseen by one another—he thought that it would be
> as sweet thus to lie so in the grave, to hear the *peaceful* sounds of the earth &
> just to know that ones dear friends were near.　(p. 92)

On 4 May, Dorothy read aloud to William in bed. He was having trouble
getting to sleep during these anxious premarital months, and her maternal
gesture soothed him, as a lullaby would a sleepless child. The fragment of
poetry she chose to read was one he had written for her while they were
living in Goslar. As she recited these lines, she must have been aware of how
readily she occupied the speaker's subject-position:

> This is the spot: —how mildly does the Sun
> Shine in between the fading leaves! the air
> In the habitual silence of this wood
> Is more than silent: and this bed of heath

Where shall we find so sweet a resting-place!
Come!—let me see thee sink into a dream
Of quiet thoughts,—protracted till thine eye
Be calm as water, when the winds are gone
And no one can tell whither.—My sweet Friend!
We two have had such happy hours together
That my heart melts in me to think of it.

('Travelling', ll. 1–11; LB, 307)

With its rich associative history, the passage was well chosen for the mood of the moment, its gentle iambic rhythms working almost hypnotically to lull the listener to sleep. The fantasy is one of total repose. In a quiet 'spot' or 'resting-place' under the shelter of trees, the 'bed of heath' provides a nest-like enclosure, where speaker and listener lie together as if in a lovers' embrace, their thoughts in total harmony. Dorothy's journal entry breathes not a word of the poem's personal significance, and mentions this ritual of reading aloud as though it were commonplace in the household: 'I repeated verses to William while he was in bed—he was soothed and I left him. "This is the Spot" over & over again.'

On 2 June, brother and sister sat 'in deep silence at the window—I on a chair & William with his hand on my shoulder. We were in deep Silence & Love, a blessed hour.' A week later, on 8 June, William wrote 'The sun has long been set,' a poem that captured the balmy warmth of a midsummer night in Town End:

The Sun has long been set:
The Stars are out by twos and threes;
The little Birds are piping yet
Among the bushes and trees;
There's a Cuckoo, and one or two thrushes;
And a noise of wind that rushes,
With a noise of water that gushes;
And the Cuckoo's sovereign cry
Fills all the hollow of the sky!

Who would go 'parading'
In London, and 'masquerading,'
On such a night of June?
With that beautiful soft half-moon,
And all these innocent blisses,
On such a night as this is!   (ll. 1–15; PTV, 204–5)

Dorothy is the muse of presence in William's poetry, and when his writing approaches this close to pure lyric utterance, as it did a number of times in

1802, one can almost imagine her alongside him speaking the words. From evidence in her journal, it seems that this poem was created in two stages. William composed a version when he was out walking by himself. Later, he 'walked on our own path & wrote the lines, he called me into the orchard & there repeated them to me—he then stayed there till 11 o clock'. Dorothy was with him to hear the poem recited. When William stayed out on his own, was he incorporating suggestions she had just made?

Perhaps they jointly remembered sitting together in this spot on 6 May, for William's poem echoes the entry Dorothy made in her *Grasmere Journal* on that day:

> A sweet morning we have put the finishing stroke to our Bower & here we are sitting in the orchard. It is one o clock. We are sitting upon a seat under the wall which I found my Brother Building up when I came to him with his apple—he had intended that it should have been done before I came. It is a nice cool shady spot. The small birds are singing—Lambs bleating, Cuckow calling—The Thrush sings by Fits, Thomas Ashburner's axe is going quietly (without passion) in the orchard—Hens are cackling, Flies humming, the women talking together at their doors—Plumb & pear trees are in Blossom, apple trees greenish—the opposite woods green, the crows are cawing. We have heard Ravens. The Ash trees are in blossom, Birds flying all about us.   (p. 96)

The poem and the journal entry form natural companion-pieces. In both, there is a quiet sense of contentment—of dwelling in nature, and wanting nothing more. Both speakers are absorbed by immediate sights and sounds, especially birdsong; both use the present tense and a pure descriptive register to convey the nearness and distinctness of sense impressions. Dorothy's journal entry switches between the simple present tense and the present continuous. In a similar way, William's poem varies its techniques of repetition. His rhymes start in an alternating pattern, ABAB, then switch to triple-rhyme, as if coming spontaneously: 'thrushes', 'rushes,' 'gushes'.[22] The poem then settles into couplets for the remaining eight lines, with feminine rhymes that create a soft falling rhythm. A sense of companionship is captured differently by the two writers, for Dorothy selects the daytime sounds of the rural neighbourhood—Thomas Ashburner's axe 'going quietly', the women 'talking together at their doors'—while in William's poem all the night sounds are nature's, and he abjures social life by disparaging London. Nonetheless, his poem conveys a sense of human companionship subtly and implicitly through its conversational register and allusive language. His question, 'Who would go parading | In London and masquerading?' alludes playfully to Burns's lyric 'The Twa Dogs', and is spoken intimately to someone who shares his happiness and will recognize the quotation.[23] Just as we almost expect the word 'serenading' to follow after 'parading' and 'masquerading', so the final rhyme 'blisses' | 'this is' hints at a ghost-rhyme, 'kisses'. The poem has the force of a confirmation of love, hovering between seductiveness and innocent pleasure.

A week later, the mood altered. On 13 June, Dorothy wrote in her journal, 'In the evening we walked first on our own path. There we walked a good while—It was a silent night. The stars were out by ones & twos but no cuckow, no little Birds' (p. 108). The tone is apprehensive, and she emphasizes the failure of nature to match up to poetic expectation. Two days later, her journal entry for 15 June reads: 'After William rose we went & sate in the orchard till dinner time. We walked a long time in the Evening upon our favourite path—the owls hooted, the night-hawk sang to itself incessantly, but there were no little Birds, no thrushes' (p. 109). The note of elegy is unmistakeable: already the high point of summer is over, and William's poem is being remembered as a thing of the past.

The next day, Dorothy was preoccupied with a pair of swallows who built their nest under her bedroom window. Like Gilbert White, she enjoyed observing birds closely. But the swallows also have a figurative dimension, featuring prominently in her journal at a significant moment in her life. Their presence calls to mind the pair of swans who came and went in 'Home at Grasmere' in 1800—emblems of Dorothy and William's love. On 16 June, Dorothy watched the swallows making 'a bustle and a little cheerful song hanging against the panes of glass, with their soft white bellies close to the glass, and their forked fish-like tails'. The tender, tactile detail of their 'soft bellies' suggests the arousal of maternal feelings connected with nest-making. Three days later, the birds 'were very busy under my window' building their nest; but on 25 June her journal records that the nest had gone:

> Poor little creatures they could not themselves be more distressed than I was I went upstairs to look at the Ruins. They lay in a large heap upon the window ledge; these swallows had been ten days employed in building this nest, & it seemed to be almost finished—I had watched them early in the morning, in the day many & many a time & in the evenings when it was almost dark I had seen them sitting together side by side in their unfinished nest both morning & night...As soon as the nest was broad enough, a sort of ledge for them they sate both mornings & evenings, but they did not pass the night there. I watched them one morning when William was at Eusemere, for more

than an hour. Every now & then there was a feeling motion in their wings a sort of tremulousness & they sang a low song to one another.   (p. 115)

Dorothy creates a vignette of her domestic life with William. Measured in clock time, the swallows' story covers a period of only ten days; but her phrasing suggests a longer period of settled companionship. Her elegy for the birds' ruined nest offers an insight into her emotions as she prepared herself anxiously for departure from Grasmere. During William's absence, her longing for his return is reflected in the 'feeling motion' and 'tremulousness' of the swallows as they sing their 'low song to one another'.

On 20 June, the Wordsworths spent a perfect day together. Having received news of the Lowther settlement, they 'talked sweetly about the disposal of our riches', and lay together in the orchard 'upon the sloping Turf'. This was a highly significant moment, marking the end of their long grievance against the Lowther family and the beginning of a more comfortable life. Dorothy's journal suggests how their mood of happiness was reflected in the surrounding beauty and composure of the vale: 'Earth & sky were so lovely that they melted our very hearts.' On 29 June she notes that the swallows are on their nest 'side by side both looking down into the garden'. On 6 July, 'The swallows have completed their beautiful nest'; and on 8 July, 'The Swallows stole in and out of their nest, & sate there *whiles* quite still, *whiles* they sung low for 2 minutes or more at a time just like a muffled Robin.' That night, their last before departing from Grasmere, Dorothy noted that the glow-worms were out. Did a memory of William's love poem 'Among all lovely things' make her write, 'Oh beautiful place! Dear Mary William'? The two names are joined here as if in a private blessing, just as William had blessed the glowworm, offering his poem first to Dorothy and then to Mary.

In the morning, it was the swallows' nest that preoccupied Dorothy as the horse arrived and she wrote her last hurried words:

> I must prepare to go—The Swallows I must leave them the well the garden the Roses all—Dear Creatures!! they sang last night after I was in bed— seemed to be singing to one another, just before they settled to rest for the night. Well I must go—Farewell.—   (p. 119)

Dorothy's final word, 'Farewell', creates a hinge from her journal to the valedictory poem William had drafted in May, known first as 'The poem on going for Mary' and later retitled 'A Farewell'. This highly wrought work had preoccupied him for several weeks. (Dorothy had copied it out on 29 May, believing it to be complete, then again on 31 May. William was altering it on 13 June, and on 17 June Dorothy convinced him it did not need altering. The extent of his absorption in this poem suggests that it was performing a therapeutic function at this anxious time.) In the poem he blesses the garden on his own and Dorothy's behalf, giving thanks for the two years they have spent tending it and enjoying its beauty. He uses the plural pronoun consistently in this poem, yet his tones are those of a lover speaking intimately to his beloved, with gentle solicitude and a renewal of devotion:

> Farewell, thou little Nook of mountain ground,
> Thou rocky corner in the lowest stair
> Of Fairfield's mighty Temple that doth bound
> One side of our whole vale with grandeur rare,
> Sweet Garden-orchard! of all spots that are
> The loveliest surely man hath ever found,
> Farewell! we leave thee to heaven's peaceful care,
> Thee and the Cottage which thou dost surround. (ll. 1–8)

The poem is suited to the complex occasion it marks, having some of the characteristics of an epithalamion, others of a valediction or elegy. It includes Dorothy and Mary in its circling embrace, for both of them have previously been associated with the word 'nook' in verse. The 'Garden-orchard', half-cultivated and half wild, is a microcosm of Grasmere vale, in much the same way as 'Emma's dell' and 'Mary's nook' were. The vale's bounding shape, with Town End at its centre, is suggested in this opening stanza, where half the rhyming words chime with 'round'. The speaker offers his poem to the 'Garden-orchard' as a threshold gift. He speaks as if this were the culminating item in a long sequence of gifts brought lovingly to enrich the place over the years:

> Dear Spot! whom we have watched with tender heed,
> Bringing thee chosen plants and blossoms blown
> Among the distant mountains, flower and weed
> Which thou hast taken to thee as thy own,
> Making all kindness registered and known;
> Thou for our sakes, though Nature's Child indeed,
> Fair in thyself and beautiful alone,
> Hast taken gifts which thou dost little need. (ll. 33–40)

William's thoughts run on the 'debt immense of endless gratitude'[24] which he and Dorothy owe to the vale, for it has given them far more than they could ever return. Trying to match gift for gift, he declares, like a chivalric suitor, that he fears his gifts are inadequate, for the vale is fair in itself, and 'beautiful alone', therefore it needs no supplementary riches.

In Spenser's 'Epithalamion', the bride's coming forth is joyously heralded in song: 'Now is my love all ready forth to come | ... Open the temple gates unto my love, | Open them wide that she may enter in.'[25] William's nuptial poem of welcoming is quieter and more subdued. Spoken on behalf of himself and Dorothy, it transforms the personal union of bride and groom into a communal ceremony in which Mary is wedded to the orchard: 'We go for one to whom ye will be dear... | She'll come to you; to you herself will wed; | And love the blessed life which we lead here' (ll. 25–32). His mood of wistfulness—almost of melancholy—comes from looking back on the 'sweet spring' just past, his last alone with Dorothy. He anticipates a future of looking back, imagining that when they return with Mary they will share with her not only this 'Garden-orchard' but its peaceful memories:

> Help us to tell her tales of years gone by
> And this sweet spring the best-beloved and best.
> Joy will be gone in its mortality,
> Something must stay to tell us of the rest.
> Here with its primroses the steep rock's breast
> Glittered at evening like a starry sky;
> And in this bush our sparrow built its nest,
> Of which I sung one song that will not die.
>
> O happy Garden! loved for hours of sleep,
> O quiet Garden! loved for waking hours,
> For soft half-slumbers, that did gently steep
> Our spirits, carrying with them dreams of flowers,
> Belov'd for days of rest in fruit-tree bowers!
> Two burning months let summer overleap,
> And, coming back with her who will be ours,
> Into thy bosom we again shall creep.   (ll. 49–64)

The last lines echo *A Midsummer Night's Dream*, where Hippolyta calms The-seus in his impatience for their 'nuptial hour'.[26] William's desires are reined in, and in his poem the bridegroom's anticipated entry into the bridal bower is imagined as a quiet communal return to Grasmere's maternal bosom. Throughout, the stanza form creates the sense of an enclosure, even of a nest, for the first and last lines rhyme, as do the middle two. In reading the poem aloud, the ear is rewarded by the couplet at the centre of each verse, held in place by the 'embrace' of two alternating rhymes: ABAB/BABA. In this way, the poem captures a sense of the orchard's wholeness at the vale's centre, while also suggesting a pattern of departure and homecoming.

The Wordsworths' return to Grasmere was to be much as William imagined it in his tender, wishful poem. But his wedding to Mary Hutchinson
was altogether different. It took place without Dorothy on 4 October 1802
at the church in Brompton-in-Swale (near the Hutchinsons' home in Gallow
Hill, Yorkshire) after a three-month absence from Grasmere. During those
three months, William and Dorothy travelled to Calais, settled affairs with
Annette Vallon, and returned to Yorkshire via London. Dorothy's retrospective narrative in her journal is full of interesting observations about their
travels; but it falls more or less silent on their meeting with Annette and
Caroline in Calais. However, in a letter of 29 September to Jane Marshall, she
confessed her mixed feelings before William's marriage: 'I have long loved
Mary Hutchinson as a Sister, and she is equally attached to me. This being so,
you will guess that I look forward with perfect happiness to this Connection
between us, but, happy as I am, I half dread that concentration of all tender
feelings, past, present and future which will come upon me on the wedding-
morning.'[27] Her fear was justified, for on the day itself she buckled under the
strain. Heavily erased in the manuscript of her journal, and providing the
culmination of its 'plotline', is this record of the astonishing ritual of ring-
giving which took place on the morning of the wedding:

> William had parted from me up stairs. I gave him the wedding ring—with
> how deep a blessing! I took it from my forefinger where I had worn it the
> whole of the night before—he slipped it again onto my finger and blessed me
> fervently...I kept myself as quiet as I could, but when I saw the two men
> running up the walk, coming to tell us it was over, I could stand it no longer
> & threw myself on the bed where I lay in stillness, neither hearing nor seeing
> any thing, till Sara came upstairs to me & said 'They are coming'.   (p. 126)

As though uttering vows at their own secret marriage ceremony, the siblings
solemnly imply an undertaking to remain together in a single household,
their mutual devotion undiminished by the day's momentous events. Dorothy's 'sacramental benediction' is 'tenderly' answered by William's pledge of
constancy.[28] The vow follows a 'give-and-take' pattern, signifying the confirmation of a bond; and the ritual is marked out by its position in the narrative as the culminating threshold gift in a summer of gifts. As she writes,
Dorothy is looking back on an event that occurred several weeks earlier, but
her prose dwells on her emotions as if she is still in shock. Everything in her
handling of this deliberate, crafted episode suggests deep feeling: the dramatic
pause as the ring changes hands, the acceleration of pace as the marriage
takes place in her absence, and then finally the climax, with her collapse into

stillness and silence. An echo of 'A slumber did my spirit seal' in the phrase 'neither hearing nor seeing anything' suggests a disturbing consciousness of this moment as a kind of death.[29] Pamela Woof speculates that Dorothy erased this passage, either soon afterwards or later in life, 'realizing as she must have, that the drama of tenderness of that morning was perhaps played over-consciously and in any case was not for other eyes—not even perhaps for W's.'[30] Another possibility is that William decided it might cause pain to Mary, who was likely to be one of the journal's readers. (The type of ink used is iron-based, and consistent with either of these conjectures.)

During their return journey to Grasmere, Dorothy's mind was on earlier homecomings. As the carriage passed through Wensley, she remembered how William and she had walked together through Wensleydale on the way to Grasmere in December 1799. Nostalgically, her memory takes possession of the village as if reclaiming a part of William himself:

> When we passed thro' the village of Wensly my heart was melted away with dear recollections, the Bridge, the little water-spout the steep hill the Church— They are among the most vivid of my own inner visions, for they were the first objects that I saw after we were left to ourselves, & had turned our whole hearts to Grasmere as a home in which we were to rest.   (p. 129)

A few pages later, her mind runs on a similar theme, but recalling an earlier occasion: 'I am always glad to see Stavely it is a place I dearly love to think of—the first mountain village that I came to with Wm when we first began our pilgrimage together.' This time she is recalling April 1794, when she walked with William from Kendal to Windy Brow. Her phrase 'when we first began our pilgrimage' echoes the spiritual language of 'Home at Grasmere', and suggests that she dates their life-journey together from that time. In 'There is a trickling water', a sonnet probably composed soon after their return to Town End, William too remembered the 1794 homecoming, and recaptured the excitement he had felt 'when first | Two glad Foot-travellers through sun and shower | My love and I came hither'. His sonnet pays homage to a name-less brook near Ambleside where they had stopped to refresh themselves in 1794, 'while thanks burst | Out of our hearts to God for that good hour'.[31] A draft of the first three lines, in Dorothy's handwriting, appears on the closing pastedown of the leather-bound *Alfoxden Notebook* which they had used in 1798. Dorothy probably entered it there in early 1802, William requisitioning the lines in the autumn for his sonnet. In this commemorative poem, perhaps created as a further gift for Dorothy, to mark their safe return, William once again acknowledged her importance in his unfolding life.

When the Wordsworths arrived home after nightfall on 6 October, they took a walk in the orchard garden—a commemorative ritual as well as a gesture of welcome to the bride. There were no glow-worms. In her journal, Dorothy was reticent about her feelings, allowing seasonal change to speak for itself: 'I cannot describe what I felt, & our dear Mary's feelings would I dare say not be easy to speak of. We went by candle light into the garden & were astonished at the growth of the Brooms, Portugal Laurels &c &c &' (p. 132). The next couple of days enabled a gradual settling in to their new lives together, and then an opportunity arose for Dorothy to be alone with Mary. Her record of their walk to Rydal quietly acknowledges and accepts their altered roles: 'Thursday, we unpacked the Boxes. On Friday 8th we baked Bread, & Mary & I walked, first upon the Hill side, & then in John's Grove, then in view of Rydale, the first walk I had taken with my Sister.'[32] Dorothy kept her *Grasmere Journal* for three further months, recording diurnal life much as she had done before the year's emotional upheaval. The journal came to an end on 16 January 1803; but in a letter to Catherine Clarkson in June, she returned to the story of the swallows and their nest which had so preoccupied her the previous summer:

> I am writing in my own room. Every now and then I hear the chirping of a little family of swallows that have their abode against the glass of my window. The nest was built last year, and it has been taken possession of again, about six weeks ago, needing no repairs whatever.[33]

The figurative dimensions of the swallows' story take on a new significance as Dorothy switches from journal mode into a more public epistolary register. Conscious of the nest's significance as a reassuring symbol of continuity, she implies her gratitude for the swallows' return: an event which parallels the story of her own 'little family'. Her expression of joy in the chirping sounds so close to her 'own little room' signals her full acceptance of changed circumstances in the household. Mary was expecting her first child, John, in a month's time.[34]

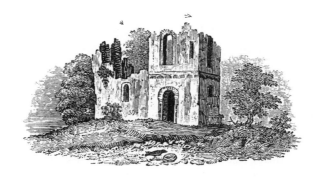

10

Scotland

'Will no one tell me what she sings?
Perhaps the plaintive numbers flow
For old, unhappy, far-off things,
And battles long ago:
Or is it some more humble lay,
Familiar matter of today?
Some natural sorrow, loss, or pain,
That has been, and may be again!'[1]

*

In the summer of 1803, Napoleon marched into Switzerland. The Peace of Amiens was broken, and England once again found itself at war with France. Travel abroad became difficult, because the Napoleonic campaigns presented hazards for British tourists. At Town End, where William's work on *The Recluse* was making little progress, the national crisis induced a mood of restlessness. Just as the household was settling into a new routine after the birth of John, an unexpected plan emerged. In search of health and a new stimulus for their writing, William and Dorothy would set off with Coleridge on a six-week tour of Scotland, leaving Mary to look after the baby. It was an awkward piece of timing; and although Mary accepted their absence with characteristic good grace, it was a relief to them all that Joanna Hutchinson was able to move into the cottage at Town End to help. For Dorothy, the wrench of leaving 'our own darling child' cast a shadow over their departure, for she had grown deeply attached to John.[2] Nonetheless, the prospect of travel, free of childcare and housework, was liberating. The magic and mystery of the Highlands drew all three companions like a magnet, holding the promise of a terra incognita where they were sure to discover inspiring people and places. William and Dorothy were conscious of the strains their relationship with Coleridge had been under for some time, and looked forward to his release from the marital strife which deepened his depression. All of them must have hoped to rebuild the intimacy and creative intensity which had thrived at Alfoxden.

Like the German trip, this one started with Coleridge as a member of the group, but saw him splitting off from the Wordsworths on discovering that his habits were incompatible with theirs. His reaction to the tour suggests that, even before they were alone, William and Dorothy had begun to re-establish the exclusive relationship they enjoyed at Goslar. Travelling together was always an absorbing experience for them, recalling earlier symbolic journeys they had undertaken as a pair—most significantly, the pilgrimage to Windy Brow in 1794, the Wye tour of 1798, and their homeward journey to Grasmere in 1799. Nostalgia, the longing for spiritual home which sometimes became a kind of sickness, united them. As they travelled through Scotland they stored memories, particularly of meetings with people, or dwellings in landscapes. The tour was restorative, for even in the most desolate scenes they found habitable places and memorably dignified lives. The writings generated by their trip—Dorothy's *Recollections of a Tour Made in Scotland, A.D. 1803*, and a number of poems by William, including 'Stepping Westward' and 'The Solitary Reaper'—were written retrospectively, after returning to Grasmere. They convey the sense of powerful shared experiences that have been distilled and shaped by memory.

Dorothy began writing about Scotland immediately after their return to Town End in September 1803. It was not her intention to publish her recollections as a book: she disliked journals of tours 'except as far as one is interested in the travellers',[3] and wrote primarily for those who couldn't join the tour: her brother John, the Hutchinson sisters, and Coleridge, who had gone off on his own for part of the holiday. She made good progress with writing throughout the autumn, and by December had covered the tour up till September 1803. She was then interrupted. As it turned out, two years were needed to complete her literary masterpiece because December 1803 to April 1805 was one of the most trying periods in her life. First came the challenge of nursing Coleridge through a breakdown at the end of 1803; then the onerous task of copying a substantial selection of William's poetry into a home-made notebook (DC MS 44) in time for Coleridge's departure to Malta in April 1804. Next, there were two dramatic family events: the birth of William and Mary's baby Dora in August 1804, which brought new domestic duties; and later the tragic death of John Wordsworth at sea in February 1805. His ship, *The Earl of Abergavenny*, had just embarked on a journey to China when it was caught in a storm and capsized a mile or so from Weymouth. Four hundred passengers were on board, fewer than a hundred of whom survived: John, their captain, went down with his ship, and £20,000 of personal investment in goods and money sank with him. The Wordsworths were stunned by the devastating news. Inevitably, Dorothy's account of the Scottish tour was influenced by the death of her brother, a traumatic event which disturbed her flow and darkened her memories. When she resumed writing, in April 1805, she was grief-stricken, and unsure she would be 'able to go on with it at all'.[4] Her coverage of the tour, from 5 September 1803 onwards, was selective and coloured by her mood, 'dropping the incidents of the ordinary days, of which many have slipped from my memory'.[5] She eventually managed to complete *Recollections*, with William's encouragement, sitting in the moss hut at the top of the orchard, on 31 May 1805. The original manuscript does not survive. A copy was made of it by Catherine Clarkson in two green leather-bound volumes during the autumn of 1805 (DC MS 50); and Dorothy made a further copy (incorporating revisions) in a red leather-bound volume (DC MS 54) between December 1805 and February 1806.[6] The existence of three additional fair copies—one of which she made herself, in 1821–2—indicates the importance that Dorothy attached to *Recollections*, as well as the book's relatively wide circulation among family and friends.[7]

William wrote very few poems about Scotland on returning from the tour in 1803. While Dorothy was writing *Recollections*, he was hard at work on other poems, including *The Prelude*. It was only in 1805, after Dorothy had completed her first fair copy, that he composed 'Glen-Almain' (May–June), 'Stepping Westward' (3 June), 'The Solitary Reaper' (5 November), and later 'Rob Roy's Grave' and 'Address to the Sons of Burns' (September 1805–February 1806). These poems were prompted not just by his own memories of the tour, bringing solace during the family's bereavement, but by reliving with Dorothy the experience of shared travel as she reconstructed the tour's details. He later published his Scottish poems in *Poems, in Two Volumes* (1807), but meanwhile Dorothy had copied several of them into MS B of *Recollections*, enabling her prose and his poetry to illuminate each other. Even without the addition of his poems, the prose of *Recollections* conveys a sense of William's companionship and imaginative presence throughout. More consciously and consistently than elsewhere, Dorothy embraced the influence of poetry he had already written or published (i.e. *before* the tour) on her ways of seeing and remembering. Her role as amanuensis for William during 1804 also influenced the process of writing about Scotland. There are important intersections between *Recollections* and passages in *The Prelude*, both shaped by a Protestant understanding of journeying as spiritual pilgrimage.

Fiona Stafford has argued that William's poetic motivation in touring Scotland was to draw sustenance from its vigorous oral culture. Tired of the commercialism of the south, he travelled north, she says, to discover the sources of the 'native mountain liberty' promoted by James Macpherson in *Ossian* and by the Gaelic-speaking mountain communities where 'heroic songs and traditions lived on to nourish future generations'.[8] But this was not a solitary tour, nor was it undertaken solely for the purpose of collecting poetic material. Dorothy was at William's side; and the siblings were engaged in acts of communal recognition and emotional replenishment which were vital to their lifelong work of healing. The trip was 'structured by graves', as Stafford points out,[9] but it also put them in touch with living Scottish people. It enabled them to deepen their knowledge of songs and legends in the remote landscapes where they still thrived; and to observe the customs and living conditions of obscure Scottish families. Whereas Coleridge's preoccupations on the journey were aesthetic—he was spellbound by waterfalls and lochs, rock formations and trees—the tour brought the Wordsworths a clearer understanding of the communal bonds formed by remembering and mourning. 'We had always one feeling', Dorothy emphasized.[10] In the finished text of *Recollections*, their creative responses to the Scottish tour can be considered side by side, with William's poems performing an illustrative function in Dorothy's narrative, much as prints did in contemporary guidebooks. Her role as observer of Scottish ways of life is complemented by his poetic engagement with historic people and places. At the same time, we can see that the intertwining of poetry and prose involved a complex form of symbiosis; for at every stage—seeing, remembering, discussing and writing—the Wordsworths drew on a shared fund of associations.

*

In the 'outlandish Hibernian vehicle' they had purchased for the trip, with 'room in it for 3 on each side, on hanging seats—A Dicky Box for the Driver',[11] the three companions set off from Keswick on 14 August, excited to see the lakes and mountains which they had often heard mentioned as 'familiar fireside names'.[12] William's appetite to explore the Highlands had been whetted in childhood by the Border Beacon near Penrith, where beacons had been lit since the reign of Henry III to warn that Scottish raids were imminent. During his schooldays his foster-mother Ann Tyson had told him 'tales half as long as an ancient romance' about the region around Loch Awe, which she remembered from her youth.[13] He had made only one very brief trip to Scotland as an adult, in 1801, but had admired the poetry of Burns since 1787. Dorothy, for her part, had often looked at maps of Scotland, following the intricate windings of sea-lochs 'till, pleasing myself with my own imaginations, I have felt a longing, almost painful, to travel among them by land or water'.[14] Familiar with the poetry of Thomson, Beattie, and Macpherson, the Wordsworths were also interested in seeing places written about in travel books over the previous three decades.[15] Their friend John Stoddart complained that travel writing about Scotland had mushroomed in recent years; but his own tour had a special appeal. Inviting readers to perceive similarities between Scottish and Lake District scenes, it included complimentary references to *Lyrical Ballads* and paid tribute to William's poetry of place.[16]

Further inspiration for the tour came from Burns, the Wordsworths' hero, who had journeyed through the Highlands in the autumn of 1787. He had long been a favourite in the household, and the Kilmarnock edition of his poems had been an important gift from William to Dorothy after their reunion in 1787. 'The communications that proceed from Burns come to mind with the life and charm of recognitions', William had acknowledged in 1799.[17] Later, in 'The Leech-Gatherer', he had identified Burns as a farmer-poet 'who walked in glory and in joy | Behind his plough, upon the mountain-side' (ll. 45–6), but whose poverty-stricken life and destitute family were cautionary reminders of human frailty. On 18 August, four days into their tour of the Lowlands, the Wordsworths' itinerary took in a visit to Burns' grave at Dumfries. In the churchyard, 'full of grave-stones and expensive monuments in all sorts of fantastic shapes' (p. 199), they found no stone to mark the spot where he was buried. With 'melancholy and painful recollections', they repeated to each other his moving plea for sympathy in 'The Bard's Epitaph':

> Is there a man, whose judgment clear,
> Can others teach the course to steer,
> Yet runs, himself, life's mad career,
>   Wild as the wave;
> Here pause—and, through the starting tear,
>   Survey this grave.[18]

For days, the memory of their visit lingered. 'There is no thought surviving in connexion with Burns' daily life that is not heart-depressing', Dorothy wrote of their mood as they left Dumfries (p. 200). Looking back across the Solway Firth, they saw the mountains of Cumberland. The thought that Burns, had he known them, might have seen this view 'with more affection for their sakes' brought sorrow as well as pleasure. At Brownhill, where they spent the next night in a lonely inn, the dangers Burns' children were exposed to now he was dead 'filled us with melancholy concern, which had a kind of connexion with ourselves' (p. 202). In his poem, 'Address to the Sons of Burns', William later drew on his memory of their sombre thoughts on this occasion. The poem is written in Standard Habbie (the six-line verse form which Burns made his own), as an act of tribute and identification. William's blessing on the destitute children is tenderly protective, urging them to take inspiration from their father, but to follow a wiser course:

> Let no mean hope your souls enslave;
> Be independent, generous, brave!
> Your Father such example gave,
>   And such revere!
> But be admonished by his Grave,
>   And think, and fear![19]

The Wordsworths were elegiac in their preoccupations for much of the Scottish tour. Both were thinking about the final home, or resting-place; and about how obscure lives—not just lives of poets—should be commemorated.

Travelling together brought them a sense of being 'neighbours in mortality'[20] with a nation whose struggle for survival against poverty and oppression they found both sorrowful and uplifting. Scotland's history provided many examples of heroic deeds that had passed into legend, holding out the consolation of an afterlife in communal memory. These intimations of immortality impressed themselves on William's and Dorothy's minds all the more forcefully because they were connected with the permanent, elemental beauty of nature.

*

After paying their respects to Burns, the three companions journeyed further north, enjoying a 'delicious spot' within sight of the magnificent Falls of Clyde. The region was steeped in memories of William Wallace, who led a resistance against the English during the Wars of Scottish Independence in the thirteenth century. Below one of the falls, Bonnington Linn, was a chasm called Wallace's Leap. Here the intrepid hero, hotly pursued by English soldiers, was reputed to have leapt to safety, taking refuge in a cave in its sandstone cliffs. The three travellers passed not one but *two* sites purporting to be Wallace's cave. 'There is scarce a noted glen in Scotland that has not a cave for Wallace or some other hero', Dorothy recalled, a little mischievously (p. 228). Coleridge made no mention of Wallace in his notebook, being more concerned to catch in words the mesmerizing sight of waterfalls in motion: 'O for evening & solitude | such Cathedral Steeples, broken Arches | so overboughed | such sounds, such shapes, such motions above the Fall'.[21] Dorothy too was impressed by Cora Linn, said to be the inspiration for James Thomson's homage, in *The Seasons*, to the 'haunted stream, that by the roots of oak | Rolls o'er the rocky channel'.[22] 'I was much affected by the first view of it', she recollected. 'The majesty and strength of the water (for I had never before seen so large a cataract), struck me with astonishment, which did not die away, giving place to more delightful feelings.'

Approaching the banks of Loch Lomond, Dorothy observed that they had entered the Highlands, 'an outlandish scene—We might have believed ourselves in North America' (p. 252). Here they found the most romantic landscapes of their tour—wild, solitary, and relatively unexplored by previous writers. From Inch-na-Vannach they saw two islands 'lost' in the lake, which was 'all in motion with travelling fields of light, or dark shadows under rainy clouds' (p. 251). Coleridge made a dismissive comment in his notebook about the guide who took them on a Rob Roy tour of Loch Katrine.[23] But for the Wordsworths, the allure of the place was inseparable from its legendary associations. Staying with the MacFarlanes, a 'handsome, healthy and happy-looking' family near his birthplace at Glengyle, they discovered how strongly Rob Roy's glamorous reputation lived on in fireside stories, for he was 'as famous here as ever Robin Hood was in the Forest of Sherwood; he also robbed from the rich, giving to the poor and defending them from oppression' (p. 268). William's poem on 'Rob Roy's Grave' gave credence to a local fiction, locating his grave 'near the head of Loch Ketterine, in one of those small, Pin-fold-like Burial-grounds, of neglected and desolate appearance, which the Traveller meets with in the Highlands of Scotland'.[24] It was 'a dismal spot', containing four or five graves overgrown with long grass, nettles, and brambles, and they were unable to read the inscriptions. 'Then clear the weeds from off his Grave', William wrote in his poem of restitution, 'And let us chaunt a passing Stave | In honour of that Hero brave.'[25]

While in the Trossachs, they learned how the Highlanders' old ways of life had been swept away in the brutal acts of repression which followed the Battle of Culloden. When the clan system disintegrated, many clansmen had left to seek new lives in America, Canada, or coastal areas in Scotland, leaving the Highlands depopulated and disenfranchized. Formerly cultivated lands were now laid waste, and everywhere derelict farmsteads and deserted herdsmen's huts told a dismal story.[26] Near Loch Lomond, they walked with a nearly blind man who was returning to his parish after several years abroad in America:

> he spoke of emigration as a glorious thing for them who had money; poor fellow! I do not think that he had brought much back with him, for he had worked his passage over: I much suspected that a bundle, which he carried upon a stick, tied in a pocket handkerchief, contained his all.   (p. 257)

From the MacFarlanes they heard about the government's restrictions on emigration, and about the conditions endured by those staying in Scotland, which were often dire. In the Highland Clearances, crofters were evicted from their homes—a process with even severer consequences than the enclosures in rural England. Exploited for cheap labour, many lived on the breadline, or close to starvation; others wandered the roads, begging, or looking for work. Meeting a beggar by Loch Lomond, Dorothy thought 'what a dreary waste must this lake be to such poor creatures, struggling with fatigue and poverty and unknown ways!' (p. 249). On meeting another woman living in 'miserable conditions' by Inversneyde, she observed: 'every step was painful toil, for she had either her child to bear or a heavy burthen. *I* walked as she did, but pleasure was my object, and if toil came along with it, even *that* was pleasure,—pleasure, at least, it would be in the remembrance' (p. 369). The grim reality of these encounters provided a disturbing contrast with the beauty of the travellers' surroundings.[27]

*

In the third week of the tour, a weary and dejected Coleridge sometimes chose to walk alone, while his friends explored the lakes by boat. Despite being impressed by the 'visionary' beauty of the Trossachs—'every intervening Distance softened by the rainy Air'[28]—he found the scenery round Loch Lomond desolate. 'Everywhere we want the "Statesmen's" Houses, & sweet spots of Cumberland Cultivation', he wrote, in homesick mood.[29] In truth, the trip had already proved too much for him. He and his companions had anticipated travelling in relative comfort, with the option of dismounting and walking whenever they wished; but Coleridge found this form of locomotion intolerable. 'I was so ill that I felt myself a burthen on them & the exercise was too much for me, & yet not enough', he confessed in a letter.[30] Under strain already, his spirits sank. The trip brought into clearer focus his alienation from William, whom he found withdrawn and uncommunicative: 'a brooder over his painful hypochondriacal Sensations...not my fittest Companion'.[31] Accusations of self-absorption were soon to become a recurrent theme in Coleridge's embittered comments about his friend, whom he saw as 'more and more benetted in hypochondriacal Fancies, living wholly among Devotees—having every the minutest Thing, almost his very Eating and Drinking, done for him by his Sister, or Wife'.[32] The Scottish tour had deepened the seam of jealousy which ran through his feelings, intensifying his sense of exclusion from William and Dorothy's intimacy. In a notebook entry written just before leaving them, he wrote with agonizing insight into his own bitterness: 'What? tho' the World praise me, I have no dear Heart that loves my Verses—I never hear them in snatches from a beloved Voice, fitted to some sweet occasion, of natural Prospect, in Winds at Night.'[33] Saddened by the rift, the Wordsworths divided their funds with him, and the three friends parted at Arrochar. Dorothy shivered at the thought of his being 'sickly and alone, travelling from place to place'.[34] However, once by himself—'such blessing there is in perfect Liberty!'[35]—Coleridge abandoned his intention to return to Keswick, and instead proceeded on a 'wild journey' through the Highlands. Suffering from gout, a swollen ankle, asthma, extreme symptoms of opium-withdrawal, and nightmares, he struck north to Inverness and walked compulsively, filling three small notebooks with detailed observations of the spectacular landscapes that unfolded around him. Averaging over thirty miles a day, he then headed south via Edinburgh to Perth. The whole journey took eight days—an epic achievement.[36]

On 29 August the Wordsworths pushed on to the north-westerly region of Argyllshire. In the Strath of Appin, where they glimpsed a sea loch, they were bewitched by the wildness of the scenery and the magic of local place names. 'The admirers of the Ossianic poetry will be interested in these, as the residence of the Mighty Fingal', Stoddart had observed in 1800.[37] Close to the sea, 'Morven' and 'Appin' were traditionally associated with the mythic Gaelic kingdom in Macpherson's translation of Ossian's epic verse. These names had a seductive power over the Wordsworths, especially in the eerie afternoon light, when 'Ossian's old friends, sunbeams and mists, as like ghosts as any in the mid-afternoon could be, were keeping company with them' (p. 320).[38] As they travelled deep into Scotland's past, Dorothy and William took in a number of sites connected with Jacobite uprisings. At Glen Coe they saw the laird's house, which 'stood sweetly in a green field under the hill near some tall trees and coppice woods' (p. 330). They found out later that the bloody massacre of 13 February 1692 had started in this very spot. Later, they travelled to the celebrated pass of Killiecrankie in Perthshire, where Highland Scottish clans supporting the ousted King James II had met and triumphantly defeated government troops on 27 July 1689. Reaching the pass at nightfall, around the hour the battle had taken place, they themselves went through it 'hearing only the roaring of the river, and seeing a black chasm with jagged-topped black hills towering above' (p. 348). Determined to see it by daylight, they returned, and saw the river Garry 'forcing its way down a deep chasm between rocks, at the foot of high rugged hills covered with wood, to a great height'. As they looked down from the road into the deep chasm through which Mackay's troops had advanced from the north, William imagined how dead bodies had fallen so thickly across the river that they temporarily dammed it. Conscious throughout their tour of the daily threat of French invasion, the Wordsworths reflected on the bravery of the Jacobites, inspirational role models for the young men of England at their own time of national crisis: 'one could not but think with some regret of the times when the now depopulated Highlands forty or fifty thousand men might have been poured down for the defence of the country',

Dorothy wrote (p. 356). On their return to Grasmere, William would honour Killiecrankie in his sonnet, 'October 1803' ('Six thousand Veterans'). His poem condemns the 'day of shame' when 'Six thousand Veterans practised in War's game' met their match against 'an equal Host that wore the Plaid, | Shepherds and Herdsmen' (ll. 1–8).

William and Dorothy reached the most northerly point of their journey on 7 September, near Blair Atholl Castle, a vast, whitewashed mansion 'commanding a prospect all round of distant mountains, a bare and cold scene' (p. 349). This Jacobite stronghold had been garrisoned by Bonnie Dundee in 1689: his body was brought here after Killiecrankie.[39] In nostalgic mood, they visited the natural Falls of Bruar in the hot sun 'for the sake of Burns', thinking of his plea that the fourth Duke of Atholl plant trees on the steep banks of the river. In 'The humble petition of Bruar water', Burns had adopted the voice of the stream, asking to be surrounded with 'lofty firs and ashes cool' and with 'fragrant birks in woodbines drest':

> Would then my noble master please
> To grant my highest wishes
>   He'll shade my banks wi' towering trees
> And bonie [sic] spreading bushes.[40]

It was a poet's plea for the sustenance and replenishment of his art, as much as identification with the wild natural sources of beauty. Sixteen years after Burns, the Wordsworths enjoyed the same rocks and stones, 'fretted and gnawed' by water: 'I do not wonder at the pleasure which Burns received from this stream', wrote Dorothy (p. 352). But she took as little delight as Gilpin had in the surrounding scenery, spoiled by insensitive planting. Although the duke had responded to Burns' petition, the hillside had been planted with firs and larches, rather than trees indigenous to Scotland.[41] She felt that winding paths through birches and mountain ashes would have been a more fitting monument to the poet than the 'whole chasm of the hillside with its formal walks' (p. 351).

Before their homeward trip, the Wordsworths returned to the Trossachs. Their encounter with 'two neatly dressed women, without hats', one of whom said in a soft friendly voice, 'What, you are stepping westward?' was to stay with them. Like a welcoming, her voice epitomized the 'true pastoral hospitality' which Johnson had observed as a characteristic of Highlanders, and which the Wordsworths had encountered everywhere on their travels.[42] It formed a striking contrast to the history of turbulence which they had been tracing in their visits to Jacobite sites, and yet there was a ghostly quality in the encounter, subliminally connected with that history. 'I cannot describe how affecting this simple expression was in that remote place, with the western sky in front, yet glowing with the departed sun', Dorothy wrote (p. 367). In William's poem 'Stepping Westward', the woman's words take on a numinous quality, suggesting a spiritual pilgrimage towards the afterlife and a sense of the fellowship between human beings in their wayfaring:

> *'What, you are stepping westward?'*— *'Yea'*
> —'T would be a wildish destiny,
> If we, who thus together roam
> In a strange Land, and far from home,
> Were in this place the guests of Chance:
> Yet who would stop, or fear to advance,
> Though home or shelter he had none,
> With such a Sky to lead him on?[43]

The word 'home', reinforced by repetition, and the haunting rhyme word, 'roam', signifies the depth of William's longing, which leads his thoughts to a resting place beyond known coordinates in a 'strange land'. Dorothy's prose is, by comparison, content with the reassurance of a nearby 'home or shelter': 'We went up to the door of our boatman's hut as to a home, and scarcely less confident of a cordial welcome than if we had been approaching our own cottage in Grasmere' (p. 368). Dorothy later connected 'The Solitary Reaper' with this part of their tour, using the poem as an accompaniment to her georgic description of reapers near Loch Voil: 'It was harvest-time, and the fields were quietly...enlivened by small companies of reapers. It is not uncommon in the more lonely parts of the Highlands to see a *single* person so employed' (p. 380). In William's poem, this peaceful harvesting scene is transfigured by the reaper's song, which fills the vale and seems unending. As an epitome of what he and Dorothy had come to value in Scotland—the sense of a connection, through the living voice, with 'old, unhappy, far-off things, | And battles long ago' (ll. 19–20)—the solitary Highland lass seemed almost to be the region's *genius loci*.

The Wordsworths' interest in the survival of Scottish songs and legends deepened in the final week of the tour. Their journey home took them eastwards on a pilgrimage to meet Walter Scott, the living embodiment and custodian of Scottish culture. Warmly welcomed at his summer home in Lasswade, they spent the week of 17–23 September being proudly shown the local sights. Scott 'limped by our side through the groves of Roslin', Dorothy remembered, 'went with us along the shores of Tiviot, and the

Tweed, led us to Melross [*sic*] Abbey and pointed out every famous hill and told some tale of every old Hall we passed by'.[44] When she later said of Scott that 'His local attachments are more strong than those of any person I ever saw', she acknowledged the basis for a lasting affinity. Scott's was not a merely antiquarian interest in local traditions; 'his whole heart and soul seem to be devoted to the Scottish Streams Yarrow and Tweed Tiviot and the rest of them which we hear in the Border Ballads, and I am sure that there is not a story ever told by the firesides in that neighbourhood that he cannot repeat and many more that are not so familiar'.[45] Two volumes of Scott's *Minstrelsy of the Scottish Border* had been published in 1802; a further volume appeared in 1803. This compilation struck a deep chord with the Wordsworths. In analysing the history of the Border ballads, Scott celebrated their peculiarly local and communal character. His observation that traditions had hitherto been especially vigorous in the South Highlands 'where, in many instances, the same families have occupied the same possessions for centuries'[46] could not fail to appeal to the writers of 'Michael' and the *Grasmere Journal*. The Wordsworths knew a great deal about the strong ties that existed between subsistence farmers and the land, and of the fireside stories which thrived in close communities. Hearing their host read aloud, in 'an enthusiastic style of chant' from the first four cantos of *The Lay of the Last Minstrel*, they re-experienced the power of the bardic voice.[47] As Dorothy recalled the last lap of her journey homeward to Grasmere, the haunting line, 'The sun shone fair on Carlisle's walls', came appropriately to mind. Quoting from 'The English Ladye and her Knight', she paid tribute to Scott's role in a thriving Border tradition. William, for his part, began a correspondence soon after the Scottish tour, sending Scott 'Yarrow Unvisited', a ballad in which he defers the pleasure of seeing the famous Braes of Yarrow to a future date. With its dialect words and litany of Border place names, the poem was a fitting acknowledgement of affinity.

*

Very soon after they returned to Town End, Dorothy began to transform the documentary evidence she had collected on the Scottish tour into an inspiring portrait of the Scots' courage and stoical resilience—a living reality, as she saw it, quite as much as a tradition preserved in legend and song. Commenting on the lives of the labouring poor, she ennobled them, just as Wordsworth had ennobled their Westmorland counterparts in *Lyrical Ballads* (1800). Describing an old man living alone, near the village of Thornhill in

Dumfriesshire, she supplied careful details about his half-furnished house, the reading matter on his shelves, the bareness of his larder—'he had no other meat or drink in the house but oat bread and cheese'—but celebrated the dignity and pride which accompanied this frugal lifestyle: 'there was a politeness and a manly freedom in this man's manners which pleased me very much' (p. 204). As she looked back on the tour, she remembered with gratitude the kindness and hospitality she had received, even from the need-iest people. Among them was their attentive hostess at Jedburgh, whose 'overflowing gaiety and strength' brought happiness to her deaf and infirm husband. In his poem 'The Matron of Jedburgh and her Husband', William paid tribute to this woman, whose character embodied the spirit of domes-tic heroism they had found in many Scottish homes: 'I praise thee, Matron! and thy due | Is praise; heroic praise, and true!'[48]

Coleridge's portrait of Scotland was altogether different. It was the land-scapes he went to see, and throughout the tour he was preoccupied by the challenge of capturing visual beauty in words. His notebooks are crowded with miniature line drawings, intended to convey the silhouettes of hills and the shapes of lakes. In his rapid al fresco jottings, he described towering rock formations, using geometric and architectural analogies: 'the Rocks now retir-ing in Bays &c; & now bulging out in Buttresses;—now in Giant Stairs, now in needle points, now in huge Towers with Chimneys on the Top.—The sin-gle Trees on the very Edge of the Top, Birch and Ash, O how lovely!'[49] He strained constantly for effects that couldn't be achieved in language: 'The Head of Glen Nevish how simple for a Painter | & in how many words & how laboriously, in what dim similitudes & slow & dragging Circumlocutions must I give it.'[50] 'O Christ', he wrote, in one of his many frustrated outbursts, 'it maddens me that I am not a painter, or that Painters are not I.'[51]

For the Wordsworths, Scotland was a place 'recollected in tranquility'.[52] They were not bound by Coleridge's obligation to capture landscapes directly before them, or tantalized by his longing for the fluid medium of paint. Although Recollections adopts the structure of a journal or travelogue—map-ping a clearly described route, intermittently mentioning dates, and record-ing events as if they have just unfolded—it was written with very little help from notes.[53] The vividness of detail suggests a quite exceptionally accurate memory, prompted doubtless by conversation. In retrospect, the journey took on a semi-figurative dimension. Six weeks of travelling together had strengthened the Wordsworths' allegiance to the Protestant tradition of way-faring on which they had drawn in previous writings. It was the austerity of this genre, more than competition with the visual arts, which shaped their memories. Dorothy occasionally used picturesque criteria to evaluate the beauty of Scottish landscapes, but her 'inhabited solitudes' have little in common with the visual representations of Scotland which illustrated contemporary tours and guidebooks.[54] In the prints which accompany Pennant's, Gilpin's and Stoddart's prose, human figures are introduced as 'staffage' to bring views into focus. She consciously rejects this picturesque technique in favour of georgic realism. Moving the human interest into the foreground, she observes shepherds and herdsmen labouring in the fields, women close to their homes, and scenes of communal domestic labour out of doors, such as linen-bleaching. Her landscape descriptions are focalized through single cottages and herdsman's huts, reinforcing her narrative's recurrent concern with home. When she takes us inside these dwellings, her descriptions are closer in spirit to seventeenth-century Flemish paintings than to anything in contemporary British art. She has a quick eye for the telling details of domestic economy: quality of furnishings, degrees of cleanliness and tidiness. She evokes the bustle of kitchens, so we get a sense of the community spirit that binds family members and neighbours together. And she takes pleasure in the way this community spirit extends to inns.

When set in barren, deserted landscapes, her descriptions endow human figures with elemental grandeur and simplicity, like the hills that surround them. Recalling an old man walking with his staff, near the village of Crawfordjohn, she writes, 'there was a scriptural solemnity in this man's figure, a sober simplicity which was most impressive' (p. 214). A single shepherd boy wearing a grey plaid, glimpsed from the great road from Longtown to Glasgow, struck her as deeply memorable: 'on a bare moor, alone with his sheep, standing, as he did, in utter quietness and silence, there was something uncommonly impressive in his appearance, a solemnity' (p. 216). Although seen from a distance, and visually arresting, these figures are not reduced to pictorial objects by their bleak surroundings, but instead provide a focus for reflection on the human spirit in adversity. Two herdsmen, seen in the fading light near the river Dochart, 'were exceedingly distinct, a beautiful picture in the quiet of a Sabbath evening, *exciting thoughts and images of almost patriarchal simplicity and grace*' (p. 341; emphasis added). These people have a striking kinship with the leech-gatherer, whose fortitude had offered William strength in his time of crisis in 1802.

Some of the sights and encounters Dorothy chose to record have an allusive quality, suggesting that she and William saw them as analogous to

the 'spots of time' which structured *The Prelude*. At Leadhills in South
Lanarkshire, they passed 'a decayed tree beside a decayed cottage', where 'the
vale seemed to partake of the desolation of the cottage, and to participate in
its decay'. Dorothy recaptures the atmosphere of desolation before introducing the human presence which gives the scene its lasting power:

> We went on, looking before us, the place losing nothing of its hold upon our
> minds, when we discovered a woman sitting right in the middle of the field,
> alone, wrapped in a grey cloak or plaid. She sat motionless all the time we
> looked at her, which might be nearly half an hour.   (pp. 212–13)

The motionless woman is at one with the visionary dreariness surrounding
her. Partly because of associations with several of William's poems—'The
Ruined Cottage', 'The Thorn', and the 'Woman on the Hill' in *The Prelude*—
she takes on a symbolic resonance in the Wordsworths' shared vocabulary of
mourning. Her history remains a blank, but Dorothy's allusive language supplies a speculative framework for her mysterious solitude. Remembering the
'Waiting for Horses' episode in *The Prelude*, where the sight of 'one blasted
tree'[55] was forever associated with their father's death, she builds a connection
between the unknown woman and her own family history ('what we had
supposed to be *one* blasted tree was eight trees, four of which were entirely
blasted'; p. 213). Dorothy stills the moment of perception, so that it resembles
a spot of time, drawing emotional and aesthetic nourishment from it.

A few miles from Tarbet on Loch Lomond as rain came on in twilight,
all three travelling companions had shared a spot of time:

> While we were walking forward, the road leading us over the top of a brow, we
> stopped suddenly at the sound of a half-articulate Gaelic hooting from the
> field close to us: it came from a little boy, whom we could see on the hill
> between us and the lake, wrapped up in a grey plaid; he was probably calling
> home the cattle for the night. His appearance was in the highest degree mov-
> ing to the imagination: mists were on the hillsides, darkness shutting in upon
> the huge avenue of mountains, torrents roaring, no house in sight to which the
> child might belong; his dress, cry, and appearance all different from anything we
> had been accustomed to. It was a text, as Wm. has since observed to me, con-
> taining in itself the whole history of the Highlander's life—his melancholy, his
> simplicity, his poverty, his superstition, and above all, that visionariness which
> results from a communion with the unworldliness of nature.   (p. 286)

Coleridge recorded very similar emotions on seeing the boy: 'Never, never
let me forget that small Herd boy, in his Tartan Plaid, dim-seen on the hilly
field, & long heard ere seen, a melancholy *Voice*, calling to his Cattle!' But

even in this notebook entry—one of the few in which he observed a High-lander—his focus moves quickly from the boy's arresting presence to the surrounding textures and movements which animate the scene: 'the Harmony of the Heath, the dancing Fern, & the ever-moving Birches...its fields of Heath...giving a sort of feeling of Shot silk and ribbon *Finery*'.[56] All three companions' response to the Highland boy differed strikingly from previous travellers' reactions to Scottish people. In 1773, Johnson and Boswell had been frightened by them: 'Some were as black and wild in their appearance as any American savages whatever', Boswell wrote.[57] For Johnson, their language was bewildering. Erse, he commented, 'is the rude speech of a barbarous people, who had few thoughts to express, and were content, as they conceived grossly, to be grossly understood'.[58] As an *unwritten* language, Erse was fluid and suspect: he complained that it 'floated in the breath of the people, and could therefore receive little improvement'.[59] Thirty years later, when the three companions stood listening to the boy's 'half-articulate Gaelic hooting', they felt quite otherwise. His power to admonish them consisted precisely in his mystery. William likened his utterance to a written 'text' that invites strangers to read and sympathize with his history.[60]

Unlike Johnson, Dorothy was no linguist; but at the centre of *Recollections* there is an ethnographic interest in the customs, language, and people of Scotland. Her fascinated absorption in the Highlands is reflected in her attentive recording of dialect words and Scottish idioms: 'ingles' (hearths), 'birks' (birches), 'burnies' (streamlets), 'callans' (children), 'great speet' (downpour), 'shiels' (mountain-huts). Sometimes she puts dialect into italics: 'we peeped into a clay *biggin* that was very *canny*' (p.198). At others she uses quotation marks to highlight phrases: 'what's your wull?', 'she keeps a dram', and 'to keep the gate' (take messages). Snatches from Scottish songs and ballads are woven into her narrative. Remembering how, at Dumbarton, the yeomanry cavalry were exercising below the castle, she quotes the line 'Dumbarton's drums beat bonny, O!' from a seventeenth-century ballad; and her conversation with a guide near Loch Achray calls to mind 'the old Scotch songs, in which you continually hear of the "pu'ing the birks"' (p. 275). Burns and the popular Scottish ballads were an inspiration to Dorothy in appreciating idiom and dialect. Her narrative pauses to explain the oddity of certain Scottish expressions: 'We were amused with the phrase "Ye'll get that" in the Highlands, which appeared to us as if it came from a perpetual feeling of the difficulty with which most things are procured' (pp. 270–1). At an inn near Ben Lomond, when the travellers asked the maid to light us a fire: 'I dinna ken whether she'll gie fire', meaning her mistress. We told her we did not wish her mistress to *give* fire, we only desired her to let *her* make a fire and we would pay for it' (p. 249).

Dorothy's analysis of the Highlanders' power of speech drew on contemporary theories of language. 'Simplicity', 'conciseness', and 'strength' were the three attributes of discourse which the Scottish minister and rhetorician Hugh Blair singled out as criteria for sublimity in his *Lectures on Rhetoric and Belles Lettres* (1783). His prime examples came from the Scriptures and Milton. Dorothy shared Blair's enthusiasm for plain expressiveness. Her imagination was quickened by the strangeness of Erse, but she took equal pleasure in hearing English when it was spoken in a Scottish accent; and she was intrigued by the terse eloquence of Scottish people who had few English words. Admiring the cleanliness of one woman's house, Dorothy noted 'a bookishness, a certain formality in this woman's language' (p. 210); and remembering the owner of a boat near Glen Coe she observed that he 'spoke after a slow and solemn manner, in book and sermon language and phrases' (p. 311), like the leech-gatherer. William's view that in low and rustic life 'the essential passions of the heart find a better soil in which they can attain their maturity, are less under restraint, and speak a plainer and more emphatic language'[61] is repeatedly endorsed in *Recollections*. Remembering a conversation with two girls near Loch Lomond, Dorothy wrote: 'I think I never heard the English language sound more sweetly than from the mouth of the elder of these girls, while she stood at the gate answering our inquiries, her face flushed with the rain; her pronunciation was clear and distinct; without difficulty, yet slow, like that of foreign speech' (p. 279). The clarity and naturalness of the girl's voice stayed in her memory as a personal touchstone:

> At this day the innocent merriment of the girls, with their kindness to us, and the beautiful figure and face of the elder, come to my mind whenever I think of the ferry-house and waterfall of Loch Lomond, and I never think of the two girls but the whole image of that romantic spot is before me, a living image, as it will be to my dying day.   (p. 283)

Dorothy's romantic views on language fed significantly into William's poems about the Scottish tour. In 'To a Highland Girl', one of the first he composed after returning to Grasmere, he remembered the girl at Loch Lomond, paying tribute to her innocence and intelligence. Nurtured by the freedom of her life in the mountains, she conveyed her thoughts through the animation of her face, he claimed—an eloquent supplement to her 'few words of English speech'. He was drawn to her strength and independence, which epitomized Scotland's history of resistance to conquest: 'So have I, not unmoved in mind, | Seen birds of tempest-loving kind, | Thus beating up against the wind.'[62]

'Stepping Westward' also developed out of Dorothy's *Recollections*. The poem's starting point was a greeting delivered by a woman in a chance encounter by Loch Katrine: 'What, you are stepping westward?' It was a custom among the Highlanders, Dorothy observed, to use the points of the compass (rather than place names and local landmarks) to give directions: '[They] always direct you by east and west, north and south—very confusing to strangers'(p. 355). This custom presumably grew up because of the vastness of the terrain, the scarcity of roads, and the importance of the sun's rising and setting to the daily rhythm of work. In the first stanza, William pays tribute to the evocative power of spoken language by placing the opening salutation in quotation marks, and answering with the archaic 'Yea': this word has both a Scottish timbre and a biblical solemnity. The woman's voice seems to come out of nowhere—abrupt, but gentle and courteous—startling the travellers into a sense that their lakeside walk is part of a longer, more mysterious pilgrimage:

> The dewy ground was dark and cold;
> Behind, all gloomy to behold;
> And stepping westward seemed to be
> A kind of *heavenly* destiny:
> I liked the greeting; 'twas a sound
> Of something without place or bound;
> And seemed to give me spiritual right
> To travel through that region bright.
>
> The voice was soft, and she who spake
> Was walking by her native Lake:
> The salutation had to me
> The very sound of courtesy:
> Its power was felt; and while my eye
> Was fixed upon the glowing sky,
> The echo of the voice enwrought
> A human sweetness with the thought
> Of travelling through the world that lay
> Before me in my endless way.[63]

Here, at the end of the poem, the rhyme-words 'eye' and 'sky', 'lay' and 'way', echo the first stanza's end-rhymes 'yea' and 'destiny', their open vowels inviting the reader on a spiritual journey which leads simultaneously homeward and onward.

In 'The Solitary Reaper', it is again the sound of a human voice that prompts the poet's imaginings: 'Behold her, single in the field, | Yon solitary Highland Lass! | Reaping and singing by herself; | *Stop here, or gently pass*' (ll. 1–4; emphasis added). Our attention is initially drawn to the reaper through the ancient rhetorical address of *'siste viator'* (stop, traveller', traditionally used on Roman roadside tombs), which William translates into the vernacular. As the poem develops, epitaphic associations give way to intimations of immortality, for it is the sound of a *living* voice that fills the vale. The reaper's song initiates a series of associations which take the traveller and reader as far afield as the exotic East, then homeward again to the islands off north-western Scotland, surrounded by the bleak Atlantic Ocean:

> No Nightingale did ever chaunt
> So sweetly to reposing bands
> Of Travellers in some shady haunt,
> Among Arabian sands:
> No sweeter voice was ever heard
> In spring-time from the Cuckoo-bird,
> Breaking the silence of the seas
> Among the farthest Hebrides.[64]

Standing alone in a field by Loch Voil, the solitary 'lass' (William takes pleasure, as Dorothy did, in this homely Scottish word) is transformed into a symbol of the power of song to reach across the barriers of nationality and cultural difference. Recognizing that William's poem shared this deep communicative power, Dorothy made two copies of it within the course of a week, to send in letters to Lady Beaumont and Catherine Clarkson.

The solitary reaper's 'plaintive numbers' flow (as the Wordsworths' did in writing about Scotland) not only 'for old, unhappy, far-off things' but for 'some natural sorrow, loss, or pain, | That has been, and may be again' (ll. 18–24). The travellers' elegiac themes when remembering the tour were influenced not only by Scotland's turbulent past but by their

own orphaned consciousness. As they looked back on the latter part
of their travels through Dorothy's narrative, their preoccupation with
mortality was intensified by a more recent loss. Many of William's most
moving poems relating to Scotland were written, Fiona Stafford
observes, 'when the shock of John Wordsworth's death seemed to
demand an active recovery of buried strengths. Then perhaps, the Scottish journey, in many ways a pilgrimage to a land where the dead
seemed to live forever, rose up to offer remembered joys and profound
emotions, to confront the paralyzing effects of bereavement.'[65] Much
the same might be said of the last section of Dorothy's *Recollections*. Her
description of returning with William to the Trossachs marks the point
at which she resumed her narrative after John's death. The special quality of her prose arises from several kinds of revisiting: the literal return
of two travellers to a place they loved; the resuming of a narrative thread
after a lapse of time; and the remembering of a place in connection
with deep sadness that had intervened during composition. The first
readers of *Recollections*—Coleridge, the Hutchinsons, the Clarksons—
would have been more strongly aware than any subsequent audience of the
painful circumstances in which some of it was written. (Dorothy's decision
to include a 'memorandum' of John's death in her fair copy drew attention
to the effect of grief on her memories, alerting friends and family members
to the emotional undercurrents which ran through its last section.) In the
context of this bereavement, it is clear that communal recollection,
the symbiosis of William's poetry and Dorothy's prose, transformed the
Trossachs into a haunted place, the source of regenerative as well as elegiac
feelings.

Writing about Scotland coincided with joys in the Wordsworths'
family as well as sorrows, and both left their mark on the texture of their
writing. Dorothy noted in her fair copy of 'Stepping Westward' that it
was composed while she and William, together with 'little Dorothy'
(baby Dora, then fifteen months old) 'were walking in the green field,
where we used to walk, by the Rothay'.[66] The green valley with its river
is a recurring topos in their literary partnership, recalling, among other
contexts, their walk through the Wye valley in 1798, and these words
from Psalm 23, to which William had movingly alluded in 'Tintern
Abbey': 'though I walk through the valley of the shadow of death, I will
fear no evil: *For thou art with me.*' In 'The Solitary Reaper', John's death

is sombrely present in the figure of the reaper, but transfigured by the renewal that Dora's infancy brought into the Wordsworths' life. A great many associations with Dorothy and her namesake became attached to William's remembered encounters with Scottish women. In this way, shared memories of the Scottish tour became sources of 'the faith that looks through death', as well as a powerful aid to the 'soothing thoughts that spring | Out of human suffering'.[67]

1. The Wordsworths' birthplace, Cockermouth: old photo. By Permission of The Wordsworth Trust, Grasmere.

William Wordsworth
H. EDRIDGE, A.R.A.
1805.

2. Henry Edridge, William Wordsworth, pencil and watercolour, 1806. By Permission of The Wordsworth Trust, Grasmere.

3. Silhouette of Dorothy Wordsworth by an unknown artist, c.1806. By Permission of The Wordsworth Trust, Grasmere.

4. James Bourne, Esthwaite Water, watercolour. By Permission of The Wordsworth Trust, Grasmere.

5. Rev. Joseph Wilkinson, Windy Brow, on the river Greta, watercolour, 1795. By Permission of The Wordsworth Trust, Grasmere.

6. S.L. May, Racedown, Dorsetshire, pencil and wash, date unknown. By Permission of The Wordsworth Trust, Grasmere.

7. James Northcote, Samuel Taylor Coleridge, oil on canvas, 1804. By Permission of The Wordsworth Trust, Grasmere.

8. Coplestone Warre Bampfylde, View of the Severn from Quantock, near Alfoxton, pencil, ink and watercolour, pre-1791. By Permission of The Wordsworth Trust, Grasmere.

9. TM Richardson, View of Town End, watercolour, 1840s. By Permission of The Wordsworth Trust, Grasmere.

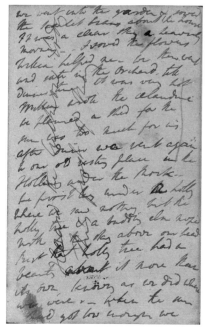

10. Page from Dorothy *Grasmere Journal*, 1 May 1802 (DC MS 19) 'The Cuckow today this first of May'. By Permission of The Wordsworth Trust, Grasmere.

11. Sir George Beaumont, Old Cottage at Applethwaite near Keswick, watercolour, 1803. By Permission of The Wordsworth Trust, Grasmere.

12. George Fennel Robson, Grasmere, watercolour, c. 1830. By Permission of The Wordsworth Trust, Grasmere.

13. Grasmere Rectory: old photo. By Permission of The Wordsworth Trust, Grasmere.

14. Thomas Creswick, Rydal Mount, oil on canvas, c. 1840–7. By Permission of The Wordsworth Trust, Grasmere.

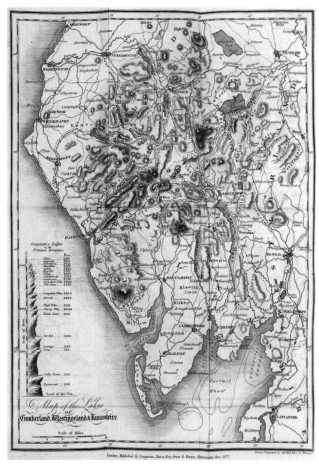

15. Rev. Joseph Wilkinson, Map of the Lakes of Cumberland Westmorland & Lancashire, 1810. By Permission of The Wordsworth Trust, Grasmere.

II

Grasmere and Coleorton

'Not in Utopia, subterraneous Fields,
Or some secreted Island, Heaven knows where,
But in the very world which is the world
Of all of us, the place in which, in the end,
We find our happiness, or not at all.'[1]

*

Whether we are reading 'Home at Grasmere' alongside the *Grasmere Journal*, or *The Prelude* alongside *Recollections of a Tour Made in Scotland*, we find the great Homeric motifs of wandering and returning home intertwined with the georgic theme of dwelling in a place of work. Increasingly, the Wordsworths distanced themselves from picturesque aesthetics and romantic tourism, finding their communal identity as writers who belonged to a local landscape and its working community. As William worked intensively on *The Prelude* in 1804, the perspective he brought to his memories of travelling on the Continent and living in France was that of a patriotic family man, permanently settled in Westmorland. Napoleon's rise to power had alienated him from the current regime in France. Although he recoiled from the French episode in his life, he did not, like Coleridge, disown his early republicanism; nor did he trivialize his relationship with Annette Vallon. Instead, he tried to understand the role of Continental travel (and his early enthusiasm for the French Revolution) as a formative stage in his developing consciousness. Wandering abroad in search of sublime prospects and Utopian communities, he had neglected the place where 'in the end | We find our happiness, or not at all'.[2] His task as a poet was to make amends.

Ever since receiving the Calvert legacy, William had understood his life as a form of honourable service predicated on the obligation to reciprocate a gift. His poetry was an expression of thanksgiving to the Lake District for fostering him in childhood and later providing him with a permanent home. If he wasted his talent, he would be, as he put it in January 1804, 'like a false steward who hath much received | And renders nothing back'.[3] The biblical word 'steward' (suggesting the parable of the talents in Matthew's Gospel) indicates how seriously he took his gift. *The Prelude* traces his education in spiritual terms, as a journey of error and self-recovery which leads eventually homewards. Ravished though he had been by the Alps as a young man, Book VI of his autobiographical epic gives less prominence to the sublimity of Mont Blanc, 'a soulless image on the eye', than to a peaceful field in the Vale of Chamonix:

> There small birds warble from the leafy trees,
> The Eagle soareth in the element;
> There doth the Reaper bind the yellow sheaf,
> The Maiden spread the haycock in the sun…
> (VI, ll. 462–5)

This harvesting scene—reminiscent of one of Bewick's georgic vignettes—could equally well be set in the Trossachs, or indeed in Grasmere. The pair of fellow-workers, one of each sex, might be viewed as an apposite emblem for William and Dorothy's cooperative labour. In *The Prelude's* overall structure the vignette signifies gratitude for the diurnal rhythms of rural life, making recompense for the barrenness of Alpine mountains and reconciling the poet to 'realities'.

William's deflation of Continental sublimity is central to *The Prelude's* moral design, highlighting his vocation as regional poet and his role as family man. At the expected climax of the epic's narrative, the crossing of the Alps, he remembers how he and Robert Jones had lost their way, inadvertently passing the correct route to the summit without noticing they had done so. The symbology of the lost wanderer recovering his true path is common in Protestant narratives and spiritual autobiographies. William redeploys it here to highlight the fundamental error tourists make in hunting for memorable experiences. These are not to be had by taking a particular route up a mountain, or standing in a particular station at its summit. They come unbidden, in the form of more mysterious and unforeseen encounters—'A leading from above, a something given'[4]—whose significance is apparent only in retrospect.[5] The moral lesson of Book VI emerges in the poet's acceptance that imagination consists in 'something evermore about to be' (l. 542). In a boldly patriotic gesture, his autobiography challenges the pre-eminence traditionally accorded to the Alps in the Grand Tour, relocating the true goal of his life's pilgrimage in Britain, at the top of Mount Snowdon. It was here, he tells us in Book XIII, that he found *spiritual* sublimity. Remembering the 'huge sea of mist' which transformed the landscape seen from the summit, he reflects on the 'sense of God' awakened in him by the 'homeless voice of waters' which rose through a gap in the vapours (XIII, ll. 60–65). 'Homeless', one of the most resonant words in his vocabulary, here connotes his identification with the voice of unseen mountain brooks, whose disembodied sound reaches him through the mist: a metaphor for his orphaned consciousness. The visual tenets of Romantic tourism are revised, and its central values displaced, by the distinctively moral tenor of his language. Words that belong to aesthetics—'admiration', 'delight', 'grand'—are drawn into the orbit of moral philosophy. Using 'Soul' and 'Imagination' as near-synonyms, the poet meditates on the way 'communion with the *invisible* world' leads to a deeper understanding of the transforming power of love (XIII, ll. 105–51; my italics).

During William's lifetime, *The Prelude* in its various forms became known in his family as the 'Poem to Coleridge', a title which acknowledged the poet's ongoing obligation to his friend. Coleridge was pressurizing him to dedicate himself wholeheartedly to *The Recluse*, a project he had sincerely promised to complete; but William's heart was unequally divided. In writing his autobiography, he showed that he had other promises to keep—with himself, his family, and the Lake District.[6] He read the first two books aloud to Coleridge before his friend left Grasmere for Malta in 1804. This recital, in its highly symbolic setting, confirmed the poem's role as a gift within a *regional* gift economy:

Wednesday, Jan 4th/In the highest & outermost of Grasmere, Wordsworth read to me the second Part of his divine Self-biography.[7]

Sacramental rituals of this kind, marking key moments in a long developing friendship, became embedded in *The Prelude*'s associative history and part of its communal life; for the 'Poem to Coleridge' was also the poem to Dorothy. Two dear companions sometimes overlapped or merged in the poet's digressions and apostrophes, reaffirming the three-way bond which had formed in the West Country during 1797–8. Coleridge's place as an honorary member of the Wordsworth household was thus reinforced by and through the poem, alongside Dorothy's central role as both sister and friend.

While William was busy working intensively on his autobiography during early 1804, Dorothy was absorbed in making fair copies of his shorter poems for Coleridge to take with him to Malta. Undertaking this onerous task required her to put *Recollections* to one side for the communal good; and in exchange—gift for gift—William paid tribute to her devotion in his autobiography. Dorothy's ongoing role as amanuensis gave an additional layer of significance to her place in *The Prelude*, for in November 1805, as she reported in a letter, she became 'engaged in making a fair and final transcript' of the entire poem.[8] Copying her brother's autobiography involved long, concentrated, and intense absorption in memories he had probably discussed with her many times; as well as conversations with her that were never recorded, and have passed into oblivion. The labour of transcription was an act of loving devotion to her brother, but not in any sense an act of subservience. Dorothy was contributing to the gift-economy of the household, and expressing her faith in William's ability one day to complete *The Recluse*, for which *The Prelude* served as a 'bond', or promissory note. Her scribal involvement in William's narrative made her an inmate of his thoughts. As she copied down his written tributes to her, they must have felt like intimate thanksgivings, not just loving acknowledgements. In this apostrophe from Book X, probably composed in December 1804, William described her guiding influence as beginning immediately after his return from France, when he had 'yielded up moral questions in despair'; and gave thanks for her companionable presence through an entire decade:

> then it was
> That the beloved Woman in whose sight
> Those days were passed, now speaking in a voice
> Of sudden admonition, like a brook
> That does but cross a lonely road, and now
> Seen, heard and felt, and caught at every turn,
> Companion never lost through many a league,
> Maintained for me a saving intercourse

With my true self; for, though impaired and changed
Much, as it seemed, yet I was no further changed
Than as a clouded, not a waning moon:
She, in the midst of all, preserved me still
A Poet, made me seek beneath that name
My office upon earth, and nowhere else.　　　*(Prelude,* X, ll. 907–20)

This long simile provides a history of Dorothy's accompanying and shaping influence on the poet's unfolding life. When William describes her as a 'companion never lost through many a league', is he picturing her as a woman walking with him on a road, or as a river that runs perpetually alongside him (he is the road), shaping his course and never allowing him to lose a sense of emerging direction? Gratitude for Dorothy, as so often in William's writing, means two things simultaneously: gratitude for her presence, a continuous state of being; and gratitude for the moral, intellectual, emotional, and spiritual influence which she began to exert on his life after their reunion in 1794. She enabled him, he says, to 'maintain' a connection with the 'true' self that had become impaired through long separation from her. She admonished him for taking a wrong turn—for changing from what he was—and she guided him back to his 'office' or vocation. The phrase 'made me seek' connotes her superior moral strength, to which he submitted gladly: it was her active intervention that helped him ground himself 'upon earth' through poetry.

'To make a gift of something to someone is to make a present of some part of oneself', Marcel Mauss observed.[9] As he brought *The Prelude* to a close in Book XIII, William expressed his gratitude to the people who had supported him thus far in his life and writing: Calvert, whose legacy had enabled him to become a poet; Coleridge, his 'joint labourer', soon to return from Malta and receive 'this Offering of my Love'; and Dorothy, 'Who ought by rights the dearest to have been | Conspicuous through this biographic verse' (XIII, ll. 340–1). His culminating apostrophe to Dorothy, 'Child of my parents! Sister of my soul!' (XIII, l. 211), associates her loving ministry with the homeward stretch of his epic journey toward self-recovery. Its figurative language is at once generic and local, evoking the Grasmere setting in which he writes, even as it suggests an allegory of his emotional development:

but for thee, sweet Friend,
My soul, too reckless of mild grace, had been
Far longer what by Nature it was framed,

> Longer retained its countenance severe,
> A rock with torrents roaring, with the clouds
> Familiar, and a favourite of the Stars;
> But thou didst plant its crevices with flowers,
> Hang it with shrubs that twinkle in the breeze,
> And teach the little birds to build their nests
> And warble in its chambers.   (XIII, ll. 227–36)

In identifying his former self with the 'countenance severe' of a mountain, he recalls 'There is an Eminence', composed soon after arriving at Town End. Dorothy had renamed the lonesome peak of Stone Arthur after William, humorously alluding to his love of solitude. Now an inmate of the vale, he felt a greater kinship with the 'little domestic slip of mountain' behind the cottage than with a distant summit. In William's extended simile, birds warbling in the 'chambers' of the rock face are metaphorically dwellers inside the home of his consciousness, and Dorothy is the spirit of awakening spring:

> When every day brought with it some new sense
> Of exquisite regard for common things,
> And all the earth was budding with these gifts
> Of more refined humanity, thy breath,
> Dear Sister, was a kind of gentler spring
> That went before my steps.   (XIII, ll. 241–6)

In 'Home at Grasmere' he had likened Dorothy's companionship to the diffusive presence of birdsong, light, music, breath: 'Where'er my footsteps turned, | Her Voice was like a hidden Bird that sang...' (ll. 109–10). Now, remembering that poem and its associated homecoming, he again gave thanks for her creative influence, imagining her one step ahead of him on the path.

*

During 1803–5—years that saw William's intensive work on *The Prelude*, the completion of Dorothy's *Recollections*, the birth of two children, and John's death—the family's attachment to Grasmere strengthened. They became more conscious of their inter-assimilation with the landscape, and more emotionally invested in their immediate surroundings. Although they did not own the cottage, it rewarded them with something akin to the security of possession. At the same time, they began to put out feelers beyond the vale. Soon after their return from Scotland, Coleridge's friend Sir George Beaumont, a painter and rich patron of the arts, gave them deeds for a plot of land in Applethwaite near Greta Hall. It was a generous gesture, designed to enable William to continue his 'high Calling' in closer proximity to Coleridge. Although the family had no desire to move, William accepted the gift graciously, promising that he would act 'as Steward of the land, with liberty to lay out the rent in planting, or any other improvement which might be thought advisable'.[10] Doubtless the gift's symbolism pleased him. At last he had become a member of the class of 'Statesmen' (freeholders) he so admired; and with this new status he gained the right to vote. In a sonnet which Dorothy copied out for him to send in a letter, he thanked Beaumont for the plot of land, and the opportunity to build 'A seemly cottage in this sunny Dell'.[11] Two months later, he received a further gift from Sir George—this time a drawing of Applethwaite Dell, featuring a 'Cottage, its dashing waters, and the corner of old Skiddaw'.[12] Beaumont's drawing, a much-cherished item in the Wordsworth household, hung above the chimney piece in the cottage at Town End for the remainder of their time at Grasmere. Corresponding to the archetypal image of home which William and Dorothy had carried with them since their exile from Cockermouth, it served as a symbolic expression of their nostalgia. The drawing's central placement was also a daily reminder of their *practical* need to find a permanent home. 'There is not a day in my life,' William confessed to Beaumont in December 1804, 'in which that exquisite little drawing of yours of Applethwaite does not affect me with a sense of harmony and grace which I cannot describe.'[13]

When Dora was born, in August 1804, the Beaumonts marked her christening with yet another gift, this time of money, which the Wordsworths saved to invest 'in planting a small plot of ground which is to be Dorothy's Grove, near our own house wherever we make our final settlement'. In her thank-you letter to Lady Beaumont, Dorothy took pleasure in foreseeing how her own role as steward of the environment would benefit Dora: 'if sun and wind prosper there they will be a shelter and a shade for her by the time she has lived twenty years, and who knows but they may be the nursery of her tenderest and best thoughts!'[14] Her letter reveals identification with her namesake. Figuring the trees as 'brethren' who will grow up alongside her niece, she subliminally recalls her own early childhood among brothers. Her pride in imagining Dora's future—'the trees are to be the Child's, *her own*' (emphasis added)—acknowledges the rarity of a girl being granted ownership of land.

There is no doubting that the 'little family of Love'[15] at Town End was extremely contented in the years leading up to John's death. It was a tight squeeze, but they could still fit into the cottage. Their 'final settlement' away from Grasmere, although still distant, was unavoidable, but they delayed moving. During the winter of 1804 they worked on a moss-hut at the top of the orchard: 'a place for my Brother to retire to for quietness on warm days in winter', Dorothy said; and 'a little parlour for all of us in the summer—It is large enough for a large party to drink tea in'.[16] On Christmas Day, William announced it was almost finished. 'We have lately built in our little rocky orchard a little circular Hut lined with moss like a wren's nest, and coated on the outside with heath', he wrote to Beaumont. In the same letter, he enclosed a 'dwarf inscription' describing this nest-like structure in terms reminiscent of his 1800 island inscriptions. The hut, he said, was 'No Pleasure-House forlorn' but rather 'A tributary Shed to chear | The little Cottage that is near'.[17] 'Come and see it, do come and see it if only for a fortnight', he urged John in a Christmas letter.[18] For months after John's death in February 1805, work on the moss-hut was suspended. It stood at the top of the orchard, like Michael's unfinished sheepfold: a symbol of dashed hopes and tragic loss. 'We see nothing here that does not remind us of our dear brother', William wrote to Southey, unable to contemplate the personal associations surrounding him.[19] Dorothy, writing to Jane Marshall, confessed the same: 'I can turn to no object that does not remind me of our loss. I see nothing that he would not have loved with me and enjoyed had he been by my side ... he loved our cottage, he helped us to furnish it, and to make the gardens—trees are growing now which he planted.'[20]

In the short term, bereavement took a heavy toll on the Wordsworths' attachment to their home, inseparably connected as it was with John's memory. But with time, the human history which steeped the place brought them solace and a sense of continuity. After a period of intensely creative work completing *The Prelude* and *Recollections*, they turned their minds back to domesticity. Together they set to rights the cottage and garden, which had 'fallen into disorder like other things'.[21] In the summer of 1805, the moss-hut was ready for use. 'We have summoned up our hearts and done everything', Dorothy wrote to Catherine Clarkson, 'and now we spend many sweet hours in this shed ... Oh my friend, we remember our Brother every moment of our lives, and begin even to feel in happiness how great a blessing the memory of him will ever be to us.'[22] Two letters sent independently to the Beaumonts in June mention their enjoyment of the moss-hut in its orchard setting. William's was written to Sir George on the 3rd, a fortnight after finishing *The Prelude*:

I write to you from the Moss-Hut at the top of my orchard, the Sun just sinking behind the hills in front of the entrance, and his light falling upon the
green moss of the side opposite me. A Linnet is singing in the tree above, and
the Children of some of our neighbours who have been today little John's
Visitors are playing below, equally noisy and happy; the green fields in the
level area of the Vale and part of the lake, lie before me in quietness.[23]

Listening to nearby sounds, and counting his blessings as a father, William
was however disturbed by the consciousness of party political strife and
warmongering that reached him through the news.[24] His letter moves on to
talk about Coleridge, and refers sadly to John's death. Before signing off, he
mentions completion of *The Prelude*, describing it as the 'portico' to *The
Recluse*—an architectural analogy which perhaps came to mind in connection with the completed 'tributary hut' where he was sitting. Dorothy's letter, written on the 11th, is more attuned to the nest-like quality of the hut.
Listening to the sound of birds after the rain, enjoying the warmth of the
enclosed space, and surveying the vale spread out before her, she figures the
entire landscape as a secure enclosure:

I write to you from the Hut, where we pass all our time except when we are
walking—it has been a rainy morning, but we are here sheltered and warm,
and in truth I think it is the sweetest place on Earth—the little wrens often
alight on the thatch and sing their low song, but this morning all the birds are
rejoicing after the rain. Before my eyes is the church and a few houses among
trees, and still beyond the hollow of Easedale which I imagine but cannot see,
and the quiet mountains shutting all up.[25]

Both writers, aware that their nesting instinct was connected with the
trauma of loss, reveal the satisfaction that grew out of completing projects
and repossessing time. But there remained the slower, ongoing work of
mourning. Dorothy's letter relates how, on Saturday 8 June, William had
brought himself to revisit Grisedale Tarn, where they had said goodbye to John
when he was last in Grasmere. 'We were in view of the head of Ulswater'
[*sic*], Dorothy remembered, 'and stood till we could see him no longer,
watching him as he *hurried* down the stony mountain. Oh! my dear Friend,
you will not wonder that we love that place.'[26] William wrote his elegy, 'I
only looked for pain and grief', in floods of tears. Using plural pronouns to
evoke an intensely communal memory, his poem was an important milestone
in the family's grieving process:

> Here did we stop, and here looked round
> While each into himself descends

For the last thought of parting Friends
That is not to be found.
Our Grasmere vale was out of sight,
Our home and his, his heart's delight,
His quiet heart's delicious home.[27]

Many places in the surrounding landscape were steeped in memories, but
Grisedale Tarn was the most painful.

*

Completing the moss-hut at Town End was not the only gardening project
William was involved in during 1805. In October he volunteered guidance
on Sir George Beaumont's plans for landscaping his extensive gardens in
Coleorton, Leicestershire. In a careful, detailed letter, he drew together some
of his and Dorothy's most strongly held environmental principles for the
benefit of their new friend. Condemning the 'age of improvement', his letter
advocates a relish for the simplicity he had championed in *Lyrical Ballads*—
'let Nature be all in all'—and celebrates the human community which gives
landscapes their meaning: 'Strip my Neighbourhood of human beings, and
I should think it one of the greatest privations I could undergo.'[28] These
were principles that could be applied anywhere, but William drew on lessons
learnt from the Scottish tour, as well as on local examples. His letter con-
trasts the sterile and dehumanised 'walks' at Blair Atholl—'without a blade
of grass or weed upon them, or anything that bore trace of a human footstep'[29]—to Lowther Woods, which had been dear to him since his reunion
with Dorothy in 1787. Revisiting them in the summer of 1805, he had met
country people 'posting to and from church' and two musicians playing the
hautboy and clarinet: examples of the community spirit that thrived in rural
places. The beauty of the woods, he anxiously noted, was now under threat.
Lord Lowther planned to create a 'manufactured walk' through the forest
ground, effacing 'the most beautiful specimen of a forest pathway ever seen
by human eyes, and which I have paced many an hour, when I was a Youth,
with some of those I best love'.[30] As a place, but also as an organizing metaphor for the companionship which gives meaning to place, the pathway was
rich in family associations. As well as the track worn by the Wordsworth
brothers in 'When first I journeyed hither', William here calls to mind the
twinned use of path and stream as figures for Dorothy's guiding spirit in *The
Prelude*. His description of the Lowther path develops into an extended
analogy, much as the river Derwent does in his autobiography: 'This path

winds on under the trees with the wantonness of a river or a living creature; and even if I may say so with the subtlety of a Spirit, contracting or enlarging itself visible or invisible as it likes.'[31] William welcomes the thought of the forest ground at Lowther 'wearing away' under the tread of successive feet because of the human history signified by walking: 'In a word, if I were disposed to write a sermon, and this is something like one, upon the subject of taste in natural beauty, I should take for my text the little pathway in Lowther Woods, and all which I had to say would begin and end in the human heart, as under the direction of the divine Nature conferring value on the objects of the senses and pointing out what is valuable in them.'[32]

William made a further visit to Lowther Woods with Dorothy in the autumn. We probably have the Beaumonts to thank for the existence of her travel journal, 'November, 1805', a self-contained account of the nine-day walking tour which culminated there.[33] 'We were as happy travellers as ever paced side by side on a holiday ramble', Dorothy wrote, enjoying a release from the demands of childcare in Town End.[34] Rather than going to Patterdale via Grisedale Tarn, they took the route over the Kirkstone Pass, 'Wm on foot, and I upon the pony, with Wm's greatcoat slung over the saddle-crutch, and a wallet containing our needments' (p. 413). Dorothy's journal emphasizes the sense of companionship which they sought, even on the bleakest heights. At the top of Kirkstone, where 'every scattered stone the size of one's head becomes a companion', they discovered the fragment of an old wall, which in this desolate, mist-shrouded setting reminded them of 'some noble monument of ancient grandeur' (p. 414). Stones, broken walls, and ruined buildings always spoke to the Wordsworths' yearning for human habitation. Years later, in 'The Pass of Kirkstone', William recaptured the desolation of this place where even the rushes seemed to 'sigh forth their ancient melodies'. His poem recoils from the terror of unpeopled solitude, preferring 'Lawns, houses, chattels, groves, and fields | All that the fertile valley shields'. Desolation had its uses though, eliciting a more thoughtful gratitude for community: 'Who comes not hither ne'er shall know | How beautiful the world below.'[35]

It was to just such a fertile valley that the Wordsworths descended after crossing the Pass. While staying with the Luffs in Patterdale, William 'pitched upon the spot where he should like to build a house better than any other he had yet seen' (p. 415). Through the good offices of his friend Thomas Wilkinson and the patronage of Lowther, he later acquired this plot.[36] Although nothing came of his plans to build on it, the purchase marked the beginning of a new, less Grasmere-centred phase in the family's relationship with the Lake District. As if empathizing with the spirit of the place, Dorothy's journal shows her curiosity about the local tales of human survival and suffering inscribed in its landscape. Travelling along the hilltops, she and William were impressed by a ruined chapel, not easily distinguishable from a sheepfold, to which a recent story attached. Here, the previous summer, an old man had taken shelter during a storm by 'laying turf and ling and stones in a corner of it from one wall to another', and thankfully survived over-night in this 'nest' (p. 418). His miraculous story ensured that the chapel was 'kept holy in the memory of some now living in Patterdale' (pp. 417–18). Dorothy's narrative dwells on the old man's lucky escape before alluding to a more ancient and tragic local tale. Twenty years earlier, two brothers had drowned on New Year's Day while skating on the ice at Brothers Water—the place taking its name from their tragedy. 'It is said that they were found locked in each other's arms' (p. 419). Doubtless William's poem 'The Brothers' came to mind; and how could the two siblings not think of the drowning in connection with John's recent death?

The Wordsworths reached Lowther Woods on 12 November. Walking here took them back in time, for they had explored these woods together in their teens. In Book VI of *The Prelude*, William remembered their sum-mer vacation rambles along the 'gentle banks | Of Emont', in the 'bye tracts' of their native region and all round Penrith. Dorothy, 'after separa-tion desolate | Restored to me', had seemed in 1787–8 'a gift then first bestowed':

> O'er paths and fields
> In all that neighbourhood, through narrow lanes
> Of eglantine, and through the shady woods,
> And o'er the Border Beacon and the Waste
> Of naked Pools and common Crags that lay
> Exposed on the bare Fell, was scattered love,
> A spirit of pleasure and youth's golden gleam.   (VI, ll. 239–45)

Perhaps alluding to these lines, Dorothy writes nostalgically in her 1805 journal about 'the very place which has been the boundary of some of the happiest of the walks of my youth... So vividly did I call to mind those walks, that, when I was in the wood, I almost seemed to see the same rich light of evening upon those trees which I had seen in those happy hours' (p. 420). Revisiting Penrith on the night of 12 November 1805, she remem-bered how 'Mary and her sister Margaret and I used to steal to each other's houses, and when we had had our *talk* over the kitchen fire, to delay the moment of parting, paced up one street and down another by moon or starlight' (p. 421). In this vivid memory of a happy female community, Dorothy's nostalgic pilgrimage reaches its end point. Building a connection with Mary, who was waiting at home for the travellers, her evocation of Penrith at night was like a keepsake for her sister-in-law, to commemorate their shared past.

*

Family life at Town End was child-centred during 1806, and even before the arrival of Thomas, Mary's third child, Dorothy observed that 'we are crammed in our little nest edge-full'.[37] In a letter revealing her attunement to seasonal rhythms and human rites of passage, she observed how Thomas's birth brought back memories of John's in 1803 'after such a clear and starlight night, the birds singing in the orchard in full assembly...the young swallows chirping in the self-same nest at the chamber window'.[38] With three children to look after, conditions in the cottage worsened, and the need to move became urgent. William was working on *The Excursion* through the summer; and he also succeeded in composing 'The Waggoner', reminiscent in some respects of Burns's 'Tam o' Shanter'. The mood of this poem reflected his affection for local people and places, commemorating settled domestic happiness in the passage describing the 'Rock of Names'. Much of Dorothy's time was taken up with childcare, so she didn't keep a journal; but she tried her hand at writing for the amusement of Johnny and Dora. 'Mary Jones and her Pet-Lamb' told the story of a little girl lost on the mountains and happily recovered by her parents. Inspired by the kind of accident that often happened in the vale, the story-line would not have been out of place in the *Lyrical Ballads*. In a lullaby, 'To my niece Dorothy, a sleepless baby', she captured the silence at Town End at night, when there was 'nothing stirring in the house | Save one wee hungry nibbling mouse'. Finally, in 'Address to a Child in the High Wind', she comforted her four-year-old nephew with a beautiful poem in rhyming couplets. It may have been intended as a companion piece to 'The Kitten and the falling leaves', a long poem composed by William for Dora when she was an infant, featuring the sounds of birds in the orchard—'Chirp and songs, and murmurings'[39]—and the movement of wind among the leaves. With its rollicking rhythm, Dorothy's poem also echoes William's 'A Whirl-Blast from behind the Hill' and 'The Barberry-Tree':

As soon as 'tis daylight tomorrow with me
You shall go to the orchard & there you will see
That he has been there, & made a great rout,
And cracked the branches, & strew'd them about.   (ll. 20-3)

William read both of Dorothy's recent poems to the Beaumonts on a visit
to Coleorton in April 1806. Although his sister disclaimed any pretensions
to authorship—'looking into my mind I find nothing there, even if I had
the gift of language and numbers, that I could have the vanity to suppose
could be of any use beyond our fireside'[40]—it is clear that William and Lady
Beaumont thought differently. Dorothy's identity as a writer was increasingly established within the circle, and William was helping to promote her
work. In due course, these poems would be published in his *Poems* (1815) as
'by a Female friend'.

Coleridge returned from his travels in 1806, irrevocably altered. During
his stay in Malta, lonely and homesick, he had succumbed to opium addiction and deep depression. As the Wordsworths worked to re-establish their
old intimacy with him, their new friendship with the Beaumonts strengthened. When the Leicestershire couple suggested they stay in the farmhouse
on their estate for eight months to escape the overcrowded cottage in Grasmere, they accepted gladly. While their hosts were away in London, the
Wordsworths enjoyed the comfort and space at Coleorton, with Coleridge
as their guest from late December till April. They repaid the Beaumonts'
hospitality by offering advice on designing and planting a Winter Garden on
the Coleorton estate.[41] Two surviving letters—one from William to Sir
George, the other from Dorothy to Lady Beaumont—show the symmetry of
this friendship. Both siblings made independent suggestions, and the garden
was a topic of discussion for the whole household that season. Dorothy took
as much pleasure in anticipating how it would look as if it was to be her
own.[42] The pattern changed in December, when William (at Lady Beaumont's invitation) submitted to her a long and minutely detailed design,
accompanied by a sketch of Dorothy's. Later on in their stay, William super-
intended work on the garden while his sister looked on admiringly: 'the plan
and I may say invention is entirely William's, and a beautiful picture or
romance it is; and when time has helped the work it will be a substantial
and true paradise'.[43] This project established his credentials as a professional
landscape designer, and six months later he was to lay out the gardens
at Allan Bank for their owner Mr Crump, a service of 'public benefit',
Dorothy thought.[44] William's relationship to the Coleorton garden sug-

gests a less hostile approach to property than he had previously shown. Family responsibilities brought with them an increasing sympathy towards the gentry he had once despised. In a letter to Sir George, he referred to his restless ambitions to find and transform a permanent place of his own: 'I have at least built five hundred houses, in five hundred different places, with garden, ground, etc.... but I have no house to cover me, and know not where to get one.'[45]

During Coleridge's stay at Coleorton, William read aloud *The Prelude* on a succession of evenings by the fireside, hoping the poem would correct his friend's despondency. He was rewarded with deep admiration and praise in Coleridge's answering poem, 'To William Wordsworth', but there was no disguising that the two men had moved apart. William was making no progress with *The Recluse*, which interested him only intermittently. On returning to Grasmere, he would briefly resume the theme of reclusion in 'The Tuft of Primroses', finding inspiration in the life of a fourth-century scholar and monk, St Basil. His narrative, prompted by Coleridge's recent company, evokes nostalgic memories of a time when the friends had shared their ideals. Basil, encouraged by his sister Macrina to practise self-denial, retires to wild mountain countryside near Annesi, where he founds a monastery. He succeeds in persuading his friend Gregory to join him there. Gradually the two monks attract an entire community of like-minded scholars, who devote themselves to a holy life of learning. The parallels with Pantisocracy, with the 1798 collaboration in Somerset, and with the group soon to become famous as the 'Lake Poets', speak for themselves. William, who became a regular churchgoer while at Coleorton, presumably hoped that his description of an exemplary monastic life would appeal to Coleridge. Town End was not, he implied, a haven where he was hiding away from his responsibilities but a place of serious dedication and communal work.

Meanwhile, however, the lyric poetry composed during the past five years showed how markedly William had diverged from the philosophical path Coleridge had mapped out for him. While still at Coleorton, he assembled his *Poems, in Two Volumes* (published in April 1807) with help from Dorothy and Sara Hutchinson, who made fair-copies to send off to the printer. This collection, more than any other, defined his identity as a poet of the domestic affections. Its organization may have been influenced by the Winter Garden project at Coleorton, for it is divided into compartments leading into each other. This enables a guided progression from homely lyrics to formal sonnet sequences in Volume One; and from poems composed during the Scottish Tour to 'Moods of my own Mind' in Volume Two, with a final compartment of miscellaneous poems, culminating in the great Ode 'Intimations of Immortality'. The volumes' shifts of perspective—from the miniaturized world of a cottage garden through to the grand vistas suggested by walking tours, political topics, and spiritual themes—suggest that William was structuring his poetic output so as to reflect its developmental integrity. The opening section of Volume One, which he intended to be subtitled 'The Orchard Pathway', contains many of the poems composed at Town End in 1802, and shows how strongly he grounded his poetic identity in the garden at home. A lyric for John is given pride of place on the first page, and the section contains numerous poems concerned with close members of his family and their circle: 'Louisa', a poem conflating Dorothy's attributes with those of Joanna Hutchinson; 'She was a phantom of delight', celebrating his marital love for Mary; 'To H. C., Six Years Old', addressed to Hartley Coleridge; 'The Kitten and the falling leaves', his couplets for Dora; and two lyrics associated with Dorothy and Mary: 'Among all lovely things my love had been', and 'I travell'd among unknown men'. The domestic subject matter of this section is balanced by more austere and public-spirited themes in 'Sonnets dedicated to Liberty', but overall the volume's register is intimate and familial. In Volume Two, the Scottish tour poems are followed by a central section devoted to nature poems composed in 1802, so the orchard at Town End features as a secluded spot to which readers return after poems about Rob Roy and Ossian. The inclusion of an excerpt from Dorothy's *Recollections* to introduce 'Stepping Westward' nicely acknowledges her collaborative presence.

The poet as family man was stamped all over *Poems, in Two Volumes*, and from its first reception onwards, readers have never been entirely comfortable with what in modern parlance would be called the 'feminine side' of William's public identity. When reviewers lambasted the collection, condemning its parochial subject matter and pedestrian verse, he took up a posture of indifference: 'My ears are stone-dead to this idle buzz, and my flesh as insensible as iron to these petty stings.'[46] But the criticisms hurt. Both he and Dorothy had anticipated a better reception for this Grasmere-centred volume in which their shared experiences at Town End and in Scotland had been immortalized. As the family returned to the cramped cottage in July 1807, their homecoming was further darkened by changes that had taken place in their absence: 'On our arrival here our spirits sank and our first walk in the evening was very melancholy', Dorothy wrote to Catherine Clarkson: 'Many persons are dead, old Mr Sympson, his son the parson, young George Dawson, the finest young Man in the vale, Jenny Hodgson our washerwoman … All the trees in Bainriggs are cut down, and even worse, the giant sycamore near the parsonage house, and all the finest firtrees that overtopped the steeple tower.'[47] The litany of familiar fireside names is doubly mournful in connection with the demise of so many trees. 'Ill word that laid them low— unfeeling Heart | Had he who could endure that they should fall!' So William protested in one of his saddest laments for the wanton destruction of a beautiful natural habitat:

> Ah what a welcome! when from absence long
> Returning, on the centre of the Vale
> I look'd a first glad look, and saw them not.
> Was it a dream! th'aerial grove, no more
> Right in the centre of the lovely vale
> Suspended like a stationary cloud
> Had vanish'd like a cloud—yet say not so …[48]

William, like Dorothy, associated the felling of trees with the human deaths that had occurred in the parish while they were absent. As his eye moved downward from the steeple of Grasmere Church it came to rest on five newly made graves in the churchyard. He vowed at a future date to tell 'the History of their un-ambitious lives' (l. 205), and true to his promise, their stories would eventually make their way into *The Excursion*, his poem of Christian consolation for the local dead. The Wordsworths' stay at Coleorton had strengthened not just their environmental principles but their religious faith, causing them to adjust their mental images of the vale. In 1800 it had been the cottage at Town End which brought the surrounding hills into focus. Now it was the church steeple, newly prominent because denuded of its 'aerial grove'. From this time forward, Grasmere church—'the last Central Home'—was to feature more and more clearly in their lives and writings.

12

The Lake District

'How closely the bonds of family connection
are held together in these retired valleys.'[1]

*

In 1808, a new stage arrived in the Wordsworths' collaboration as West-morland writers. The family's public role in their community emerged in response to the shocking tragedy of a local couple, George and Sarah Green, who died in the snow on 19 March. The Greens had been returning over the hills to their home in Easedale when they lost their way and perished overnight. Six of their eight children—all under the age of sixteen, one 'an infant at the breast'—waited patiently at home for two nights before raising the alarm. Writing to William on 23 March (he was visiting a sick Coleridge in London at the time), Dorothy tried to piece together the circumstances: 'They were probably bewildered by a mist before daylight was gone, and may either have fallen down a precipice or perished with cold.' Her letter communicates the agony of an entire neighbourhood as it waited for the search-party to find the bodies:

> many men went out to search upon the Fells. Yesterday between 50 and 60 were out, and to-day almost as many, but all in vain... Mary and I have been up at the house this morning, two of the elder daughters are come home, and all wait with trembling and fear, yet with most earnest wishes, the time when the poor creatures may be brought home and carried to their graves. It is a heart-rending sight—so many little, *little* creatures.[2]

The children's predicament touched the Wordsworths deeply. One of the Greens' daughters, Sally, had been working as a servant at Town End, so they knew her parents; but until catastrophe fell, they had not appreciated that hers was the poorest family in the vale. Although the Greens owned a small estate, it was heavily mortgaged; and the family had never received assistance from the parish. Their means had been reduced 'till scarcely anything but the Land was left'.[3]

Moved by Dorothy's letter, William encouraged her to write a narrative of the tragedy as part of a fund-raising effort to support the orphaned children. (The money would be used to place them with respectable local families, and to ensure that they were given a basic education.) Her account was circulated among friends under the title *A Narrative of George and Sarah Green*. Later, when pressed to publish the story more widely, she resisted, sensing the importance of protecting the children's privacy. William wrote (but did not publish) a poem about the tragedy as well as a brief prose account of it, partly based on Dorothy's *Narrative*, for the subscription book. During April, he sent off letters to influential friends appealing for donations. Mary was on the committee which organized the management of funds for the orphans.[4] The Wordsworths' joint effort amounted to an expression of sympathy for the children's bereavement, a practical gesture of help, and a political intervention. Rallying support for individual parish care, they implicitly condemned its alternative, the humiliating and impersonal workhouse system.

'Who weeps for strangers? Many wept | For George and Sarah Green.'[5] So begins William's poem about the tragedy—an epitaph in quatrains which boldly names the dead, immortalizing them like the folk heroes of ballad tradition. He appears to be questioning the limits of sympathy, much as Dorothy does when she observes, 'I cannot give *you* the same feelings that

I have for [the Greens] as Neighbours and Fellow-inhabitants of this Vale; therefore what is in my mind a full and living picture will be to you but a feeble sketch.'[6] For both writers the local character of sympathy was not just a fact of life but a measure of authentic feeling. Public benevolence seemed an empty abstraction when compared with the close ties that bonded human beings in the Vale of Grasmere. Dorothy's *Narrative*, 'Addressed to a Friend' (probably Joanna Hutchinson), shows her reaching out beyond her immediate neighbourhood to elicit sympathy. With conversational intimacy, she draws her readers into the Greens' tragedy as if it were a fireside story, much as the speaker does in 'Michael': 'You remember a single Cottage at the foot of Blentern Gill:—it is the only dwelling on the Western Side of the upper reaches of the Vale of Easedale, and close under the mountain...' (p. 143). We can see in her prose the shaping influence of William's 'local eclogues'.[7] She describes communal remembering, a process central to 'The Brothers' and 'Michael', as a fundamental principle of cohesiveness:

> It is, when any unusual event happens, affecting to listen to the fireside talk in our Cottages; you then find how faithfully the inner histories of Families, their lesser and greater cares, their peculiar habits, and ways of life are recorded in the breasts of their Fellow-inhabitants of the Vale.   (pp. 52–3)

With an eye for telling domestic detail that resembles Gaskell's in *Mary Barton*, Dorothy conveys a 'full and living picture' of ordinary lives in a small community united by grief. Her storytelling, economical and restrained, resists sensationalism. Local place names—Blentern Gill, Mill Beck, Dungeon Gill—root the tragedy in a familiar landscape. Dorothy gives circumstantial details of the Greens' poverty: the ageing cow; the meagre supply of food in the kitchen; the 'one oaken cupboard which was so bright with rubbing that it was plain it had been prized as an ornament and a treasure' (p. 55). Precise vignettes capture the family's varied responses to the aftermath of death. In the parlour where the coffins were placed, the younger girls 'gathered about the kitchen fire, partly amused, perhaps, by the unusual sight of so many persons in their house' (p. 54). Whereas the eleven-year-old Jane stepped immediately into her mothering role with a 'calmness amounting almost to dignity', the eight-year-old John Green stood at the funeral 'like a Statue of Despair' (p. 56). And all the while, as Dorothy notes laconically, the natural rhythms of life continued: '[Mary and I] went out of doors, and were much moved by the rude and simple objects before us—the noisy stream, the craggy mountain down which the old Man and his Wife had hoped to make their way on that unhappy night—the little garden, untilled—with its box-tree and a few peeping flowers' (p. 55).

Our faith in Dorothy's *Narrative* as an authentic chronicle makes the central drama all the more moving. We learn that the Greens' land, which 'had been in the possession of the Family for many generations', was now so heavily mortgaged that they would have lost it had they lived (p. 48). It was a poignant example of the predicament faced by many in the vale, including the Ashburners, whose story Dorothy had related in her *Grasmere Journal*.[8] Recalling 'Michael', Dorothy captures the intensity of the family's attachment to their smallholding: 'You will wonder how they lived at all; and indeed I can scarcely tell you. They used to sell a few peats in the summer, which they dug out of *their own hearts' heart, their Land*' (p. 49; my italics). Like William, she believed passionately in the importance of a settled connection with the land as the proper foundation for moral happiness: the virtuous character of the Green children had developed, she says, because their parents' employment was exclusively 'centred there', in the patrimonial fields. This kind of attachment would not be possible, she concluded, 'where people are only transitory occupants of the soil on which they live' (p. 75).

Bereavement, by eliciting fellow-feeling, provides the foundation for community; and the Wordsworths' own sorrows drew them into fellowship with their neighbours. The story of a pair of adults, dying in the snow and leaving their children orphaned, touched on two traumatic family memories. Their father, John Wordsworth, had died in December 1783 after being out all night without shelter on Cold Fell. Ann Wordsworth had died five years earlier, in March 1778. Dorothy's shocked identification with the Green family (parents and children alike) is palpable in a personal digression. She recounts an earlier, near fatal, experience of her own above Easedale Tarn, on the spot where George's and Sarah's footprints were discovered. She had left her brother at Stikell Tarn and was 'unable to see a yard before me, or to go a step further over the Crags':

> A mist came on after I had parted with him, and I wandered long, not knowing whither. When at last the mist cleared away I found myself at the edge of the Precipice, and trembled at the Gulph below, which appeared immeasurable. Happily I had some hours of daylight before me; and after a laborious walk I arrived home in the evening. (pp. 45–6)

On a literal level, the passage records Dorothy's feelings about a spot that is doubly charged with associations of danger and dread. But her figurative

handling of landscape distils her life story into a single spot of time, giving
a retrospective glimpse of the childhood trauma of bereavement. Separation
from William is followed by bewilderment and terror, then the relief of
reunion. She is remembering her brother as the boy looking round for his
'lost guide' in the 'Woman on the Hill' episode in *The Prelude*; and also his
standing on the edge of a 'huge sea of mist' in 'The Climbing of Snowdon'
(XI, l. 312; XIII, l. 43). Her associative imagination flickers between her own
memories of separation from him and two moments of isolation in his
autobiography.

In the final pages of the *Narrative*, Dorothy quotes from 'The Ruined Cottage' (newly reworked, with a Christian emphasis, for *The Excursion*), remembering the hold Margaret's story had on the Pedlar and the listening poet:
'I feel | The story linger in my heart... | ...my spirit clings | To that poor
Woman' (I, ll. 812–15). William's response to the Greens' tragedy was no less
empathetic. Writing to Richard Sharp in April, he captured the desolation of
the Greens' deserted house, which, he said, 'in its appearance and situation,
strikingly accords with the melancholy catastrophe: a brawling Brook close
by, and huge stones scattered on every side'. The building seemed to merge
with the identities of people who had once lived there, 'as if it had grown out
of the mountain, an indigenous Dwelling, for indigenous Inhabitants'(MY i,
230). Witnessing the children's bereavement doubtless stirred some of
William's traumatic early memories, but it also reopened more recent
wounds.[9] In his epitaph for the Greens, his figurative language suggests a
barely suppressed echo of the disaster which took his brother's life:

> Now do these sternly-featur'd Hills
> Look gently on this Grave;
> And quiet now is the depth of air
> As a sea without a wave...
>
> O Darkness of the Grave! How calm,
> After the living night,
> The last and dreary living one
> Of sorrow and affright![10]

Identifying with the stillness and quietness of the grave, William does not
dwell, as Dorothy does, on the plight of the Greens' orphaned children.
Instead, his poem focuses almost exclusively on the sacred bond of love
connecting George and Sarah, who were briefly separated in death but lay
undivided in Grasmere churchyard:

O sacred Marriage-bed of Death
That holds them side by side
In bond of love, in bond of God,
Which may not be untied![11]

By contrast, Dorothy's *Narrative* seeks consolation in the living web of relationships that survives (and is strengthened by) death. Written almost exactly thirty years after she and William lost their mother, the *Narrative of George and Sarah Green* may be read as her long-delayed answer to the 'Mathew' poems William had composed while in Germany in 1798. Just as he had recalled the positive benefits of fostering in tributes to his Hawkshead schoolteacher, so Dorothy finds solace for the Greens' tragedy in the households that gave the orphans a home:

> I must say that the general feelings have been purely kind and benevolent, arising from compassion for the forlorn condition of the Orphans and from a respectful regard for the memory of their Parents who have left in them a living example of their own virtuous conduct. (p. 73)

Dorothy dwells on the gentle humanity of John Fleming towards his eight-year-old namesake, observing that 'he took hold of him and patted his head as lovingly as if he had been his Grandfather, saying "Never fear, mun! Thou shalt go on the hills after the sheep!"' (p. 70). This sketch is of a piece with William's portraits of William Taylor in the 'Mathew' poems and old Walter Ewbank in 'The Brothers'. It offers compelling evidence of the adequacy of fostering: an experience the Wordsworths both remembered with gratitude. In this way, private and public consolations intermingle in Dorothy's response to William's encouragement 'to leave behind a record of human sympathies and moral sentiments, as they were called forth, or brought to remembrance, by the distressful event'.[12]

*

The cottage at Town End was home, but it had become unbearably cramped; and by 1808 the Wordsworths had reluctantly accepted that moving to a bigger house was a priority. (The Greens' tragedy occurred at a time when they could ill afford to make room for an extra member of the household; but they kept 'little Sally' Green on, as their personal contribution to the appeal.) William had been counting on the income from his long narrative poem *The White Doe of Rylstone* to fund their move. However, at the last minute, fearful of hostile reviews, he postponed publication, provoking an outburst from his sister: 'Without money what can we do? New house! New furniture! Such a large family! Two servants and little Sally! We cannot go on so another half-year.'[13] Although Dorothy recognized that poetry was first and foremost a vocation, William's reluctance to make it a lucrative profession had its disadvantages. In this case her brother's scruples won the day, but the incident is a reminder that she could sometimes spring into action as manager. ('Many & many a time have I been twitted by my wife and sister for having forgotten this dedication of myself to the stern law-giver', William was to observe in old age, drily alluding to his recurrent failure to live up to the resolutions he had made in his 'Ode to Duty'.)[14]

In the early summer of 1808, the Wordsworths moved from Town End to Allan Bank, a large Georgian villa overlooking Grasmere Lake, where William and Mary's fourth child, Catherine, was born in September (their fifth, Willy, following in May 1810). Dorothy took pleasure in the views eastward to 'the mighty mountains of Fairfield and Seat Sandal, now green to the very summits', but there was no disguising the fact that leaving Town End was a wrench: 'the dear cottage! I will not talk of it. To-day the loveliness of the outside, the laburnums being in the freshness of their beauty, made me quite sad—and all within, how desolate!'[15] A year later, Thomas De Quincey, who would be its next occupant, arranged that Dorothy should oversee preparations for his arrival. Throughout the summer of 1809, she and Sara made regular visits: 'It is quite a pleasure to go down to the old spot and linger about as if we were again at home there', she wrote on 6 May: 'Yesterday I sat half an hour musing by myself in the moss-hut, and for the first time this season I heard the cuckow there.'[16] Her nostalgia was intensified by anxieties about the destruction of woodlands, which she was witnessing on a daily basis in the vale. Under Nab Scar, 'trees of centuries growth inrooted among and overhanging the mighty crags' had been levelled: 'There is no other spot which we may have prized year after year that we can ever look upon without apprehensions that next year, next month, or even tomorrow it may be deformed and ravaged.'[17] While the vested interests of local gentry—Mr North, Lady Fleming—were spoiling the local landscape, the orchard at Town End remained a paradisal refuge. After De Quincey moved into Town End, Dorothy continued to think of the place longingly: 'we have now almost a home still, at the old and dearest spot of all'.[18] Two years later, when he polled the ash tree and cut down the hedge all round the orchard—'every Holly, Heckberry, Hazel, and every twig that skreened [*sic*] it'—Sara Hutchinson reported that Dorothy was 'so hurt and angry that she can never speak to him more'.[19]

During their two years at Allan Bank, the Wordsworths were intermittently living under the same roof as Coleridge, who had embarked on a new periodical, *The Friend* (with William and De Quincey as collaborators), but soon found himself flagging. Dorothy's letters during this period give a lively picture of comings and goings in the household: child-rearing and attending to Coleridge's needs being intermixed with intense creative activities. As Coleridge struggled with his unrequited love for Sara Hutchinson and moved to and fro between London, Keswick, and Grasmere, his friendship with the Wordsworths deteriorated. This prepared the way for the terrible rift of October 1810, which lasted for two years and never entirely healed. Despite emotional tensions (and chimneys which smoked intolerably), William was productive, publishing three important prose works in quick succession before returning to work on Book V of *The Excursion* in the winter.[20] Disappointed with the reception of *Poems, in Two Volumes*, he wrote his outspoken political essay *The Convention of Cintra* for *The Friend* in 1809, then turned his mind to more familiar subjects. The Greens' tragedy may have played a part in crystallizing his thoughts on how the dead should be memorialized, preparing the way for his *Essays on Epitaphs*. Here he reached back into memories of John's death, and behind that his parents', drawing together ideas about language, mortality, and commemoration that had been gestating since the Scottish tour. In 'Michael' and 'The Brothers', he had celebrated a rural community in which stories of the local dead were told by the fireside. The *Essays* explored the possibility of a transparent language that would transmute individual or local grief into something universal. The concern to connect the particularities of an individual life with general truths arose from a need to answer the charge of insularity which had been levelled against him in reviews of his poems.

There was nothing insular in either the *Convention of Cintra* or *Essays on Epitaphs*; but the impulse behind *Guide to the Lakes* was defiantly regional. First published anonymously, to accompany illustrations by the artist Joseph Wilkinson, it appeared in 1810 under the title of *Select Views in Cumberland, Westmoreland, and Lancashire*. Written from a hill rather than a vale, the book ranged more widely than the Grasmere-centred poems of 1800–2, encompassing a grand survey of Lakeland scenery, as well as of its inhabitants' ways of life. The term 'prose poem' is suggestive as a way of understanding the differences between its rolling periods, grand effects, smooth transitions, and the more intimate, informal prose of Dorothy's journals. Even so, it was an expression of the Wordsworths' shared environmental beliefs and aesthetic principles. In a letter of November 1810, Dorothy observed that William had just employed her 'to compose a description or two for the finishing of his work for Wilkinson';[21] and doubtless her conversation fed into the book's composition throughout.

The target audience for *Select Views* was the tourists who were flocking to the Lakes as an alternative to travelling abroad. Just as in *The Prelude* William had dismissed a purely visual understanding of beauty as superficial—the eye being 'the most despotic of our senses' (XI, l. 174)—so now he implied that tourists were too easily satisfied with viewing picturesque prospects: 'It is upon the *mind* which a traveller brings along with him that his acquisitions . . . must principally depend' (*Guide to the Lakes*, p. 98). The book is less a guide than homage to the Lake District, celebrating the 'ennobling interchange' between the region and the shepherds who lived and worked there. As in 'The Brothers' and 'Michael', William extols the virtues of 'the humble sons of the hills' who 'had a consciousness that the land, which they walked over and tilled, had for more than five hundred years been possessed by men of their name and blood' (p. 74). Until sixty years ago, 'a community of shepherds and agriculturalists, proprietors, for the most part, of the lands which they occupied and cultivated', had lived in equality.[22] Recent methods of manufacture, however, had reduced the independence of this 'republic':

> The lands of these *statesmen* being mortgaged, and the owners constrained to part with them, they fall into the hands of wealthy purchasers, who ... erect new mansions out of the ruins of ancient cottages, whose little enclosures, with all the wild graces that grew out of them, disappear.   (p. 92)

Although there was no way of reversing the destruction of the subsistence farming community, there was still time to arrest the environmental damage that was following in its wake. William set out to protect the Lake District from the depredations of newcomers who whitewashed buildings and put up pretentious new villas. He warned strongly against the defacement of local beauty which would surely follow as the Lake District fell 'almost entirely into the possession of gentry, either strangers or natives' (p. 92). Plantations of conifers were threatening the varied unity of natural woodland. William inveighed against them, as Dorothy had done in the grounds of Blair Atholl in 1803. The natural beauty of the Lake District was inseparable, to their way of thinking, from its long history of organic evolution.

If woodlands were evidence of 'the fine gradations by which in Nature one thing passes into another' (p. 79), so too were the subtle, permeable borders separating arable and pasture land from the fells. Lake District architecture told the same story. Whereas newcomers were increasingly building white-washed houses prominently, so as to optimize their views, older-established farmhouses nestled into sheltered places, camouflaged by their subdued colours among the surrounding rock and bracken. In this way, they became 'gently incorporated with the works of Nature' (p. 86).

Select Views has been identified as a founding text of modern environmentalism. Its figurative language reveals how closely the Wordsworths' ecological concerns were bound up with the history of their resettlement in the region. Several of the metaphors used to describe organic processes of interaction, such as 'incorporate' and 'intermixture', might apply equally well to their cooperation as regional writers. William and Dorothy were 'indigenous' siblings, whose cohabitation attached them more securely to their origins. The intermingling of their writings followed an organic pattern, producing a natural unity. *Select Views* contains many echoes from, allusions to, and associative connections with their shared work. A number of passages bear the imprint of Dorothy, or of ideas they discussed so closely and so often that it would be difficult to identify who originated them. Some have a figurative dimension over and above their immediate aesthetic content. Take, for instance, the discussion of the roofs and sides of houses:

> These dwellings, mostly built ... of rough unhewn stone, are roofed with slates, which were rudely taken from the quarry before the present art of splitting them was understood, and are, therefore, rough and uneven in their surface, so that both the coverings and sides of the houses have furnished places of rest for the seeds of lichens, mosses, ferns, and flowers. Hence buildings, which in their very form call to mind the processes of Nature, do thus, clothed in part with a vegetable garb, appear to be received into the bosom of the living principle of things, as it acts and exists among the woods and fields.   (p. 71)

The gradual naturalization of rooftops and walls is in itself a powerful symbol of environmental symbiosis; but there is also a connection, here, with the imagery William used in *The Prelude* to describe Dorothy's influence on his own creative life:

> But thou didst plant its crevices with flowers,
> Hang it with shrubs that twinkle in the breeze,
> And teach the little birds to build their nests
> And warble in its chambers.   (XIII, ll. 233–6)

Streams, too, take on a partly figurative resonance in the *Guide* because they are so often connected with Dorothy in William's poems. He sees streams (like paths and lanes) as 'an ever ready guide', leading the nature-lover into 'all the recesses of the country, so that the hidden treasures may . . . be laid open to his eyes' (p. 72). Their fluid, winding properties connote a 'wise passiveness' that is open to emerging knowledge.

*

A year after the anonymous publication of *Select Views*, the Wordsworths—together with Sara Hutchinson, now a permanent member of the household—moved from Allan Bank with its smoking chimneys to Grasmere Rectory, a damp house in the village. Here, the quiet stability of relationships in the household was put to a severe test by two shocking family bereavements. In June 1812, four-year-old Catherine died from convulsions. William and Mary were away from Grasmere at the time, so it was left to the omnicompetent Dorothy to arrange for her burial in their absence. This terrible blow was followed all too speedily by the death of Thomas, aged six, in December of the same year. Mary was inconsolable, and the tragedy of the children's deaths might have permanently damaged a less resilient family, but not this one. William's tenderness and physical passion for his wife had already become apparent in love letters that passed between them while they were apart during 1810.[23] That their mutual attachment strengthened in the aftermath of tragedy was in part thanks to Dorothy's tireless sympathy. 'It would have pitied the hardest heart to witness what he has gone through', she wrote of her brother, relieved that in January 1813 he turned back to *The Excursion* for therapeutic release. He began by adding lines to the Solitary's narrative in Book III: some of the details allude to the Wordsworth family's bereavement, and composition was rapid, suggesting a rush of eloquent grief.[24] *The Excursion*'s theme of 'Despondency Corrected' took on an urgent relevance as the family came to terms with their loss, making this a poem of private consolation as much as a public articulation of their deepening Christian faith. In Book VI, most of which had been drafted by the end of 1812, William had described a graveyard where death and life are interwoven. These lines, recalling 'The Brothers', were appropriate to the Wordsworths' predicament:

> Green is the Church-yard—beautiful and green;
> Ridge rising gently by the side of ridge:
> A heaving surface—almost wholly free
> From interruption of sepulchral stones,

And mantled o'er with aboriginal turf
And everlasting flowers. These Dalesmen trust
The lingering gleam of their departed Lives
To oral records and the silent heart;
Depository faithful, and more kind
Than fondest Epitaphs.   (VI, ll. 621–30; E, 211)

From Grasmere Rectory, the Wordsworths looked out each day towards the graves where Thomas and Catherine were buried. Despite their trust in the comforting power of communal memory, this daily reminder of the children's deaths became too painful to bear. In 1813, having decided a further move was essential, they embarked on a new life at Rydal Mount, two miles from Grasmere. Leaving behind the rectory and its associations, they trusted that in this new setting they would find 'the life where hope and memory are as one'.[25]

Their instincts were right. Keen as always on the outdoor life which nourishes health and creativity, the family came to love the substantial house overlooking Ambleside which was to be their home for the next forty years. Enjoying views of Wansfell to the south-east—and westward, beyond Rydal Water, to Silver How—they took pleasure in its large hillside gardens, lovingly developed by William. Here he built a terrace where he could walk to and fro composing poetry, and a moss-hut like the one at Town End to symbolize the continuity of the family's local attachments. Although their unpretentious way of life continued much as it had in Grasmere, this new situation (away from village life and close to Rydal Hall) brought them into contact with the Ambleside gentry: a novelty that Dorothy greeted apprehensively. 'The simplicity of the dear Town End Cottage comes before your eyes', she wrote to Catherine Clarkson, 'and you are tempted to say "are they changed, are they setting up for fine Folks? for making parties—giving Dinners etc etc?"'[26] Her wariness proved well founded, for William's obligations to his patron, Sir William Lowther, heralded a shift in the family's political and class affiliations.

During their early adulthood, the name Lowther had been synonymous for the Wordsworths with the greed and selfishness they had experienced at the hands of 'Wicked Jimmy', the first Earl of Lonsdale. They knew themselves to be in kinder hands when his distant cousin and successor, Sir William, restored their rightful inheritance in 1803. The family's gratitude toward Sir William had been growing over the years with further signs of his generosity. He helped them to purchase Broad How in 1806, and in

1813 his influence secured for William the post of Distributor of Stamps throughout Westmorland, Whitehaven, and parts of Cumberland. In return, William campaigned on Lowther's political behalf. This new relationship played an important part in healing the breach between the two families. As William found his way back into the Lowther fold, he was following the path of his father and grandfather, both of whom had worked as attorneys for the Lowthers. Defending the interests of the landed gentry was not his prime motive. The work he did on Sir William's behalf was consistent with his instinct to work as a custodian of the Lake District, a region he perceived to be under threat from the depredations of nouveau riche offcomers. His political allegiances shifted as he grew older, but he was consistently driven by a responsibility to honour 'the filial bond of nature' that connected his family to their native region. There were local examples aplenty of 'false stewards' who took from their environment without giving back to it. (James Lowther, who hoarded his resources, cheating his loyal servant and exploiting the land, was a case in point.) True stewardship, as William saw it, involved taking care of the land *without owning it*—a service his father and grandfather had faithfully performed. In a symbolic sense, this notion of faithful stewardship forms the ethical backbone of Christian environmentalism: Man's duty is to serve God by taking good care of the earth's resources, regarding them not as possessions or entitlements but as wondrous gifts, carrying responsibilities. Increasingly, William's actions and writings came to embody this system of belief.

*

The diarist Henry Crabb Robinson told Charles Lamb in November 1816 that he 'never saw a man so happy in three wives' as William. This characteristically warm, witty, and generous remark gives us an insight into the household at Rydal Mount four years after Thomas and Catherine's deaths. Much had been done to distract the family from their grief; but although they showed no signs of regretting their acceptance among the gentry, they paid a high price for this new way of life. William's vigorous electioneering commitments inevitably consumed much of his attention; and further calls on his time came with his acceptance of the post of Distributor of Stamps— a job which took him away from home for long stretches, altering the balance of the household and reducing opportunities for creative collaboration. During the first few years after moving, he composed very little new material. However, poems that had been in the pipeline for a while soon began to appear in print. In 1814 (while he was on a brief tour of Scotland with Mary), *The Excursion* was published, and a year later his *Poems* (1815) in two octavo volumes. This was followed almost immediately by *The White Doe of Rylstone*, which Dorothy had been pressurizing him to publish for years.

Rydal Mount did not prompt a sequence on the naming of places, as Town End had done; for the area immediately surrounding the house was already familiar. However, in 1818–19, William gathered together a number of sonnets he had been writing over the years about the river Duddon, publishing it in 1820 as an itinerary sequence. (No original drafts survive. Mary made a fair copy of twenty-one of the thirty sonnets in a small quarto notebook at the end of 1818; the remainder appear in other notebooks.)[27] The poems revisit in memory places he had been familiar with in his youth, as well as others he had come to know through more recent trips. Seeking 'the birth-place of a native Stream',[28] his sequence traces the Duddon's progress from the highest point of Wrynose Pass (almost 1,300 feet above sea level) down to the village of Seathwaite; from there to Broughton-in-Furness (where he had sometimes stayed during his university vacations), and so to the Duddon Estuary and the Irish Sea. Each sonnet represents a 'station' or stopping-place for observation and reflection on local people, places and customs. Taken as a unified whole, the sequence is an experiment in topographical writing akin to *An Evening Walk*, both in the regional pride it expresses and its handling of the riverside journey as metaphor.

In choosing to write about the Duddon, William aligned himself with a well-established eighteenth-century tradition. Streams and rivers, named and unnamed, had often been used in English poetry as metaphors for the rhythmic flow of music, memory, and time. Many contemporaries and predecessors—including Thomas Gray, Anna Seward, William Lisle Bowles, Mark Akenside—had combined the revisit genre with the river theme. Others before them, such as Drayton in *Poly-Olbion*, had celebrated their national pride by naming and praising rivers. 'The power of waters over the minds of Poets has been acknowledged from the earliest ages', William observed in his Postscript to *The River Duddon*, giving Virgil's *Georgics* as an example, along with this simple Scottish quatrain:

> The Muse nae Poet ever fand her
> Till by himsel' he learned to wander.
> Adown some trotting burn's meander,
> AND NA'THINK LANG[29]

In 1798, Coleridge had chosen this very quotation from Burns as an epigraph for *The Brook*, a projected poem which had preoccupied him in Somerset as a possible medium for reflection 'on nature, men, and society'. His plan for the poem—as ambitious in scope as *The Prelude* or *The Recluse*—had been to trace the progress of Alfoxden stream, starting with the source known as Lady's Fountain in Danesborough Hill, and following it out to the sea. Recalling the project in *Biographia Literaria*, Coleridge felt that it gave 'equal room and freedom for description, incident, and impassioned reflections':

> Such a subject I conceived myself to have found in a stream, traced from its source in the hills among the yellow-red moss and conical glass-shaped tufts of bent, to the first break or fall, where its drops became audible, and it begins to form a channel; thence to the peat and turf barn, itself built of the same dark squares as it sheltered; to the sheep-fold; to the first cultivated plot of ground; to the lonely cottage and its bleak garden won from the heath; to the hamlet, the villages, the market-town, the manufactories, and the seaport.[30]

Originally, Coleridge's impressions of Alfoxden stream had been recorded in his 1798 Notebook while in the Wordsworths' company. His later formulation of the plan in *Biographia* brought vividly onto the page his memories of a familiar, deeply loved valley in the Quantocks, which he had explored with his friends. The beautiful intricacy and richness of his description resembles Dorothy's journals, reminding us of the habits of minute observation they had in common. *The Brook* had remained unwritten, like *The Recluse*, but its fluvial analogy for moral development and human progress had organized *The Prelude*, and William returned to this analogy explicitly when writing his *River Duddon* sonnets.[31] Seeing the continuing relevance of *The Brook* to *The Recluse*, he transferred Coleridge's original Somerset plan to the Duddon Valley. He was not plagiarizing Coleridge's idea, he felt, so much as choosing to develop a genre of moral topography which had its origins in communal creativity. Hauntingly, he presented his sequence to the public as a gesture of recognition to his friend across the years of their estrangement: 'There is a sympathy in streams: "one calleth to another."'[32]

Community, communal memory, and regional identity are the central themes of William's sonnet sequence. The Duddon ran along the boundary between the old counties of Westmorland and Cumberland, and in following its progress he connected his identity as a Westmorland writer with his Cumberland origins. In a note, he identified the river's source at a point of intersection between the three separate Lake District counties in which he had lived as infant, schoolboy, and man. His intention, motivated by gratitude, was to 'dignify the spot' of their interconnection:

> It is with the little river Duddon as it is with most other rivers, Ganges and Nile not excepted, —many springs might claim the honour of being its head. In my own fancy I have fixed its rise near the noted Shire-stones placed at the meeting point of the counties Westmoreland, Cumberland and Lancashire. They stand by the wayside on the top of the Wrynose Pass, and it used to be reckoned a proud thing to say, that by touching them at the same time with feet and hands one had been in the three counties at once. At what point of its course the stream takes the name of Duddon I do not know.[33]

William's sonnets paid homage to this 'cradled Nursling of the mountain',[34] associating it with centuries of Lake District history (and even prehistory), into which his own life had been quietly subsumed. The imagined tour takes place in the course of a single day. Although the poet is solitary, there is a sense of companionship throughout—not just with the river itself, but with the local inhabitants he stops to observe, and people he remembers from his youth: 'friends and kindred tenderly beloved; | Some who had early mandates to depart' (XXI, ll. 3–4). At Seathwaite stepping-stones, he imagines a pair of local lovers negotiating the river's turbulence (X); and at Pen Crag, he looks down towards a peaceful scene in Dunnerdale, 'with Dwellings sprinkled o'er, | And one small Hamlet, under a green hill' (XIII, ll. 1–2). Seathwaite chapel prompts gratitude for the endurance of Protestant faith in a small Lakeland community (XVIII), and 'Sheepwashing' commemorates the peaceful cooperation of the river with the farmers who live and work beside it.

The dignified lives of ordinary people had inspired William in 1800 to write his 'local eclogues' for *Lyrical Ballads*; and in 1814 to publish his 'Narratives of calm and humble life' in *The Excursion* (VIII, l. 6; E, 259). So too, they had prompted Dorothy to chronicle the 'inner histories of Families' in the *Grasmere Journal* and the *Narrative of George and Sarah Green*.[35] Thinking about the obscure lives of Dalesfolk in *The River Duddon*, William drew attention to the human history the river had witnessed—the 'glad meetings, tender partings' of unidentified lovers (XXVIII, l. 11); the deeds performed by 'the loyal and the brave' whose names had never made it into song. Praising the innumerable dead, 'who lie | In the blank earth, neglected and forlorn' (XXIX, ll. 9–10), he made restitution for their unrecorded lives in his homage to their 'native stream'. For an audience that was recovering from the Napoleonic wars and consciously taking pride in Englishness, the passionately regional emphasis of the Duddon Sonnets was instantly appealing, and ensured their 'wonderful popularity'.[36] William highlighted the Christian tenor of the sequence in his introductory poem about the local minstrels whose custom it was to go their rounds at Christmas time, playing outside people's houses. He saw this and other ceremonies (such as rush-bearing in the summer) as important rituals binding members of the local community together. He addressed this opening poem to Christopher Wordsworth, the brother with whom he had shared a notebook while at Hawkshead, and who had planned one day to write a poem in praise of the North. Christopher, now a settled southerner, had recently been appointed Master of Trinity College, Cambridge, and in addressing him William was writing as one member of the establishment to another across the North/South divide. Respectful of the 'choice' that had taken Christopher from his 'native hills', he reminded his absent brother of the bonds of kinship and loyalty which still connected him to the Lake District, if only through memories of childhood. 'The greeting given, the music played | In honour of each household name' were more than usually important, he implied, in a family that had been scattered in different directions far too early.[37]

When the sonnets appeared in print, they were accompanied not only by a second edition of 'Topographical Description' (the prose written by William for *Select Views*), but also by a prose memoir of the Reverend Robert Walker, a notable pastor of Newfield church in Seathwaite, who had been greatly loved for his work as a schoolteacher and parish priest. William's memoir paid tribute to his thrift and industry, his honoured place in the community, and his fondness for 'old customs and usages'.[38] Walker's exemplary Christian life was in keeping with the moral tenor of the Duddon sonnets, providing evidence of the 'little, nameless, unremembered acts | Of kindness and of love' that are the foundation of community.[39] William's choice of commemorative prose as an accompaniment for his homage to the Duddon was significant, acknowledging that a medium often regarded as the inferior relative of verse might be 'the acknowledged voice of life'. This act of recognition had its parallel in the Wordsworth household, where William's poetry and Dorothy's prose had been commingling over the course of many years.

*

William often likened creativity to the movement of rivers or streams, and just as frequently associated the 'voice' of waters with communal origins or shared homecomings. When he first drafted the sonnet which appears as XXVI in the Duddon sequence, he began it with the line 'Dear Native brooks' and wrote it (probably with the river Derwent in mind) as a tribute to his Cumberland origins. By requisitioning the poem for his later sequence, he acknowledged that brooks—whatever their name, history, and geographical location—had also a *personal* meaning, to which he was 'bound . . . by a tender chain'.[40] It was as if he imagined them flowing from one place and time to another, changing their names but always performing the same 'function' (a word which resonates in the final line of 'After-Thought', the concluding sonnet in this sequence). From 1798 onwards, a familial theme kept recurring in this pattern of identification. When evoking the tranquil, nurturing voice of the Wye in 'Tintern Abbey', William had subliminally linked it with memories of the Derwent, and with his sister's companionship: 'How oft, in spirit, have I turned to thee | Oh sylvan Wye! Thou wanderer through the woods, | How often has my spirit turned to thee!' (ll. 56–8). Exiled in Germany with her during 1798, he repeated this association, recalling how the Derwent's 'ceaseless music' used to fill their childhood home at Cockermouth, its steady cadence tempering 'Our human waywardness' much as the Wye had done.[41] Once resettled in the Lake District, streams in and around Grasmere Vale provided daily reminders of restorative homecoming and companionable belonging. In 1800, William linked Dorothy with the brook which ran 'with a young man's speed' beside him up Easedale to 'Emma's Dell'—'my other home, | My dwelling, and my out-of-doors abode';[42] and in 1802 he immortalized a nameless 'trickle' near Ambleside, associating it with their shared pilgrimage to Windy Brow eight years earlier. Dorothy herself, grateful to be an 'inmate' of the vale, used a 'foaming streamlet' as a poetic figure for her glad arrival in Grasmere, a signal that her association with brooks had become a habitual trope in the household. The ever-increasing abundance of rivers, streams, and fluvial metaphors in William's poetry suggests Dorothy's ubiquitous presence in his thoughts, memories, and creative processes. In *The Prelude* Book X, he observed that her influence on him had at one time seemed like 'a brook | That does but cross a lonely road'; whereas now she was 'seen, heard and felt, and caught at every turn, | Companion never lost through many a league' (ll. 910–13). The emphasis William increasingly placed in his writings on what Karl Kroeber has called 'ecological holiness' was deeply indebted to the role Dorothy played in his life.[43] He saw her influence in emotional terms: as a restoring of intuition to the meddling intellect, which had led him astray in his quest to understand the grounds of 'moral happiness'. More and more, he identified her as the human embodiment of a spiritual strength which he had formerly associated with the river Wye:

> The anchor of my purest thoughts, the nurse,
> The guide, the guardian of my heart, and soul
> Of all my moral being.[44]

By 1820, brooks and rivers had accumulated a richly associative meaning, for they connoted Dorothy's guiding spirit as well as nature's power 'to heal and to restore'.[45] When William addressed the Duddon as 'my partner and my guide' in the concluding sonnet, his immediate circle of readers doubtless understood (through its long history of associations) a tacit reference to his sister.

The Wordsworths' habit of sharing and exchanging memories in conversation fed into their experience and understanding of creativity as a fluid process, open to the confluence of identities. (I am reminded here of Mauss's description of gift exchange: 'Souls are mixed with things; things with souls. Lives are mingled together, and this is how, among persons and things so intermingled, each emerges from their own sphere and mixes together.')[46] Dorothy's preference was always for an anonymous role in their collaboration, but this need not be read as a sign that she believed herself to be inferior. Although she was, in an economic sense, dependent—playing a conventionally subservient role in the domestic routines of family life—her labour was not alienated, and she knew her gifts to be greatly valued. 'When gift exchange achieves a convivial communion of spirits, there is no call for liberty,' Lewis Hyde writes, 'it is only when our attachments become moribund that we long to break them'.[47] The Wordsworth household successfully operated a *double economy* in relation to creativity. Before publication, the siblings' shared labour followed the pattern of a household gift economy, serving as a communal means to a communal end; but at the point of publication, the products of cooperative labour went out into the marketplace, where they became commodities associated with the single name 'William Wordsworth'. We see here a potential conflict between community and individual advancement. Hyde warns of the danger that in a group which derives its cohesion from the circulation of gifts, 'the conversion of gifts to commodities will have the effect of fragmenting the group, or even destroying it'.[48] This danger was avoided in the Wordsworth family, however, by keeping the two categories—gift and commodity—distinct. For instance, fair copies of some of Dorothy's writing circulated among friends and family, but remained unpublished, as did quite a lot of William's. *The Prelude* retained its status as a gift—'The Poem for Coleridge'—throughout the poet's life. William went on revising his poems after they had been published, a signal that they had a developing life in his imagination even after appearing in print. Although some aspects of the 'cottage industry' at Rydal Mount might appear to the modern reader exploitative, we miss the point of the family's communal enterprise if we insist that Dorothy, Mary, Sara, and Dora should have received a wage for their work. They did well to keep some aspects of their communal life out of the marketplace.

Gratitude is 'the moral memory of mankind',[49] and one of the distinguishing features of a gift economy. As we have seen, William often acknowledged Dorothy's intellectual, emotional and spiritual importance, paying tribute to her explicitly on numerous occasions. He also used subtle devices of allusion and figurative language to express his admiration of her creative qualities. These devices are not always accessible to a modern audience, because they belong partly to literary conventions of compliment and tribute, partly to a private discourse of grieving, devotion, gratitude, and reparation. They need to be read carefully and sympathetically if we are to understand the *non-hierarchical* contract of the heart which was the basis for the siblings' creative partnership. Increasingly, as William achieved fame, a shift became discernible in the way he acknowledged Dorothy's contribution. In the first edition of *Select Views*, published anonymously, her ideas were quietly incorporated into William's writing; but a more developed collaboration emerged when he later published this book (without its illustrations, which he disliked) under his own name. The *Guide* appeared in three separate forms: first, in 1820, under the title 'A Topographical Description of the Lakes, in the North of England' (to accompany *The River Duddon ... and Other Poems*); and two years later as a separate volume, *A Description of the Scenery of the Lakes in the North of England*, which sold out immediately and was reprinted in 1823, with additions. It was in the 1822 edition, in a section entitled 'Excursions to the top of Scawfell and on the Banks of Ullswater', that William included two substantial pieces of Dorothy's prose. The first was a revised version of the 'November 1805' journal which I discussed in chapter 11. The second was part of a letter she had written to the Reverend William Johnson (formerly a curate at Grasmere) in October 1818.[50] By including these two passages, William acknowledged Dorothy's independent voice as a writer. In *A Description of the Scenery of the Lakes* (1823), he identified her 1818 writing as an 'extract from a letter to a

Friend', reordering it a little but leaving much of her landscape description unchanged.[51] She here relates a strenuous walk from Borrowdale up Scafell Pike in the company of her friend Miss Barker and a local 'statesman-shepherd'. (The shepherd is unnamed, but his comments about the unfolding landscape and changing weather are reported or quoted on several occasions. Dorothy refers to him appreciatively as 'our prophetic Guide' and 'our wise Man of the Mountains'.) Her prose style is smoother and more decorous than in her journals, but it reveals her undiminished talent. Take this description of the bleak landscape at the summit of Scafell Pike, where she sees the scattered rocks as if they were the remains of a vast skeleton on a prehistoric burial site; then focuses more closely on their texture, softened by lichen:

> not a blade of grass is to be seen—Cushions or tufts of moss, parched and brown; between huge blocks and stones that lie in heaps on all sides to a great distance, like skeletons or bones of the earth not needed at the creation, and there left to be covered with never-dying lichens, which the clouds and dews nourish; and adorn with colours of vivid and exquisite beauty.   (p. 110)

Dorothy observes the symbiosis of rock and vegetation with an interest in 'the fine gradations by which in Nature one thing passes away into another' that William had noticed in his study of organic processes (p. 79). It is a striking passage, in keeping with the Wordsworths' recurrent theme of centuries-long patterns of growth and acclimatization.

In between this 1818 extract and the revised version of Dorothy's 'November 1805' journal, William placed a poem of his own, 'To—on her first ascent to the summit of Helvellyn', which he had written for a neighbour (Miss Blackett) in 1816, and first published in 1820. The poem nicely complements Dorothy's prose, widening our sense of the community of enthusiastic walkers in the Wordsworth circle. By including it, William introduces an ambiguity in the transition from letter to journal, for it is unclear who is the unnamed author of the 'journal written for one acquainted with the general features of the country' which follows immediately after the poem (p. 112). The first readers of A Description must have been aware that a different voice had entered the text, because of the journal format, the use of the pronoun 'we', and the reference to Nelson's death on Saturday 10 November 1805, which anchored this piece of writing securely in historical time. But they would not necessarily have concluded that the letter and the journal were written by the same person. The overall effect is one of a harmonious counterpointing of voices rather than a seamless joining of poetry and prose. Implicitly, the writers' identities matter less than their common purpose and intrinsic compatibility.

In revising Dorothy's 'November 1805' journal, William preserves the particularity of diurnal experience by retaining the journal format, and with it much that is typical of her authentic ways of observing and writing, such as the observation that 'there was never a drop [of rain] on our hair or clothes larger than the smallest pearls on a lady's ring' (p. 113). But irregularities in her style are smoothed, and references to an intimate circle of named friends and relatives—Mary, 'dear Coleridge', the Clarksons, and Mr Luff— are removed. If the familiarity of her prose is somewhat lost in the process, the inclusion of this piece is nonetheless in the spirit of the Wordsworths' joint regionalism. William celebrates the communal importance of local attachments, immortalizing a favourite walk and its family associations. Although Dorothy is not acknowledged by name, her contribution is given an important place in the concluding pages of the *Guide*, immediately preceding William's ode 'On the Pass of Kirkstone'. Side by side in print, the two writers pay tribute to the mountains and valleys that stretched from Grasmere Vale north-west to Cockermouth and Penrith. It was a landscape saturated in shared memories that dated as far back as their childhood. As we read through the 'Excursions'—progressing from William's to Dorothy's prose, and taking in William's intermingled poems en route—we see how creatively, over the years, their symbiotic identities had blended with their surroundings.

13

The Continent

'We left the hut at Trientz musing on the strange connexions of events in human life; how improbable, thirty years ago, that W should ever return thither!—and *we* to be his companions! And to pass a night within the hollow of that "aboriginal Vale" was a thing that the most romantic of our fancies could not have helped us even to dream of!'[1]

*

In 1820, middle age had begun to take its toll on the Wordsworth family. William was suffering from inflammation of the eyes; while Dorothy— who with only six teeth left had 'a true old woman's mouth and chin'— decided a false set was necessary, and departed for London to have them fitted.[2] Soon afterwards, in search of health and new literary material, all three Wordsworth adults set off together on a four-month tour of the Continent. Eager to share the excitement of travel abroad, which had been impossible during the Napoleonic wars, they were also fulfilling a promise to visit Annette Vallon. (Her daughter Caroline had recently married, and now had two young daughters.) They took with them 'the new Edition of William's poems'—this was the four-volume *Collected Poems* of 1820—which had 'just been put into our hands bound up in an unfinished state'.[3] Sara Hutchinson stayed behind at Rydal Mount, looking out for letters from the travellers and following the latest royal scandal in the newspapers. January had seen the coronation of King George IV and the eruption of the Queen Caroline affair, with the unpopular new king putting his estranged wife on trial for alleged adultery. His action provoked outrage among the masses. During the eleven weeks of the Queen's trial over the summer, a reform movement rose up in her defence. Most members of the household at Rydal Mount took sides with the aggrieved queen, and were glad to be abroad during such unruly times. (William, Mary and Dorothy were considerably less tolerant than Sara of the king; nonetheless they took a mild interest while they were abroad in some of the places where Caroline had reputedly conducted an affair with her servant, Pergami.)

The eighteenth-century Grand Tour, typically organized around the cultural centres of Europe, had by 1820 been reshaped by the diverse objectives of English tourists. The Wordsworths planned their route carefully, taking expert advice from their friend Richard Sharp about which scenes to view and where to stay. (Two years later, 'Conversation' Sharp would recommend an almost identical itinerary to the political economist David Ricardo.) They all looked forward to viewing the Alpine landscapes that featured in contemporary poetry and travel writings; but they had a personal journey in mind. 'Switzerland was our end and aim', Dorothy wrote, identifying wishes they had cherished since their youth, 'when that romantic country was first shut out from the traveller.'[4] It was thirty years since William had walked through Europe with Robert Jones. Although the 1820 itinerary moved in an opposite direction from the 1790 tour (following the new road built by Napoleon's army, not the old muleteer's track remembered in *The Prelude*), it enabled Dorothy and Mary to explore the places William had visited as a student.

It was a nostalgic pilgrimage, but with little opportunity for the intimacy enjoyed in Scotland. This time, William and Dorothy were accompanied by Mary, her cousin Thomas Monkhouse, his wife Jane, her sister Miss Horrocks, and their maid. The tour had been planned as a honeymoon trip for the Monkhouses, but when the party approached the Alps, the going became too rough for Jane. Whereas Dorothy and Mary were fired up by a spirit of adventure, Jane was 'of a very delicate constitution and unable at present to keep pace with us'.[5] It was decided that she and her sister would rest at

Geneva while Thomas Monkhouse (somewhat selfishly) pushed on to the Alps with the Wordsworths. The party split in two on 11 August, reuniting in September. At Lucerne, the enthusiastic walkers were joined by their bachelor friend Henry Crabb Robinson, a middle-aged barrister whose early career as a foreign correspondent had given him considerable experience of travel in Europe. A voracious reader and careful listener, he habitually kept a diary and wrote voluminous letters packed with witty and wise observations about culture, politics, and people. (Whig in his opinions, Unitarian in his faith, and a close friend of the anti-slave trade pioneer Thomas Clarkson, he once described himself disarmingly as having 'a neutral apathetic character'. Yet when it came to politics, he was unhesitatingly outspoken— the Queen Caroline affair, for instance, he dismissed with the word 'disgraceful'.)[6] His intellectual openness and gift for friendship ensured that he was always welcome in the Wordsworth family, who were delighted that he was able to join them in their exploration of Switzerland and the Italian lakes. He was 'inclined to Boswellise' in William's company,[7] but the holiday also deepened his friendship with Dorothy, whom he greatly admired. His language skills and experience as a traveller were to prove invaluable.

Reflecting on the varied groupings which had been possible in so large a party of travellers, Dorothy later identified one of the tour's key successes: 'We set forward together, forming different companies—or sometimes solitary—the peculiar charm of pedestrian travelling, especially when the party is large—fresh society always ready—and solitude to be taken at will.'[8] Four members of the party kept journals during the tour, but Jane Monkhouse's does not survive. Mary and Dorothy recorded their impressions of Continental ways of life; while Crabb Robinson wrote about conversations, encounters, and incidents in his familiar gossipy style. He felt his journal was perfunctory by comparison with the women's, commenting that he was especially 'humbled' by Mary's powers of observation. She and Dorothy had succeeded in making a record of the tour which 'put mine to shame', he confessed.[9] Although none of Dorothy's notes survive, Mary's four small notebooks do. The two women used their notes, on their return to Rydal, to create independent journals. Mary produced a finished version by March 1821, and when dedicating her neatly penned quarto volume to Dora referred to it as 'a mere transcript of the hasty notes, made by snatches, during our Journey'.[10] This wasn't quite true, for she added many quotations from William's poetry; but her journal does preserve the fresh immediacy of impressions, often using the present tense and dashes. She wrote with a consciousness that her style might be deficient, deferring repeatedly to Dorothy's superior skills. As she saw it, there was a clear hierarchy of writers in the household: 'as D is journalist general I shall in future, go on giving our route without comments, for, to describe where there is so much,—at every step something beyond description, is not a work for me'.[11]

With her reputation as 'journalist general' to keep up, Dorothy was even more anxious than Mary about her writing, which began in February 1821. In March, she complained that 'Mary seems to have succeeded so well in the brief way that I can hardly hope my lengthiness will interest in like degree.'[12] It took until August 1821 to complete the first draft, which she then began copying out in October. ('D is still busy with her Journal', Mary wrote in November, 'She has an arduous task…and will make a complete book of it.')[13] None of the initial drafts survive. The only extant manuscript—a handsome pair of volumes, bound in marbled boards—was in the hand of an unidentified friend, who began transcribing it in November 1825. It runs to 745 quarto pages. Although Dorothy claimed that 'My object is not to make a Book but to leave to my Niece a neatly penned Memorial of those few interesting months of our lives',[14] the polished format of the volumes—with running headers, a list of contents, several coloured prints, and a tally of miles covered on each lap of the journey—suggests a more ambitious plan. Crabb Robinson, seeing the journal's market potential, urged her to shorten and publish it, but Dorothy made only a few suggestions for cutting before handing her manuscript over to the copyist. 'As to compressing—or re-writing I shall never do it,' she wrote in 1825, 'for it well answers the purpose intended, of reviving recollections.'[15] Her thoroughness was justified, she felt, by the fact that its many details were 'lingering places of memory; and therefore, for my sake, not to be neglected'.[16]

Characteristically, William's poetic response to the tour was delayed until a year after the family had returned home. In 1821, he drew on his memories, stimulated by Mary's and Dorothy's accounts, to write thirty-eight poems on miscellaneous subjects in a wide variety of genres and forms. They came fast, between November 1821 and March 1822. In a letter, Dorothy referred to William's dependence on her during the early stages of their composition 'when he was pondering over his recollections, and asking me for hints and thoughts'.[17] He had originally intended to write only a few poems, to accompany or illustrate Dorothy's prose, following the pattern of *Recollections of a Tour Made in Scotland*. ('Wm is writing Poems to intersperse—several very beautiful ones he has already done', Mary wrote in a letter dated 5 November 1821.)[18] With Robinson's encouragement, the family began to consider a collaborative volume, even envisaging a second tour of the Continent on the proceeds. However, by the middle of January 1822, Dorothy reported that William's work 'has grown to such importance...that I have long ceased to consider it in connection with my own narrative',[19] and by March, his material had expanded further. The sequence was published in 1822, as *Memorials of a Tour on the Continent, 1820*. Dorothy copied some of the poems into *Journal of a Tour on the Continent* at appropriate places, providing evidence of the original collaborative plan.

The creativity engendered by the Continental tour had a fascinating dynamic, enabling three subject positions to emerge within a single household. There is some indication that creative processes took the writers in different directions, and that the long-standing cooperative habits of the siblings altered as a result of Mary's involvement. Whereas Mary constantly deferred to and cross-referenced Dorothy's narrative, Dorothy took care not to consult Mary's while she was writing; in this way, the two women's accounts of their experiences remained distinct. Were there rivalries in the family? A semi-figurative passage from Dorothy's journal, commenting on the movement of streams at Interlaken, may reveal her fear that the women's narratives would eventually be subsumed:

> I have seen a muddy and a transparent streamlet, at a few yards' distance hurrying down the same steep:—in one instance the two joined at the bottom, travelled side by side in the same track, remaining distinct though joined together, as if each were jealous of its own character. Yielding to mild necessity, they slowly blended, ere both, in turbulent disrespect, were swallowed up by the master-torrent.[20]

As it turned out, William's 'master-torrent' of poetry did not 'swallow up' the women's streams of prose but took a separate course. Crabb Robinson observed that 'it would have been well if Wordsworth would have allowed one of these journals to be published and his Poems intermixed. It would have been popular;'[21] but the length of Dorothy's journal precluded this option. Despite a wish that one day his poems might appear in print alongside edited sections of the journals, both women's accounts of the tour remained unpublished in their lifetime.[22] Substantial extracts from Dorothy's were however included as head-notes, with the attribution 'Extract from a Journal', in the 1827 edition of William's *Memorials of a Tour on the Continent*.

*

Both journals suggest that as the Wordsworths travelled, the women were preoccupied by William's youthful journey in 1790. Thoughts of Annette may have also have been strong at the outset of the tour, for they were retravelling the route William and Dorothy had taken in 1802, just before his marriage to Mary. Near Dover, seeing a group of boys playing a game of cricket, both women remembered (and both journals quote) William's patriotic sonnet of 1802, 'Dear Fellow-Traveller! Here we are once more', in which a game of cricket features as a symbol of Englishness. This commemorative quotation, which drew Dorothy and Mary's journals briefly together, signified their consciousness of a shared present inhabited by the past. Even in setting out, they anticipated the Wordsworthian pleasure of homecoming.

At Calais, Dorothy looked around the city she and William had explored with Annette and Caroline all those years ago. Mary, on French soil for the first time, was taken up with the 'first shock of difference' as she adjusted to hearing spoken French and seeing 'a line of white-capped Fish-women with their brown faces'.[23] William would in 1821 respond to her mention of 'Fish-women' with a poem, but no evidence survives of his reaction, on Tuesday 11 July, to these hardy working women in whom Dorothy noted 'something of liveliness, of mental activity'.[24] His mind may have been on other things. In a mood to reconstruct the past as nearly as possible, he had visited Robert Jones just before the trip, hoping to persuade his friend to join the party on their travels; but Jones had declined. By the time the Wordsworths arrived at Bruges, William had become absorbed in 'hurting himself' (as Mary put it) with a sonnet about Jones's parsonage in Oxfordshire.[25] The poem, which distracted him from his immediate surroundings, is evidence of the elegiac mood in which he embarked on his journey through post-Napoleonic Europe. Recurring to thought-patterns shared with Dorothy while travelling through Scotland in 1803, he observes the permeable boundary between past and present, the living and the dead:

> wheresoe'er the stealing footstep tends,
> Garden, and that Domain where Kindred, Friends,
> And Neighbours rest together, here confound
> Their several features—mingled like the sound
> Of many waters, or as evening blends
> With shady night.[26]

The graveyard in Oxfordshire where the 'stealing footstep tends' is metaphorically connected with the terrain covered on the Continental tour. The

Wordsworths' journey through Europe, where many had lost their lives during the Napoleonic wars, would involve both a personal reckoning with the passage of time and a communal recognition of large-scale suffering and change. The sonnet's setting, although not immediately relevant to the city where it was composed, also reflects something of the 'tender melancholy' which Dorothy found in 'pensive images of monastic life among the quiet goings-on of a thinly peopled city'.[27] After returning home, William made amends for his inattentiveness during this part of the tour with two sonnets about Bruges, evocative of the serenity of this ancient place saved from 'the injuries of time'.[28] Honouring his fellow-travellers' powers of observation, these poems drew closely on Mary's description of 'graceful nun-like women in their long cloaks, treading with swan-like motion those silent avenues of majestic architecture', and on Dorothy's affinity with still streets where 'you might fancy that the Builder's hammer was never heard' and where 'no change is going on, except through the silent progress of time'.[29]

As the party travelled through Northern France and the Netherlands, the women recorded the experience in different ways. Mary, struggling with her ignorance of languages, wrote as a tourist. Interspersing glimpses from carriages with stationary or pedestrian views, her curiosity was checked by moments of revulsion, especially from the Catholic rituals she found oppressive. Attending mass at Calais, she noted its 'tawdry' decorations and 'flippant... ceremonies', contrasting these with a 'striking female Figure, in rags' who sat alone on the steps to the altar.[30] With her farming background, she wrote authentically about agriculture; but her confidence failed her when it came to historical topics, and she recoiled from the task of writing about Waterloo. A single vivid detail, observed in a hotel at Genappe—'two Bullet shots in the wainscot of the room' which during the battle had been 'heaped with dead, & dying'—captures her shocked response to the terrible events of 18 June 1815.[31] Dorothy's journal, shaping the experiences of each day carefully, reflects her greater assurance as a travel writer. She writes with an eye for telling details. Noting a lonely beggar with her dog in the cathedral at Calais, she describes 'her melancholy and sickly aspect', and dwells on 'the change in the woman's skinny, doleful face' on being given a penny.[32] The encounter, worthy of a scene from Sterne's *A Sentimental Journey*, was perhaps inspired by spending the night in a bedroom whose door was inscribed 'Sterne's room', with a print of the celebrated author hanging over the fireplace. In such circumstantial details, Dorothy disclosed her literary taste and standing. Some of her observations on social and economic conditions (especially in the Netherlands) recall Mary Wollstonecraft's style of reportage, which had earlier influenced the *Hamburg Journal* of 1798. Ernest De Selincourt's edition omits many of the grittier passages, especially concerning the poor. At Dunkirk, Dorothy noted that numerous beggars seemed to be evidence of 'abject poverty'; but 'where do they live? I have seen no dwellings that seem to belong to very poor people'.[33] At Alost, she observed that the people were 'dirty, ragged,—bold, and the children obstinate sing-song beggars, following our carriages while breath would serve'.[34]

Everywhere she went, Dorothy saw the centres of European civilization as fragile edifices, subject to the powerful forces of human ambition, nature, and time. Writing about the 'venerable antiquity' of Ghent, she describes 'multitudes of swallows... wheeling round' the cathedral roof, their 'restless motions and plaintive call' imparting 'a stillness to every object'. Responding to the swallows as prefigurations of a 'period when that once superb but now decaying structure shall be "lorded over and possessed by nature"', she remembers and revises lines from *The Prelude* in which William had described hills 'lorded over and possessed | By naked huts'.[35] The apocalyptic implications of her prose parallel Anna Laetitia Barbauld's 'Eighteen Hundred and Eleven', with its prophecy of a future in which empire will be overthrown, and tourists will wander through the ancient ruins of London, finding in 'each splendid square, and still untrodden street' memorials to the vanity of human wishes.[36] At one time, the Wordsworths had been ardent Francophiles. There was a world of difference between William's revolutionary sentiments as he walked though Europe in 1790 and the sombre feelings of this middle-aged family—Anglican Tories, members of the Establishment—as they made their way towards Waterloo. The Emperor Napoleon's long tyrannical rule had ended in 1815, but what had been the cost? Like many British patriots, they visited the assembly room at Brussels to hear details of the ball given by the Duchess of Richmond the night before the battle, 'from which some of our young officers hurried away in their dancing shoes, to meet the Enemy—and, of these, how *many* were brought back, in the course of a few hours, dead, dying, or wounded!' Dorothy does not recoil, as Mary does, from the terrible events of Waterloo, but listens to an eyewitness, who relays these details 'with lively gestures and animated language'.[37]

By 1820, the battlefield of Waterloo had featured in some of the most celebrated art and literature of the day. Southey, in *A Poet's Pilgrimage to Waterloo*, had related how, three months after the battle, he toured the site, contemplating with mingled feelings of sadness and triumph the victory of the combined armies of the Seventh Coalition over Napoleon's Grande Armée:

> Set where thou wilt thy foot, thou scarce can tread
> Here on a spot unhallowed by the dead...
> Earth had received into her silent womb
> Her slaughtered creatures: horse and man they lay,
> And friend and foe, within the general tomb.[38]

A year later, in exile from England, Byron too had stood in 'this place of skulls,| The grave of France, the deadly Waterloo'. In his sensationally popular poem *Childe Harold's Pilgrimage* (1816), the hero muses on the fate of 'un-returning brave', prophesying that their deaths will soon pass into oblivion:

> Ere evening to be trodden like the grass
> Which now beneath them, but above shall grow
> In its next verdure, when this fiery mass
> Of living valour, rolling on the foe
> And burning with high hope, shall molder cold and low.[39]

Turner had visited the battlefield in 1817 to make preliminary sketches for *The Field of Waterloo*, exhibited in London in 1818—no celebration of heroic victory, this, but a dark, apocalyptic study of violence and suffering. The Wordsworths, too, made their pilgrimage not to gloat over the defeat of Napoleon—'that audacious charlatan and remorseless desperado'[40]—but to reflect on the horror and waste of war. They were taken round by a guide who had previously shown the sights to Southey. At the time of his visit, the material signs of war—shoes, belts, hats, gun-flints—were still 'scattered all around' the battlefield; but by 1820 they had disappeared. Dorothy's journal conveys the calm oblivious workings of nature:

> the wide fields were covered with luxuriant crops,—just as they had been before the battles, except that now the corn was nearly ripe, and *then* it was green. We stood upon grass, and corn fields where *heaps* of our countrymen lay buried beneath our feet. There was little to be seen; but much to be felt;—sorrow and sadness, and even something like horror breathed out of the ground as we stood upon it![41]

William, in his 1821 sonnet 'After visiting the field of Waterloo', drew on a rich tradition of heroic writing as well as his own memory of the feelings prompted by this 'far-famed spot', where so many had died or mourned the dead. Like Byron, and like Dorothy, his attention was held by the absence of visible memorials of the battle in a field where 'wind-swept fields of corn...roll'd|In dreary billows'.[42] His poem condemns the hollowness of patriotic sentiment, describing a feeling that is much closer to shock, or survivor's guilt, or shame. He concludes with an image drawn directly from Dorothy's journal:

> If the wide prospect seemed an envious seal
> Of great prospects; we felt as Men *should* feel
> With such vast hoards of hidden carnage near,
> And horror breathing from the silent ground!   (ll. 11–14)

Waterloo, the highlight of the first part of the tour, coloured the way in which Dorothy (and, in places, Mary) saw and wrote about their journey to Cologne. Filled with a consciousness of change, the travellers looked everywhere for reminders of 'the former dignity, wealth and commerce of these great cities, and their hard struggles for liberty'.[43] *Journal of a Tour on the Continent* dwells on the damage wrought by war on communities in the Netherlands and Germany. Poverty was a striking feature in places once noted for their beauty: 'a flashy meanness, a slight patchery of things falling to pieces is everywhere visible'.[44] Even in Aix-La-Chapelle, romantically associated with Charlemagne, the party caught sight of a 'squalid half-naked woman' looking out after the rattling carriages as they went past.[45] Mary's journal records her dismay at shabby streets, 'women with naked bosoms', 'squalid Mothers and sickly babes'.[46] In every town they passed through, 'the veil of romance was withdrawn; and we were compelled to think of human distress and poverty'.[47]

Recollecting their journey in tranquillity, William's poems covering this section of the tour are mellow in tone. His sonnet 'Between Namur and Liege' mentions only briefly the 'crimson stains' of war, turning instead to 'smooth meadow-ground, serene and still!'[48] Whatever he was noticing in 1820 as he travelled through the Rhineland, by 1821 William remembers the chateaux and towns only dimly, as a sequence of beetling ramparts and cloistral arches, seen from a carriage which took him 'Backward, in rapid evanescence' through time. His sonnet 'In a carriage, upon the banks of the Rhine' confesses the sadness of a 'defrauded heart', but comes to terms with mutability:

> Yet why repine?
> Pedestrian liberty shall yet be mine
> To muse, to creep, to halt at will, to gaze:

Freedom which youth with copious hand supplied,
May in fit measure bless my later days.   (ll. 10–14; SIP, 364)

Remembering how William and Robert Jones had 'floated down the stream in their little Bark', Dorothy's own nostalgia blends with and deepens his: 'Often did my fancy place them with a freight of happiness in the centre of some bending reach overlooked by tower or castle.'[49] She notes resemblances between the Rhine and the Wye, recalling her 'glad eagerness of hope' during the walking tour of 1798, when she was alone with her brother and 'all the world was fresh and new'.[50] It was not until the Alpine stretch of the journey that all three members of the family found themselves actively engaged in tracking down the places William remembered from thirty years ago.

*

Arriving at Lake Constance on 1 August 1820, the Alps were shrouded in mist, obscuring what should have been a 'glittering prospect'. Dorothy's narrative pauses to recall how William, returning from Europe, had told her his youthful tales of travel:'I remembered the shapeless wishes of my youth—wishes without hope—my brother's wanderings thirty years ago, and the tales brought to me the following Christmas holidays at Forncett; and often repeated while we paced together on the gravel walk in the parsonage garden, by moon or star light.'[51] Inspired by his conversation, memories, and writing, Switzerland had become for Dorothy something between an inaccessible Eden and a promised land. As a young woman, her 'shapeless wishes' to journey there had been 'without hope', because of the impracticality of travel for unmarried women. Domestic duties and war had continued to put obstacles in her way till now. But here she was, in middle age, on the brink of experiencing everything that the Alps had to offer: the mighty waterfall at Shaffhausen where she was to be 'gloriously wetted and stunned and deafened by the waters of the Rhine'; Mont Blanc with its 'pikes, towers, needles and wide wastes of everlasting snow, in dazzling brightness'; and the terrible solitudes of the Wetterhorn where 'all night, and all day, and forever, the Vale of Meiringen is sounding with torrents'.[52]

Once the party had separated from Jane Monkhouse, the pedestrian tour was truly under way. With two mules to carry their baggage, and 'having somewhat the appearance of trampers',[53] the Wordsworths entered into three weeks of strenuous walking in Switzerland. They travelled over the St Gothard Pass into Italy on 21 August, where they spent a couple of weeks exploring Lombardy and Milan. After crossing the Simplon Pass into the

Haute-Savoie on 9–11 September, they descended into Chamonix for the culmination of their Alpine adventure. During the entire tour they themselves had no accidents or injuries, but they walked for a few days in the company of two students from Geneva University, one of whom (an American, Frederick William Goddard) drowned in the lake of Zurich soon after parting company with them at the top of the Rigi. The news caught up with the Wordsworths later, casting a shadow over their memories of the early part of the tour. This aside, as an inspiring and health-giving holiday, the summer proved an outstanding success. Priding herself on her increasing health and fitness, Dorothy pointed out how much further she had been able to walk than Thomas Monkhouse—in all weathers, as her family did in the Lake District, for 'a wetting was, amongst *us* at least, no great evil'.[54] When a carriage of gentlemen, driving past Val Vedro, turned to look at the torrent without even stopping, she congratulated herself on being on foot: 'for a hundred reasons the pleasantest mode of travelling in a mountainous country'.[55] She might be visiting all the tourist prospects, but her toughness as a pedestrian, 'happy in my freedom', distinguished her from that class of travellers.[56]

Dorothy's journal emphasizes the communal pleasures of wayfaring. She felt, as any serious walker does, a sense of comradeship with those she met on the heights. At the top of the Swiss mountain of the Rigi (nearly 6,000 feet high), she enjoyed not just the 'ocean of mountain summits' but a group of miscellaneous travellers: 'ladies, middle-aged men, students from the Universities, without hat or cap, rough-headed, bare-necked—all on the look-out—all met together as friends, as if being uplifted from the world did but bring human beings nearer to each other'.[57] Her linguistic proficiency enabled her to gain a wealth of local knowledge. 'D. is an adept in making her way, for she never hesitates,' Mary commented in a letter, 'going into the Kitchens, talks to everybody there—and in the villages, on the roads, and makes friends and gains information and gabbers German everywhere. She astonishes us all.'[58] Dorothy relates how she got to know a postilion, chatting with him as they jogged alongside each other, and how she was repeatedly congratulated on her good German. She records her conversations with people from all walks of life: a Frenchman whose property had been pillaged before the Revolution; a German who had served in the pay of the English; a landlord who told her about the conditions of people living in the cantons of Schwyz and Uri—how Napoleon's army had pillaged the mountain communities, how people were driven from their homes. She established a friendship with Pierre, a guide, whose family had lived for five hundred years in the Vale of Chamonix, and who felt for the place the same kind of intense local attachment the Wordsworths had to the Lakes.[59]

'Travelling like everything must be learned', Crabb Robinson later observed in a letter to Dorothy. 'It is not everybody who are native geniuses like you and me, in that more than other arts. But certainly you and I—sex age and degree being all considered—are very good travellers.'[60] The compliment was a heartfelt recognition of the pleasure he had experienced in her company, and of the many skills he observed her exercising while on the tour. Looking back on their travels in her journal, Dorothy distanced herself from tourist traditions of travel literature, defining a more intimate relationship with the landscapes she saw. Nonetheless, she wrote about Alpine landscapes with a confident awareness that she was adapting aesthetic techniques used by the great travel writers who preceded her. Of the Falls at Schaffhausen, she observed, 'I took no description ... at the time; nor will I now attempt to describe them. Coxe and other travellers have done it better than I could do'; then proceeded to give a lively description, animated by colour, movement, and figurative language:

> Below, in the ferment and hurly-burly, drifting snow, and masses resembling collected snow, mixed with sparkling green billows. We walked upon the platform as dizzy as if we had been on the deck of a ship in a storm.[61]

Dorothy was captivated, like Turner, by the rapidly shifting cloudscapes and swirling vapours which she watched from the heights. At the top of the Rigi she observed how 'thick masses of clouds, and light smoky mists alike drove away with inconceivable rapidity ... What would not the exhibition-contrivers of London or Paris give for such power of rapid transformation!'[62] Her descriptive register, accustomed to dealing with the nearer horizons and lower peaks of the Lake District, was challenged by the massive scale of these mountains. She used the analogy of the ocean, and long rolling sentences with subordinate clauses, to capture their sublimity.[63] Her language also strained to convey the danger and suffering endured with the perpetual threat of avalanches. At Goldau, where a former village lay buried in ruins, she noted that 'masses of barren rubbish lie close to the houses, where, but a few years past, nothing was seen but fruitful fields'.[64] The village of Gheslenen gave her 'impressions of awful grandeur never to be effaced; yet mingled with dismal sympathies in the lot of some of our fellow-creatures'.

At Martigny, where a burst lake had ended forty lives in a single day, she paused to absorb the scale of the disaster and its effects on the region.[65] Descending into the valley of the Rhone, the geological formations told a dismal story—of 'the northern Barrier that, year by year, is wasting away, and scattering over the level of the vale barrenness that defies all industry of man'.[66] These desolate scenes were all the more striking for their contrast with the peaceful valleys of Switzerland, reminiscent of home:

> All things were quiet: the weak tinkling of bells of cattle (here pasturing in the vale) seemed but to add to the stillness which accompanied every image of social life at that hour, when the day's labour was ended.[67]

Travel writers often made comparisons between the Alps and the Lake District, either to sing the praises of Alpine sublimity or to promote the rival attractions of Britain, but in the Wordsworth family allusions to the Lakes played a personal, associative role. Occasionally, comments in the journals suggest homesickness. Dorothy longed for the 'blue-grey, pebbly bed' of a Westmorland mountain stream, while Mary observed that the lakes are 'not to be compared to our own in colour, nor clearness…nothing like the inverted landscapes with all their bright & lovely hues & forms as upon the lakes of Grasmere Rydal &c.'[68] For the most part, however, the Swiss valleys elicited a perpetual delight in similarity. Near Lungern in the canton of Obwalden, Mary noted 'a Vale which seemed like one of our own'; and near the Vale of Urseren 'an area, so like that at the top of Easedale…we might have fancied we were there'.[69] Dorothy likened the avalanches below the Wetterhorn to the screes of Wasdale; the Aar Pass to the Duddon; the village of Lungern to Grasmere. Homely resemblances continued after the party had reached Lombardy: Lago di Piano, she noted, 'sweetly surprised us', like 'a little *Loughrigg Tarn*'.[70]

*

William's retrospective accounts of his 1790 tour—in *Descriptive Sketches* (1793) and *The Prelude* Book VI (1804)—were remembered by all three travellers as they experienced and wrote about the 1820 tour. But whereas Mary alluded more often in her journal to *Descriptive Sketches*, Dorothy recurred just as frequently to *The Prelude*, entering into her brother's auto-biographical reconstruction of his youthful travels. (Both women had been involved in making fair copies of *The Prelude*, but Dorothy's immersion in its narrative was deeper.) Several timelines run through the Alpine section of *Journal of a Tour on the Continent*. As Dorothy checks her observations against William's relayed impressions (oral and written), she is preoccupied by the passage of time, the challenge of retrieving past experience, and the subjective nature of viewing. There are emotional difficulties for her—not just in approaching a significant episode of her brother's life from which she had been excluded, but in closing the gaps left in William's retrospective narration. And as always, when she was describing places away from home, there is the sense of observing and evaluating new places with reference to familiar Westmorland scenes. All of this gives her prose a complex, allusive texture, revealing the associative patterns of her thinking.

Her impressions shade almost imperceptibly into William's as the narrative shuttles between their shared present and his separate past. At the top of St Gothard Pass, she sympathized with his feelings of 'sadness' and 'disappointment' when he was told unexpectedly that 'the Alps were crossed'.[71] Together with Mary, she looked for the place where, separated from Jones, he became lost in a thunderstorm near Gravedona, her own frustration in locating the spot mirroring his perplexity in 1790, until she eventually noticed the path across the valley.[72] Dorothy's interest in recovering the 1790 tour was no act of dutiful subservience to her brother's wishes, but an attempt to enter empathetically into his past. She shows particular attentiveness to moments of disappointment, anxiety, and loss in *The Prelude*'s narrative, as if trying to create an authentic map of William's developing consciousness. On one occasion, her enthusiasm to retrieve past experience surpassed his. Her journal relates how, in the Simplon Pass, the party happened on the spital (highway shelter), eight storeys high, where William and his companions had spent an awful night, 'stunned | By noise of waters'.[73] In 1790, a torrent came 'thundering down a chasm of the mountains on the opposite side of the glen', whereas in 1820 there was only a rivulet that 'chearfully bounded down to the Vedro'.[74] Even so, William's memory of this night spent among the precipices and vapours was so disturbing that he chose not to re-enter the building. 'I now regret not having the courage to pass the threshold alone', Dorothy wrote in her journal: 'I had a strong desire to see what was going on within doors for the sake of tales of thirty years gone by: but could not persuade W. to accompany me.'[75]

Journal of a Tour on the Continent repeatedly draws attention to the practical difficulties of recovering the past, for the party was travelling on 'the track of all nations' (Napoleon's road)—'clearing crags, bridging chasms, bestriding precipices, or stretched out in sweeping bold curves'—not on the original winding track William had travelled in 1790.[76] The Wordsworths separated briefly from the main party, choosing instead to walk on the old road, 'Wm. because he had travelled it before, and Mary and I from sympathy with his feeling'. Disoriented not just by their different route in 1820 but by their direction of travel, William took pleasure in moments of exact recognition, as when he discovered the track which had led him inadvertently to cross the Alps:

> W was waiting to shew [*sic*] us the track, on the green precipice. It was impossible for me to say how much it had moved him, when he discovered it was the very same which had tempted him in his youth. The feelings of that time came back with the freshness of yesterday, accompanied with a dim vision of thirty years of life between.[77]

According to the evidence of both Dorothy's and Mary's journals, all three travellers were delighted to discover, at Chamonix, that the 'aboriginal vale' remembered in *The Prelude* was unchanged:

> While standing on the brow of the precipice above this shady deep recess, the very image of pastoral life, stillness and seclusion Wm came up to me, and, if my feelings had been moved before, how much more interesting did the spot become when he told me it was the same dell, that '*aboriginal vale*', that '*green recess*' so often mentioned by him—the first of the kind that he had passed through in Switzerland, and 'now' said he, 'I find that my remembrance for thirty years has been scarcely less vivid than the reality before my eyes!'[78]

Occurring nearly at the end of their tour, after they had crossed the Alps into Savoy, the rediscovery of this 'aboriginal vale' provides the climax of Dorothy's narrative. Associated with memories of Westmorland, the Wye Valley, and Edenic images of Grasmere that went back as far as William's boyhood, this 'deep recess, the very image of pastoral life' features in her narrative as a kind of haven, signifying the completion of an emotional journey. 'Mary and I sate beside a streamlet and wrote in the sunshine', she records, while William 'stretched himself at length on bench' in a nearby chalet, and probably slept.[79]

*

By highlighting the sense in which the Continental tour was a revisiting of William's past, did Dorothy hope to guide him towards an appropriate unifying theme for the poems he began writing in 1821? If so, she may have been puzzled by his response. Just as he declined her request to accompany him into the highway shelter at Simplon, so he chose *not* to write about his

rediscovery of the Edenic 'recess' in Chamonix. Among the forty poems in
Memorials of a Tour on the Continent, there is only one about personal memories of the Continental tour of 1790. In 'Author's Voyage down the Rhine
(Thirty Years Ago)', William writes nostalgically of a landscape glimpsed in
passing and never seen again: 'We saw the living Landscapes of the
Rhine, | Reach after reach, salute us and depart.'[80] The typical Wordsworthian
concern with revisiting is nowhere near as explicit here as it is in 'Tintern
Abbey' or 'Yarrow Re-visited'. On a personal level at least, the poet appears
to be conscious of an immeasurable gulf between the present and the past.
'Elegiac Stanzas', written at Crabb Robinson's suggestion to commemorate
the untimely death of Frederick Goddard, suggests that he identified with
the drowned American student. After descending from the Rigi, the Wordsworths had parted with him 'at an hour and on a spot well suited to those
who were to meet no more'.[81] It would be hard to miss the symbolism.
Goddard had died at the age of twenty while on a walking holiday with his
friend in the Alps: exactly the age William had been in 1790 when he
climbed the same mountains with Robert Jones.

William's passion for Switzerland nonetheless remained undiminished by
the passage of thirty years. *In Descriptive Sketches* (1793), he had vowed his
lifelong devotion to the Swiss and Savoyard Alps: 'And thou! Fair favoured
region! which my soul | Shall love till Life has broke her golden bowl, | Till
Death's cold touch her cistern-wheel assail.'[82] The cantons of Switzerland,
each with their own form of independent democratic government, embodied a spirit of local republicanism which had shaped his political ideals as a
young writer. Here, William wrote in 1793, the uncorrupted shepherd lived
'Bless'd with his herd, as in the patriarch's age':

> The slave of none, of beasts alone the lord,
> He marches with his flute, his book, and sword,
> Well taught by this to feel his rights ...[83]

William's youthful hero-worship of the Swiss peasantry had developed into
a more mature understanding of agrarian economics over the years, but he
maintained his belief that affinities linked the Swiss mountain communities
with the farmers and shepherds of the Lake District. Ever since the French
invasion of 1798, he had sided with the people of Switzerland in their struggle to resist conquest by France and Austria. Now, after the restoration of
Swiss independence, his devotion to the country redoubled. On returning
from the Continent, he set to work on a new edition of his *Guide to the Lakes*.

Some of his revisions suggested a clear analogy between Lakeland farming communities and those in the Alps.[84] As he turned in 1821 to the composition of his Memorial poems, he continued to reflect on this analogy.

Like the coloured prints of Swiss women in national costumes which appear in Dorothy's *Journal of a Tour on the Continent*, his poems testify to his enduring political sympathies. In 'The Town of Schwytz', he hails the spirit of Swiss liberty, which was threatened when 'foreign Soldiers were seen upon the frontiers of this small Canton, to impose upon it the laws of their governors'.[85] In 'The Church of San Salvador', he sings the praises of historical figures associated with the Old Swiss Confederacy and its struggle against Austrian conquest: Arnold Winkelried, whose bravery at the battle of Sempach (1386) was 'one of the most famous in the annals of Swiss heroism';[86] and William Tell, a fifteenth-century hero 'cast in Nature's mould, | Deliverer of the steadfast rocks | And of the ancient hills' (ll. 40–2; SIP, 376). Turning to more recent history, his ballad 'Memorial, near the Outlet of the Lake Thun' pays homage to the captain general of the Swiss forces who led a resistance against the French in 1798. Mary and William had accidentally passed by an inscription to Reding on 'a stone seat directly fronting the setting sun' near Thun. Mary transcribed it on the final page of her second notebook, honouring the important place this hero had in their family's consciousness.[87] Back at Rydal, both she and Dorothy transferred the inscription into their journals. 'Wherever you find a stone seat or memorial inscription', Dorothy wrote, 'it is in harmony with tender, elevated, or devotional feelings,—the musings upon time and eternity which must visit all but the most unthinking minds in a solitude like this, surrounded by objects so sublime.'[88]

Some of William's poems were inspired by Dorothy's evocation of the Continent as a vast landscape disfigured by the ruins of Napoleon's empire. A column of granite intended for the Emperor's triumphal arch at Milan lay by the wayside in the Simplon Pass—'I wish it may remain prostrate on the mountain for ages to come', Dorothy wrote.[89] William's poem on the subject reflects on the overweening ambition of tyrants:

> Memento uninscribed of Pride o'erthrown;
> Vanity's hieroglyphic; a choice trope
> In Fortune's rhetoric.[90]

Ruined buildings, monuments and memorial sites, striking relics, and memento mori are highlighted by both William and Dorothy, but the levelling sense of loss is offset by poignant images of survival. At the ancient ruins of Fort

Fuentes near Lake Como—'everywhere something to remind one of former splendour, and of devastation and tumult'[91]—a marble statue of a child rested in the brambles, uninjured by the explosion that had driven it downhill. William added some striking details to Dorothy's tender description of the statue, which 'lay bedded like an Infant in its cradle amongst the low green bushes' (CJ, 245). In his poem, a lizard basks in the infant's palm, a snake is twined round his neck, and nature silently encroaches among the ruins. In a country where even the mountains told 'a plain tale both of perpetual and fitful wasting',[92] every stage of the Wordsworths' journey brought reminders of mutability. Mary honoured the heroic 'industry of the Husbandmen & their daring & patient perseverance, struggling among those crumbling & overwhelming materials'.[93] Dorothy wrote movingly about 'frequent memorials' marking places where wayfarers had died in Alpine avalanches, and especially the small wooden crosses placed under stones, 'so slightly put together that a child might break them to pieces:—yet they lie from year to year as safe as in a sanctuary'.[94] William observed a similar cooperation of nature with human history wherever signs of religious devotion had outlasted Napoleon's conquest. In the Catholic cantons, shrines and wayside oratories were everywhere to be seen. 'Composed in one of the Catholic Cantons' alludes to the 'knee-worn cell' found on many a village lawn, and to the 'Chapel far withdrawn | That lurks by lonely ways' (ll. 11–12; SIP, 408). In these humble edifices, something of the primitive spirit of Christianity lived on, just as it did in remote chapels throughout Cumberland and Westmorland.

*

Memorials of a Tour on the Continent is less autobiographical than might be expected from so personal a journey. Nonetheless, the sequence reflects on the workings of memory in ways that were germane to William and Dorothy's lifelong concern with exile and nostalgia, as in

'On hearing the "Ranz des Vaches" on the top of the Pass of St Gothard'

I listen—but no faculty of mine
Avails those modulations to detect,
Which, heard in foreign lands, the Swiss affect
With tenderest passion; leaving him to pine
(So fame reports) and die; his sweet-breath'd kine
Remembering, and green Alpine pastures deck'd
With vernal flowers. Yet may we not reject
The tale as fabulous.—Here while I recline

> Mindful how others love this simple Strain
> Even here, upon this glorious Mountain (named
> Of God himself from dread pre-eminence)
> Aspiring thoughts by memory are reclaimed;
> And, thro' the Music's touching influence,
> The joys of distant home my heart enchain.[95]

'Ranz des Vaches' ('Kuhe-Reyen') was a type of melody played by Swiss herdsmen, traditionally on the horn, as they drove their cattle to and from pasture. The haunting tunes were associated with the crepuscular hours of dawn and dusk and the musical sound of cattle-bells on Alpine mountains. Hearing these bells for the first time, Mary described them in her second travel notebook as 'that Alpine sound which years ago William prepared my ears instantly to understand upon the first hearing'.[96] In *Descriptive Sketches* William had written about the 'Ranz des Vaches' in connection with nostalgia (*mal de suisse*), noting that Swiss mercenaries were forbidden to sing these tunes, believed to evoke so powerful a longing for home that they might lead exiled soldiers to desertion, sickness, or even death.[97] In 1821, his emotional affinity with the soldiers is clear. Composed at Rydal, and remembering two tours of the Continent which were thirty years apart, the sonnet celebrates the power of music to bridge the gulfs of time and space. If the speaker's nostalgia arises out of a sense of exile from his past, he finds in the melody's 'touching influence' both 'thoughts by memory reclaimed' and 'joys of distant home' (ll. 12-14; SIP, 374).

Thoughts of home recur several times in *Memorials of a Tour on the Continent*, as though two intentions—to celebrate Continental wandering, and to reinforce attachment to Westmorland—have become intertwined. 'Stanzas, Composed in the Semplon Pass' creates the illusion of a poem written *in situ*, like 'This Lime-Tree Bower my Prison' or 'Tintern Abbey'. After casting a longing look toward the shady woods of Vallombrosa, the speaker bids farewell to the warm southern 'climate of myrtles' and turns northward to the mist-shrouded 'land of my Sires'. Using plural pronouns, William suggests the family's communal pleasure in their movement homeward:

> Tho' the burthen of toil with dear friends we divide,
> Tho' by the same zephyr our temples are fann'd,
> As we rest in the cool orange-bower side by side,
> A yearning survives which few hearts shall withstand:
> Each step hath its value while homeward we move;—

> O joy when the girdle of England appears!
> What moment in life is so conscious of love,
> So rich in the tenderest sweetness of tears?   (ll. 25–32; SIP, 388)

In 'The Eclipse of the Sun', William remembers how an event that was witnessed all over Europe had concentrated his mind on home. Situating himself 'beneath Italian skies', he writes in the present tense, wondering what a familiar Westmorland landscape must have looked like in his absence under the estranging darkness of the sun's eclipse: 'O Ye, who guard and grace my Home | While in far-distant lands we roam, | Enquiring thoughts are turned to you' (ll. 67–9; SIP, 384). This poem lacks the intensity of 'Stepping Westward', but the rhyme words 'home' and 'roam' call that poem to mind, suggesting the spiritual yearning which came into play whenever the Wordsworths travelled.

As their accounts of the Continental tour came to an end, thoughts of home surfaced more often in Mary's journal than in Dorothy's. *Journal of a Tour on the Continent* has an elegiac tone as it bids farewell to the border between France and Switzerland, as if that region has become a home from home. Dorothy dwells nostalgically on features of the landscape that, by the time she writes this section of the tour, have become vague memories: 'the pastoral solitudes of wide-spread hills—of narrow vallies, silent but for the wandering sound of cattle bells—or if a stream be there it murmurs gently'.[98] Both journals are discreetly uninformative about the Wordsworths' movements in Paris, where they met Caroline Vallon and her husband. (Crabb Robinson was trusted with William's secret, but the children knew nothing of it.) The final section of Dorothy's journal emphasizes the adventure of the party's near escape from shipwreck at Boulogne; and Mary records her feeling of relief to be back in Dover. Her description of sheltering cattle as 'a home-feeling sight'[99] prompted a sonnet by William, 'After Landing—The Valley of Dover, November, 1820', in which he expressed his gratitude for the 'majestic herds of Cattle free | To ruminate—couched on the grassy lea' (ll. 6–7; SIP, 396). Doubtless remembering his return to Dover in 1802, this poem conveys the same mood of patriotic contentment with his native country that he had captured in 'Dear Fellow-traveller! Here we are once more'. All three writers were appreciative of the sights and sounds which confirmed their homecoming.

On arrival in England, the Wordsworths went first to see their brother Christopher in Cambridge, and then took their separate ways. William and Mary went north to Westmorland, breaking their journey at Coleorton, while Dorothy remained south in January, dividing time between Cambridge and the Clarksons at Playford Hall near Ipswich. Mary's journal concluded at Rydal Mount on 7 December. Snow had fallen overnight, and 'all our good neighbours and friends rejoiced to see us'.[100] Dorothy, in due course, briefly recorded the fact of arriving at home. By contrast, William wrote no poem of domestic homecoming, as he had done on the Scottish tour. Instead, looking back in 'Desultory Stanzas'— composed after receiving proof-sheets in 1822—he ranged freely over his memories:

> All that I saw returns upon my view,
> All that I heard comes back upon my ear,
> All that I felt this moment doth renew;
> And where the foot with no unmanly fear
> Recoil'd—and wings alone could travel—there
> I move at ease, and meet contending themes
> That press upon me, crossing the career
> Of recollections vivid as the dreams
> Of midnight,—cities—plains—forest, and mighty streams!
>
> (ll. 10–18 ; SIP 404)

Despite the powerful use of anaphora—'All that I saw ... All that I heard ... All that I felt'—and a rousing sense of energy, the prevailing tone is elegiac, with undercurrents of regret at opportunities lost or foregone. In a letter, Dorothy congratulated Henry Crabb Robinson on inspiring 'Desultory Stanzas', observing somewhat ruefully that he had succeeded where she had failed: 'I mentioned that very subject and he then thought he could make nothing of it:—You certainly have the gift of setting him on fire.'[101] Her self-deprecation was unnecessary. Crabb Robinson's encouragement certainly helped William to see in the great bridge of Lucerne a metaphor for the unifying processes of memory, history, and spiritual aspiration; but the poem is equally inspired by Dorothy's evocation of Switzerland as a site of mutability and decay. The poet describes the Alps, a 'gigantic crew, | Who triumphed o'er diluvian power', as no more than 'a wreck and residue | Whose only business is to perish' (ll. 20–3):

> —but no more;
> Time creepeth softly as the liquid flood;
> Life slips from underneath us, like the floor
> Of that wide rainbow-arch whereon we stood,
> Earth stretched below, Heaven in our neighbourhood. (ll. 82–6)

Both William and Dorothy, in recollecting their encounter with the 'crumbling' Alps, had evoked the unremitting attrition of time on the 'beautiful and permanent forms of nature'.[102] William's culminating poem confirms that human memorials, too, are subject to the inexorable process of destruction.

14

Wanderlust

'Travelling agrees with me wonderfully. I am as much Peter Bell as ever...I find nothing so feeding to my mind as change of scene, and rambling about; and my labours, such as they are, can be carried on better in the fields and on the roads than any where else.'[1]

*

When arriving at Grasmere in 1799, William had announced his and Dorothy's plan to honour their 'obligation of gratitude' to Westmorland by transforming the bit of steep rocky land behind Town End into a garden. By the time they reached middle age, Christianity had become central to their way of life, bringing a different order of gratitude into play; yet their shared thankfulness, as they looked back on twenty-five years in the region, still centred on their surroundings. 'I never had a higher relish for the beauties of Nature than during this spring, nor enjoyed myself more', William wrote in 1825 to George Beaumont:

Theologians may puzzle their heads about dogmas as they will, the religion of gratitude cannot mislead us. Of that we are sure, and Gratitude is the handmaid to Hope, and hope the harbinger of Faith. I look abroad upon Nature, I think of the best part of our species, I lean upon my Friends, and I meditate upon the Scriptures... and my creed rises up of itself with the ease of an exhalation, yet a Fabric of adamant.[2]

Rydal Mount was no more the Wordsworths' property than Town End had been; but over the years it had come to seem their own. When Lady Fleming announced her plan to terminate the lease in July 1826, William retaliated by purchasing an adjoining piece of land to build on. His 'Inscription', composed when he feared that they would be leaving, bade farewell to the terrace he had built at the side of the house, which had become a favourite place for composition. Describing how his steps 'repeated to and fro | At morn, at noon, and under moonlight skies, | Through the vicissitudes of many a year'[3] had kept the weeds from growing, he expresses his deep sense of affinity with this beautiful pathway. The image of the pacing poet is both familiar and familial. It recalls William's habitual pacing as he composed in Dorothy's company on the orchard path at Town End, and the memory of their brother John, pacing to and fro in the fir-grove nearby. After successfully retaining their tenancy of Rydal Mount, he wrote another inscription, 'intended for a stone', to commemorate a tranquil summer spent in 'Dora's Field'. William's family had the stone engraved with this inscription while he was away on his travels. It was more like a covenant binding him to return than a gravestone where visitors might, as he put it, 'heave a gentle sigh for him, | As one of the Departed' (ll. 7–8; LP, 217).

'I was never leaner in my life', Dorothy wrote in 1821; 'I can walk with as little fatigue as when I was 20.'[4] William, too, despite the inflammation of the eyes which periodically disabled him, was by all accounts exceptionally fit for his age. As he approached his sixtieth birthday, Dorothy observed, 'He is still the crack skater on Rydal Lake, and, as to climbing of mountains, the hardiest and the youngest are yet hardly a match for him.'[5] Even so, life was not always easy in the Wordsworth household during the 1820s. There were uncertainties about the future of the three surviving children: John, who graduated from Oxford in 1826, and had difficulties finding a suitable curacy; Willy, who struggled at Charterhouse, and was later dependent on his father to find him a job; and Dora, who stayed at home with her parents, over-protected by her father because of ill-health, till her late marriage in 1841. William's responsibilities as a Stamp Distributor continued to consume more time than he had anticipated. He also committed himself with increasing vigour to Tory politics, loyally campaigning on behalf of William Lowther. Between 1822 and 1835—years in which he did much travelling and led an active social life among the neighbouring gentry—he produced no new collections. This was a time for taking stock of past achievements, bringing old work up to date, and enjoying the delayed rewards of literary success. Repeatedly postponing *The Recluse*, he was the subject of repeated nagging from Dorothy, who had grown anxious about his prospects of completing it: 'After fifty years of age there is no time to spare, and unfinished works should not, if it be possible, be left behind.'[6] William laboured instead on revision of existing poems. In 1824, the first collected American edition of his poems was published, and in 1827, his important five volume *Collected Works* appeared, including a revised version of *The Excursion*. A year later his poetical works were pirated in a single volume by Galignani in Paris, a sign that he had achieved recognition abroad. He and his family invested considerable time and energy in the preparation of volumes for the press, Sara Hutchinson and Dora working as his amanuenses as well as Dorothy and Mary. This cooperative labour consolidated his reputation late in life, building a solid foundation for his success as a Victorian poet.

As he became famous, William's relationship with Dorothy entered a new stage. Excursions to London frequently took him away from the rural life to which they were suited. A consciousness of the public sphere impinged more noticeably on the household's creative activities. Steadfast devotion to Mary, and increasing attachment to Dora, 'the apple of [his] eye',[7] changed the nature of his dependency on his sister. Equally, Dorothy's bonds with Sara and Joanna Hutchinson became more important as she aged. Because they were frequently apart, the Wordsworths' writings often grew out of independent experiences. Conscious though they continued to be of each other's influence, their works were not as intricately intertwined as they had been in the past, and there was more of a time lag between one stage and the next in their ongoing dialogue. Dorothy's writings developed in new ways as she spent more time away from William; and both writers turned less often to day-to-day life than to memories for confirmation of each other's love. Fundamental affinities between the writings of brother and sister nonetheless remained. Travelling away from home and homecoming provided them with common rituals, themes, and structural devices. For both, recollection went on being of paramount importance; and they each drew nostalgically on *shared* memories, especially of past tours.

Inevitably, the siblings had occasional disagreements. In 1825, for instance, Dorothy entered into correspondence with Walter Scott, asking him to settle a dispute that had arisen about whether or not she and William had accompanied their friend to Lichfield in 1806 to meet the poet Anna Seward. Twenty years had passed since their alleged visit, yet Dorothy claimed to remember many of its incidental details vividly: the wallflowers that grew on the old town walls; the unexpectedly short stature of their hostess; the upstairs room in which they had all sat talking, entered by a door on the left at the top of the stairs. William, however, flatly denied that they had accompanied Scott any further than the cathedral, as they had only fifteen minutes to spend on their Lichfield visit. Diplomatically or otherwise, Scott couldn't solve the mystery. He had no memory of being with either of them when he paid a visit to Anna Seward, and was mildly amused by all the fuss. Dorothy tried to maintain patience during what she humorously referred to as the 'Seward Dispute'; but as William joined the second round of letters, it became clear that the accuracy of memory was no trivial matter in the Wordsworth household. Her tone came near to despair as she acknowledged that she might either have dreamt the whole visit up, or pieced it together from other people's impressions. 'So it must be', she wrote on 25 June 1825; 'Yet the conclusion is mortifying, and will principally tend to make me doubt my internal testimony respecting past events connected with external objects.' It would be rash to read into this episode a premonition of dementia, the condition that in a decade's time would severely affect Dorothy's short-term memory, causing her to live more and more in the distant past. But her brief panic in 1825 serves as a reminder of how important shared memories were to her; and also high-lights the insecurity that accompanies any kind of memory failure—especially for a writer so preoccupied with veracity.[8]

*

Dorothy's failing health was to cast a long shadow over her middle age. The first signs of strain began to appear during the 1820s, with friends observing how tired she became when responding to repeated calls on her time and energy. Even so, she could still walk twenty miles a day, averaging three or four miles an hour over rough ground; and during the first eight years after the Continental tour of 1820 she was productive, finding inspiration for new writing not only in local surroundings but also in travels elsewhere. A number of creative projects got under way while she was separated from William. In September

to October 1822 she took a seven-week tour in Scotland with Joanna Hutchinson. The companions travelled in the opposite direction from the 1803 tour,
via Scott country to Edinburgh (in a coach appropriately named 'Walter
Scott'), west to Stirling and Glasgow, before pushing on to the Highlands and
the Isle of Bute, then circling back to Glasgow, and homeward. Although
Joanna's rheumatoid condition proved burdensome, holding Dorothy back on
several occasions, their slow pace gave her some productive solitude.

Recording her impressions of Scotland in a notebook while travelling,
Dorothy later made two expansions towards a fuller, more polished account
of the tour.[9] Though differing in some stylistic respects from earlier writings,
her *Journal of my Second Tour in Scotland* is an interesting variant on the revisit
mode she and William had evolved over a lifetime. Instead of describing an
itinerary structured by traditional tourist landmarks, Dorothy commented on
how Scotland had changed in the last nineteen years, mapping her journey
through personal associations. The revisit structure is already pronounced in
the notebook version of the tour (MS 98a). Walking to Arrochar with Joanna,
she remembered descending the same pass with William and Coleridge in their
Irish jaunting car: '*My* approach now slower, & I was glad, both for the sake of
past & present times' (JST, 8). Arrochar inevitably brought back the sad memory of parting from Coleridge; and writing about Tarbet prompted her, in the
second version of the tour (MS 98b), to remember the coffee and fowls
'dropped into the water when poor Coleridge was with us, & of our coasting
the Bay in a vessel even more crazy than this' (p. 53). The Trossachs, which in
1803 had inspired the Wordsworths' most evocative writing, were richly overlaid with associations. The notebook indicates that as Dorothy approached
Loch Lomond these crowded in upon her. She gladly recognized the 'proud
summit' of Inch Davannoch, from which the travellers had viewed 'so sublime
a prospect' in 1803; and describes looking out for the island which she had
imagined then as an ideal home: 'I missed the [Islet] with the ruins and could
not find our own cottage Isle' (p. 5). Saddened by the absence of an expected
landmark, Dorothy's thoughts in the journal dwell on mutability. She remembers how a chance encounter had inspired William's poem 'To a Highland
Girl' nineteen years earlier; and, in a sombre afterword to that poem, wonders
what has become of the girl's youth and beauty:

> Ferry house at Inversneyds just the same, excepting *now* a glass window. A Girl
> now standing at the door, but her I cannot fancy our Highland Girl, & the
> Babe, which its Grandame rocked, while the Babe squalled, now must be
> grown-up to toil & perhaps hardship or is it in a quiet grave?   (p. 5)

Her narrative is much preoccupied, often in unspoken ways, with William, and with the waning of creative power. Towards the end of the tour her frequent recording of moonlight scenes and the movement of streams suggests a need to map her journey through semi-figurative images and motifs from the past. (In the Wordsworths' writing, as we have seen, moonlight was associated with the creative stimulus of each other's presence, and streams with creative development and confluence.)

Much less well known than her early journals, *My Second Tour* is especially interesting for what it tells us about Dorothy's habits of revision. Thanks to the survival of all three manuscripts, we are able to trace the discrete stages through which her journal passed, and its evolving character. Dorothy's brief, staccato notebook entries while in transit are often no more than mnemonic devices to prompt later description and reflection:

> Cobler to right, huge stones scattered over glen. One hut in first reach, none in 2nd, white house in 3rd. Broken sash windows. Lieutenant. Stones. Fish. Father. Drunkenness. Shabby clothes, dirty shirt.   (pp. 10–11)

Even so, just as an artist can capture the essence of a scene by making a rapid sketch, so the notebook creates memorable vignettes from ordinary sights glimpsed in passing: 'Three children beside giant house, a Single Robin at the window. Cattle in the fields—as beautiful as if all were a living innocence' (p. 13). Preoccupied, as always, by the conditions endured by those she encountered on her travels, her notes convey their broken lives starkly, in a minimum of words:

> Mistress pretty tall woman, a Tear on her cheek. Three or 4 pretty children, all in a crowd. Within J said lay a dead child, nicely set out. I entered fire in centre chearful, cakes Baking, house small & melancholy.   (p. 14)

There is a vitality in rapid sketches that is sometimes lacking in more polished drafts. For instance, her laconic mention of the 'dead child, nicely set out' is later expanded into a detailed description of the family surrounding the child's body, 'covered with a clean linen cloth' (p. 123). Highlighting the scene's pathos, Dorothy creates a moral tableau by dwelling on the mother's melancholy—'I perceived a tear on her cheek'—and makes explicit the woman's kindness, which 'seemed to proceed from habitual good-will and hospitality' (p. 124). She also draws attention to her own presence as a woman of sensibility, 'musing on poverty, & peace, on death & the grave' (p. 123).

The expanded version of *My Second Tour* indicates Dorothy's increasing consciousness of readers beyond the family circle. Despite her reservations about the novel as a form, she handles narrative with a novelistic awareness of suspense. In a section of the tour relating to the journey from Crawford to Moffat which she added in the final draft, MS 99, she describes her fears as she travelled, encountering or imagining danger. Followed by two men whom they believed to be thieves or worse, the companions later discovered their mistake, and made light of it. Dorothy uses anticlimax (a device familiar to readers of Ann Radcliffe) to add tension and humour to this episode. Her authorial persona is also stronger than in previous journals. In her observations of Scottish life, she is more preoccupied than she had been in 1803 with articulating her Christian faith. Equally, her outspoken comments on Robert Owen's New Lanark factory-town reflect impatience with educational systems that ignore spiritual reverence in the teaching of botany and geography. She promotes the nature philosophy she shares with William, by this stage a Christian reformulation of the views he had expressed in Book V of *The Prelude*.

Dorothy's preoccupation with Scotland lasted a good while after her return to Rydal Mount. Before completing her 1822 tour, she revised her 1803 *Recollections* in the hopes of publishing it, and thus making some money for a further 'ramble'. Seeing an opening for herself as a travel writer—a genre she had once despised—she approached Samuel Rogers with a serious proposal for publication. This came to nothing, for reasons that have not been established. (Crabb Robinson, reading the final version in 1833, wished she had filled it with William's and her conversation, rather than minute description; so perhaps the volume's length deterred publication, though readers such as De Quincey thought it very fine.)[10] After writing up the 1822 tour, Dorothy returned to the more informal diary writing in which she had found her voice as a young woman. In May and June 1824, she made visits to Oxford, London, Cambridge, and Ipswich; and in December of that year she began to record daily events in a journal which she was to keep until 1833. The majority of the *Rydal Journal* is unpublished. It survives in fifteen notebooks, some hand-sewn, and is in places almost illegible. Mostly it takes the form of observations much sparser than those in the *Grasmere Journal*, as if its main purpose was to serve as a rudimentary mnemonic device. While at Rydal, memorable events are not recorded, and details of day-to-day happenings are rarely developed. She did, however, closely monitor the weather, catching in deft phrases its shifting identity: 'Darkness—dull moonlight—misty rain';[11] 'A warm misty mizzling bird-chaunting morning'.[12] Her use of dashes, anticipating Emily Dickinson's poetry, conveys a rapid, almost breathless sense of her connection with the constantly changing sky-scape:

> Thaw—heavy rain—clear before day—Walk on Terrace—amber Clouds— To Ambleside with Wm and Dora—Full Moon—tip toe—on dark Cloud— lost again.[13]

Moods of the mind are not explicitly analysed, but she records fluctuations of light and temperature so persistently that her writing serves almost as a mood-diary: 'Very close—and hot—Thunder showers—head-ache...Letters to Coleridge etc. Great thunders elsewhere—Man killed on lake';[14] 'Lovely Evening—Walk with Wm. on Terrace—Ruby Lights on Lake'.[15]

Some of the *Rydal Journal's* fullest and happiest entries concern the time she spent with her sister-in-law Joanna Hutchinson in 1826 on Thomas Hutchinson's new farm at Brinsop Court, near Hereford. Originally intending to stay only two months, Dorothy decided to prolong her visit because William was absorbed in an electioneering campaign before the general election: she was away from him for eight months, longer than any separation since their childhood. On holiday, with the time and leisure to observe the Herefordshire landscape as winter turned to spring, her journal regained a descriptive richness and detail reminiscent of days at Alfoxden and Grasmere: 'Green pastures in valley spotted with sheep—venerable pear trees— crested and tufted with mistletoe—branched with grey moss—Woods above.'[16] Joanna's companionship is a constant, felt presence in the journal; and William too haunts Dorothy's prose, as if she is conversing with him in her thoughts. On 2 March, for instance (remembering a walk they took by Brothers Water in the spring of 1802, and quoting the poem William had composed that day) she writes: '32 Cattle feeding like one on slope opposite my window—Birds singing but sound absorbed by grating of Mill.' A month later, exploring the Wye valley, she recalls his words in 'Tintern Abbey':

> Visited by 'something of a sad perplexity'—and shocked at the changes about New Weir—No longer the beauty of wild desolation and grandeur which I recall.[17]

The quotation marks signal her sense of William's voice speaking; and she borrows the word 'wild' to reinforce a sense of personal loss. While with the Hutchinsons, she also wrote two poems which show the continuing importance of memory to her health and happiness. In 'Lines to JH from Gwendovennant', she uses simple seasonal contrasts to express joy's transience. As William had asked Dorothy to return in memory to the Wye, so she in her turn asks Joanna to protect herself against sadness by returning literally to a particular place, beloved of them both. In 'A Holiday at Gwendovennant', she recalls times in her early childhood when she had played with her brothers, and celebrates a picnic with the Hutchinsons amid an entourage of children. The poem's mood is nostalgic, emphasizing the importance of festivals for binding together family members: 'each shall be a resting-place | For memory, & divide the race | Of childhood's smooth and happy years' (ll. 159–61).

Another exception to the usual brevity of entries in the *Rydal Journal* came in June–July 1828. During this month Dorothy stayed on the Isle of Man, where Joanna and her brother Henry Hutchinson (a retired sailor) were now living. Although her account of the trip is not a self-contained journal like the Scottish tour, it resembles a travelogue. Beginning at Rydal, Dorothy traces her solitary trip to Whitehaven via Cockermouth ('Lime trees gone from my Father's Court', she observed wistfully of her birthplace);[18] then describes her journey by steamship and her arrival at the Isle of Man, where she was united with Henry and Joanna. As she explored the island, she combined a tourist's perspective with insider knowledge gleaned from her hosts. The journal provides a vivid account of an island community, showing a strong interest (as the *Hamburg Journal* had done) in domestic scenes and especially women's ways of life. At Douglas on 28 June Dorothy captures the bustle of market day—women wearing 'round hats, like the Welsh'; panniers 'made of matted straw'; country people speaking more Manx than English, 'a sound…not coarse or harsh' (p. 403). The following day she notes how the same place is transformed by the quiet of sabbath: the street to the Post Office 'narrow as an Italian street, and cool', the stairs 'worn down with much treading, and everything reminding one of gentry life at Penrith 40 years back' (p. 404). In the company of Joanna, she visits the harbour:

> Saw the steam packet depart for Liverpool. Ladies in immense hats, and as fine as milliners and their own various tastes can make them. Beauish Tars, their pleasure boats in harbour, with splendid flags; two or three working sailors in bright blue jackets, their badges on their breast, straw hats trimmed with blue ribands. For the first time I saw the Cumberland hills; but dimly. Sea very bright; talked with old sailor and tried his spectacles.   (p. 405)

Natural objects are seen freshly, with the eye-on-the-object accuracy which so impressed Virginia Woolf: 'The moon rose large and dull, like an ill-cleaned brass plate, slowly surmounts the haze, and sends over the calm sea a faint bright pillar' (p. 402).

*

Although they spent less time together as they aged, the Wordsworths' writings in the late 1820s testify to their continuing closeness. They had many symbols for their reciprocal love, drawn from detailed observation of their surroundings. Often natural objects formed into semi-figurative clusters by virtue of having been often noticed together on local walks. In her *Grasmere Journal* for April 1802, Dorothy had noticed a single primrose growing near Glow-worm rock, a favourite stopping place on the road from Town End to Rydal; and six years later her description prompted William's poem about retirement in Grasmere, 'The Tuft of Primroses'. Glow-worms and primroses had an interlinked life in the Wordsworths' shared emotional history, as this lyric of 1829 confirmed:

> A Rock there is whose homely front
> The passing Traveller slights
> Yet there the glow-worms hang their lamps
> Like stars, at various heights;
> And one coy Primrose to that Rock
> The vernal breeze invites.[19]

Drawing on many accumulated personal associations, William gave thanks in his poem for the contribution this small flower had made to his emotional and spiritual life over the years. The primrose was 'A lasting link in Nature's chain | From highest Heaven let down', its perennial regrowth a sign of God's beneficence:

> The flowers still faithful to their stems
> Their fellowship renew;
> The stems are faithful to the root
> That worketh out of view
> And to the rocks the root adheres
> In every fibre true.   (ll. 13–18)

The importance of this poem as an expression of the household's bond with the region is signalled by the exactness with which Dorothy noted the circumstances of composition as she made her fair copy—'Written in March 1829 on seeing a Primrose-tuft of flowers flourishing in the chink of a rock in which that Primrose-tuft had been seen by us to flourish for twenty nine seasons'.[20] Such elaborate specificity suggests that she saw the poem as belonging to the 'Inscription' genre, normally used to commemorate connections between people and places. William was to revise the poem again and again, for it held a special significance in the painful years which saw a sharp deterioration in Dorothy's health. Manuscript versions survive in three forms: a fair copy by Mary Wordsworth of an early short version; a rough draft in William's hand (in the same notebook) of the longer version; and finally a fair copy of the completed poem in Dorothy's hand. The family's cooperative work on this poem nicely reflects its communal significance.

Dorothy's first severe bout of illness came only a month after the first draft of 'The Primrose of the Rock'. From November 1828, she had been keeping house for her nephew John in his curacy at Whitwick, a colliery village near Coleorton. In April 1829, while still away from home, she was struck down with an 'internal inflammation' from which she almost failed to recover. 'What a shock that was to our poor hearts', William wrote to Crabb Robinson, once she was out of the worst danger: 'Were She to depart the Phasis [sic] of my Moon would be robbed of light to a degree that I have not courage to think of.'[21] By the second week in May, she was well enough to leave Whitwick with Mary, paying an extended visit to her aunt Elizabeth Rawson on the way home. She arrived back at Rydal Mount on 8 September, but soon took to her bed, regaining strength slowly. In her invalid state, she relied on Dora to fulfil her duties in the household, acknowledging affectionately how her niece 'takes all care from her mother & me—as an Amanuensis to her Father—& Reader—spares our aged hands, eyes, & voices'.[22] Another attack of illness, with no apparent cause, struck her down in December 1831. The symptoms pointed to a diagnosis of gallstones, a condition which the family doctor appears not to have understood. 'Her recovery from each attack is slower and slower', William observed sadly in a letter to his brother Christopher.[23]

'That woman's so light she's made for walking.'[24] Proud that they referred to herself, Dorothy had recorded these words, overheard when she was exploring the Isle of Man, in 1828. Physical fitness had always been crucial to her emotional well-being, and to her creative life with her brother. Now she was unable to leave Rydal Mount, her enjoyment of the natural world was confined to what she could see from her window (or from the garden, into which she sometimes ventured). The household lived in dread of her recurring bouts of ill health, which were further complicated by progressive arteriosclerosis; but according to letters written by family members, Dorothy herself remained cheerful. She took pleasure in the arrival of visitors, in reading or listening to William read aloud, and in memories of happier times. 'Her friends might suppose that, having been so fond of the country, its prospects, and exercise she would have been in bad spirits under confinement,' William wrote, 'but it is not so—she finds compensation in reading, and her time never hangs heavy.'[25] The *Rydal Journal* indicates the extraordinary range of her taste in books. She not only read (or reread) the canonical English poets—Shakespeare and Spenser, Donne and Herbert, Milton, Collins, Cowper, and Crabbe—but the classics too: Dante, Tasso, Diderot, and Cervantes; and she transcribed Virgil. She also kept in touch with contemporary reviews, studied the Bible regularly, and built up her knowledge of sermons and devotional books. There was time for the enjoyment of her reading, as there had not been when the children were younger: this was some recompense for being physically inactive. But despite her good cheer, everyone at Rydal Mount was increasingly depressed by fears for her. 'I shall not dwell upon her state which weighs incessantly upon every thought of my heart', William wrote in January 1833.[26] A month later Sara Hutchinson wrote to Sara Coleridge, more plainly:

> alas! My dear friend, I fear she will not be long with us. Her weakness and languor are truly deplorable—indeed without the help of stimulants you could scarcely believe her alive … Mr Carr [the family doctor and Ambleside surgeon] gives us no hope of recovery—Her poor Brother strives to hope against hope—& to him we dare not breathe the fears which oppress us.[27]

During the spring and early summer, Dorothy rallied, thanks in large part to the loving attention she received at home. An extra servant was hired to attend to her basic needs, and the whole family helped with her daily palliative care. Mary and Sara were tirelessly attentive. Dora washed Dorothy, remembering how her aunt had done the same for her when she was a child. William regularly massaged her swollen feet, read to her, and pulled her out on the terrace in her carriage when it was fine. On receiving a copy of *Essays of Elia* in May 1833, he shared with her the delights of Lamb's prose: 'I read Love me and love my Dog to my poor Sister this morning while I was rubbing her legs at the same time.—She was much pleased.'[28] By then Dorothy was managing to walk with sticks; and by 16 July she had resumed her journal; but the improvement was not to last. At the beginning of December 1834, she was in bed for three weeks, and thereafter her health was steadily worsening.

The effects of Dorothy's decline on William were incalculable. Quite apart from grief, and the strain of helping to look after an invalid, there was a very real threat to his work. Walking with his sister—observing and remembering, in familiar or unfamiliar landscapes—had been so central a part of his adult life that it was hard to imagine a different kind of future.

In 1814, he had found that touring Scotland with Mary yielded creative results, partly because Dorothy was associated with the places he was visiting. Other attempts at poetic touring had been less successful. In 1828, when he travelled through the Rhineland and Holland with Dora and Coleridge, only one poem had emerged from the trip; and his five-week tour of Ireland in September 1829 proved equally unproductive. When it became clear that Dorothy was unlikely ever again to accompany him on his travels, the prospects for his continuing happiness and productivity looked bleak. There was no alternative but to look for solace from surrogate companions. By the time he set off for Scotland with Dora in August 1831, his daughter was fulfilling the expectation that she would play a supportive and companionable role, standing in for her aunt. The Scottish tour was designed to lift William's spirits, distracting him from his anxieties about the forthcoming Reform Bill, to which he was opposed. (In late spring 1831, Parliament was dissolved. The bill was introduced for the second time, and passed by the Commons in late September; then rejected by the Lords in October.) William felt 'averse ... to all hot Reformations; i.e. to every sudden change in political institutions upon a large scale',[29] and increasingly drew on a vocabulary reminiscent of Edmund Burke to express his conservatism: 'Where men will not ... look back, they cannot be expected to look forward; and therefore, caring for the present only, they care for *that* merely as it affects their own importance. Hence a blind selfishness is at the bottom of all that is going forward.'[30] Although a holiday would not diminish the misery caused by Dorothy's ill health, it might briefly take his mind off what he called 'the deplorable state of the country'.[31]

In the Wordsworth family, travels to Scotland were like pilgrimages to a creative source: brother and sister had taken turns (in 1814 and 1822) in bringing back their renewed impressions of the country, like health-giving tonics, to the sibling left behind. William's 1831 tour with Dora proved no exception to this family ritual. Often walking twenty miles a day, father and daughter went to Abbotsford, where they visited the banks of Yarrow with Walter Scott (soon to depart for Italy, and already dying) then on to Edinburgh and Stirling, the Highlands, and west to Mull, returning home via Inveraray, Glasgow, Lanark, Carlisle and Penrith. Like Dorothy a decade earlier, William was dismayed by changes that had taken place. Just as she had complained in her *Second Tour* about tourists trekking to see spots made famous by Scott, so he lamented the advent of steamboats, observed sadly that bagpipes were no longer played and kilts seldom worn; and objected to Celtic herdsmen using umbrellas.[32] Despite—or perhaps because of—the evidence of 'manners withering to the root', the tour proved to be deeply thought-provoking. Meditating on the vital role played by centuries-old customs and traditions, he looked around and saw enough to secure his continuing devotion to Scotland. A Highland brooch worn 'at the breast of some grave Dame' prompted speculation about the origins of this family heirloom, handed down through many generations. A pair of mountain peaks, known as the 'Shepherds of Etive Glen', proved that there was more to Scottish history than violent clan rivalry, for peaceful traditions lived on in local place names. A highland hut, with cracked walls and unused pathway, called for sympathy with the 'lonely Poor'. An overgrown graveyard 'Part fenced by man, part by a rugged steep', where wild animals came and went, provided a solemn setting for thoughts of nature's beneficence.[33]

The prevailing mood of the poems written during and after the tour was elegiac: 'coloured', William later acknowledged, 'by the remembrance of my recent visit to Sir Walter Scott, and the melancholy errand on which he was going'.[34] Dorothy's declining health, never out of his thoughts, gave an additional edge to his sombre reflections on human mortality:

> There's not a nook within this solemn Pass,
> But were an apt confessional for One
> Taught by his summer spent, his autumn gone,
> That Life is but a tale of morning grass,
> Withered at eve.[35]

Memories of Dorothy in her prime came thick and fast as William revisited places he had explored with her in 1803. His creativity was as always stimulated by the combination of walking and remembering. By the time the travellers returned to Rydal, he had laid the foundations for a new and highly unified collection, *Yarrow Revisited and Other Poems*, published in 1835. The title poem alludes to his two previous tours of Scotland, inviting readers to make connections between them. Remembering how Dorothy was alongside him in 1803 as they postponed their enjoyment of the Yarrow, he reuses the phrase 'winsome marrow' (a Scottish endearment in Hamilton's poem 'The Braes of Yarrow') to acknowledge her continuing presence in his thoughts. The poem concludes by giving thanks for the river's ongoing life:

> To dream-light dear while yet unseen
> Dear to the common sunshine,
> And dearer still, as now I feel,
> To memory's shadowy moonshine!   (ll. 109–12)

Hearing William read this poem aloud when he returned, Dorothy would doubtless have recognized in its final line a thankful acknowledgement of her role as muse. Ever since *An Evening Walk*, he had used the moon as a symbol of the hope, joy, and creativity he associated with Dorothy. In 1831, as he meditated on the creative power of memory, he was recalling his blessing in 'Tintern Abbey'—'Therefore let the moon | Shine on thee in thy solitary walk' (ll. 135–6).

Missing companions and missed opportunities are recurring motifs in the Wordsworths' writings about Scotland, arising naturally from their revisits. On a steep hill in the valley of Glen Croe, which William and Dorothy climbed together in 1803, they had found the famous seat—a stopping-point for travellers, mentioned by Boswell in his *Tour of the Hebrides*—which bore the inscription 'Rest and be Thankful'. The spot features in *Recollections of a Tour Made in Scotland*; Dorothy looked out for it when she retraced her steps in 1822, but failed to find it. William and Dora were luckier. His poem 'Rest and be Thankful' makes restitution to Dorothy for the opportunity she missed, and expresses gratitude for the seat's continuing presence. At Bothwell Castle, the tables were turned, and it was William who missed out on reliving the past. He had visited the castle in 1803 with Dorothy, and she had described it in her *Recollections*, but stormy weather prevented a revisit in 1831. Not to be deterred, he turned disappointment into an opportunity. His poem 'Bothwell Castle' celebrates the power of memory to soften regret, reaching out beyond the immediate context of disappointment to offer solace for much deeper losses:

> Better to thank a dear and long-past day
> For joy its sunny hours were free to give
> Than blame the present, that our wish hath crost.
> Memory, like Sleep, hath powers which dreams obey,
> Dreams, vivid dreams, that are not fugitive:
> How little that she cherishes is lost![36]

This sonnet belongs to a genre of healing poems, developed as long ago as 1797 in 'This Lime-Tree Bower My Prison' and perfected by the Wordsworth circle over the years. In such poems, re-creation from memory is doubly consolatory—to the poet himself, and to the recipient of his gift.

'Composed in Roslin Chapel, during a storm', another revisit poem, was prompted by a day spent in a beautiful disused chapel while the rain poured

down incessantly as it so often does in Scotland. Remembering its composition years later, William emphasized its extempore nature—'*Here* this Sonnet was composed'—but his poem so closely resembles a passage in
Dorothy's *Recollections* that we may assume he recalled or consulted it while
writing. Describing the same chapel, Dorothy's eye had been drawn to a
group of ferns growing in a niche alongside carvings of foliage in stone.
She had turned this sight into a beautiful word-picture, as skilful and intricate as a Victorian miniature:

> The stone both of the roof and walls is sculptured with leaves and flowers, so
> delicately wrought that I could have admired them for hours, and the whole
> of their ground work is stained by time with the softest colours; some of those
> leaves and flowers were tinged perfectly green, and at one part the effect was
> most exquisite: three or four leaves of a small fern, resembling that which we
> call adder's tongue, grew round a cluster of them at the top of a pillar, and the
> natural product and the artificial were so intermingled that at first it was not
> easy to distinguish the living plant from the other, they being of an equally
> determined green, though the fern was of a deeper shade.[37]

Whether or not William again saw this species of fern in 1831, his sonnet
follows the direction of Dorothy's thought, fascinated by her minutely
detailed observation of art and nature intermingling:

> From what bank
> Came those live herbs? by what hand were they sown
> Where dew falls not, where rain-drops seem unknown?
> Yet in the Temple they a friendly niche
> Share with their sculptured fellows, that, green-grown,
> Copy their beauty more and more, and preach,
> Though mute, of all things blending into one.[38]

Like other images of symbiosis in his writing, this one suggests not only an
appreciation of *nature's* mellowing influence but also a subliminal recognition of his sister's. The friendly cohabitation of 'live herbs' and their 'sculp-
tured fellows' might be read as a simile for their collaboration. Just as art
'copies' nature 'more and more', so William echoes Dorothy's prose. And just
as the line between their writings is 'not easy to distinguish', so they both
define beauty as a 'blending' of all things into one.

Scotland, in the company of Dora, provided William with the rejuvenat-
ing change he needed. For more than a month, he 'scarcely saw a newspaper,
or heard of their contents', so that when he came back to Rydal Mount, it
seemed as if he had 'waked from a dream that was never to return'.[39] Even

while touring he was unusually productive, composing five sonnets between 22 and 28 September. Ten days after returning home, he had completed the entire sequence. (Dorothy made fair copies of most of these, in DC MS 106.) Transcribing accurately is a demanding task, needing steady concentration: in this case, it required Dorothy to set aside her disappointment at being left behind, and enter into William's imaginative reconstruction of his and Dora's tour. Perhaps the copying process resuscitated memories of her own creativity in Scotland. When the collection went to press, it contained two substantial passages from *Recollections*, identified by William as 'from the journal of a Lady, my fellow-traveller in Scotland, in the autumn of 1803'.[40] One of these provided further information about the Wordsworths' visit to Bothwell Castle on that earlier trip; but the second, a description of the inside of a Highland hut with beams 'glossy as black rocks, on a sunny day, encased in ice', was included for purely aesthetic reasons.[41] Among Dorothy's finest pieces of prose, it recalls her state of reverie as she lay alone in 1803, listening to the sound of waves beating against the shore of Loch Katrine:

> I went to bed some time before the rest of family: the door was shut between us, and they had a bright fire, which I could not see, but the light it sent up among the varnished rafters and beams, which crossed each other in almost as intricate and fantastic a manner as I have seen the under boughs of a large beech tree withered by the depth of shade above, produced the most beautiful effect that can be conceived. It was like what I should suppose an underground cave or temple to be, with a dripping or moist roof, and the moonlight entering upon it by some means or other; and yet the colours were more like those of melted gems.[42]

Appearing at the end of *Yarrow Revisited*, this passage (slightly revised from the original) drew attention to Dorothy's importance as a touring companion and writer. William's decision to publish it, along with another long excerpt from *Recollections*, was an important recognition of their intertwined creativity. It also signified his longing for continuity between present and past selves, and may have helped to compensate for her exclusion from the 1831 tour.

*

In 1833, once again seeking the creative stimulus which came from travelling, William set off on a fifth tour of Scotland, this time accompanied by his son John and Henry Crabb Robinson. His objective was to explore places he had not had time to visit with Dora. 'I have been taking a peep at the Hebrides', he wrote to John Kenyon on 23 September. 'My tour, which was only for a fortnight, included the Isle of Man (visited for the first time), Staffa, Iona, and a return thro' Burns country, Renfrewshire and Airshire. The weather was mixed, but upon the whole I and my companions...were well repaid.'[43] The first part of their itinerary followed Dorothy's 1822 tour, pausing at Cockermouth and proceeding by steamboat from Whitehaven to the Isle of Man. William's letters home were full of solicitude for his ailing sister, containing descriptions 'chiefly for dearest Dorothy' of places she had seen in 1822. 'I thought far too much about your fatiguing walks in the Isle of Man and wished many times for you all to see the objects which pleased me so much.'[44] Dorothy's prior sentimental attachment to the island is clearly signalled in William's words of approval as he summarizes the trip: 'Upon the whole, Dearest D. I liked your Isle of Man better than I expected.'[45] Thereafter, his tour took him to places she had not explored, making her a captive audience for his impressions.

No poems were composed while the travellers were en route, but after his return to Rydal William wrote a series of sonnets, and this time it was Dora who made fair copies (DC MS 128). The sequence lingers lovingly on Lake District subject matter for quite a while before turning to the Scottish tour itself. A farewell sonnet to Rydal is followed by ten further poems about places on the way to Whitehaven, as if delaying the substance of the tour to make room for material that had greater sentimental value. Perhaps prompted by Dorothy's nostalgic pilgrimage to their birthplace in 1822, William's own visit to Cockermouth inspired a cluster of sonnets. 'In sight of the town of Cockermouth' begins movingly with lines honouring the Wordsworths' parental graves, and linking these with the graves of Thomas and Catherine. In a lighter tone, 'Address from the spirit of Cockermouth Castle' recaptures William's adventures in the castle's dungeon, and his chasing of butterflies across its 'green courts'. In this poem, William remembers 'To a Butterfly', composed in 1802, in which he had joined Dorothy's early memories with his own. Ten sonnets grew out of William's visit to the Isle of Man, but despite Dorothy's familiarity with this terrain, few of them drew on material from her journal of 1822, though they did allude to places she knew: Douglas, Bala-Sala, Tynwald Hill. After returning to Rydal, conversation with her about the remaining part of William's tour may well have stimulated a number of poems, but no evidence of this process survives. We can imagine Dorothy reading or listening to his three sonnets about the cave of Staffa with special interest; and she was probably touched

by a poem about the field in which Burns saw his mountain daisy. The final
sonnet offers a self-portrait which would have appealed to the whole family.
Describing his habit of frequently walking with his head bent to the ground,
William recalls the pensive poet of 'A Night-Piece':

> Most sweet it is with unuplifted eyes
> To pace the ground, if path be there or none,
> While a fair region round the Traveller lies
> Which he forebears again to look upon;
> Pleased rather with some soft ideal scene,
> The work of Fancy, or some happy tone
> Of meditation, slipping in between
> The beauty coming and the beauty gone.[46]

This sonnet beautifully captures the poet's sense of being suspended between
real and imagined travel, as if anticipating that future tours to Scotland will
be impossible, whereas journeys in the mind can go on and on.

*

William's wanderlust did not diminish with the passing years. Although he
never again visited Scotland, he did set off with Crabb Robinson on yet
another tour in the spring of 1837, this time to Italy. The trip fulfilled his
long-postponed ambition to complete the traditional 'Grand Tour' of Europe
by visiting Rome. This ambition had been reawakened by Scott's departure
for warmer climes in 1831 and by Samuel Rogers' book on Italy, three copies
of which the author sent to the Wordsworths in 1834. Dorothy was 'affected
even to the shedding of tears' on receiving one of them as a gift, for she too
had long harboured a wish to return to Italian places associated with happier and healthier times, and had indeed plotted such a return with Crabb
Robinson.[47] Writing to her from London before setting out, William regret-
ted his sudden departure: 'How I wish you could have gone with us; but I
shall think of you every where, and often shall we talk of you.'[48] It was with
some misgivings that he left Mary to take care of Dorothy, aware of the
sacrifice she was making. An unsympathetic reader might accuse him of
selfishness in taking time away from Rydal Mount during his sister's decline,
but the emotional strain caused by her illness—and his need to produce
new poetry—should be set against the difficulties his absence created.[49]
There is no surviving evidence that Mary felt resentment when he went
away; but Dorothy did occasionally complain in her journal of feeling
neglected: 'This day William and Mary left us in the car to go to London',

she wrote, on 17 February 1835 (Dora was also bed-bound at this time). 'Both in good spirits till the last parting came—when I was overcome ... [I] shall only state my sorrow that our friendship is so little prized and that they can so easily part from the helpless invalides.'

The Italian tour (which had been planned with advice from Richard Sharp, like the tour of 1820) followed a highly ambitious itinerary for two elderly men. After travelling south from Calais to Marseilles, they headed to Rome, Florence, Bologna, Milan, Como, Iseo, and Garda. From there they travelled to Austria, arriving in June, and making their way home through Germany. In Dorothy's absence, William became the primary chronicler *in prose* of experiences he planned to write about later in poetry. A letter describing his journey from Calais through northern France (which Isabella Fenwick forwarded to Mary, Dorothy, and Dora) set out his plan: 'To spare your eyes and save time I shall write journal-wise.'[50] He remained true to his promise, providing an informal narrative reminiscent in many respects of Dorothy's travel journals, which he sent off in letters to the womenfolk waiting at home. He selected details that would appeal to their nostalgia. At Paris he recalled how, walking in the Tuileries gardens in 1820, he and his companions had watched a group of boys rolling and hiding among withered leaves. At the Ponte Mario in Rome, he discovered a pine tree 'looking like a little cloud in the sky, with a slender stalk to connect it with its native earth'.[51] Learning that the pine had been saved from felling by Sir George Beaumont, he 'touched the bark of the magnificent tree and could almost have kissed it out of love for his memory'.[52] Other places in Italy were saturated with family associations, which he was quick to communicate. At Lake Como and Cadenabbia, the 1820 tour came upon him 'as fresh as if [it] happened the day before', and 'very often could I, for my hearts relief, have burst into tears'.[53]

Much of the tour impressed him deeply. Lake Albano, he wrote, was 'surrounded with romantic beauty and every part of it is renowned in history and fable'.[54] The fall of Terni was 'much the most impressive waterfall I ever saw'.[55] But he found travelling with his active and sociable companion stressful, and repeatedly said of the tour while travelling 'it is too late'.[56] His long, marvellous letters show how alive he was to foreign landscapes and culture, but also how much he longed for home. 'I think of you all a thousand times a day and often wish I were back again at dear Rydal', he wrote from Lake Albano in May.[57] In June, he confessed to Dora that his spirits had been 'depressed' by not receiving a letter. At Munich in July, he observed wistfully that 'A man must travel alone, I mean without one of his family, to feel what his family is to him!'[58] The Italian tour of 1837 worked as a stimulus for poetry, but only after he had returned to Rydal Mount. Here, surrounded once again by the people and hills he loved, he composed a final travel sequence, *Memorials of a Tour in Italy*, later published as a subsection of *Poems, Chiefly of Early and Late Years* (1842), with a touching dedication to Crabb Robinson. The most appealing poems in the sequence are those which succeed in bridging Westmorland and the Continent. 'Musings at Aquapendente' opens with reminiscences of Scott's departure for Italy, comparing Italian rural landscapes with the Lake District. 'The Pine of Monte Mario at Rome' describes how 'thoughts of home, | Death-parted friends, and days too swift in flight' overwhelmed him, supplanting 'the whole majesty of Rome'.[59] These poems are balanced by the very last, 'Composed on May Morning, 1838', to commemorate homecoming. Here William writes as a settled native of Westmorland, comparing his 'old love of you, dear Hills' with his 'new love of many a rival image brought | From far'.[60] Like a lover torn between two women, he begs forgiveness for 'wandering of...thought', and rededicates himself to his native region. 'One enjoys objects while they are present but they are never truly endeared till they have been lodged some time in the memory', William observed to his friend George Ticknor.[61] He might appropriately have added, 'till they have been shared with family'.

15

Rydal

'Glad sight wherever new with old
Is joined through some dear homeborn tie;
The life of all that we behold
Depends upon that mystery.'[1]

*

As Dorothy's health degenerated and one after another of their friends died, awareness of mortality weighed heavily in the Wordsworth household. Sir George Beaumont's death on 7 February 1827 affected the entire family deeply. 'Nearly five and twenty years have I known him intimately, and neither myself nor my family ever received a cold or unkind look from him', William wrote to Samuel Rogers.[2] When Lady Beaumont followed him two years later, Dora confessed what a blow this was to her parents. The 'last link of a most interesting chain of thought, recollection, association & affection' had been 'snapped for ever', and with it 'an uninterrupted friendship of seven and twenty years standing'.[3] A tally of close friends who died in the next eight years—William Calvert in 1829, Walter Scott in 1832, James Losh in 1833, Coleridge and Lamb in 1834, John Fleming, Richard Sharp, and Robert Jones in 1835—is by no means comprehensive. In January 1834, William reported that in the previous three or four months 'No less than 14 of our Relatives, or valued acquaintance have been removed'.[4] When writing of Coleridge's death, his language expressed the visceral shock of mortality: 'though . . . I have seen little of him for the last twenty years, his mind has been habitually present with me, with an accompanying feeling that he was still in the flesh. That frail tie is broken, and I, and most of those who are nearest and dearest to me must prepare and endeavour to follow him.'[5] The year 1835 was the gloomiest of all. In April, two days before his sixty-fifth birthday, William observed, 'How a thought of the presence of living friends brightens particular spots, and what a shade falls over them when those friends have passed away.' Two months later, Sara Hutchinson's sudden fatal illness proved how right he was. Dorothy was too shocked to respond to the loss of her closest female companion. 'My tears are all to shed', she wrote,[6] taking refuge in the anticipation of her own demise: 'I do not feel that I have lost her, I am brought nearer to her.'[7] William, watching his sister's precarious health anxiously, wrote in tears: Sara's loss, he said, was 'irreparable to us all'.[8]

Life was never quite the same at Rydal Mount after 1835. As the Wordsworths knew from experience stretching back to their early childhood, one loss associatively calls up another. When William learnt that Hogg the 'Ettrick Shepherd' had died on 21 November, he composed his 'Extempore Effusion upon the Death of James Hogg'. The title is misleading, for it implies that the poem is a spontaneous outpouring of grief for a single person, whereas in fact it expressed a cumulative grieving that had already spanned several years. Many losses are lamented within the poem's brief time-frame:

> Like clouds that rake the mountain-summits,
> Or waves that own no curbing hand,
> How fast has brother followed brother,
> From sunshine to the sunless land!
>
> Yet I, whose lids from infant slumbers
> Were earlier raised, remain to hear
> A timid voice, that asks in whispers,
> 'Who next will drop and disappear?'   (ll. 21–8)

A subtle allusion to 'Kubla Khan'—'From sunshine to the sunless land'—recalls the dazzling early years of Coleridge's genius, before opium addiction blighted his life and wrecked his marriage. In the line 'how fast has brother followed brother', William subliminally returns to the first terrible loss of his adulthood—that of his brother John in 1805. Outliving was a lonely privilege. 'Extempore Effusion' is a poignant expression of survivor's guilt, spoken on behalf of a lost generation: its sombre, measured tones convey the meditative power that is characteristic of William's greatest elegies.

Despite the 'timid voice' reminding him of his own mortality, William lived on for a further fifteen years. His gloomy pronouncements on current literary tastes—'these are bad times for publishing Poetry, in short nothing but low prices—and utilitarian works seem to go down'[9]—proved baseless, for he had already made considerable progress with creating the taste by which he was to be enjoyed. *Yarrow Revisited and Other Poems* (1835) sold more copies than any volume he had previously published—1,500 within nine months—and went into its third edition in 1839. Nor did his success end there. Between 1839 and 1850, his *Poetical Works* were reissued nine times. As his fame increased, so did his readers' interest in meeting him. Throughout the 1830s, a stream of English and American literati visited Rydal Mount. Public honours showered upon him: in 1838 and 1839, Durham and Oxford Universities awarded him honorary degrees; and in 1843, on the death of Southey, he became Poet Laureate. For all the satisfaction this belated acclaim brought, it bored him. He was 'never thoroughly happy but in the country', as Crabb Robinson explained,[10] and felt alienated by the metropolis, where he was lionized. 'O, my dear Friend,' he complained to Isabella Fenwick in 1841, 'the hollowness of London society . . . and not only the hollowness but the tediousness especially among Dabblers in Literature—to me their talk, and their flattery above all, is insupportable.'[11] As he looked back on his long connection with the Lake District, memories became a form of sustained thanksgiving for the choice he had made in 1799 to live in seclusion. In a sonnet addressed to Wansfell (a nearby summit, seen every day from Rydal Mount), he rebuked himself for taking its beauty for granted, honouring the glory this summit had 'lavished on our quiet days'. Blending Christian faith with fatherly solicitude, his poem is a moving tribute spoken on behalf of an entire family:

> Bountiful Son of Earth! when we are gone
> From every object dear to mortal sight,
> As soon we shall be, may these words attest

How oft, to elevate our spirits, shone
Thy visionary majesties of light,
How in thy pensive glooms our hearts found rest.[12]

Such poems had a valedictory mood, for William was taking the opportunity to leave a clear record of his gratitude before he died. The memory of his father's sudden intestate death may well have influenced the way in which he ordered and arranged a lifetime's recollections into a unity he could bequeath to the generations who survived him.

*

There was a remarkable consistency in the 'home-born' ties linking William's public and private activities during the last two decades of his life. In the 1830s and 1840s, he fought for two important public causes. The first, reforming the law of copyright, had been an active concern of his for a considerable time. 'The wrongs of literary men are crying out for redress on all sides', he had proclaimed in 1819: 'It appears to me that towards no class of his Majesty's Subjects are the laws so unjust and oppressive.'[13] Although some progress had occurred since then, the law still prevented the families of authors from benefiting from the sale of their works once the authors had died. In a petition to Parliament, in letters to prominent politicians, and in a number of late poems, William championed the claims of surviving families to a share in the booksellers' profits. His own reputation had been established within his lifetime; but he was mindful of his old age, of the future of his children and grandchildren, and of writers whose lives were shorter than his. Engaging in a vigorous campaign to extend copyright from twenty-eight to sixty years, he worked in alliance with Thomas Noon Talfourd, barrister and MP, who took this cause to Parliament, and succeeded in changing the law in 1842. William's aims in the campaign were altruistic, but impelled by a different instinct from the one that led to the anonymous and collaborative publication of *Lyrical Ballads* in 1798. Then, poetry had been distinct from material property, and the notion of inherited wealth had been abhorrent. Throughout his life, William had remained ambivalent towards property and success. Deploring the newly emerging celebrity culture, he had resisted the pressure to be popular like Scott or Byron, preferring to envisage an audience that was 'fit...though few' ('Home at Grasmere', ll. 972–3). Circumstances had enabled him to stay relatively aloof from the literary marketplace, and to preserve a gift economy for his and Dorothy's writing, at least before publication. In the Wordsworth household, the intrinsic value of poetry as a creative, therapeutic, and devotional medium mattered a great deal more than the money it raised. The economics of authorship, however, had impinged as the family expanded and a larger income became necessary. In old age, never having inherited or owned a home, William gave careful thought to how the earning power of collections published under his name might go on ensuring the family's livelihood. He continued to see poems as inalienable possessions; but he now looked beyond his death for a financial reward that was commensurate with the labour they had cost and the market value they had accrued. Poetry had been a family concern in the Wordsworth household ever since 1800. *All the women at Rydal Mount—Dorothy, Mary, Sara Hutchinson, and Dora—had made active contributions. ('He held a pen with reluctance and impatience,' his nephew Christopher wrote, 'but he wielded many pens in the hands of others.')[14] Now William was famous, it was fitting that those who survived him should reap the rewards of work to which they had collectively devoted so much of their lives.

The second public cause he championed in the 1840s was environmental. In 1844, a proposal was put forward for a railway line from Oxenholme to Windermere, preparatory to extending the line further north. Not only would the peaceful surroundings at Rydal Mount be spoiled, but on the other side of the Lake District the planned railway would pass close by John Wordsworth's vicarage in Brigham, cutting through his garden. 'A vile job contrived by juggling speculators': in this bitter phrase, William gave vent in private to his hatred of all that the Windermere railway line stood for.[15] His implacable opposition to the plan arose from his loyal commitment to the Lake District and its accumulated memories. He responded immediately with a literary campaign, writing poems and letters to the editor of the *Morning Post*. Historic sites such as Furness Abbey provided a focus for his outrage:

> Is there no nook of English ground secure
> From rash assault? . . .
> And must he too the ruthless change bemoan
> Who scorns a false utilitarian lure
> Mid his paternal fields at random thrown?
> . . .
> Plead for thy peace, thou beautiful romance
> Of nature; and, if human hearts be dead,
> Speak, passing winds: ye torrents, with your strong
> And constant voice, protest against the wrong.[16]

Addressing members of the Board of Trade and the House of Commons, he argued that easier access to the Lake District would be of little benefit to outsiders. The region's beauty was an acquired taste, he claimed, the pre-rogative of those who lived locally, absorbing its influence day by day: 'the perception of what has acquired the name of picturesque and romantic scenery is so far from being intuitive, that it can be produced only by a slow and gradual process of culture'.[17] Instead of exporting artisans from indus-trial cities to the countryside, would it not be better, he argued, to lead them towards an appreciation of *their own* local surroundings, from which they could draw sustained pleasure, health, and moral improvement? He cited Burns, the people's poet, as a fellow believer in the importance of local attachments. Burns, he claimed, was 'little affected by the sight of one spot in preference to another, unless where it derived an interest from history, tradition, or local associations'.[18] Although the elitist tenor and territorial tone of this argument proved unpopular, his protest succeeded in enlisting support, and prevented the railway from extending any further than Wind-ermere. There was nothing new in William's environmentalist position, grounded as it was in the laws of association he had spent his life observing. When using the phrase 'paternal fields', he referred to the small plots of land farmed through many generations by the likes of the shepherd Michael. As he had felt in 1800, so he felt now: that these 'little tract[s] of land' served as 'a kind of permanent rallying point for domestic feelings, as a tablet upon which they are written which makes them objects of memory in a thou-sand instances when they would otherwise be forgotten'.[19] William's concern for the Lake District's future intertwined with his wish that his own family's regional identity—its deep sense of belonging to Westmor-land—should continue through generations to come. His fears for Dora, whose health had always been fragile, and for Dorothy, who looked increas-ingly likely to die before him, intensified his regional attachments.

*

By a tragic irony, the years that consolidated William's poetic reputation saw a dramatic deterioration in Dorothy's health. In 1833, she fell very seriously ill; but worse followed two years later, with the onset of a debilitating men-tal condition that was to blight the remainder of her life. It was the sudden shock of Sara Hutchinson's death in June 1835 which provoked alarming new symptoms. 'Since Sarah's [*sic*] departure', William wrote on 6 August, Dorothy's mind had been 'so confused as to passing events, that we have no distinct knowledge of what she may actually have to support in the way of bodily pain'.[20] The disappearance of her short-term memory (a classic sign of senile dementia) intensified her emotional attachment to the past: 'She remembers and recollects all but recent things perfectly, and her understanding is, as far as her strength will allow her to think, clear as it ever was.'[21] Unable to walk, or remember anything she had recently read, she stayed in her room, which she kept at an unbearably warm temperature—insisting on having a fire lighted, even during the summer. Increasingly, Mary observed, she became incontinent and demanding, 'like a very *clever tyrannical* spoilt child'. Mary attributed Dorothy's 'restless feelings' to 'something amiss going on in the head which she rubs perpetually', and noted that she was unable to find quiet for her reading: 'nor will she often listen to it—she says she is too busy with her own feelings'.[22] She developed a 'gnawing appetite', periodically uncontrollable, and put on a great deal of weight.[23] William and Mary tried to wean her off opiates, causing her to become increasingly irritable. She responded with fits of rage, and even violence: 'she would terrify strangers to death', Mary confided in a letter.[24] Edith Southey had undergone a similar collapse in 1834: Southey coped by having her admitted to a mental institution for the insane at York, and three years later, with no hope of recovery, she returned home to die. By contrast, the treatment Dorothy received was deeply enlightened and humane, enabling her to live at home, surrounded by those she loved, for twenty more years.

Dorothy's grand-nephew Gordon Graham Wordsworth, when arranging the family papers, decided that the entries in her *Rydal Journal* between 1831 and 1833 were 'so full of her malady that I have had no hesitation in excising and destroying them after making a copy of every record that seemed to me of permanent interest'.[25] As a result, stubs are all that remain of eighteen leaves in one of the notebooks. Entries in the journal between 1834 and 1835, her last coherent year, are intermittent and mostly brief. Aside from inventories of her fluctuating symptoms—'pain—sickness—headache—perspiration—heat and cold'[26]—they are consistent with her voice in the *Grasmere Journal*. They show her attentive to goings-on in the household: Dora's bouts of illness, Mary's perpetual kindness, Crabb Robinson's willingness to sit patiently, hour after hour, entertaining her. The visits and deaths of friends are noted. 'How recent the deaths of poor Coleridge and Charles Lamb!' she wrote in January 1835, 'and should Mr Fleming go Wm will have to mourn over one who was his dearest friend in youth!!'[27] Her prose captures the beauty of the changing seasons, the busy life of birds and insects on warm days, her continuing efforts to do a little gardening, the pleasure of being taken out in a wheelchair (her 'Baby Ride'), or transported in the 'family phaeton' to revisit her favourite haunts:

I have been sticking leafy bright green twigs of Elder among my Spring and winter flowers—my garden of *all the* seasons visited by the Bees who solace me with their gentle humming while the birds warble sweetly.[28]

Dora and Mrs E. Took me to Grassmere Lake [*sic*]—never more beautiful— the Oaks changing their first yellow to the purest of bright green hues—all things partook of life and happiness—As I said to Wm.—there was a calm brilliancy surpassing any thing I ever saw at that hour.[29]

She treasures, much as in the Grasmere years, the thought of occasional physical closeness to her brother—'A lovely day—dear William even purposed bearing me in his arms to the terrace to view his last improvement'[30]—and records, at other times, how their lives run in quiet parallel:

Had a delightful airing…on green terrace with James alone—Wm. lying on grass-plot shaded with Umbrella etc, and I passed him unperceived of him, and not perceiving him though close to him. The day charming—a newly-fledged Thrush could not fly to the top of the wall—The little wren very busy—Robin and white moth—tired but a sound sleep quite set me up again—the air now does me much good—I feel it day by day.[31]

At least in its edited form, the journal is remarkably free of anger and self-pity. Dorothy was grateful for the opportunity to re-enter the world outside her sickroom; but when cooped up inside she gave thanks for the ministrations of nature: 'I prudently contented myself with sitting before the window and was never more cheared—with sun-set and moon-rising—and clouds gathering and melting away. It was perfect healing.'[32] Even though her disability was severe, she was able to follow the example set by Coleridge in 'This Lime-Tree Bower my Prison', vicariously enjoying the pleasures from which she was excluded. 'Wm came to me rejoiced to hear thickly falling rain after so long a pause', she wrote on 10 December 1834: 'I could not but feel a touch of sympathy with him in memory of many a moist tramp.'

The poems Dorothy composed between 1832 and 1835 are more mercurial than her journal, alternating between despair and acceptance of her invalid state. In 'Lines intended for Edith Southey's album' (1832), she reminds herself that the trials of illness are helpful to the soul. The same year, in 'Lines written…on a day of surpassing beauty', she listens to peaceful country sounds drifting into her room, comforting herself with pious thoughts of an afterlife. Usually the devoutness of her Christian faith is uppermost, but the tone of 'To Thomas Carr, my medical attendant' (1835) is plaintive: 'Five years of sickness and of pain | This weary frame has travelled o'er'; and in a brief poem of protest addressed to John Carter, her anger sounds out loud and clear:

> When shall I tread your garden path?
> Or climb your sheltering hill?
> When shall I wander, free as air,
> And track the foaming rill?
>
> A prisoner on my pillowed couch
> Five years in feebleness I've lain,
> Oh! shall I e'er with vigorous step
> Travel the hills again?

Three lines of verse written in the back pages of her last notebook reveal that Dorothy may have had insight into her deteriorating mental condition in 1835: 'My tremulous prayers feeble hands | Refuse to labour with the mind | And that too oft is misty dark & blind.' Thereafter, she experienced intervals of mental clarity, during which she wrote a few letters and poems. 'Christmas Day' (1837), which celebrates anniversaries as rituals for bringing together family members, recalls the nostalgic poem about local minstrels that William had addressed to their brother Christopher in 1820. Always a poignant day for Dorothy, 25 December was her birthday: through nine years of her childhood, she had not been included in the family's Christmas festivities at Cockermouth.

The *Rydal Journal* comes to a sudden end in November 1835. Two years later, Dorothy confessed in a letter, 'A madman might as well attempt to relate the history of his own doings, and those of his fellows in confinement, as I to tell you one hundredth part of what I have felt, suffered and done.'[33] That same year, on Christmas Day, William wrote to his publisher, Edward Moxon, acknowledging that in his judgement Dorothy was no longer capable of preparing her 'journal' (Presumably *Recollections of a Tour Made in Scotland*) for publication:

> I *had* hoped that my carrying my Sister's journal thro' the press might prove a salutary interest to her—but as I no longer can cherish that hope, I must defer the publication—we find that the work perhaps would not interest her at all, or if it did, like every thing that excites her, it would do her harm.[34]

Her last surviving letter, one of the very few she wrote after the onset of dementia, was to Dora in the spring of 1838. It begins on an uncharacteristic note, protesting against the *obligation* to communicate: 'They say I must write a letter—and what shall it be? News—news I must seek for news. My own thoughts are a wilderness—'not pierceable by power of any star'— News then is my resting place—news! news!'[35] Dorothy's quotation from Spenser's *The Fairie Queene* shows the persistence of her extraordinary memory for poetry. Then, with a sudden shift of register, she turns to her community of female friends, living and dead:

> Poor Peggy Benson lies in Grasmere Church-yard beside her once beautiful Mother. Fanny Haigh is gone to a better world. My Friend Mrs Rawson has ended her ninety and two years pilgrimage—and *I* have fought and fretted and striven—and am here beside the fire. The Doves behind me at the small window—the laburnum with its naked seed-pods shivers before my window and the pine trees rock from their base.—More I cannot write so farewell! and may God bless you and your kind good Friend Miss Fenwick to whom I send love and all the best of wishes.[36]

The litany of names is solemn, but unsentimental—the religious connotations of 'better world' and 'pilgrimage' offset by a laconic realism that acknowledges physical decay and the struggles of old age ('once beautiful Mother'; '*I* have fought and fretted and striven'). Nature, as always in her writing, is present as the continuum within which human lives unfold. The doves are trusty companions, like the swallows who built their nests outside her window at Town End in 1802. But the laburnum shivers, its seed-pods vulnerably naked; and the pine trees rock from their base.

*

'In tenderness of heart I do not honestly believe [she] was ever exceeded by any of God's Creatures', William confessed to Lamb on 17 May 1833: 'Her loving kindness has no bounds.'[37] To the end of his life, Dorothy remained William's beloved sister, his ideal reader, and muse, the person to whom above all others he dedicated his poetry. Although the Wordsworths' literary dialogue became one-sided when Dorothy stopped writing, her influence and contribution did not end, for she had intervals of lucidity, valuable to their shared emotional and creative life. The memory of Dorothy in her prime lived on alongside the infirm sister, shaping the poems William wrote during the 1830s. Some implicitly addressed her; some included her in a general address to the household; others alluded directly or indirectly to her decline. As Dorothy adapted to the constraints of her sickroom at Rydal Mount, so William's poetry turned to themes of sickness and healing. These were increasingly popular subjects, especially in album verses and sentimental fiction during the Victorian period. Felicia Hemans's collection *Scenes and Hymns for Life*—a copy of which William received as a gift from the author— contained a poem in this genre. In a letter thanking Hemans for her gift, William mentioned finding the poem ('Flowers and Music in a Room of Sickness') 'especially touching' on account of Dorothy, 'who has long been an invalid, confined almost to her chamber'.[38] A few months after reading it, he wrote 'The Redbreast', drawing on his impressions of Dorothy shortly before her dementia set in. Out of respect for her privacy, he provided an alternative setting for the sickroom, and concealed her identity behind that of a man 'who long hath lain, | With languid limbs and patient head, | Reposing on a lone sick-bed'.[39] Family members must have read 'The Redbreast' with Dorothy clearly in mind, for it alludes to her experience of being visited in her sickroom by a robin. William later recalled how the bird 'took up its abode with her, and at night used to perch upon a nail from which a picture had hung. It used to sing and fan her face with its wing in a manner that was very touching.'[40] In Thomson's *The Seasons*, the robin is hailed as a bird 'sacred to the household gods'[41] and ever since 1798, robins had symbolized hope, love, and renewal in the Wordsworth household. The bird's companionship was a sure sign that Dorothy's intimate bond with nature continued even in sickness: 'not like a beggar he is come, | But enters as a looked-for guest' (ll. 4–5). Her lifelong attachment to robins also influenced Sara Hutchinson's poem addressed 'To the Redbreast', which contains a stanza composed by William, and describes the bird as a 'harbinger | Of everlasting spring'. To commemorate Sara's life, this poem was published in 1836 alongside Dorothy's 'Loving and Liking: Irregular Verses Addressed to a child', which William tactfully identified as 'by a female friend of the author'. The positioning of the two poems next to each other within the volume recognized the close proximity in which the two women had lived, and William's love for them both.

'There is always something very touching in his way of speaking of his sister', a neighbour observed of William in old age: 'the tones of his voice become more gentle and solemn. It is as if the sadness connected with her present condition was too much for him to dwell upon in connection with the past.'[42] As Dorothy's dependency increased, so did William's preoccupation with sibling relationships. Ever since first meeting Lamb in 1797, he had identified with his friend's devotion to his sister Mary; and comparisons between the two pairs of siblings were commonplace in their circle of friends.[43] In his story 'Mackery End, in Hertfordshire', which is based on his relationship with Mary, Lamb referred to their close relationship—grounded in cohabitation and collaboration—as 'a sort of double singleness'.[44] This was a phrase that applied just as appropriately to the Wordsworths, as they doubtless recognized. In a late revision to 'Farewell Lines', written when the Lambs were leaving London for Enfield, William described Charles and Mary as 'Two glowworms in such nearness that they shared, | As seemed, their soft self-satisfying light'.[45] It was a simile steeped in familial associations, reflecting back on his and Dorothy's symbiotic relationship. After the devastating blow of Charles Lamb's death in December 1834, William observed, 'It seems to us upon reflection that his Sister will bear the loss of him better than he could have borne that of her', an empathetic comment that once again revealed the strength of his identification.[46] Members of the Wordsworth circle would have understood that the poet's epitaph for Charles Lamb was not just a tribute to the steadfast patience with which he had cared for his sister over a period of thirty years; it was also a declaration of William's renewed love and loyalty to Dorothy in her increasingly dependent state:

> Her love
> (What weakness prompts the voice to tell it here?)
> Was as the love of mothers; and when years,
> Lifting the boy to man's estate, had called
> The long-protected to assume the part
> Of a protector, the first filial tie
> Was undissolved; and, in or out of sight,
> Remained imperishably interwoven
> With life itself.[47]

William's similes, both here and in subsequent lines, describe the intertwined fates of brother and sister, recalling earlier poems about familial bonds such as 'The Brothers', 'When to the Attractions of the Busy World', and 'A Tradition of Darley Dale'. In an elegy for one family, William writes a poem of consolation for another:

> Thus, 'mid a shifting world,
> Did they together testify of time
> And season's difference—a double tree
> With two collateral stems sprung from one root...[48]

No record survives of Dorothy's response to this touching epitaph; but two years after William composed it, in one of her very few letters, she revealed her empathy with Mary Lamb, who 'still survives—a solitary twig—patiently enduring the storm of life. In losing her Brother she lost her all—all but the remembrance of him, which cheers her the day through.'[49]

During the painful years of Dorothy's decline, much of William's poetry spoke directly to the concerns of his household and their immediate circle of friends, offering solace to a dying generation. He had a sympathetic listener in Southey, who was also coping with mental illness in the family. In a sonnet sent to Southey as a gift after Edith died, William reached deep into his own experience of loss and grief, consoling his friend with the thought that Edith's years of insanity had not been pointless. Like the idiot boy of *Lyrical Ballads*, whose life was 'hidden with God', her spiritual identity had remained intact, he believed, until the end. In the first draft of his poem, William openly revealed the personal grounds of his identification with Southey: 'While o'er my stricken Sister's couch I bend | Like consolation comes with gentle force.'[50] The published version was less transparently confessional because Mary intervened, not wanting lines that might give pain to her sister-in-law to appear in print. William relied on the women in the household to guide him in such delicate matters. Poetry was a family concern, and important decisions were collective.[51] The same sensitivity entered into his decision to acknowledge Dorothy's contributions to his work anonymously. When *Yarrow Revisited* went to press in 1835, he included 'The Sun has long been set'—a favourite poem of hers—at her request, but referred to her as 'a friend who was present when the lines were thrown off as an impromptu'.[52] Her own poem 'The Floating Island at Hawkshead' appeared in *Poems* 1842 as by 'DW': the use of her initials being a significant development in the way he approached their creative collaboration.

*

In October 1833, Catherine Clarkson wrote to Henry Crabb Robinson just after reading her way through 'heaps of old letters', many written by their mutual friend Dorothy. 'What a heart and what a head they discover! What puffs we hear of women, and even of men, who have made books and done charities, and all that, but whose doings and thinkings and feelings are not to be compared with hers!'[53] There was something elegiac in the way members of the Wordsworth circle began to write about Dorothy's intellect and character as they watched her declining into inactivity.

Coleridge, for instance, referred to her in the same year as 'a Woman of Genius, as well as manifold acquirements' who 'but for the absorption of her whole Soul in her Brother's fame and writings would, perhaps, in a different style have been as great a Poet as himself'.[54] This was missing the point, for Dorothy's *prose* was her main claim to fame, as other readers had begun to appreciate, though rather too late to be of any practical use. De Quincey's essay entitled 'William Wordsworth' (*Tait's Magazine*, 1839) included the first serious published account of her creative talent. The essay was ambivalent towards William, but unstintingly generous in the tribute it paid to Dorothy in her prime, praising her for her 'originality and native freshness of intellect', and remembering her as 'an intellectual creature from her cradle, with much of her illustrious brother's peculiarity of mind'.[55] De Quincey alluded in his essay not just to Dorothy's unpublished journals, but to her conversation, observing that she would make 'many a sudden remark or ejaculation, extorted by something or other that struck her eye, in the clouds, or in colouring, or in accidents of light and shade, of form or combination of form' (p. 399). Judging her alongside the picturesque writers of the day, he found no one her equal for descriptive naturalism. She had a 'power of catching and expressing all the hidden beauties of natural scenery', he wrote, 'with a felicity of diction, a truth, and strength, that far transcend Gilpin' (p. 399). He singled out for special praise her *Recollections of a Tour Made in Scotland*, copies of which had been circulating in the Wordsworth circle for many years. This book, De Quincey wrote, 'is absolutely unique in its class: and, though it never could be very popular, from the minuteness of its details ... and the luxuriation of its descriptions, yet I believe no person has ever been favoured with a sight of it, that has not yearned for its publication' (p. 400).

De Quincey's appraisal of Dorothy's talent was generous and insightful; but he overstepped the mark by speculating openly about the possible causes of her illness. He diagnosed a depressive temperament, which had come to the fore as her nephews grew up and she lost her nurturing role in the household. His public analysis of her decline struck a deeply uncomfortable note, especially by introducing imputations of wasted talent, frustrated energy, and weakness of the will:

> I fear that Miss Wordsworth has suffered not much less than Coleridge: and, in any general expression of it, from the same cause—viz, an excess of pleasurable excitement and luxurious sensibility, sustained in youth by a constitutional

glow from animal causes, but drooping as soon as that was withdrawn...It would have been far better had Miss Wordsworth condescended a little to the ordinary mode of pursuing literature; better for her own happiness if she *had* been a bluestocking; or at least, if she had been, in good earnest, a writer for the press, with the pleasant cares and solicitudes of one who has some little ventures, as it were, on that vast ocean.   (p. 400)

The hint that her 'relaxation of the will and its potential energies' resembled Coleridge's was bound to cause pain to her family. Even though De Quincey's 'love and respectful pity' were sincere, his elegy was scarcely tactful: 'Farewell, Miss Wordsworth! farewell, impassioned Dorothy! I have not seen you for many a day—shall, too probably, never see you again perhaps; but shall attend your steps with tender interest, so long as I hear of you living' (p. 401).

For the many visitors who made the pilgrimage to Rydal Mount, Dorothy's deteriorating condition was less a sentimental prospect than a harrowing fact. Her family made no secret of her illness, around which the household's activities revolved. Referred to by William on one occasion as 'my dear ruin of a Sister',[56] she outlived him by five years—sometimes an object of pity or revulsion to outsiders, but always secure in her family's unconditional love. In September 1848, the Duke of Argyll described how, soon after meeting her, he heard William give an impassioned reading of 'Tintern Abbey' in its entirety. The poet's delivery impressed him deeply, especially when he came to the concluding lines, which he read with a 'fervour and almost passion' that were 'very striking and beautiful'. The strong emphasis that William put on the words 'My dear, dear friend' struck the Duke as odd, until he realized that 'the old paralytic and doited woman' he had seen earlier that day was the sister thus addressed. It was melancholy, he concluded, to think that 'the vacant silly stare which we had seen in the morning was from the "wild eyes" of 1798'.[57] But would Dorothy have continued staring so vacantly had she been present to hear this recital, as she doubtless was on many such occasions? Throughout their adult lives, 'Tintern Abbey' held a special place in the Wordsworths' affections. William often read the poem aloud in company, and Dorothy mentioned it frequently in her writing as a source of 'tranquil restoration'. By virtue of the poem's importance in their emotional lives, the Wye Valley had become a place of pilgrimage for family members, prompting further acts of recollection across the years. When Mary was away from William in 1812, she visited Tintern Abbey, and wrote him a letter describing the valley's enchanting beauty. He replied with a recapitulation of the river's soothing power, connecting it as on many previous occasions with his sister: 'I have been reading at Lamb's the Tintern abbey, and repeated a 100 times to my self the passage O Sylvan Wye thou Wanderer through the woods, thinking of past times, & Dorothy, dear Dorothy, and you my darling.'[58] As the three Wordsworths grew old together, William's blessing on Dorothy—'My dear, dear Friend'—never lost its resonance, for these words were deeply embedded in the family's communal memory:

> When thy mind
> Shall be a mansion for all lovely forms,
> Thy memory be as a dwelling-place
> For all sweet sounds and harmonies; Oh! then,
> If solitude, or fear, or pain, or grief,
> Should be thy portion, with what healing thoughts
> Of tender joy wilt thou remember me.   (ll. 140–6)

Reading 'Tintern Abbey' aloud was, I believe, a key component in the palliative care that William provided for his sister throughout her illness, and played a very significant role in strengthening family bonds as she declined. I am reminded, here, of Lewis Hyde's words, 'The gift and its bearers share a spirit which is kept alive by its motion among them, and which in turn keeps them both alive.'[59] In spring 1832, when Dora brought in the first spring flowers 'Culled from the precincts of our home, | From nooks to Memory dear', Dorothy reciprocated with 'Thoughts on my sick-bed', a touching poem of gratitude for the consolation this poem gave her. Reviewing the 'careless days' when she and her brother had been 'Companions of Nature', she remembered their symbolic pilgrimage in 1798 and William's address to her as the Muse of memory:[60]

> No prisoner in this lonely room,
> I *saw* the green banks of the Wye,
> Recalling thy prophetic words—
> Bard, brother, friend from infancy![61]

Although wistful in tone, her poem expresses a glad participation in shared memories, an abiding belief in the restorative power of place, and acceptance of the important creative role William had prophesied for her.

After Dorothy's short-term memory disappeared, she no longer found it possible to concentrate fully on books when they were read aloud to her, unless this was done slowly and very painstakingly. When the household assembled to enjoy Harriet Martineau's *Life in the Sick Room*—'they like to read it together; one, of course, reading aloud to the rest'[62]—Dorothy was unable to keep pace. She 'could not bear sustained attention to any book', although she 'would be quite capable of appreciating a little at a time'.[63] The recital of familiar poems provided a much more reliable therapeutic tool. In 1835, Crabb Robinson noted that Dorothy was 'fond of repeating the favourite small poems of her brother, as well as a few of her own. And this she did in so sweet a tone as to be quite pathetic.'[64] He concluded (much as William had done when writing to Southey about Edith) that 'the temporary obscurations of a noble mind can never obliterate the recollections of its inherent and essential worth'.[65] Just as 'Tintern Abbey' was a set piece that William regularly performed for visitors and family, so Dorothy had her own favourite, 'The Floating Island at Hawkshead, an Incident in the Schemes of Nature'. Although she had written this poem in the 1820s before her senile dementia set in, its relevance to her medical condition must have been apparent to her listeners. The poetic image of a 'slip of earth, | By throbbing waves long undermined, | Loosed from its hold' (ll. 5–7) powerfully connotes her islanded and drifting consciousness—doomed eventually to 'pass away' and 'fertilize some other ground', but still teeming with life:

> There berries ripen, flowerets bloom;
> There insects live their lives—and die:
> A peopled *world* it is; in size a tiny room.   (ll. 14–16)

In 1840, when her condition became severe, Dorothy could talk 'nothing absolutely insane or irrational' for a while, but had 'little command of herself' and had a disagreeable habit of 'blowing loudly & making a nondescript sound more shrill than the cry of a partridge or a turkey'.[66] However, she continued to have periods of clarity in which her behaviour appeared normal, and never more so than when reading poetry aloud. Crabb Robinson was not the only one to notice that she could be withdrawn from her strange screaming noises 'by a request to repeat Verses which she does with affecting sweetness, quite pathetically'.[67] Another visitor (Mrs Inge, wife of the President of Worcester College, Oxford) observed that 'There was a marvelous gleam and radiance in her face as she repeated some of her brother's lines.'[68] In 1844, after a visit to Rydal Mount, William Bennett described how he and his family heard Dorothy reciting her poems in the garden. She did so, Bennett wrote, 'in the most clear and beautiful accents, and with that modulation and emphasis which only the poet can give to his own productions'. While she performed, she 'closed her eyes, and giving herself up to the full feeling of it, threw her whole soul into the poetry'.[69] In the conversation that followed, she was completely coherent, telling her listeners about her illness and the death of her brother John. She even quoted his last words, reputedly spoken just before the *Earl of Abergavenny* sank, and treasured for nearly thirty years. One could not look for clearer testimony of her absorption in the past.

The transformation observed in Dorothy by several visitors and friends is explicable in neurological terms if we consider poetry's rhythmic properties. Oliver Sacks, in his book *Musicophilia*, has drawn on thirty years of clinical experience to demonstrate the therapeutic power of rhythm for patients suffering from Alzheimer's, amnesia, strokes, traumas, and various forms of encephalitis. 'Musical emotion and musical memory can survive long after other forms of memory have disappeared', he observes.[70] The response to musical rhythm can be very useful as a mnemonic that activates sensory and motor activities in the brain simultaneously:

> Music has the power to embed sequences and to do this when other forms of organisation fail…Entire books can be held in memory—*The Iliad* and *The Odyssey*, famously, could be recited at length because, like ballads, they had rhythm and rhyme. How much such recitation depends on musical rhythm and how much purely on linguistic rhyming is difficult to tell, but these are surely related—both 'rhyme' and 'rhythm' derive from the Greek, carrying the conjoined meanings of measure, motion, and stream. An articulate stream, a melody or prosody, is necessary to carry one along, and this is something that unites language and music, and may underlie their perhaps common origins.[71]

Even without any overt movement such as tapping a foot to keep time, listening to music activates motor cortex and subcortical motor systems. Sacks even claims that *imagining* music can be as potent, neurally, as hearing it. Likewise, when learnt by rote, poems provide a remarkable therapeutic tool, enabling direct contact with memories and their associated emotions. Dorothy's temporary recovery when reciting poetry may have appeared miraculous to those who were meeting her for the first time. But for members of the Wordsworth family, the importance of rhythm to physical and mental health was intuitively understood. (Sacks's observation that '*An articulate stream, a melody or prosody, is necessary to carry one along*' sounds almost like a gloss on their understanding of the soothing power of rhythmic memory.) Reading aloud was not simply a last resort the family turned to during her sickness but a lifelong household ritual. In the spring of 1802, Dorothy had read aloud 'over and over again' to William the following lines, knowing they would lull him to sleep. Their power as a soothing mantra derived partly from that fact that he had reused

them in several poetic contexts over the years, on each occasion tacitly calling
to mind the circumstances of their original composition:

> Come!—let me see thee sink into a dream
> Of quiet thoughts,—protracted till thine eye
> Be calm as water, when the winds are gone
> And no one can tell whither. My sweet Friend!
> We two have had such happy hours together
> That my heart melts in me to think of it.
>
> ('Travelling', ll. 6–11; LB, 307)

Throughout adulthood, William's poems had been at the centre of Dorothy's
consciousness, shaping the household's communal life. Not only had she copied and recopied his work over a period of thirty years, but she carried them
in her long-term memory, drawing on them for sustenance when they were
needed. Like him, she also knew by heart a vast range of poems by other
writers. 'If I read Milton, or any favourite Author, and pause,' William observed
during her dementia, 'she goes on with the passage from memory; but she
forgets instantly the circumstances of the day.'[72] A sense of rhythm had surfaced on numerous occasions in her early journals, making her 'more than half
a poet'; and the poetry she wrote in her fifties played a restorative role during
bouts of illness as she grew old. After losing her capacity to walk, write, and
retrieve short-term memories, the recital of poems served as a restorative way
of 'keeping time'. Poetry's intensely *communal* function within the household
enabled her to sustain old-established bonds with family members, and even
(as Bennett's letter testifies) to create new bonds outside the family.

16

Home

'A point of life between my Parents' dust,
And your's, my buried Little-ones! am I;
And to those graves looking habitually
In kindred quiet I repose my trust.'[1]

*

Dorothy was too unwell to accompany William and Mary when they
travelled to Bath in 1841 to witness Dora's marriage to Edward
Quillinan. Her absence prevented her from offering support on the wed-
ding-day itself, and from sympathizing with William's failure to attend the
wedding ceremony—a repetition of her own collapse on 4 October 1802.
Nor did she join the family party in their nostalgic pilgrimage to Alfoxden.
But from her sickroom at Rydal Mount, she must have been intermittently
aware of these and other family rituals as they unfolded during the 1840s.
William continued to read his work aloud to her, so she may have noticed

how often his late poems returned to familiar places and themes, commemorating their life together. 'A Night-Thought', for instance, composed
in 1842, describes the moon's emergence from behind the clouds, a motif
associated with the *Alfoxden Journal* and 'A Night-Piece' (1798), both fresh
in the poet's mind after his recent visit to Alfoxden. 'The Wishing-Gate
Destroyed' pays elegiac tribute to one of Dorothy's favourite local landmarks, mentioned often in the *Grasmere Journal* as a stopping-place on walks
from Town End. 'Suggested upon Loughrigg Fell', occasioned by walking in
one of Dorothy's favourite spots, focuses on the delicate beauty of a mountain daisy, recalling lyrics William had written for her in the orchard at Town
End. Dorothy is the implied listener for these late poems, but William does
not dwell exclusively on memories of his life with her, any more than he
had done in 'Poems on the Naming of Places'. A late addition to that group,
'Forth from a jutting ridge'(1845), relates how Mary and Sara Hutchinson
had often helped each other to climb one or other of two neighbouring
peaks at the top of Bainriggs Wood, and how he named the peaks 'Mary and
Sara Point' after them. The poem celebrates sibling cooperation, and the
power of sisterly love to outlast death, in lines that speak to and for all members of the Wordsworths' close-knit household, living and dead.

The importance of local associations to memory's restorative power
remained a constant throughout the Wordsworths' lives, and even in sickness the gift economy that sustained their creative collaboration continued.
Dorothy's dementia prompted William to make therapeutic use of their
lifelong habit of remembering: in this respect he intuitively anticipated
modern medicine. Doctors nowadays routinely advise nurses, carers, and
families of patients suffering from Alzheimer's to stimulate patients' long-
term memories in conversation. Recollections of home are especially beneficial in restoring a sense of stability and calm to highly distressed people
whose grasp of recent events is at best tenuous.[2] As anyone with experience of talking to such patients knows, the act of remembering can be
mutually beneficial, especially where carers are family members. Many of
William's late poems, read aloud in the sickroom at Rydal Mount, can be
interpreted as invitations to revisit, or as soothing forms of shared revisita-
tion. Reconnecting the brother and sister to the homes they had lived in,
they may well have helped temporarily to restore their sense of communal
identity. According to one of the Wordsworths' neighbours, Dorothy in her
old age spoke constantly 'of their early days, but more of the years they
spent together in other parts of England than those at Grasmere'.[3] William

too observed, 'My poor sister…talks much of her Aunt…of Halifax and all her early connections there; nothing indeed seems to employ her thoughts so much.'[4] In a context where long-term memories were much stronger than short-term ones, even Town End—'the old and dearest place of all'— was less vivid and present to Dorothy's consciousness than her happy years in yorkshire.

One of William's most important actions as an old man was to dictate to his friend Isabella Fenwick a series of fascinating autobiographical notes. Ranging over the entirety of his career, and rooting each poem in the location that had prompted it, these served as an archive of family memories as well as an exercise in therapeutic associationism. Many were a tribute to the sustaining importance of daily life, much as the *Grasmere Journal* had been. Insofar as William imagined an ideal reader for them, it was Dorothy in her prime; and the sense of Dorothy's shadowy presence gives the memories he selected their nostalgic poignancy. In his descriptions of Alfoxden, recently revisited without her, the days of 1798 came back with all the happiness of their associations still intact. Commenting on 'It is the First mild Day of March' (retitled 'To my Sister' as an act of homage) William observed that the larch mentioned in the opening stanza was still standing, forty-one years after he wrote his poem. The sight of leaves skipping and dancing in the woods near Alfoxden had inspired 'A Whirl Blast from behind the Hill' in 1798: the same woods were still there, he remarked, 'in unimpaired beauty'.[5] Speaking to his sister through these notes, William confirmed the special place that spring 1798 continued to have in their imaginative and emotional lives.

The *Fenwick Notes* also honoured the importance of later, more settled homes. In his memories of Town End, Dorothy was alongside William, not just as a household presence— 'My Sister and I were in the habit of having the tea-kettle in our little sitting room'[6]—but as a companionable reader, inspiring and shaping the direction of his poetry. Introducing 'Miscellaneous Sonnets', he recalled how 'in the cottage of Town-End, one afternoon, in 1801, my Sister read to me the Sonnets of Milton'.[7] Some poems prompted him to plot the narrative of their life together, highlighting significant emotional events. The sixth of his 'Miscellaneous Sonnets' was written, he observed, in recollection of their winter journey from Kendal to Grasmere in 1799, a journey often remembered by both siblings as a pilgrimage toward their longed-for home. Rydal, the house in which the Wordsworths had lived longest, featured in his memory as a place where

habitual associations had accumulated over forty years. Sonnet 44 was
suggested, William said, 'in front of Rydal Mount, the rocky parapet being
the summit of Loughrigg Fell opposite'.[8] Here, through diurnal repetition,
'the same objects seen from the same place' had awakened a continuous
chain of feelings. Likewise, the poem 'If with old love of you dear hills' was
inspired by affection for the 'far Terrace' at Rydal Mount 'where I have
murmured out many thousands of my Verses'.[9]

Dorothy's acknowledged centrality to the process of remembering is apparent not only in the substance of William's late memories but in their form and
texture. 'The Affliction of Margaret' was 'taken from the case of a poor widow
who lived in the town of Penrith'; 'The Sailor's Mother' from that of a woman
he met 'near the Wishing-Gate, on the high road that then led from Grasmere
to Ambleside'.[10] Dorothy's ways of noticing, recording and chronicling had
encouraged William to respect 'the realities of life' by incorporating prosaic
details into his poems. Just as it mattered, in the first version of 'The Leech-
Gatherer', to remember the old man's exact words as her journal had recorded
them, so now he sought to establish the authenticity of his poetry, beyond the
shadow of a doubt, by tracing its human interest back to a specific person, or its
composition back to a particular spot. Many of the 'facts' recorded by William
in these notes have since come under question, as scholars have unearthed
countermanding evidence; but that is not my concern here. (He was old when
he dictated them, and his memory was fallible.) I am interested by his continuing adherence to the *principle of veracity*, so strongly present in Dorothy's journals.
One of Simon Lee's expressions was 'word for word from his own lips'.[11] An
incident from real life found its way into 'As on a sunny bank' with 'every particular...exactly as I have related'.[12] 'Hint from the mountains' was prompted
by a 'particular bunch' of ferns 'noticed in the Pass of Dunmail-Raise'.[13] Dorothy presided over the *Fenwick Notes* not simply as the poet's beloved sister but as
the muse of memory—a role she had occupied ever since walking at his side
through the Wye Valley in 1798.

*

One by one, members of the family at Rydal Mount died, each cared for
during their last days by their survivors. When Dora became terminally ill
with tuberculosis in 1847, only six years after her marriage to Quillinan,
nothing could take the edge off William's grief. Whereas Mary's Christian
faith consoled her at the end of her daughter's life, his was largely ineffec-
tual. On 9 July, at the age of forty-four, Dora died, leaving him stunned and

inarticulate: 'We bear up under our affliction as well as God enables us to do,' he wrote to Moxon, 'but O my dear Friend our loss is immeasurable.'[14] In the months that followed, the only activity that stirred him out of his immovable grief was attending to Dorothy, who had 'sunk still further in insensibility' after Dora's death.[15] Crabb Robinson, visiting Rydal Mount as usual in December—'No Crabb, no Christmas!'[16]—was saddened by the family's low spirits, and shocked by how absolutely his friend had withdrawn from all social contact. 'I suffer most in head and mind before I leave my bed in a morning', William confessed to Isabella Fenwick. 'Daily used she to come to my bedside and greet me and her Mother and *now* the blank is terrible.'[17] His spirits rallied a little in 1848, when for the first time he was able to resume his favourite walks and revisit places that reminded him of Dora; but the emotional strain had taken its toll. In the long cold winter of 1850, he contracted pneumonia and became seriously unwell. The shock of his ensuing fragility acted as a powerful stimulus to Dorothy. Just as, during the years at Town End, she had watched over his premarital anxieties with considerable devotion, so now his perilous condition revived her maternal instincts. According to Quillinan, her personality underwent a complete transformation, and she appeared 'as much herself as she ever was in her life, and has an almost absolute command of her own will'.[18] But this improvement was not to last long. When William died on 23 April 1850, she went into a long-drawn-out decline, and for five further years it was her turn to be tended by Mary.[19] On 25 January 1855, a month after her eighty-fourth birthday, she died. 'Our dear sister', Mary wrote in a letter, was 'released after her gradual but fitful sinking and some few hours of peaceful and anxious waiting.'[20] Dorothy was buried in Grasmere churchyard near the remains of William, three of his children, and Sara Hutchinson. It was left to Mary to oversee the publication of *The Prelude* (she gave it a title which honoured the poet's longer-term ambition to write *The Recluse*), and to support her nephew, Christopher Wordsworth, in writing a biography. Mary lived until 1859, a 'Solitary Lingerer',[21] before joining her family in the 'last Central Home'. Rydal Mount, the family's home of forty years standing, passed into other hands with her death, which left 'a sad rent in the structure of my friendships', as Crabb Robinson put it.[22]

Locals in the neighbourhood of Rydal Mount were later to remember William as a remote figure, somewhat disconnected from his community, and Dorothy as a clever communicative woman to whom her brother always deferred. 'Well, fwoaks said she was cliverest mon of the

two at his job, and he allays went to her when he was puzzelt. Dorothy
hed t'wits, tho' she went wrang, ye kna.'[23] There were mischievous
rumours that the siblings had been lovers, as well as a more credible
suspicion that Dorothy had played a leading role in the creation of William's poetry. 'Mr Wordsworth went bumming and booing about, and
she, Miss Dorothy, kept close behint him, and she picked up the bits as
he let 'em fall, and tak 'em down, and put 'em on paper for him.'[24] De
Quincey had drawn attention to Dorothy's talent as a writer in 1839;
and William had published segments of her journals on several occasions since 1807. However, it was not until the publication of Christopher Wordsworth's *Memoir* of the poet in 1851 that the *Grasmere Journal*
began to emerge into the public sphere, enabling Dorothy's talent to be
more widely appreciated. Meanwhile, when Matthew Arnold paid tribute to William's poetry in his 'Memorial Verses' (1850), he made no
mention of the poet's sister:

> Time may restore us in his course
> Goethe's sage mind and Byron's force;
> But where will Europe's latter hour
> Again find Wordsworth's healing power?
> Others will teach us how to dare,
> And against fear our breast to steel;
> Others will strengthen us to bear—
> But who, ah! who, will make us feel?[25]

Arnold was not old enough to have known Dorothy in her prime; and in
his elegy the name 'Wordsworth' refers appropriately to William's singular
authorial voice, not to the communal experiences, memories, conversations,
and creative processes which shaped his poetry. Nonetheless, Arnold recognized the empathetic and relational nature of Wordsworthian creativity:

> He found us when the age had bound
> Our souls in its benumbing round;
> He spoke, and loosed our heart in tears.
> He laid us as we lay at birth
> On the cool flowery lap of earth,
> Smiles broke from us and we had ease;
> The hills were round us, and the breeze
> Went o'er the sun-lit fields again;
> Our foreheads felt the wind and rain.
> Our youth return'd; for there was shed
> On spirits that had long been dead,

Spirits dried up and closely furl'd,
The freshness of the early world.[26]

The 'healing power' identified in these lines as the hallmark of William's poetic genius arose out of the Wordsworths' shared psychological needs, strengthening with the passage of time as their creative identities commingled. We have seen how their longing for home emerged in response to the early traumas they suffered, together and apart; and how the symbolic significance of homecoming sustained them through subsequent bereavements and losses. The fundamentally therapeutic nature of their collaborative processes—walking, talking, remembering, and grieving—was important at every stage of their adult lives, enabling them to consolidate family bonds and recover their sense of regional belonging. The volumes that emerged from Town End, Allan Bank, and Rydal Mount were products of their joint labour and expressions of their shared devotion to Westmorland; but they were also articulations of their belief in the healing power of love.

Hazlitt's beautiful (albeit barbed) observation, 'He lives in the busy solitude of his own heart; in the deep silence of thought', recognized the meditative power of William's poetry, but not its communal nature and purpose.[27] To rebut his unfair but influential allegations of aloofness and egotism, one need only return to lines William wrote in 1800 describing his sister: 'She who dwells with me, whom I have loved | With such communion, that no place on earth | Can ever be a solitude to me.'[28] These lines remind us that the profoundly empathetic quality of William's writing was grounded in his relationship with Dorothy, whose accompanying thoughts and creative processes mingled with his own. Acknowledging 'the curious links | With which the perishable hours of life | Are bound together',[29] associationism served a reparative purpose in the family, both as a system of belief and as a creative practice. After their reunion in 1787, William made recompense to Dorothy for their early separation with poems that drew on shared associations. In later years, when Dorothy was no longer able to walk or write, communal memories supplied her with a medicine that was akin to nature's healing. Ever more securely grounded in the domestic sphere, William's poetry brought comfort to his sister; but his companionable voice—'confiding, advising, consoling'[30]—also reached out beyond the intimate family circle at Rydal Mount and provided, as

Arnold saw it, a form of healthful nourishment to Victorian readers during 'this iron time | Of doubts, disputes, distractions, fears' ('Memorial Verses', ll. 43–4). Its medicinal properties have been felt by generations of readers and writers ever since. Keats, who knew that the world was 'full of Misery and Heartbreak, Pain, Sickness and Oppression', observed that William thought more deeply 'into the human heart' than any other poet, and learned from reading his work how the 'burden of the Mystery' might be lightened.[31] ('The great end | Of Poesy', he wrote, was 'that it should be a friend | To soothe the cares, and lift the thoughts of man.')[32] John Stuart Mill emerged from a breakdown through reading his poems—'In them I seemed to draw from a source of inward joy, of sympathetic and imaginative pleasure, which could be shared in by all human beings.'[33] Many others have found in his understanding of human emotions a 'medicine' for their state of mind. Edward Thomas's identification with William's homesickness helped him to craft his own therapeutic prose of place when walking through the Home Counties in the decade leading up to the First World War. Wordsworthians in our own time include, pre-eminently, Seamus Heaney and Alice Oswald.

Since the beginning of the twentieth century, readers have acknowledged that Dorothy's prose, as much as William's poetry, has a healing power. 'If the written word could cure rheumatism, I think hers might—like a dock-leaf laid to a sting', Woolf once observed.[34] Increasingly, visitors make the pilgrimage to Dove Cottage for Dorothy's sake as well as William's, valuing what this iconic literary partnership goes on signifying, emotionally and spiritually. The humanist ideal of 'ennobling interchange' still survives as a wholesome model of creativity, even in a global capitalist economy; and increasingly there is need of it:

> The true commerce of art is a gift exchange, and where that commerce can proceed on its own terms we shall be heirs to the fruits of gift exchange…to a creative spirit whose fertility is not exhausted in use, to the sense of plenitude which is the mark of all erotic exchange, to a storehouse of works that can serve as agents of transformation, and to a sense of an inhabitable world—an awareness, that is, of our solidarity with whatever we take to be the source of our gifts, be it the community or the race, nature, or the gods.[35]

My book has drawn attention away from how celebrity is achieved in a competitive literary marketplace, to the more important question of how a gift economy between creative writers thrives in a local environment. William and Dorothy devoted their lives to a unique form of inalienable labour, the therapeutic value of which was—and is—inestimable. Throughout adulthood, their associative rituals and mnemonic practices bonded them in a sacred non-sexual union. In the Wordsworth household, collaborative writing was at no stage seen as a species of property in which each contributor held a share but as commerce of the spirit in which creative artefacts circulated as tokens of kinship, love, and gratitude to the natural world.

List of Abbreviations

All quotations from WW's poetry are taken from Stephen Gill's *Oxford Authors* edition (2012), unless otherwise noted. I have used Ernest De Selincourt's edition of DW's prose, except in cases where a more recent scholarly edition is available; and quotations from DW's poetry refer to Susan Levin's Longman Cultural Edition. The following abbreviations of primary materials have been used throughout.

Alfoxden Journal	*The Grasmere and Alfoxden Journals*, ed. Pamela Woof (Oxford: Oxford University Press, 2002).
BL	*Biographia Literaria*, ed. James Engell and W. Jackson Bate, 2 vols, *The Collected Works of Samuel Taylor Coleridge*, Bollingen Series lxxv Princeton, NJ: Princeton University Press, 1983).
BTW	Henry Crabb Robinson, *Books and their Writers*, ed. Edith J. Morley, 3 vols (London: J. M. Dent and Sons, 1938).
BW	*Benjamin the Waggoner*, ed. Paul F. Betz (Ithaca, NY: Cornell University Press, 1981).
CJ	Dorothy Wordsworth, *Journal of a Tour on the Continent 1820*; *Journals of Dorothy Wordsworth*, ed. Ernest De Selincourt (London: Macmillan, 1941), vol. ii.
Common Reader	Virgimia Woolf, *The Common Reader: Second Series*, ed. Andrew McNeillie (London: Hogarth Press, 1986).
CWM	Christopher Wordsworth, *Memoirs of William Wordsworth*, 2 vols (London: E. Moxon, 1851).
DC MS	Dove Cottage Manuscript.
DC MS 90	Dorothy Wordsworth, *Journal of a Tour on the Continent 1820*.
DS	*Descriptive Sketches*, ed. Eric Birdsall with the assistance of Paul M. Zall (Ithaca, NY: Cornell University Press, 1984).
DWJ	*Journals of Dorothy Wordsworth*, ed. Ernest De Selincourt, 2 vols (London: Macmillan, 1941).
DWL	*Letters of Dora Wordsworth*, ed. Howard P. Vincent (Chicago: Pickard & Company, 1944).
E	*The Excursion*, ed. Sally Bushell, James A. Butler, and Michael C. Jaye with the assistance of David García (Ithaca, NY: Cornell University Press).

EPF	*Early Poems and Fragments, 1785–1797*, ed. Carol Landon and Jared Curtis (Ithaca, NY: Cornell University Press, 1997).
EW	*An Evening Walk*, ed. James Averill (Ithaca, NY: Cornell University Press, 1984).
EY	*The Letters of William and Dorothy Wordsworth: The Early Years, 1787–1805*, ed. Ernest De Selincourt, rev. Chester L. Shaver (Oxford: Clarendon Press, 1967).
FN	*The Fenwick Notes of William Wordsworth*, ed. Jared Curtis (London: Bristol Classical Press, 1993).
Grasmere Journal	*The Grasmere and Alfoxden Journals*, ed. Pamela Woof (Oxford: Oxford University Press, 2002).
Gray	*Thomas Gray's Journal of his Visit to the Lake District in October 1769*, ed. William Roberts (Liverpool: Liverpool University Press, 2001).
Griggs	*Collected Letters of Samuel Taylor Coleridge*, ed. Earl Leslie Griggs, 6 vols (Oxford: Clarendon Press, 1956–71).
Guide to the Lakes	William Wordsworth, *Guide to the Lakes*, ed. Ernest De Selincourt, with a preface by Stephen Gill (London: Frances Lincoln, 2004).
Hazlitt	*The Selected Writings of William Hazlitt*, ed. Duncan Wu, 9 vols (London: Pickering and Chatto, 1998).
HCRC	*The Correspondence of Henry Crabb Robinson with the Wordsworth Circle*, ed. Edith J. Morley, 2 vols (Oxford: Clarendon Press, 1927).
HCRD	Henry Crabb Robinson, *Diary*, in *Diary, Reminiscences, and Correspondence*, ed. Thomas Sadler, 3 vols (London: Macmillan and Co., 1869), vol iii.
HG	*Home at Grasmere*, ed. Beth Darlington (Ithaca, NY: Cornell University Press, 1977).
HJ	Dorothy Wordsworth, *Journal of my tour in Hamburg. The Continental Journals 1798–1820*, edited with a new introduction by Helen Boden (Bristol: Thoemmes Press, 1995).
Hofer	Johannes Hofer, 'Medical Dissertation on Nostalgia by Johannes Hofer, 1688', trans. Carolyn Kiser Anspach, *Bulletin of the Institute of the History of Medicine*, 2 (1934), 376–91.
Hyde	Lewis Hyde, *The Gift: How the Creative Spirit Transforms the World* (Edinburgh: Canongate Books, 2007).
Journey to Western Islands	Samuel Johnson, *A Journey to the Western Islands of Scotland* and James Boswell, *The Journal of a Tour to the Hebrides*, ed. Peter Levi (London: Penguin, 1984).

JST	*Journal of my Second Tour in Scotland, 1822: A Complete Edition of Dove Cottage Manuscript 98 and Dove Cottage Manuscript 99*, ed. Jiro Nagasawa (Tokyo: Kenkyusha, 1989).
Ketcham Transcript	Karl Ketcham (ed.), *Selections from the Rydal Journal, with a Critical Introduction and Notes* (Unpublished; Wordsworth Trust archive.)
Lamb	*The Letters of Charles and Mary Lamb,* ed. Edwin Marrs, Jr, 3 vols (Ithaca, NY: Cornell University Press, 1975).
LB	*'Lyrical Ballads' and Other Poems, 1797–1800*, ed. James Butler and Karen Green (Ithaca, NY: Cornell University Press, 1992).
Longman DW	*Dorothy Wordsworth*, ed. Susan M. Levin. Longman Cultural Edition (New York: Longman, 2009).
LP	*Last Poems, 1821–1850*, ed. Jared Curtis (Ithaca, NY: Cornell University Press, 1999).
LY	*The Letters of William and Dorothy Wordsworth: The Later Years, 1821–53*, ed. Ernest De Selincourt, rev. Alan G. Hill, 4 vols (Oxford: Clarendon Press, 1978–88).
Mauss	Marcel Mauss, *The Gift: Forms and Functions of Exchange in Archaic Societies* (London: Routledge and Kegan Paul, 1923; repr. 1969).
Mays	*The Collected Works of Samuel Taylor Coleridge*, vol. 16, ed. J. C. C. Mays, *Poetical Works*, 2 vols (Princeton, NJ: Princeton University Press, 2001).
McCracken	David McCracken, *Wordsworth and the Lakes: A guide to the poems and their places* (Oxford: Oxford University Press, 1984).
MWJ	*Mary Wordsworth's Journal of the Continental Tour* 1820 (DC MS 92), http://www.daybooks.com/diaries/wordsworth.
MWL	*The Letters of Mary Wordsworth* (Oxford: Oxford University Press, 1958).
MY	*The Letters of William and Dorothy Wordsworth: The Middle Years, 1806–1820*, ed. Ernest De Selincourt, rev. Mary Moorman and Alan G. Hill, 2 vols (Oxford: Clarendon Press, 1969–70).
Narrative	Dorothy Wordsworth, *George and Sarah Green, A Narrative* ed. Ernest De Selincourt (Oxford: Clarendon Press, 1936).
Notebooks	*The Notebooks of Samuel Taylor Coleridge*, ed. Kathleen Coburn, 5 vols in 10 (Princeton, NJ: Princeton University Press, 1957–2002).
PTV	*Poems, in Two Volumes, and Other Poems, 1800–1807*, ed. Jared Curtis (Ithaca, NY: Cornell University Press, 1983).
RCP	*The Ruined Cottage and The Pedlar*, ed. James Butler (Ithaca, NY: Cornell University Press).

Recollections	*Recollections of a Tour Made in Scotland, A.D. 1803; Journals of Dorothy Wordsworth*, ed. Ernest De Selincourt, 2 vols (London: Macmillan, 1941).
Reminiscences	*Reminiscences of Wordsworth among the Peasantry of Westmoreland*, complied by Hardwicke Drummond Rawnsley (London: Dillon's, 1968).
Selected Prose	*William Wordsworth Selected Prose* ed. John O. Hayden (Harmondsworth: Penguin, 1988).
SHL	*Letters of Sara Hutchinson*, ed. Kathleen Coburn (London: Routledge and Kegan Paul, 1954).
SIP	*Sonnet Series and Itinerary Poems, 1820–45*, ed. Geoffrey Jackson (Ithaca, NY: Cornell University Press, 2004).
SP	*Shorter Poems, 1807–1820*, ed. Carl H. Ketcham (Ithaca, NY: Cornell University Press, 1989).
SPP	*The Salisbury Plain Poems of William Wordsworth*, ed. Stephen Gill (Ithaca, NY: Cornell University Press, 1975).
Stoddart	John Stoddart, *Remarks on Local Scenery and Manners in Scotland during the years 1799 and 1800*, 2 vols (London: William Miller, 1801).
Suppl	*The Letters of William and Dorothy Wordsworth*, viii: *A Supplement to the Letters*, ed. Alan G. Hill (Oxford: Clarendon Press, 2000).
To the Hebrides	*Samuel Johnson's Journey to the Western Islands of Scotland and James Boswell's Journal of a Tour to the Hebrides*, ed. Ronald Black (Edinburgh: Birlinn, 2007).
TP	*The Tuft of Primroses, with Other Late Poems for The Recluse*, ed. Joseph F. Kishel (Ithaca, NY: Cornell University Press, 1986).
TPP	*The Prelude, 1798–1799*, ed. Stephen Parrish (Ithaca, NY: Cornell University Press, 1977).
Wollstonecraft	*The Works of Mary Wollstonecraft*, ed. Janet Todd and Marilyn Butler, vi: *Letters Written in Sweden, Norway, and Denmark* (London: Pickering, 1989).
WPW	Wordsworth, *Poetical Works*, ed. Ernest De Selincourt, 5 vols, (Oxford: Clarendon Press, 1946).
WW Poems	*William Wordsworth*, ed. Stephen Gill, Twenty-First Century Oxford Authors (Oxford: Oxford University Press, 2012).
WW Prel	*William Wordsworth, The Prelude: The Four Texts*, ed. Jonathan Wordsworth (Harmondsworth: Penguin, 1995).

Notes

PREFACE

1. EY, 568.
2. Griggs i, 451.
3. *Common Reader* ii, 169.
4. When Woolf observed that William and Dorothy's love for each other resembled that of Heathcliff and Cathy in Brontë's *Wuthering Heights*, she succeeded in evoking their passionate affinity—emotional, physical, and spiritual—without literally implying incest. As recently developed by Frances Wilson (2008), however, the analogy with Heathcliff and Cathy's lawless passion has stronger sexual overtones (see 150–3) and takes us back to the argument mounted famously by F. W. Bateson (1956). The possibility of repressed sexual attraction is discussed with sensitivity and attentiveness to textual evidence by Reiman (1978) and Johnston (1988), among others.
5. 'Home at Grasmere', l. 78.
6. 'Home at Grasmere', ll. 261–2.
7. LY ii, 536.
8. *Prelude*, XII, ll. 376.
9. 'Tintern Abbey', l. 32.

CHAPTER I

1. 'Home at Grasmere', ll. 175–6.
2. Lowther used his wealth to control nine parliamentary boroughs in the North West—the 'Lowther Ninepins'.
3. *WW Prel*, xxv.
4. EY, 616.
5. EY, 663.
6. EY, 65.
7. *Two-Part Prelude* II, ll. 261.
8. VIII, ll. 221.
9. EY, 15–16.
10. EY, 9–10.
11. EY, 3.

12. EY, 88.

13. EY, 88.

14. The argument is compelling, and well worth reading in full: see Freud (1917).

15. EY, 88.

16. EY, 88.

17. EY, 663.

18. Mauss (1923; repr. 1969).

19. Mauss, 16.

20. Mauss, 25–6.

21. Mauss, 19.

22. Hyde, 39.

23. Hyde, 37.

24. Hyde, 60.

25. Mauss, 58.

26. 'The Vale of Esthwaite', ll. 243–71; EPF, 442.

27. EY, 16.

28. EY, 8.

29. 'The whole character of Edwin resembles much what William was when I first knew him after my leaving Halifax'; EY, 101.

30. The name Mary had featured in two of WW's unpublished poems, written during 1786–7. One of these, a ballad, was based on a local story of heartbreak which he had heard from Ann Tyson; the other, 'Beauty & Moonlight', is a haunting love poem in couplets set beside 'Winander's stream'. There is nothing to suggest he had Mary Hutchinson in mind in these poems.

31. EY, 46.

32. EY, 23.

33. EY, 23.

34. EY, 99.

35. EY, 92.

36. EY, 83.

37. *Gentleman's Magazine*, 64 (March 1794), 252–3.

38. See Fink (1958), 74–118.

39. EW, 44.

40. EW, 27.

41. Preface to *Descriptive Sketches* (1793); DS, 32.

42. EY, 35.

43. EY, 36.

44. EY, 47.

45. EY, 74.

46. *Paradise Lost* XII, ll. 648–9.

47. EY, 89.

48. EY, 96, 98.

49. The best detailed account of WW's time in London is given by Roe (1988).
50. EY, 118, 120.
51. ll. 782–3; DS, 116.
52. BL i, ch. 4.
53. EY, 88.
54. EY, 93.
55. EY, 93.
56. EY, 91.
57. EY, 94.
58. EY, 99.
59. EY, 101–2.
60. EY, 101. The phrase is echoed by WW five years later, in 'Tintern Abbey'.
61. EY, 108, 91.

CHAPTER 2

1. 'There is a trickling water', ll. 9–14; PTV, 530.
2. EY, 151. The whereabouts of the first of these volumes is not known; but the second survives in the Wordsworth Collection at the Jerwood Centre, Grasmere. Its inscription reads:'D Wordsworth | The Gift of Mr Wm Rawson | August 18th 1795.' See Wu (1993), 2, 118.
3. EY, 113–14.
4. Gray, 2 October 1769, 39.
5. EY, 115.
6. Leslie (1845), 15.
7. Christopher Cookson had changed his name to Crackanthorpe (his mother's maiden name) when he married; and his widow kept this name after his death in 1792.
8. EY, 116–17.
9. l. 8; EPF, 752.
10. EY, 89.
11. This separate notebook (DC MS 9) contains a mixture of fair copy with interleaved and pasted-in passages from the 1793 volume. All the writing is in WW's hand; and probably belongs to the summer of 1794. See EW, 12.
12. See Sheats (1973), 95; Jonathan Wordsworth (1969), 186; and Piper (1962), 73n. Jump (1986) attributes WW's appreciation for 'enhanced perception of the natural world' to his recent reading of Mark Akenside's *The Pleasures of the Imagination*.
13. I have supplied the alternate reading of l. 191. The one usually quoted is 'Blest are those spirits tremblingly awake' (EW, 137).
14. For Hartley's use of the metaphor of links in a chain to describe the building up of memories, see Hartley (1998), ch. 3, sect. IV.
15. 'Septimi, Gades', ll. 10–12; EPF, 762.

16. The friend is identified later in the poem as 'Mary'—a name used several times in WW's early poetry without reference to Mary Hutchinson, his future wife.

17. WW's description in December 1798 of 'uneasiness at my stomach and side, with a dull pain about my heart', during their exile in Germany, is significant in this context (EY, 236).

18. Hofer, 383.

19. Hofer, 383.

20. Hofer 381.

21. Hofer, 384. Nowadays, such alterations in the chemistry of the brain would probably be referred to as 'inflammatory conditions', 'lesions', and in some cases 'encephalitis'.

22. Hofer, 386.

23. WPW i, 78; note to l. 632.

24. Darwin (2004), ix, 82–3. Darwin's definition of nostalgia indicates that he knew about Hofer's 1688 dissertation through Zwinger's 1710 reprint, which included a transcription of the musical notes for 'Kuhe-Reyen' (see Hofer, 389, 376).

25. He addresses this in a poem written while on the Continental tour of 1820.

26. See 'When first I journeyed hither' and 'The Brothers'.

27. Hofer, 389.

28. Wu (2002) has discussed WW's delayed mourning, especially for his father.

29. Wildschut et al. (2006).

30. A phrase WW used in his Note to 'The Thorn'; WW Poems, 728.

31. See Matlak (1997), 114. Wu (1993) gives 1796–7 as a suggested date of reading.

32. For the best account of Coleridge's connection with Beddoes, see Vickers (2004).

33. 'Brunonian' medicine followed the Scottish physician John Brown (a student of William Cullen's at Edinburgh), who approached all illnesses as symptomatic of either too much or too little stimulation. Brown's book Elementa Medicinae was an important influence on Beddoes.

34. EY, 616.

35. 'On returning to a cottage, a favourite residence of the author, after a long absence', ll. 1–5; EPF, 770.

36. ll. 1–6; LB, 274.

37. Goodman (2008), 196.

38. 'Salisbury Plain', ll. 386–7; SPP, 33.

39. EY, 118.

40. EY, 146.

41. EY, 150.

42. EY, 161.

43. EY, 161.

44. EY, 154.

45. EY, 161.

46. EY, 169.

47. EY, 161.
48. Unfortunately, the diary has never been found; see Woof (1995).
49. EY, 281.
50. EY, 117, 115.
51. EY, 162.
52. EY, 154.
53. EY, 159.
54. EY, 172.
55. EY, 189.
56. EY, 189.
57. EY, 366.
58. Hazlitt ii, 23; 'On the Love of the Country', published in *The Round Table* in 1817.
59. ll. 127–8; EW, 135.
60. Griggs i, 414.
61. Hartley (1998), i, 31, 34f, 374f. ch. 1, sect. I; Proposition V; ch. 1, sect. I, Proposition VI; ch. 3, sect. IV; Proposition XC.
62. Griggs i, 154.
63. Blake's observation was recorded by Henry Crabb Robinson in 1827; HCRD ii, 382.
64. EY, 101–2.
65. Ch. 1; sect. Hartley (1998) II, Proposition XIV.

CHAPTER 3

1. *Prelude*, X, ll. 907–17.
2. EY, 189.
3. *Paradise Lost* IX, ll. 910.
4. *Paradise Lost* IX, ll. 908–16.
5. Griggs i, 330.
6. Griggs i, 330–1.
7. See the first draft of 'This Lime-Tree Bower my Prison'; Mays i, 353–4.
8. Griggs i, 334.
9. WPW i, 329.
10. Lamb i, 117.
11. Coleridge, 'This Lime-Tree Bower My Prison', ll. 37–41.
12. Griggs i, 334.
13. EY, 190.
14. Roe (2010).
15. Quoted in Holmes (1989), 156.
16. Thelwall (1801), 'Lines, written at Bridgwater', ll. 130, 129, 131.
17. EY, 222.
18. Coleridge, 'Frost at Midnight', ll. 54–5.

19. Thelwall, ed. Thompson (2001), 112.
20. I have examined elsewhere how Goethe's chemical account of friendship in *Elective Affinities* applies to their case. Newlyn (2001), xxiii–xxxiv.
21. Letter, 1819; Keats, ed. Gittings (2002), 299.
22. Conversation recorded in a letter from the Reverend Alexander Dyce to H. N. Coleridge.
23. Griggs i, 422.
24. Woof (2002): see the note on this journal entry.
25. Her phrase for the view from the south of the house; EY, 191.
26. 'Advertisement' to LB.
27. 'Preface' to LB.
28. *Alfoxden Journal*, 142.
29. 'A Night-Piece', ll. 1–23.
30. FN, 13.
31. 'Expostulation and Reply', ll. 17–24.
32. See Stafford (2010).
33. Matlak (1997).
34. Hazlitt ix, 104.
35. WPW ii, 527.
36. Hazlitt ix, 104.
37. '*From the verso of a loose foolscap sheet on which an early draft of* "The Old Cumberland Beggar" *is written*'; see WPW v, 340.
38. Roe (1992) links the loco-descriptive opening of 'Tintern Abbey' with an entry in the *Alfoxden Journal* for 24 February 1798, suggesting that WW's imagination 'responded to Dorothy's prose rather than to his own immediate observation' (120).
39. In his introduction to *Dorothy Wordsworth: Selections from the Journals* (1992), Hamilton correctly identifies the *Grasmere Journal* as 'a modern georgic: a mode of writing which draws little distinction between art and labour' (xxvii).
40. See Hartman (1987) for WW's interest in the 'un-remarkable'.
41. Barrell (1988) characterizes WW's tone as patronizing; whereas Grob (1998) argues that WW is solicitous towards DW.
42. 'This Lime-Tree Bower My Prison', ll. 37–8.

CHAPTER 4

1. EY, 223.
2. EY, 213.
3. EY, 213.
4. EY, 213.
5. EY, 221.
6. EY, 222.
7. EY, 223.

8. HJ, 21.

9. Lamb i, 152.

10. Griggs i, 416.

11. Griggs i, 415–16.

12. 'hearing oftentimes | The still, sad music of humanity' (ll. 91–2). The word 'still', carrying additional temporal resonances, is important in 'Tintern Abbey'. Eleven lines later, WW writes, 'Therefore am I still | A lover of the meadows and the woods' (ll. 103–4).

13. Johnston (1998), 612.

14. Griggs i, 431.

15. Coleridge observed that 'K spoke fluently, altho' with a most glorious Havock of Genders & Syntax' (Griggs i, 436).

16. EY, 229.

17. Griggs i, 420.

18. Griggs i, 431.

19. Griggs i, 432.

20. Wollstonecraft vi, 339–40.

21. Wollstonecraft vi, 340.

22. Wollstonecraft vi, 343.

23. 'Essay on Morals', *Selected Prose*, 105.

24. Coleridge notes that on 27 September he and WW discovered the red-light district in Altona, where they found the prostitutes 'all in one street', adding that up till then 'we had seen none even in the streets, & no beggars' (Griggs i, 456).

25. Jews were 'horribly, unnaturally oppressed and persecuted all throughout Germany', Coleridge observed in a letter (Griggs i, 473).

26. Griggs i, 455–6.

27. Griggs i, 456.

28. EY, 230.

29. EY, 229–30.

30. In modern parlance, this degree of susceptibility to light would go by the name of Seasonal Affective Disorder. Coleridge would later associate dull light with low spirits in his 'Dejection: an Ode'.

31. Griggs i, 397.

32. EY, 255.

33. This is Coleridge's description of the city, on briefly visiting it in May 1799 (Griggs i, 514).

34. Griggs i, 459.

35. 'Coleridge is in a very different world from what we stir in, he is all in high life, among Barons, counts and countesses...It would have been impossible for us to have lived as he does; we should have been ruined' (EY, 245).

36. 'Hexameters'; Griggs i, 452.

37. 'By the Fireside', l. 229; Browning, ed. Alan Roberts (2009), 172.

CHAPTER 5

1. ll. 1–6; *WW Prel*, 3.
2. EY, 245.
3. ll. 6–15; *WW Prel*, 3.
4. *Two-Part Prelude*, I, l. 5; *WW Poems*, 164. Future line references in the *Two-Part Prelude* will be to this version of the poem, and will follow quotations in the text.
5. 'Frost at Midnight', ll. 45–7.
6. 'Frost at Midnight', l. 43.
7. l. 13; *WW Prel*, 3.
8. EY, 255.
9. Bachelard (1994), 7.
10. EY, 238.
11. In a letter to her brother she writes that 'Coleridge is in a very different world from what we stir in, he is all in high life, among Barons, counts and countesses' (EY, 245).
12. EY, 238–9.
13. EY, 241.
14. 'A Night Piece', ll. 21–3.
15. 'Frost at Midnight', ll. 54–62.
16. Johnston (1998) has suggested that these passages 'were offered to Coleridge as love tokens, part of the timeless ritual of courtship in which one displays to the beloved one's life in its entirety up to the moment the two lovers met' (639).
17. EY, 616.
18. See also how the metaphor of transplantation features in 'To the Reverend George Coleridge', discussed briefly in ch. 3.
19. Richard Onorato, David Ellis, and Douglas Wilson have all used a Freudian methodology to discuss the poet's processes of transference. Wu (2002) resituates the idea of transference in the context of eighteenth-century psychology.
20. Bachelard (1994), 104.
21. 'Essay on Morals', *Selected Prose*, 106.
22. The fostering metaphor was introduced in a later revision to Book I: see *Prelude* (1805) I, ll. 305-6; *WW Poems*, 309.
23. DW acknowledged in a half-wistful, half-guilty letter to her Aunt Rawson, on 13 June 1798, that they could not take care of him while travelling (EY, 220). Coleridge's poem 'The Foster-Mother's Tale' was published in *Lyrical Ballads* just after their departure—a valedictory gesture to the boy whose moral growth the Wordsworths had monitored.
24. 'Elegy III', ll. 21–2; LB, 299.
25. The poet couples these two words when he refers to the old man, in 'Elegy V', as 'Our common friend and father'; l. 4; LB, 301.
26. In this respect, Mathew prefigures the Old Cumberland Beggar and the Waggoner.

27. Griggs i, 479.
28. 'Frost at Midnight', l. 54.
29. 'Tintern Abbey', ll. 137–8.
30. WW, addressing DW, describes 'the shooting lights | Of thy wild eyes'; 'Tintern Abbey', ll. 119–20.
31. In the Fenwick Note, he identifies 'the extensive woods that still stretch from the side of Esthwaite Lake towards Graythwaite, the seat of the ancient family of Sandys' (FN, 13).
32. ll. 10–11; LB, 302.
33. ll. 17–22; LB, 302.
34. Internal evidence identifies the central episode as an outing that took place during WW's schooldays at Hawkshead—DW not being present. But in the long version he uses the present tense, describing an incident he has just witnessed.
35. This is the poem's unavoidable meaning if we identify her as 'Lucy'.
36. Johnston (1998), 652.
37. Rigby (2004), 228.
38. Robert Pogue Harrison (1992) reminds us that forests are symbols of a human ancestry that reaches further back than civilization. In literary history, they are often connected with enchantment, and with the unconscious.
39. 'Nutting' was not included in *The Prelude* of 1805, but one of its offshoots, 'I would not strike a flower', provides a gloss on the passage in Book X where WW thanks DW for the 'saving intercourse' she helped him to maintain with his 'true self' (ll. 914–15). In this passage, he expands the ethical and ecological message of 'Nutting' and outlines a personal creed. He turns to the example of a 'beloved maid', whose sympathy for nature is his inspiration:

> For she is Nature's inmate, and her heart
> Is everywhere; even the unnoticed heath
> That o'er the mountains spread its prodigal bells
> Lives in her love. (ll. 24–8; LB, 312–13)

This description of a 'beloved maid' later found its way into the 1805 *Prelude* (XI, ll. 218–22) as an expression of WW's gratitude to both the women closest to him in his adult life. The identity of the 'gentle maid' changed between the manuscript, where she was clearly associated with DW, and *The Prelude*, where the phrase applied equally well to Mary Hutchinson. 'Tactfully or otherwise', as Jonathan Wordsworth puts it (*WW Prel*, 646), this is an indication that the exclusive love WW felt for his sister adapted to include his wife.

40. EY, 253.
41. EY, 250–1.
42. EY, 252.
43. Griggs i, 484.

44. Griggs i, 490.
45. Griggs i, 491.
46. EY, 259.
47. *Notebooks* i, 515.
48. EY, 241.
49. Griggs i, 484.
50. *Notebooks* i, 508.
51. EY, 272.
52. *Prelude* (1805), I, ll. 9–14.

CHAPTER 6

1. 'A Sketch'; Longman DW, 183.
2. Sixteen years afterwards, prompted by snowfall in December, DW could distinctly recall their arrival, 'on the shortest day of the year... at 5 o'clock in the evening' (MY ii, 259).
3. Gray, 8 October 1769, 88.
4. EY, 274.
5. They travelled almost all the way on foot. At Kendal they paused to buy furniture, and took the post-chaise to Grasmere for the last leg of their journey.
6. EY, 274.
7. EY, 278.
8. EY, 279.
9. EY, 274.
10. EY, 275.
11. Coleridge would also doubtless have heard in these words a subliminal echo of 'Three years she grew in sun and shower': 'And hers shall be the breathing balm | And hers the silence and the calm | Of mute insensate things' (ll. 16–18).
12. 'Home at Grasmere', ll. 125–8.
13. *Recollections of the Lakes and Lake Poets*, 122. The travel writer Thomas West describes this as 'the more advantageous station' from which to 'view this romantic vale'. West (1784; repr. 1989), 80.
14. WW sees the butterflies (but not himself) through the filter of literary allusion—'winged creatures that are Lords | Without restraint of all which they behold'—linking them with the castaway in Cowper's poem, 'The Solitude of Alexander Selkirk': 'I am monarch of all I survey; | My right there is none to dispute; | From the centre all round to the sea | I am lord of the fowl and the brute' (ll. 1–4; *Poems* i, 403).
15. Revising this passage twenty years later, WW underscored the importance of returning as a *shared* experience, motivated by the Wordsworths' orphaned state. See MS D; HG, 43.
16. Quoted by Vogler (1984), who also connects the name with Julia Kristeva's concept of the 'semiotic'—'a phase of rhythmic babble that precedes the acquisition

of speech and marks the period in which the child is still bound up with the presence of the mother's body'.

17. 'Frost at Midnight', ll. 1–2.

18. The word is used here in the sense that Coleridge intends it, when he writes in 'Dejection' of the 'new Earth and new Heaven' granted to the mind as it is 'wedded' to nature (ll. 68–9).

19. The sense of holy dedication in this poem is connected with the ongoing project of *The Recluse*, the philosophical poem planned with Coleridge in 1798.

20. Hartman (1971), 172.

21. Bachelard (1994), 99.

22. Griggs i, 582.

23. John Wordsworth, *Letters*, ed. Ketcham (1969), 95.

24. In 'Tintern Abbey' he links the untidiness of hedgerows with the movement of blank verse, describing the way 'little lines | Of sportive wood' have 'run wild' (ll. 16–17).

25. Keats letter, 21 September 1819.

26. EY, 295.

27. Coleridge's honeymoon cottage in 'The Eolian Harp' is filled with the scent of a nearby bean-field, and 'o'ergrown | With white-lowered jasmin, and the broad-leafed myrtle, | Meet emblems they of Innocence and Love!' (ll. 3–5). The jasmines and myrtles reappear, accompanied by the 'tallest rose' which 'peeped in at the chamber-window' in 'Reflections on leaving a Place of Retirement', ll. 1–6.

28. *Guide to the Lakes*, 86.

29. Note to *Grasmere Journal*, 177.

30. Griggs i, 613–14.

31. 'Inscription for an Outhouse', ll. 14–16; LB, 182.

32. ll. 2–8; LB, 180.

33. WW was later to take up the cause in his *Guide to the Lakes*, where he objects to buildings not 'gently incorporated with the works of nature' (86).

34. The solitary of Esthwaite was too self-involved to accept the companionship of the stonechat and the dancing sand-piper, who had approached him as 'visitants' in 'Lines left upon a seat'. WW subliminally remembers them here.

35. For further information on Pocklington, see Brown (2010).

36. ll. 2–8; EPF, 752.

37. EPF, 750.

38. 2 Corinthians 5: 1.

39. Hyde, 42.

40. Neither Coleridge's *Notebooks* nor DW's cryptic journal entries allow us to prove with any certainty who 'built' the poem in its final published form. But both these sources suggest that the seat and the poem were rebuilt in Coleridge's presence, and with his help.

41. *Notebooks* i, 830.
42. *Notebooks* i, 830.

CHAPTER 7

1. 'Home at Grasmere', ll. 659–67.
2. *Grasmere Journal*, 2.
3. See *Grasmere Journal*, 5, 26, 28.
4. See Hartman (1978). This use of capitals in 'Poems on the Naming of Places' reinforces the idea of inscription.
5. McKracken, 193.
6. *Grasmere Journal*, 2.
7. 'The moving accident is not my trade', WW announces, in the opening poem of the volume, 'Hart-Leap Well' (l. 97).
8. *WW Poems*, 697n.
9. McFarland (1981) uses this term.
10. The members of this group are identified by the initials carved on the 'Rock of Names' beside Thirlmere in May 1800: W. W., M. H., D. W., S. T. C., J. W., S. H. (Joanna replaces Sara Hutchinson in the 'Poems on the Naming of Places'.)
11. Bate (1991), 87.
12. Journal for 29 September 1824; *Prose*, ed. Tibble (1951), 110.
13. See my discussion of 'Bob's Lane' in (Newlyn, 2007).
14. FN, 18. WW visited Emma's dell in 1836, with Coleridge's nephew, and observed that a man had drowned in this very spot. Easedale was also associated with the deaths of George and Sarah Green in 1808. See McCracken, 109–10.
15. McCracken, 107.
16. EY, 189.
17. McCracken, 109.
18. In much the same way, WW had relied on the suitability of Town End for their new life together, securing their tenancy of it in her absence.
19. *Paradise Lost*, IX, ll. 456.
20. 'To M. H.', ll. 15–24. 'Wordsworth stated unequivocally that it is 'in Rydal Upper Park' but the poem says—rightly, as it turns out—'The Travellers know it not, and 'twill remain| Unknown to them'; McCracken, 194.
21. 'Home at Grasmere', ll. 168–70.
22. We might link the speaker with the hermit who dwells in the woods in Coleridge's 'The Ancient Mariner', the friar in 'The Foster-Mother's Tale', or the equally sylvan hermit in 'Tintern Abbey'. Bate (1991) has noted that a number of words in this description connote holiness, linking the 'calm recess' with 'a monastery or other place of religious retreat'; 95.
23. FN, 18.
24. BL ii, 104.

25. See *Poly-Olbion* (1622), Song XXX, ll. 155–64; quoted by Coleridge in *BL* ii, 104. Bate (1991) discusses WW's echo of the passage (99).

26. *Grasmere Journal*, 14.

27. 'The Nightingale', l. 15.

28. *Grasmere Journal*, 23–4.

29. *Grasmere Journal*, 25.

30. *Grasmere Journal*, 25.

31. WW was revising his 1798 poem 'The Discharged Soldier' at the time 'A Narrow Girdle' was written, and a number of verbal echoes connect these two studies of men wasted by poverty and hardship. The lines 'for my single self I looked at them, | Forgetful of the body they sustained' is a verbatim quotation from the earlier poem.

32. WW and DW had already met him on 3 October 1800—an encounter recorded in detail in her journal. They may have discussed his loneliness and poverty during the writing of 'A narrow girdle', but WW did not write the poem about him until two years later.

33. 'Come near—thin, pale, can scarce speak—or throw out his fishing-rod' (*Notebooks* i, 761.)

34. Barrell (1980).

35. 'Home at Grasmere', ll. 444–5.

36. De Quincey observed in his *Recollections* that it was DW rather than WW who 'took upon herself the whole expenses of the flying colloquies exchanged with stragglers on the road' (211).

37. *Grasmere Journal*, 3.

38. 'Home at Grasmere', ll. 620–2. See Stafford (2008).

39. 'Home at Grasmere', l. 635.

40. EY, 314–15.

41. EY, 649.

42. *Notebooks* i, 541.

43. *Notebooks* i, 541.

44. 'Journey out of Essex', *Autobiographical Writings*, ed. Robinson (1983), 160.

45. FN, 10. WW used an interleaved copy of Coleridge's *Poems* (1796) at an early stage of composition; then moved on to a notebook, which was later used by DW for her *Grasmere Journal* of February 1802–January 1803. These two manuscripts contain draft material of lines which either occur in 'Michael' or were intended for it. The hand is WW's.

46. *Grasmere Journal*, 26.

47. EY, 322.

48. EY, 315.

49. The phrase is Edward Thomas's. Bate (1991) has analysed the connection between the 'Household Poems' composed by Thomas for his family, and WW's 'Poems on the Naming of Places'.

50. 'Michael', ll. 457–9.

CHAPTER 8

1. *Grasmere Journal*, 2.
2. The first notebook (DC MS 20), which DW used for her journal between 14 May and 22 December 1800, contained material from her seven months in Germany—jottings, sums, lists of clothes and groceries, phrases in German and English—as well as some material written down while in Sockburn (epitaphs, a version of WW's 'The Forsaken Indian Woman' in DW's hand, and two small drawings). The second notebook (DC MS 25), in which she recorded events from 10 October 1801 to 14 February 1802, dated back to 1798. At one end it contained sums and expenses from Hamburg and a list of reading matter jotted in the margins; at the other end DW had written her *Hamburg Journal* from 14 September to 1 October, 1798. In addition, WW had used it in late 1799–1800 for drafts of 'The Brothers' and 'Poems on the Naming of Places' I, III, and V. The fourth and final notebook contained the *Grasmere Journal* from 4 May 1802 to 16 January 1803. Before that, WW had used it to draft material for 'Michael' composed in 1800 and some stanzas for 'Ruth', as well as passages copied from Descartes in WW's hand. (For a more detailed account of the contents of each journal, see Woof's notes to the *Grasmere Journal*.)
3. Typically, swallows make their nests from mud and plant fibres against beams in buildings. DW writes about a pair of swallows building outside her window during the spring and summer of 1802, and their return the following year. See my next chapter.
4. *Grasmere Journal*, 66 (and note on 219–20); 104 (and note on 250).
5. Anderson (1795), xi, 780.
6. 'Home at Grasmere', ll. 620–2. See Stafford (2008).
7. Woof (1992), 173.
8. See Wolfson (1988), 139–66.
9. On Thursday 4 February 1802, she was 'enchanted' by reading 'The Idiot Boy'; and the following day she 'got into sad thoughts' after reading LB. See *Grasmere Journal*, 74–5.
10. *Common Reader* ii, 170.
11. 'Tintern Abbey', ll. 24–36.
12. 'The Pedlar', ll. 178–80; spring 1798 variant: see J. Wordsworth (1969), 175; RCP, 345.
13. For the concept of de-familiarization, see Shklovsky; in Lodge (1988), 20.
14. *Grasmere Journal*, ix.
15. *Grasmere Journal*, 39, 48, 84.
16. *Grasmere Journal*, ix.
17. *Common Reader* ii, 171.
18. *Common Reader* ii, 166–7.
19. 'Tintern Abbey', l. 31.
20. *WW Poems*, 64.

21. Woof (1992), 176.
22. By contrast with the two poems written just before, this one is improvisatory and spontaneous. 'Alice Fell' was written at the request of Mr Graham, and 'Beggars' followed DW's journal closely.
23. 'Home at Grasmere', l. 622.
24. Heaney (2008), 24.
25. PTV, 323; Sara Hutchinson's fair copy of the first version of 'Resolution and Independence'.
26. EY, 366–7.
27. EY, 766.
28. EY, 367. Gittings and Manton (1985) observe rather censoriously that 'Dorothy's automatic rush to justify William was not only ridiculous in itself; it pointed the way to dangers which even Coleridge was quick to notice barely a year later' (151–2).
29. Heaney (2008), 24.
30. Hazlitt reported in his essay 'My First Acquaintance with Poets' (1823) that Coleridge lamented 'something corporeal' in his friend's writing—'a *matter-of-factness*, a clinging to the palpable'. (Hazlitt ix, 104.)
31. Heaney (2008), 26.
32. Gill (1989), 195.
33. The phrase is Woof's; see ch. 3 above.
34. Woodmansee (2002), 9.
35. The poem, composed between March 1804 and April 1807, was later published in *Poems, in Two Volumes* (1807).
36. *WW Poems*, 73.
37. *FN*, 14.
38. 'It was an April Morning', ll. 37–9.
39. Mabey (2008), 174.
40. *An Evening Walk* (1794), l. 128; this passage is discussed in ch. 2.

CHAPTER 9

1. 'The Orchard Pathway', ll. 1–6; PTV, 63.
2. l. 52; BW, 118.
3. On 20 April Coleridge records in his Notebook, 'Cut my name & Dorothy's over the S.H. at Sara's rock' (*Notebooks* i, 1163); and on 4 May 1802, Dorothy writes in her journal, 'We parted from Coleridge at Sara's Crag after having looked at the Letters which C carved in the morning. I kissed them all. Wm deepened the T with C's penknife. We sate afterwards on the wall, seeing the sun go down & the reflections in the still water' (*Grasmere Journal*, 95).
4. EY, 332–3. The letter is written in two parts, the first in DW's hand, the second in WW's.

5. EY, 359.
6. EY, 348. In this, the first version of the poem, the woman is named as 'Emma'; later this is changed to Lucy. See 'Among all lovely things my love had been', ll. 13–20.
7. EY, 348.
8. EY, 348.
9. Perry (2004), 109.
10. Perry (2004), 142.
11. 'My heart leaps up when I behold', l. 9.
12. *Grasmere Journal*, 27, 79, 82, 91, 93.
13. ll. 10–11; EPF, 762.
14. 'To a Butterfly' ('Stay near me'), l. 8.
15. 'To a Butterfly' ('I've watched you'), ll. 10–11.
16. The poem resembles verses DW later wrote for WW and Mary's children, and after publication in 1807 it was skilfully parodied in *The Simpliciad* (1808).
17. ll. 12–14; PTV, 76.
18. The allusion is to Book XI of *Paradise Lost* (l. 186) where, as the note to the poem says, 'Adam points out to Eve the ominous sign of the Eagle chasing "two birds of gayest plume", and the gentle Hart and Hind pursued by their enemy.'
19. In his poem 'A Farewell', WW alludes to the sparrow's nest and to his poem about it. DW refers in her journal for Friday 7 May to the nest, packed with tiny fledglings: 'The sparrows are now fully fledged. The nest is so full that they lie upon one another, they sit quietly in their nest with closed mouths' (*Grasmere Journal*, 97).
20. FN, 8.
21. John 14: 2.
22. There is an extra internal rhyme at line 4, 'bushes', which would be a full rhyme in Westmorland dialect.
23. 'The Twa Dogs', ll. 153–4: 'at operas and plays parading, | Mortgaging, gambling, masquerading'.
24. Milton, *Paradise Lost*, IV, ll. 52.
25. Spenser, 'Epithalamion', ll. 110, 204–5.
26. 'Four days will quickly steep themselves in night; | Four nights will quickly dream away the time; | And then the moon, like to a silver bow | New-bent in heaven, shall behold the night | Of our solemnities' (act I, sc. i, 7–11).
27. EY, 377.
28. See Woof (1988), 46.
29. 'A slumber did my spirit seal; | I had no human fears: | She seemed a thing that could not feel | The touch of earthly years' (ll. 1–4).
30. *Grasmere Journal*, note, 266.
31. 'There is a trickling water', ll. 9–12;, PTV, 530.
32. *Grasmere Journal*, 132. On 31 October, Dorothy visited Sara's gate with Mary, another commemorative ritual.

33. EY, 393.
34. EY, 394; he was born a month earlier than expected, on 18 June.

CHAPTER 10

1. 'The Solitary Reaper', ll. 17–24.
2. EY, 397.
3. EY, 421.
4. *Recollections*, 344.
5. *Recollections*, 344.
6. De Selincourt refers to these two MSS as A and B respectively, reproducing B in his edition, from which I quote.
7. Sara Hutchinson made two copies in 1806 (DC MS 55: Ci and Cii), the first of which she prepared for Coleridge as a gift, to mark his return from Malta in 1806. DW's later copy (DC MS 97) was written in 1822–3, at a time when she was hoping to get the book published.
8. Stafford (2007), 99.
9. Stafford (2007), 101.
10. *Recollections*, 214.
11. *Recollections*, 255; Griggs ii, 975.
12. *Recollections*, 309.
13. On arrival at Bunawe, DW records that the travellers observed the place 'with pleasure for poor Ann Tyson's sake'; *Recollections*, 309.
14. *Recollections*, 289.
15. Most famously by Samuel Johnson in his ethnographic study, *Journey to the Western Islands of Scotland* (1773), and James Boswell in his anecdotal and opinionated *Journal of a Tour to the Hebrides* (1773); by William Gilpin in his aesthetic guidebook, *Observations, Relative chiefly to Picturesque Beauty* (1789); and by John Stoddart in *Remarks on Local Scenery and Manners in Scotland during the years 1799 and 1800*.
16. Stoddart compares a valley in the Strath of Appin with Grasmere, and quotes from the opening of 'Tintern Abbey' to evoke its pastoral seclusion (ii, 20). He alludes to 'The Brothers' as 'a local eclogue, of a new, and original species' (ii, 30). He also quotes from WW's address to DW in 'Tintern Abbey' (ii, 340).
17. EY, 256.
18. Burns, 'A Bard's Epitaph', ll. 13-18.
19. 'Address to the Sons of Burns, after visiting their Father's Grave', ll. 19–24.
20. A phrase of WW's, from 'To a Sexton' (composed in Goslar), l. 28.
21. *Notebooks* i, 1450
22. *The Seasons*, 'Summer', ll. 12–13.
23. 'Went with the Jacobin Traitor of a Boatman to Rob Roy's Cave.' *Notebooks* i, 1469.
24. WW's head-note to 'Rob Roy's Grave'; *WW Poems*, 250.

25. 'At Rob Roy's Grave', ll. 6–8; *Recollections,* 373.
26. See, for instance, *Recollections*, 291, 331, 372.
27. Elizabeth Bohls (1995) writes about DW's awkward self-estrangement.
28. *Notebooks* i, 1471.
29. *Notebooks* i, 1468.
30. Griggs ii, 994.
31. Griggs ii, 1010.
32. Griggs ii, 1013.
33. *Notebooks* i, 1463.
34. *Recollections*, 290.
35. Griggs ii, 979.
36. Griggs ii, 982.
37. Stoddart ii, 17.
38. James Hogg, in his patriotic ballad 'The Stewarts of Appin', would later celebrate the way in which local associations with Ossian's heroic deeds mingled with those of the Stewart clan.
39. 'Bonnie Dundee' was John Graham of Claverhouse, who received fatal musket wounds in the battle.
40. 'The humble petition of Bruar water', ll. 73, 77, 33–6.
41. The Duke of Atholl (nicknamed 'Planter John') made the first plantations in the winter of 1796–97. They were in European larch and Scots pine.
42. *Journey to Western Islands*, 55.
43. 'Stepping Westward', ll. 1–8.
44. EY, 590.
45. EY, 590–1.
46. Henderson (1932), i, 166–7.
47. *Tait's Edinburgh Magazine*, iv, New Series (1837), 219.
48. 'The Matron of Jedburgh and her Husband', ll. 33–4.
49. *Notebooks* i, 1452.
50. *Notebooks* i, 1489.
51. *Notebooks* i, 1495.
52. *WW Poems*, 73.
53. 'By the bye I am writing not a journal for we took no notes, but *recollections* of our Tour in the form of a journal', she wrote to Mrs Clarkson on 13 November 1803 (EY, 421). Nonetheless, she did take occasional notes, and made her own sketches of rivers, which survive in DC MS 54. See *Recollections of a Tour Made in Scotland*, ed. Carol Kyros Walker (1997), 20.
54. For a full evaluation of DW's indebtedness to the picturesque tradition in *Recollections*, see John Glendening (1997), 121–55.
55. I, l. 363; *WW Poems*, 172.
56. *Notebooks* i, 1471.
57. *To the Hebrides*, 237–8.
58. *Journey to Western Islands*, 207.

59. *Journey to Western Islands*, 208.
60. One is reminded of the discharged soldier and the blind beggar in *The Prelude*: figures whose internal worlds the narrator cannot hope to reach.
61. 'Preface' to LB 1800; *WW Poems,* 59.
62. 'To a Highland Girl', ll. 42–4.
63. 'Stepping Westward', ll. 9–26.
65. Stafford (2007), 108.
66. WPW iii, 444.
67. 'Ode' ('There was a time'), ll. 186–8.
64. 'The Solitary Reaper', ll. 9–16.

CHAPTER 11

1. *The Prelude* (1805) X, ll. 723–7.
2. *The Prelude* (1805) X, ll. 726–7.
3. *The Prelude* (1805), I, ll. 270–1.
4. 'Resolution and Independence', l. 51.
5. See Perry (2001) on the role of 'accidence' in WW's approach to experience and narrative.
6. 'The woods are lovely, dark and deep, | But I have promises to keep, | And miles to go before I sleep, | And miles to go before I sleep.' Robert Frost, 'Stopping by Woods on a Snowy Evening', ll. 13–16.
7. *Notebooks* i, 1801.
8. EY, 650.
9. Mauss, 16.
10. EY, 408.
11. 'Beaumont, it was thy wish that I should rear', l. 2; PTV, 532.
12. EY, 483.
13. EY, 517.
14. EY, 502.
15. Moorman (1968), ii, 39.
16. EY, 521.
17. EY, 518.
18. EY, 523.
19. EY, 542.
20. EY, 559–60.
21. EY, 598.
22. EY, 597.
23. EY, 593.
24. EY, 593.
25. EY, 598.
26. EY, 598–9.
27. 'I only looked for pain and grief', ll. 41–7.

28. EY, 627.
29. EY, 625–6.
30. EY, 626.
31. EY, 626.
32. EY, 628.
33. De Selincourt suggests that Lady Beaumont—having heard about Lowther in the Wordsworths' letters—may have encouraged DW to write an account of the tour (DWJ i, xiv–xv).
34. DWJ i, 414.
35. 'Ode. The pass of Kirkstone', ll. 40, 27–8, 73–4. Walker (1988) discusses intersections between WW's poem and DW's journal.
36. MY i, 74, 76.
37. MY i, 10.
38. MY i, 43.
39. l. 50; PTV, 95.
40. MY i, 24.
41. Noyes (1968) gives a careful account of the project.
42. MY i, 99.
43. MY i, 138.
44. MY i, 161.
45. MY i, 76.
46. MY i, 150.
47. MY i, 158–9.
48. ll. 94–105; TP, 41–2.

CHAPTER 12

1. *Narrative*, 65.
2. MY i, 201–2.
3. MY i, 205.
4. MY i, 207–14.
5. ll. 1–2; SP, 47.
6. *Narrative*, 86. I am unpersuaded by Michelle Levy's argument (2003) that DW differed sharply from WW in her views on the efficacy of sympathy and charity.
7. The phrase used by John Stoddart to describe WW's pastoral poems, 'The Brothers' and 'Michael'.
8. The Ashburners' predicament provided WW with the germ of his poem 'Repentance'.
9. He had recently visited the house at Cockermouth with Mary (MY i, 230); DW alludes to their visit in a letter written on 19 September 1807; MY i, 165.
10. I quote from the first version of WW's poem, as sent to Coleridge on 19 April (MY i, 220).

11. In the revised version of this poem which appears in WPW, the penultimate line reads: 'In bond of peace, in bond of love' (l. 35; WPW iv, 376).
12. *Narrative*, 8.
13. MY i, 207.
14. FN, 40.
15. MY i, 252–3.
16. MY i, 337.
17. MY i, 337–8.
18. MY i, 376.
19. SHL, 36.
20. A fair copy of Book V survives, written by Mary Wordsworth.
21. MY i, 449.
22. Despite his deepening conservatism, the terminology he uses to describe this community of 'statesmen' is far from Burkean. It was, he says, 'a perfect Republic of Shepherds and Agriculturalists . . . *a pure Commonwealth*' (74).
23. Published in an edition edited by Darlington (1981).
24. MY ii, 535.
25. *The Excursion*, III, l. 407.
26. MY ii, 114.
27. SIP, 49.
28. Sonnet I.
29. SIP, 77.
30. BL i, 195–6.
31. WPW iii, 503.
32. SIP, 99.
33. SIP, 99.
34. 'The River Duddon' sonnets, IV, l. 1; SIP, 58 ; all further references to the Duddon sonnets are to SIP, by line and sonnet number.
35. *Narrative*, 53.
36. WPW iii, 505.
37. 'To the Rev. Dr W—', ll. 16–20.
38. SIP, 91.
39. 'Tintern Abbey', ll. 35–6; SIP, 78.
40. For the first version, see SP, 583, 643. The revised one is printed in SIP, 71.
41. *Two-Part Prelude*, I, ll. 9–11.
42. 'It was an April Morning', ll. 3, 40–1.
43. Kroeber (1990), 179–96.
44. 'Tintern Abbey', ll. 110–12.
45. Sonnet VIII, l. 13.
46. Mauss, 25–6.
47. Hyde, 73.
48. Hyde, 77.
49. Georg Simmel, quoted by Hyde, 91.

50. It was only in 1835, technically its fifth edition, that the book was published under the name by which it is now known, *A Guide through the District of the Lakes*.
51. *Guide to the Lakes*, 108.

CHAPTER 13

1. CJ, 294.
2. MY ii, 572.
3. MWJ, 10 July.
4. CJ, 23. Mary's journal, too, clearly signals her sense that the Alps provided their journey's 'end and aim'; MWJ, 6 July.
5. MWL, 60.
6. HCRD iii, 38; 196.
7. HCRD iii, 339.
8. CJ, 262.
9. HCRD ii, 259; BTW i, 271.
10. Letter to Dora Wordsworth; MWJ, 20 February 1821.
11. MWJ, 7 August.
12. LY i, 115.
13. MWL, 81.
14. LY i, 271.
15. LY i, 337.
16. DC MS 90, i, 376.
17. LY l, 113.
18. MWL, 81.
19. LY i, 104.
20. CJ, 116.
21. BTW i, 272.
22. De Selincourt reduced the length of DW's journal by about a quarter, and Helen Boden reprints De Selincourt's text. Neither Mary's travel notebooks nor her journal have been published in book form.
23. MWJ, 11 July.
24. CJ, 10.
25. MWJ, 14 July.
26. 'A Parsonage in Oxfordshire', ll. 4–9; SIP, 232–3.
27. CJ, 23.
28. See sonnets II and III of *Memorials*, both entitled 'Bruges'; SIP, 359-60.
29. MWJ, 13 July; CJ, 19, 21.
30. MWJ, 12 July.
31. MWJ, 18 July.
32. CJ, 12.
33. DC MS 90, i, 23.

34. DC MS 90, i, 44.
35. CJ, 22; *Prelude*, VI, ll. 449–50.
36. Barbauld, 'Eighteen Hundred and Eleven', l. 170.
37. CJ, 27.
38. *A Poet's Pilgrimage to Waterloo* (London, 1816), 62, 66; Part One, III (The Field of Battle'; xxvi, xxxv.
39. *Childe Harold*, Canto III, ll. 239–43.
40. MY ii, 280.
41. CJ, 29.
42. 'After Visiting the Field of Waterloo', ll. 7–8; SIP, 231.
43. DC MS 90, i, 57.
44. CJ, 36.
45. CJ, 35.
46. MWJ, 19 July.
47. DC MS 90, i, 124–5.
48. ll. 3, 14; SIP, 361–2.
49. CJ, 57.
50. CJ, 38.
51. CJ, 86.
52. CJ, 89, 282, 132.
53. CJ, 150.
54. CJ, 180.
55. CJ, 259.
56. CJ, 135.
57. CJ, 158.
58. MWL, 61.
59. CJ, 86, 89, 172, 289.
60. HCRC i, 101.
61. CJ, 89–90.
62. CJ, 161.
63. CJ, 96.
64. CJ, 165.
65. DC MS 90, ii, 34, 213–14.
66. DC MS 90, ii, 210.
67. CJ, 129.
68. CJ, 171; MWJ, 20 August.
69. MWJ, 13 and 24 August.
70. CJ, 125, 128, 130, 135, 214.
71. CJ, 260.
72. CJ, 219.
73. *The Prelude* VI, ll. 578–9.
74. CJ, 259.
75. CJ, 259.

76. CJ, 266.
77. CJ, 260–1.
78. CJ, 280.
79. CJ, 281.
80. ll. 3–4; SIP, 763.
81. 1827 headnote to 'Elegiac stanzas'; SIP, 392.
82. ll. 740–2; DS, 110.
83. ll. 532–4; DS, 90.
84. 'I have in the press a little book on the Lakes, containing some illustrative remarks on Swiss scenery…The part relating to Switzerland is new' (LY i, 120).
85. WW's note; SIP, 415.
86. WW's note; SIP, 376.
87. MWJ, 7 August.
88. CJ, 105–6.
89. CJ, 257.
90. 'The Column intended by Buonaparte for a triumphal edifice in Milan', ll. 7–9; SIP, 387.
91. SIP, 377.
92. CJ, 163.
93. MWJ, 11 September.
94. CJ, 185–6.
95. SIP, 374.
96. MW Notebook II, unpublished.
97. Rousseau, in his *Dictionnaire de Musique* (1767), claimed that Swiss mercenaries were threatened with severe punishment to prevent them from singing their Swiss songs, evocative of homeland. See my discussion of homesickness in chapter two above.
98. CJ, 312.
99. MWJ, 8 November.
100. MWJ, 7 December.
101. LY i, 113.
102. *WW Poems*, 59.

CHAPTER 14

1. LY ii, 439.
2. LY i, 351.
3. 'Inscription' ('The massy ways, carried across the Height'), ll. 7–9; LP, 57.
4. LY i, 62.
5. LY ii, 191.
6. LY i, 50. De Selincourt provides a useful list of references to *The Recluse* in the correspondence of the Wordsworth circle; see WPW v, 367.

7. HCRD iii, 79.

8. The issue of who accompanied Scott to meet Anna Seward was never satisfactorily resolved; but if I had to put my money on anyone's testimony, it would be DW's becuase of the detail of her recollection. Had she kept going with her *Grasmere Journal* after 1803 we would probably be able to check this out.

9. The notebook is DC MS 98a; the two expansions are DC MS 98b and DC MS 99.

10. HCRD ii, 29. For De Quincey's very different assessment of the book, see my next chapter.

11. 1 June 1825.

12. 13 March 1834.

13. 6 December 1824.

14. 6 May 1825.

15. 16 July 1825.

16. 25 February 1826.

17. 25 April 1826.

18. De Selincourt reads this sentence as 'Life gone from my father's court' (DWJ ii, 401); Ketcham supplies the alternative reading, which I have adopted; see Ketcham Transcript, 51.

19. 'The Primrose of the Rock', ll. 1–6; LP, 169–70.

20. LP, 168.

21. LY ii, 60, 69.

22. DWL, 64.

23. LY ii, 521.

24. JST, 410.

25. LY ii, 504.

26. LY ii, 584.

27. SHL, 391.

28. LY ii, 620.

29. LY ii, 407–8.

30. LY ii, 557.

31. LY ii, 448.

32. See the sixth sonnet in the sequence which begins with the words 'The Pibroch's Note'; LP, 497–8.

33. See 'The Highland Broach'; 'In the sound of Mull'; 'The Avon'; 'Highland Hut'; 'A place of Burial in the South of Scotland'.

34. FN, 48.

35. 'The Trosachs', ll. 1–5; SIP, 497.

36. 'Bothwell Castle', ll. 9–14; SIP, 507.

37. DWJ i, 387–8; SIP, 529.

38. 'Composed in Roslin Chapel, during a storm', ll. 8–14; SIP, 496–7.

39. LY ii, 449.

40. SIP, 520.

41. SIP, 521.
42. SIP, 522.
43. LY ii, 641.
44. LY ii, 630, 632.
45. LY ii, 631.
46. 'Conclusion', ll. 1–8; SIP, 607–8.
47. LY ii, 687.
48. LY iii, 373.
49. On a previous occasion, in May 1832, he had cancelled a trip because she was 'in so weak and alarming [a] state of health'; LY ii, 520.
50. LY iii, 378.
51. LY iii, 396.
52. LY iii, 398.
53. LY iii, 417.
54. LY iii, 403.
55. LY iii, 405.
56. HCRD iii, 138.
57. LY iii, 404.
58. LY iii, 429.
59. 'The Pine of Monte Mario at Rome', 10–12; SIP, 757.
60. 'Composed on May Morning, 1838', 1–3; SIP, 788.
61. LY iv, 396.

CHAPTER 15

1. 'Glad sight wherever new with old', ll. 1–4; LP, 373.
2. LY i, 519.
3. DWL, 55.
4. LY ii, 688.
5. LY ii, 728.
6. LY iii, 41.
7. LY iii, 73, 74.
8. LY iii, 74.
9. LY ii, 669.
10. HCRD iii, 128.
11. LY iv, 210.
12. 'Wansfell! this Household has a favoured lot', ll. 9–14; LP, 372.
13. MY ii, 534.
14. CWM ii, 5.
15. LY iv, 655.
16. 'Sonnet on the Projected Kendal and Windermere Railway', ll. 1–2, 6–8, 8–14.
17. Letter to the *Morning Post*, 9 December 1844; *Selected Prose*, 82.
18. Letter to the *Morning Post*, 12 October 1844; *Selected Prose*, 82.

19. EY, 314–15.
20. LY iii, 83.
21. LY ii, 564.
22. Quoted De Selincourt (1933), 395.
23. LY ii, 564.
24. MWL, 218.
25. Ketcham Transcript, 25.
26. 19 February 1834.
27. 9 January 1835.
28. 10 March 1834.
29. 22 May 1834.
30. 23 November 1834.
31. 24 May 1834.
32. 29 July 1833; quoted in introduction to Ketcham Transcript, 15.
33. LY iii, 472.
34. LY iii, 506.
35. LY iii, 528.
36. LY iii, 528.
37. LY ii, 621.
38. LY ii, 736.
39. ll. 31–3; LP, 281.
40. FN, 10.
41. 'Winter', l. 246.
42. CWM ii, 439–40.
43. Crabb Robinson, for instance, observed that DW 'in her youth and middle age...stood in somewhat the same relation to her brother William as dear Mary Lamb to her brother Charles'. HCRD iii, 78.
44. *Elia*, ed. Bate (1987), 86.
45. ll. 18–19; LP, 87.
46. LY iii, 2.
47. 'Epitaph' (Text of 1836), ll. 86–94; LP, 303.
48. 'Epitaph' (Text of 1836), ll. 94–7; LP, 303.
49. LY iii, 524–5.
50. 'To R. S.', ll. 11–12; LP, 323.
51. LY iii, 524–5.
52. LP, 247.
53. HCRD iii, 35.
54. Griggs vi, 959.
55. De Quincey, ed. Lindop (2003), xix, 399, 397.
56. LY iv, 146.
57. WPW ii, 517.
58. Suppl, 108.
59. Hyde, 37.

60. 'Thoughts on my sick-bed', ll. 33–52.
61. 'Thoughts on my sick-bed', ll. 45–8.
62. HCRD iii, 235.
63. HCRD iii, 236.
64. HCRD iii, 78.
65. HCRD iii, 78.
66. HCRC i, 421.
67. HCRC i, 421.
68. Moorman (1968), ii, 607.
69. Barker (2000), 776.
70. Sacks (2008), 373.
71. Sacks (2008), 259–60.
72. LY iii, 98.

CHAPTER 16

1. 'In Sight of the Town of Cockermouth', ll. 1–4; SIP, 577.
2. Chaudhury (2008).
3. CWM ii, 440.
4. LY iii, 507.
5. FN, 11.
6. Note to 'Personal Talk'; FN, 21.
7. FN, 19.
8. FN, 22.
9. FN, 77.
10. FN, 9.
11. FN, 37.
12. FN, 87.
13. FN, 11.
14. LY iv, 854.
15. HCRD iii, 335.
16. HCRD iii, 79.
17. LY iv, 860.
18. Quoted De Selincourt (1933), 399.
19. Mary, by contrast was 'admirably calm and composed. No complaint or lamentation from her.' HCRD iii, 365.
20. MWL, 352.
21. MWL, 353.
22. HCRD iii, 469.
23. *Reminiscences*, 36.
24. *Reminiscences*, 13.
25. Arnold, 'Memorial Verses April 1850', ll. 60–7.
26. 'Memorial Verses', ll. 45–57.

27. The poet of *The Excursion*, Hazlitt famously complained, saw 'nothing but him-
    self and the universe'; Hazlitt ii, 114.
28. 'There is an Eminence', ll. 14–16.
29. 'The Pedlar', ll. 78–80; Wordsworth, Jonathan (1969), 175.
30. Trickett (1990), 51.
31. Letter to J. H. Reynolds, 3 May 1818.
32. 'Sleep and Poetry', ll. 245–7.
33. Mill, ed. Robson (1989), 121.
34. Woolf, *Letters* iv, 79–80.
35. Hyde, 161.

Bibliography

PRIMARY MATERIALS

Anderson, Robert (ed.), *The Works of the British Poets with Prefaces, Biographical and Critical*, 14 vols (London and Edinburgh: John & Arthur Arch; Bell & Bradfute; and J. Mundell & Co., 1795–1807).

Arnold, Matthew, *The Poems of Matthew Arnold*, ed. Kenneth Allott, Longmans Annotated English Poets (London: Longmans, 1965).

Barbauld, Anna Letitia, *The Works of Anna Lætitia Barbauld; with a memoir*, 2 vols, Romantic Women Poets, 1770–1830 (London: Routledge/Thoemmes Press, 1996).

Beddoes, Thomas, *Hygeia: or Essays Moral and Medical, on the Causes Affecting the Personal State of our Middling and Affluent Classes*, 3 vols (Bristol: J. Mills, 1802–3).

Bewick, Thomas, *The Works of Thomas Bewick*, 5 vols (Newcastle: Emerson Charnley, 1818–32).

Bewick, Thomas, *Memorial Edition of Thomas Bewick's Works*, 5 vols (Newcastle-upon-Tyne: B Quaritch, 1885–7).

Blair, Hugh, *Lectures on Rhetoric and Belles Lettres*, 2 vols (London and Edinburgh: W. Strahan; T. Cadell; and W. Creech, 1783).

Browning, Robert, *The Major Works*, ed. Alan Roberts (Oxford: Oxford University Press, 2009).

Burns, Robert, *The Poems and Songs of Robert Burns*, ed. James Kinsley, 3 vols (Oxford: Clarendon Press, 1968).

Byron, George Gordon Byron, Baron, *The Complete Poetical Works*, ed. Jerome J. McGann, 7 vols (Oxford: Clarendon Press, 1980–93).

Clare, John, *The Prose of John Clare*, ed. J. W. and Anne Tibble (London: Routledge, 1951).

—— *Autobiographical Writings*, ed. Eric Robinson (Oxford: Oxford University Press, 1983).

Coleridge, Samuel Taylor, *Collected Letters of Samuel Taylor Coleridge*, ed. Earl Leslie Griggs, 6 vols (Oxford: Clarendon Press, 1956–71).

—— *The Notebooks of Samuel Taylor Coleridge*, ed. Kathleen Coburn, 5 vols in 10 (Princeton, NJ: Princeton University Press, 1957–2002).

—— *The Collected Works of Samuel Taylor Coleridge*, vol. 7, ed. James Engels and W. Jackson Bate, *Biographia Literaria*, 2 vols (Princeton, NJ: Princeton University Press, 1983).

—— *The Major Works*, ed. H. J. Jackson (Oxford: Oxford University Press, 1985).

—— *The Collected Works of Samuel Taylor Coleridge*, vol. 16, ed. J. C. C. Mays, *Poetical Works*, 2 vols (Princeton, NJ: Princeton University Press, 2001).

Cowper, William, *The Poems of William Cowper*, ed. John D. Baird and Charles Ryskamp (Oxford: Clarendon Press, 1980–95).

Darwin, Erasmus, *The Collected Works of Erasmus Darwin*, introd. Martin Priestman, 9 vols (Bristol: Thoemmes Continuum, 2004).

De Quincey, Thomas, *The Works of Thomas De Quincey*, ed. Grevel Lindop, 21 vols (London: Pickering & Chatto, 2003).

Gilpin, William, *Observations on Several Parts of England: Particularly the Mountains and Lakes of Cumberland and Westmorland, Relative Chiefly to Picturesque Beauty, Made in the Year 1772*; 3rd edition in 2 vols (London: T. Cadell and W. Davies, 1808).

Gray, Thomas, *Thomas Gray's Journal of his Visit to the Lake District in October 1769*, ed. William Roberts (Liverpool: Liverpool University Press, 2001).

—— *A Tour of the English Lakes with Thomas Gray and Joseph Farington RA*, compiled by John R. Murray (London: Frances Lincoln, 2011).

Hartley, David, *Observations on Man: His Frame, His Duty, and His Expectations*, 2 vols (Poole: Woodstock Books, 1998).

Hazlitt, William, *The Selected Writings of William Hazlitt*, ed. Duncan Wu, 9 vols (London: Pickering and Chatto, 1998).

Henderson, T. F. *Minstrelsy of the Scottish Border*, 4 vols (Edinburgh: Oliver and Boyd, 1932).

Hofer, Johannes, 'Medical Dissertation on Nostalgia by Johannes Hofer, 1688', trans. Carolyn Kiser Anspach, *Bulletin of the Institute of the History of Medicine*, 2 (1934), 376–91.

Hutchinson, Sara, *Letters of Sara Hutchinson*, ed. Kathleen Coburn (London: Routledge and Kegan Paul, 1954).

Johnson, Samuel, *A Journey to the Western Islands of Scotland* and James Boswell, *The Journal of a Tour to the Hebrides*, ed. Peter Levi (London: Penguin, 1984).

——, *Samuel Johnson's Journey to the Western Islands of Scotland and James Boswell's Journal of a Tour to the Hebrides*, ed. Ronald Black (Edinburgh: Birlinn, 2007).

Keats, John, *Selected Letters*, ed. Robert Gittings, rev. Jon Mee (Oxford: Oxford University Press, 2002).

Lamb, Charles, *Elia and the Last Essays of Elia*, ed. Jonathan Bate (Oxford: Oxford University Press, 1987).

Lamb, Charles, and Lamb, Mary, *The Letters of Charles and Mary Anne Lamb*, ed. Edwin W. Marrs, Jr, 3 vols (Ithaca, NY: Cornell University Press, 1975).

Leslie, C. R., *Memoirs of the Life of John Constable*, 2nd edition (London: Longman, Brown, Green, and Longmans, 1845).

Lubbock, Tom, Tattersfield, Nigel, and Uglow, Jenny, *Thomas Bewick: Tale-Pieces* (Birmingham: Ikon Gallery, 2009).

Mant, Richard, *The Simpliciad: A Satirico-Didactic Poem containing hints for the poets of the new school* (1808; Oxford: Woodstock Press, 1981).

Mill, John Stuart, *Autobiography*, ed. John M. Robson (London: Penguin Books, 1989).

Milton, John, *Paradise Lost,* ed. Alastair Fowler, second edition, Longman Annotated English Poets (Harlow: Pearson Longman, 2007).

Pennant, Thomas, *A Tour in Scotland, 1769* (1771), introduced by Brian D. Osborne (Edinburgh: Birlinn, 2000).

Priestley, Joseph, *A Course of Lectures on Oratory and Criticism* (London: J. Johnson, 1771).

——*Hartley's theory of the human mind, on the principle of the association of ideas; with essays relating to the subject of it* (London: J. Johnson, 1775).

Robinson, Henry Crabb, *Diary, Reminiscences, and Correspondence*, ed. Thomas Sadler, 3 vols (London: Macmillan, 1869).

——*The Correspondence of Henry Crabb Robinson with the Wordsworth Circle*, ed. Edith J. Morley, 2 vols (Oxford: Clarendon Press, 1927).

——, *Books and their Writers*, ed. Edith J. Morley (London: J. M. Dent and Sons, 1938).

Southey, Robert, *A Poet's Pilgrimage to Waterloo* (London: Longman, Hurst, Rees, Orme, and Brown, 1816).

Stoddart, John, *Remarks on Local Scenery and Manners in Scotland during the years 1799 and 1800*, 2 vols (London: William Miller, 1801).

Thelwall, John, *Poems chiefly written in retirement*, 1801 (Oxford: Woodstock Books, 1989).

The Peripatetic, ed. Judith Thompson (Detroit: Wayne State University Press, 2001).

Thomson, James, *The Seasons,* ed. James Sambrook (Oxford: The Clarendon Press, 1981).

West, Thomas, *Guide to the Lakes* (London and Kendal: Richardson, Urquhart and Pennington, 1778).

——*A Guide to the Lakes in Cumberland, Westmorland and Lancashire* (Oxford: Woodstock Books, 1989).

Wilkinson, Thomas, *Tours to the British Mountains: with the descriptive poems of Lowther, and Emont Vale* (London: Taylor and Hessey, 1824).

Wollstonecraft, Mary, *The Works of Mary Wollstonecraft*, ed. Janet Todd and Marilyn Butler, vi: *Letters Written in Sweden, Norway, and Denmark* (London: Pickering, 1989).

Woolf, Virginia, *The Letters of Virginia Woolf*, ed. Nigel Nicolson, 6 vols (London: Hogarth Press, 1975–1980).

Woof, Robert, *Treasures of the Wordsworth Trust* (Grasmere: Wordsworth Trust, 2005).

Wordsworth, Christopher, *The Early Wordsworthian Milieu: A Notebook of Christopher Wordsworth with a few entries by William Wordsworth*, ed. Z. S. Fink (Oxford: Clarendon Press, 1958).

Wordsworth, Dora, *Letters of Dora Wordsworth*, ed. Howard P. Vincent (Chicago: Pickard & Company, 1944).

Wordsworth, Dorothy, *George and Sarah Green, A Narrative*, ed. Ernest de Selincourt (Oxford: Clarendon Press, 1936).

——*Journals of Dorothy Wordsworth*, ed. Ernest De Selincourt, 2 vols (London: Macmillan, 1941).

——*Home at Grasmere: Extracts from the Journal of Dorothy Wordsworth and from the Poems of William Wordsworth*, ed. Colette Clark (Harmondsworth: Penguin, 1960).

——*Journal of my Second Tour in Scotland, 1822: A Complete Edition of Dove Cottage Manuscript 98 and Dove Cottage Manuscript 99*, ed. Jiro Nagasawa (Tokyo: Kenkyusha, 1989).

——*Dorothy Wordsworth: Selections from the Journals*, ed. Paul Hamilton (London: William Pickering, 1992).

Wordsworth, Dorothy, *Journal of my tour in Hamburgh. The Continental Journals 1798–1820*, ed. Helen Boden (Bristol: Thoemmes Press, 1995).

——*Recollections of a Tour Made in Scotland* (1803), ed. Carol Kyros Walker (New Haven, CT: Yale University Press, 1997).

——*The Grasmere and Alfoxden Journals*, ed. Pamela Woof (Oxford: Oxford University Press, 2002).

——*Dorothy Wordsworth*, ed. Susan Levin. Longman Cultural Edition (New York, San Francisco, and Boston: Longman, 2009).

——'Journal of a Tour on the Continent 1820' (DC MS 90). Unpublished manuscript.

——'Selections from the Rydal Journal, with a Critical Introduction and Notes', ed. Karl Ketcham (unpublished; Wordsworth Trust archive).

Wordsworth, John, *The Letters of John Wordsworth*, ed. Carl H. Ketcham (Ithaca, NY: Cornell University Press, 1969).

Wordsworth, Mary, *The Letters of Mary Wordsworth* (Oxford: Oxford University Press, 1958).

Wordsworth, William *Poetical Works*, ed. Ernest De Selincourt, 5 vols (Oxford: Clarendon Press, 1946).

—— *William Wordsworth*, ed. Stephen Gill. Twenty-First Century Oxford Authors (Oxford: Oxford University Press, 2012).

——*The Salisbury Plain Poems of William Wordsworth*, ed. Stephen Gill (Ithaca, NY: Cornell University Press, 1975).

——*The Prelude, 1798–1799*, ed. Stephen Parrish (Ithaca, NY: Cornell University Press, 1977).

——*Home at Grasmere*, ed. Beth Darlington (Ithaca, NY: Cornell University Press, 1977).

——*Benjamin the Waggoner*, ed. Paul F. Betz (Ithaca, NY: Cornell University Press, 1981).

——*Poems, in Two Volumes, and Other Poems, 1800–1807*, ed. Jared Curtis (Ithaca, NY: Cornell University Press, 1983).

——*An Evening Walk*, ed. James Averill (Ithaca, NY: Cornell University Press, 1984).

——*Descriptive Sketches*, ed. Eric Birdsall with the assistance of Paul M. Zall (Ithaca, NY: Cornell University Press, 1984).

——*The Tuft of Primroses, with Other Late Poems for The Recluse*, ed. Joseph F. Kishel (Ithaca, NY: Cornell University Press, 1986).

——*William Wordsworth Selected Prose* ed. John O. Hayden (Harmondsworth: Penguin, 1988).

——*Shorter Poems, 1807–1820*, ed. Carl H. Ketcham (Ithaca, NY: Cornell University Press, 1989).

——*The Ruined Cottage and The Pedlar*, ed. James Butler (Ithaca, NY: Cornell University Press).

——*'Lyrical Ballads' and Other Poems, 1797–1800*, ed. James Butler and Karen Green (Ithaca, NY: Cornell University Press, 1992).

——*The Fenwick Notes of William Wordsworth*, ed. Jared Curtis (London: Bristol Classical Press, 1993).

——*William Wordsworth, The Prelude: The Four Texts*, ed. Jonathan Wordsworth (Harmondsworth: Penguin, 1995).

——*Early Poems and Fragments, 1785–1797*, ed. Carol Landon and Jared Curtis (Ithaca, NY: Cornell University Press, 1997).

——*Last Poems, 1821–1850*, ed. Jared Curtis (Ithaca, NY: Cornell University Press, 1999).

——*Guide to the Lakes*, ed. Ernest De Selincourt, with a preface by Stephen Gill (London: Frances Lincoln, 2004).

——*Sonnet Series and Itinerary Poems, 1820–45*, ed. Geoffrey Jackson (Ithaca, NY: Cornell University Press, 2004).

——*The Excursion*, ed. Sally Bushell, James A. Butler, and Michael C. Jaye, with the assistance of David García (Ithaca, NY: Cornell University Press, 2007).

——and Wordsworth, Mary, *The Love Letters of William and Mary Wordsworth* ed. Beth Darlington (Ithaca, NY: Cornell University Press, 1981).

——and Wordsworth, Dorothy, *The Letters of William and Dorothy Wordsworth*, i: *The Early Years, 1787–1805*, ed. Ernest De Selincourt, rev. Chester L. Shaver (Oxford: Clarendon Press, 1967).

——*The Letters of William and Dorothy Wordsworth*, ii, iii: *The Middle Years, 1806–1820*, ed. Ernest De Selincourt, rev. Mary Moorman and Alan G. Hill (Oxford: Clarendon Press, 1969–70).

——*The Letters of William and Dorothy Wordsworth*, iv–vii: *The Later Years*, 1821–53, ed. Ernest De Selincourt, rev. Alan G. Hill (Oxford: Clarendon Press, 1978–88).

—— *The Letters of William and Dorothy Wordsworth*, viii: *A Supplement to the Letters*, ed. Alan G. Hill (Oxford: Clarendon Press, 2000).

BIOGRAPHIES

Ashton, Helen, *William and Dorothy* (New York: Macmillan, 1938).

—— and Davies, Katherine, *I Had a Sister: A Study of Mary Lamb, Dorothy Wordsworth, Caroline Herschel and Cassandra Austen* (London: L. Dickson, 1937).

Barker, Juliet, *Wordsworth: A Life* (Harmondsworth: Penguin, 2000).

Byatt, A. S, *Unruly Times: Wordsworth and Coleridge in their Time* (London: Vintage, 1997).

De Selincourt, Ernest, *Dorothy Wordsworth: A Biography* (Oxford: Clarendon Press, 1933).

Ellis, Amanda, *Rebels and Conservatives: Dorothy and William Wordsworth and their Circle* (Bloomington, IN: Indiana University Press, 1997).

Frances Wilson, *The Ballad of Dorothy Wordsworth* (London: Faber, 2008).

Gill, Stephen, *William Wordsworth: A Life* (Oxford: Clarendon Press, 1989).

Gittings, Robert, and Manton, Jo, *Dorothy Wordsworth* (Oxford: Oxford University Press, 1985).

Gunn, Elizabeth, *A Passion for the Particular: Dorothy Wordsworth, A Portrait* (London: Gollancz, 1981).

Hebron, Stephen, *Dove Cottage* (Grasmere: Wordsworth Trust, 2009).

Holmes, Richard, *Coleridge: Early Visions* (London: Hodder and Stoughton, 1989).

—— *Coleridge: Darker Reflections* (London: Harper Collins, 1998).

Hughes-Hallett, Penelope, *Home at Grasmere: The Wordsworths and the Lakes* (London: Collins and Brown, 1993).

Johnston, Kenneth, *The Hidden Wordsworth: Poet, Lover, Rebel, Spy* (New York: W. W. Norton, 1998).

Jones, Kathleen, *A Passionate Sisterhood: The Sisters, Wives and Daughters of the Lake Poets* (London: Virago, 1998).

Knight, William A., *Coleridge and Wordsworth In The West Country—Their Friendship, Work, and Surroundings* (New York: Charles Scriber's Sons, 1914).

Lee, Edmund, *Dorothy Wordsworth: The Story of a Sister's Love* (London: James Clarke, 1886).

Legouis, Emile, *The Early Life of William Wordsworth: 1770–1798*, trans. J. W. Matthews (London: J. M. Dent & Co., 1921).

Maclean, Caroline Macdonald, *Dorothy and William Wordsworth* (Cambridge: Cambridge University Press, 1927).

Manley, Seon, *Dorothy and William Wordsworth: The Heart of a Circle of Friends* (New York: Vanguard Press, 1974).

Mayberry, Tom, *Coleridge and Wordsworth: The Crucible of Friendship* (Trowbridge: Alan Sutton, 1994).

McCracken, David, *Wordsworth and the Lakes: A Guide to the Poems and Their Places* (Oxford: Oxford University Press, 1984).

Moorman, Mary, *William Wordsworth: A Biography*, 2 vols (London: Oxford University Press, 1968).

Orel, Harold (ed.), *William Wordsworth, Interviews and Recollections* (Basingstoke: Palgrave Macmillan, 2005).

Rawnsley, H. D. (ed.), *Reminiscences of Wordsworth among the Peasantry of Westmoreland* (London: Jackson, 1968).

Sisman, Adam, *The Friendship: Wordsworth and Coleridge* (London: Harper Press, 2006).

Walker, Carol Kyros, *Breaking Away: Coleridge in Scotland* (New Haven, CT: Yale University Press, 2002).

Wordsworth, Christopher, *Memoirs of William Wordsworth*, 2 vols (London: E. Moxon, 1851).

Worthen, John, *The Gang: Coleridge, the Hutchinsons, and the Wordsworths in 1802* (New Haven, CT: Yale University Press, 2001).

Wu, Duncan, *Wordsworth: An Inner Life* (Oxford: Blackwell, 2002).

CRITICAL STUDIES OF THE WORDSWORTHS

Baron, Michael, *Language and Relationship in Wordsworth's Writing* (London: Longman, 1995).

Bate, Jonathan, *Romantic Ecology: Wordsworth and the Environmental Tradition* (London: Routledge, 1991).

Bateson, F. W., *Wordsworth: A Re-interpretation* (London: Longmans, Green, 1956).

Benis, Toby R., *Romanticism on the Road: The Marginal Gains of Wordsworth's Homeless* (Basingstoke: Palgrave Macmillan, 2000).

Bennett, Andrew, *Wordsworth Writing* (Cambridge: Cambridge University Press, 2008).

Blank, G. Kim, *Wordsworth and Feeling: The Poetry of an Adult Child* (Madison, NJ: Fairleigh Dickinson University Press, 1995).

Buchanan, Carol, *Wordsworth's Gardens* (Lubbock, TX: Texas Tech University Press, 2001).

Cervelli, Kenneth R., *Dorothy Wordsworth's Ecology* (London: Routledge, 2007).

Chandler, James K., *Wordsworth's Second Nature: A Study of the Poetry and Politics* (Chicago: University of Chicago Press, 1984).

Easson, Angus, *The Lapidary Wordsworth: Epitaphs and Inscriptions* (Winchester: King Alfred's College, 1981).

Eigerman, Hyman, *The Poetry of Dorothy Wordsworth* (New York: Columbia University Press, 1940).

Ellis, David, *Wordsworth, Freud and the Spots of Time: Interpretation in 'The Prelude'* (Cambridge: Cambridge University Press, 1985).

Fay, Elizabeth A., *Becoming Wordsworthian: A Performative Aesthetics* (Amherst, MA: University of Massachusetts Press, 1995).

Fletcher, Pauline, and Murphy, John (eds), *Wordsworth in Context* (Lewisburg, PA: Bucknell University Press, 1992).

Fosso, Kurt, *Buried Communities: Wordsworth and the Bonds of Mourning* (Albany, NY: State University of New York Press, 2004).

Friedman, Michael, *The Making of a Tory Humanist: William Wordsworth and the Idea of Community* (New York: Columbia University Press, 1979).

Fry, Paul H., *Wordsworth and the Poetry of What We Are* (New Haven, CT: Yale University Press, 2008).

Gill, Stephen, *Wordsworths's Revisitings* (Oxford: Oxford University Press, 2011).

Gilpin, George H. (ed.), *Critical Essays on William Wordsworth* (Boston, MA: G. K. Hall, 1990).

Gravil, Richard, *Wordsworth's Bardic Vocation, 1787–1842* (Basingstoke: Palgrave Macmillan, 2003).

Hanley, Keith, *Wordsworth: A Poet's History* (Basingstoke: Palgrave, 2001).

Harrison, Margaret, *Earth, Air, Sky and Water* (Grasmere: Wordsworth Trust, 2006).

Hartman, Geoffrey, *Wordsworth's Poetry* (Cambridge, MA: Harvard University Press, 1971).

——'Wordsworth, Inscriptions, and Nature Poetry', *Beyond Formalism: Literary Essays 1958–1970* (New Haven, CT: Yale University Press, 1978).

—— *The Unremarkable Wordsworth* (London: Methuen, 1987).

Hayden, Donald E., *Wordsworth's Travels in Scotland* (Tulsa, OK: University of Tulsa Press, 1985).

Johnston, Kenneth R. and Ruoff, Gene W. (eds), *The Age of William Wordsworth: Critical Essays on the Romantic Tradition* (New Brunswick, NJ: Rutgers University Press, 1987).

Jones, Mark, *The 'Lucy Poems': A Case Study in Literary Knowledge* (Toronto: University of Toronto Press, 1995).

Kneale, J. Douglas, *Monumental Writing: Aspects of Rhetoric in Wordsworth's Poetry* (Lincoln, NE: University of Nebraska Press, 1988).

Kroeber, Karl, *Romantic Landscape Vision: Constable and Wordsworth* (Madison, WI: University of Wisconsin Press, 1975).

Langan, Celeste, *Romantic Vagrancy: Wordsworth and the Simulation of Freedom* (Cambridge: Cambridge University Press, 1995).

Levin, Susan M., *Dorothy Wordsworth and Romanticism* (Jefferson, NC: McFarland, 2009).

Lindenberger, Herbert, *On Wordsworth's Prelude* (Princeton, NJ: Princeton University Press, 1963).

McCracken, David, *Wordsworth and the Lake District: A Guide to the Poems and their Places* (Oxford: Oxford University Press, 1984).

Magnuson, Paul, *Coleridge and Wordsworth: A Lyrical Dialogue* (Princeton, NJ: Princeton University Press, 1988).

Matlak, Richard E., *The Poetry of Relationship: The Wordsworths and Coleridge, 1797–1800* (New York: St Martin's Press, 1997).

Nichols, Ashton, *The Revolutionary 'I': Wordsworth and the Politics of Self-Presentation* (New York: St Martin's Press, 1998).

Noyes, Russell, *Wordsworth and the Art of Landscape* (Bloomington, IN: Indiana University Press, 1968).

Onorato, Richard J., *The Character of the Poet: Wordsworth in 'The Prelude'* (Princeton, NJ: Princeton University Press, 1971).

Oswald, Peter, Oswald, Alice, and Woof, Robert (eds), '*Earth has not anything to shew more fair': A Bicentenary Celebration of Wordsworth's Sonnet 'Composed upon Westminster Bridge, 3 September 1802'* (Grasmere: Shakespeare's Globe and the Wordsworth Trust, 2002).

Page, Judith W., *Wordsworth and the Cultivation of Women* (Berkeley, CA: University of California Press, 1994).

Prynne, J. H., *Field Notes: 'The Solitary Reaper' and Others* (Cambridge: Barque Press, 2007).

Reed, Mark, *Wordsworth: The Chronology of the Early Years, 1770–1799* (Cambridge, MA: Harvard University Press, 1967).

—— *Wordsworth: The Chronology of the Middle Years, 1800–1815* (Cambridge, MA: Harvard University Press, 1975).

Roe, Nicholas, *Wordsworth and Coleridge: The Radical Years* (Oxford: Clarendon Press, 1988).

Ruoff, Gene W., *Wordsworth and Coleridge: The Making of the Major Lyrics, 1802–1804* (New Brunswick, NJ: Rutgers University Press, 1989).

Sheats, Paul D., *The Making of Wordsworth's Poetry 1785–98* (Cambridge, MA: Harvard University Press, 1973).

Simonsen, Peter, *Wordsworth and Word-preserving Arts: Typographic Inscription, Ekphrasis and Posterity in the Later Work* (Basingstoke: Palgrave Macmillan, 2007).

Trott, Nicola, and Perry, Seamus (eds), *1800: The New 'Lyrical Ballads'*, Romanticism in Perspective: Texts, Cultures, Histories (Basingstoke: Palgrave, 2001).

Wilson, Douglas B., *The Romantic Dream: Wordsworth and the Poetics of the Unconscious* (Lincoln, NE: University of Nebraska Press, 1993).

Woof, Pamela, *Dorothy Wordsworth, Writer* (Grasmere: Wordsworth Trust, 1988).

—— and Harley, Madeline, *The Wordsworths and the Daffodils* (Grasmere: Wordsworth Trust, 2002).

Wordsworth, Jonathan, *The Music of Humanity* (Oxford: Clarendon Press, 1969).

—— *William Wordsworth: The Borders of Vision* (Oxford: Clarendon Press, 1982).

Wu, Duncan, *Wordsworth's Reading 1770–1799* (Cambridge: Cambridge University Press, 1993).

Wyatt, John, *Wordsworth's Poems of travel, 1819–42: 'Such Sweet Wayfaring'* (Basingstoke: Palgrave Macmillan, 1999).

GENERAL STUDIES

Aaron, Jane, *A Double Singleness: Gender and the Writings of Charles and Mary Lamb* (Oxford: Oxford University Press, 1991).

Alexander, Meena, *Women in Romanticism: Mary Wollstonecraft, Dorothy Wordsworth and Mary Shelley* (Savage, MD: Barnes and Noble, 1989).

Austin, Linda M., *Nostalgia in Transition, 1780–1917* (Charlottesville, VA: University of Virginia Press, 2007).

Bachelard, Gaston, *The Poetics of Space* (Boston, MA: Beacon Press, 1994).

Bardazzi, Giovanni, and Grosrichard, Alain (eds), *Dénouement des Lumières et Invention Romantique*, Histoire des Idées et Critique Littéraire Series, 407 (Geneva: Droz, 2003).

Barrell, John, *The Dark Side of the Landscape: The Rural Poor in English Painting* (Cambridge: Cambridge University Press, 1980).

——*Poetry, Language and Politics* (Manchester: Manchester University Press, 1988).

Bate, Jonathan, *The Song of the Earth* (London: Picador, 2000).

Batten, Guinn, *The Orphaned Imagination: Melancholy and Commodity Culture in English Romanticism* (Durham, NC: Duke University Press, 1998).

Benstock, Shari (ed.), *The Private Self: Theory and Practice of Women's Autobiographical Writings* (Chapel Hill, NC: University of North Carolina Press, 1988).

Bohls, Elizabeth A., *Women Travel Writers and the Language of Aesthetics, 1716–1818* (Cambridge: Cambridge University Press, 1995).

Bowlby, John, *Attachment and Loss*, 3 vols (London: Pimlico, 1997–2010).

Brinkley, Robert and Hanley, Keith (eds), *Romantic Revisions* (Cambridge: Cambridge University Press, 1992).

Brown, M. E., *A Man of No Taste Whatsoever: Joseph Pocklington 1736–1817* (Milton Keynes: Author House, 2010).

Bushell, Sally, *Text as Process: Creative Composition in Wordsworth, Tennyson, and Dickinson* (Charlottesville, VA: University of Virginia Press, 2009).

Chaudhury, Habib, *Remembering Home: Rediscovering the Self in Dementia* (Baltimore, MD: Johns Hopkins University Press, 2008).

Crisafulli, Lilla Maria, and Pietropoli, Cecilia (eds), *Romantic Women Poets: Genre and Gender* (Amsterdam: Rodopi, 2007).

Dolan, Brian, *Ladies of the Grand Tour* (London: Harper Collins, 2002).

Duff, David and Jones, Catherine (eds), *Scotland, Ireland, and the Romantic Aesthetic* (Lewisburg, PA: Bucknell University Press, 2007).

Evans, Dylan, *Emotion: A Very Short Introduction* (Oxford: Oxford University Press, 2003)

Farrell, Michael P., *Collaborative Circles: Friendship Dynamics and Creative Work* (Chicago: Chicago University Press, 2001).

Foster, Jonathan K., *Memory: A Very Short Introduction* (Oxford: Oxford University Press, 2009).

Fothergill, Robert A., *Private Chronicles: A Study of English Diaries* (Oxford: Oxford University Press, 1974).

Freud, Sigmund, *The Standard Edition of the Complete Psychological Works of Sigmund Freud*, gen. ed. James Strachey, 24 vols (London: Hogarth Press and the Institute of Psycho-Analysis, 1953–74), vol. 14: *On the* History of the Psycho-Analytic Movement, Papers on Metapsychology, and Other Works.

Gilroy, Amanda (ed.), *Romantic Geographies: Discourses of Travel, 1775–1844* (Manchester: Manchester University Press, 2000).

Glendening, John, *The High Road: Romantic Tourism, Scotland and Literature, 1720–1820* (Basingstoke: Palgrave Macmillan, 1997).

Godelier, Maurice, *The Enigma of the Gift* (Cambridge: Polity Press, 1999).

Hebron, Stephen, Shields, Conan, and Wilcox, Timothy (eds), *The Solitude of Mountains: Constable and the Lake District* (Grasmere: Wordsworth Trust, 2006).

Hacking, Ian, *Mad Travellers: Reflections on the Reality of Transient Mental Illness* (Cambridge, MA: Harvard University Press, 2002).

Hagglund, Betty, *Tourists and Travellers: Women's Non-Fictional Writing about Scotland, 1770–1830* (Bristol: Channel View Publications, 2010).

Hall, Jean, *A Mind That Feeds Upon Infinity: The Deep Self in English Romantic Poetry* (London: Associated University Presses, 1991).

Harrison, Robert Pogue, *Forests: The Shadow of Civilisation* (Chicago: University of Chicago Press, 1992).

Hartman, Geoffrey H., *Beyond Formalism: Literary Essays, 1958–1970* (New Haven, CT: Yale University Press, 1970).

Heinzelman, Kurt, *The Economics of the Imagination* (Amherst, MA: Massachusetts University Press, 1980).

Homans, Margaret, *Women Writers and Poetic Identity: Dorothy Wordsworth, Emily Brontë, and Emily Dickinson* (Princeton, NJ: Princeton University Press, 1980).

—— *Bearing the Word: Language and Female Experience in Nineteenth-Century Women's Writing* (Chicago: Chicago University Press, 1986).

Hyde, Lewis, *The Gift: How the Creative Spirit Transforms the World* (Edinburgh: Canongate Books, 2007).

—— *Common as Air: Revolution, Art, and Ownership* (New York: Farrar, Straus and Giroux, 2010).

Jarvis, Robin, *Romantic Writing and Pedestrian Travel* (Basingstoke: Palgrave Macmillan, 1997).

John-Steiner, Vera, *Creative Collaboration* (Oxford: Oxford University Press, 2000).

Kamijima, Kenkishi (ed.), *Centre and Circumference: Essays in English Romanticism* (Tokyo: Kirihara for the Association of English Romanticism in Japan, 1995).

Keith, W. J., *The Poetry of Nature: Rural Perspectives in Poetry from Wordsworth to the Present* (Toronto: University of Toronto Press, 1980).

Kinsley, Zoë, *Women Writing the Home Tour: 1682–1812* (Aldershot: Ashgate, 2008).

Klein, Melanie, *Love, Guilt and Reparation and Other Works, 1921–1945* (London: Vintage, 1998).

Krawczyk, Scott, *Romantic Literary Families*, Nineteenth-Century Major Lives and Letters (Basingstoke: Palgrave Macmillan, 2009).

Lambert, Ladina Bezzola, and Ochsner, Andrea (eds), *Moment to Monument: The Making and Unmaking of Cultural Significance*, Cultural Studies Series, 32 (Beilefeld: Transcript, 2009).

Lee, Hermione, *Body-Parts: Essays on Life-Writing* (London: Pimlico, 2008).

—— *Biography: A Very Short Introduction* (Oxford: Oxford University Press, 2009).

Mabey, Richard, *Nature Cure* (London: Vintage Books, 2008).

McDayter, Ghislaine, Batten, Guinn, and Milligan, Barry, *Romantic Generations: Essays in Honor of Robert F. Gleckner* (Lewisburg, PA: Bucknell University Press, 2001).

McFarland, Thomas, *Romanticism and the Forms of Ruin* (Princeton, NJ: Princeton University Press, 1981).

Malpas, J. E., *Place and Experience: A Philosophical Topography* (Cambridge: Cambridge University Press, 1999).

Manning, Peter J., *Reading Romantics: Text and Context* (Oxford: Oxford University Press, 1990).

Mauss, Marcel, *The Gift: Forms and Functions of Exchange in Archaic Societies* (London: Routledge and Kegan Paul, 1923; repr. 1969).

Mellor, Anne K. (ed.), *Romanticism and Feminism* (Bloomington, IN: Indiana University Press, 1988).

—— *Romanticism and Gender* (New York: Routledge, 1993).

Miller, Christopher R., *The Invention of Evening: Perception and Time in Romantic Poetry* (Cambridge: Cambridge University Press, 2006).

Newlyn, Lucy, *Coleridge, Wordsworth, and the Language of Allusion*, 2nd edition (Oxford: Oxford University Press, 2001).

—— *Branch-Lines: Edward Thomas and Contemporary Poetry* (London: Enitharmon Press, 2007).

Oerlemans, Onno, *Romanticism and the Materiality of Nature* (Toronto: University of Toronto Press, 2002).

Olney, James, *Studies in Autobiography* (New York: Oxford University Press, 1988).

O'Shea, Michael, *The Brain: A Very Short Introduction* (Oxford: Oxford University Press, 2006).

Østermark-Johansen, Lene, *Romantic Generations: Text, Authority and Posterity in British Romanticism* (Copenhagen: Museum Tusculanum Press, University of Copenhagen, 2003).

Peer, Larry H. (ed.), *Inventing the Individual: Romanticism and the Idea of Individualism* (Provo, UT: International Conference on Romanticism, 2002).

Perry, Ruth, *Novel Relations: The Transformation of Kinship in English literature and Culture 1748–1818* (Cambridge: Cambridge University Press, 2004).

—— and Brownley, Martine Watson (eds), *Mothering the Mind: Twelve Studies of Writers and their Silent Partners* (New York: Holmes and Meier, 1984).

Phillips, Adam, and Taylor, Barbara, *On Kindness* (London: Penguin, 2009).

Pinker, Stephen, *The Language Instinct: The New Science of Language and Mind* (New York: Harper Collins, 1994).

Piper, H. W., *The Active Universe: Pantheism and the Concept of the Imagination in the English Romantic Poets* (London: Athlone Press, 1962).

Richardson, Alan, *British Romanticism and the Science of Mind* (Cambridge: Cambridge University Press, 2001).

Richter, Gerhard (ed.), *Literary Paternity, Literary Friendship: Essays in Honor of Stanley Corngold*, University of North Carolina Studies in the Germanic Languages and Literatures, 125 (Chapel Hill, NC: University of North Carolina Press, 2002).

Ricks, Christopher, *Allusion to the Poets* (Oxford: Oxford University Press, 2004).

Rigby, Kate, *Topographies of the Sacred: The Poetics of Place in European Romanticism* (Charlottesville, VA: University of Virginia Press, 2004).

Robinson, Jeffrey C., *The Walk: Notes on a Romantic Image* (Norman, OK: University of Oklahoma Press, 1989).

Roe, Nicholas, *The Politics of Nature: Wordsworth and Some Contemporaries* (Basingstoke: Palgrave Macmillan, 1992).

——(ed.), *English Romantic Writers and the West Country* (Basingstoke: Palgrave Macmillan, 2010).

Runco, Mark A., and Pritzker, Stephen R. (eds), *Encyclopedia of Creativity*, 2 vols (San Diego, CA: Academic Press, 1999).

Sacks, Oliver, *Musicophilia: Tales of Music and the Brain* (London: Vintage, 2008).

Solnit, Rebecca, *Wanderlust: A History of Walking* (New York: Verso, 2002).

Spencer, Jane, *Literary Relations: Kinship and the Canon 1660–1830* (Oxford: Oxford University Press, 2005).

Stafford, Fiona, *Local Attachments: The Province of Poetry* (Oxford: Oxford University Press, 2010).

Stelzig, Eugene (ed.), *Romantic Autobiography in England* (Farnham: Ashgate, 2009).

Stone, Marjorie, and Thompson, Judith, *Literary Couplings: Writing Couples, Collaborators, and the Construction of Authorship* (Madison, WI: University of Wisconsin Press, 2006).

Tadmor, Naomi, *Family and Friends in Eighteenth-Century England: Household, Kinship, and Patronage* (Cambridge: Cambridge University Press, 2001).

Vickers, Neil, *Coleridge and the Doctors, 1795–1806* (Oxford: Clarendon Press, 2004).

Vygotsky, Lev, *Thought and Language*, ed. Alex Kozulin (Cambridge, MA: MIT Press, 1986).

Wallace, Anne D., *Walking, Literature, and English Culture: The Origins and Uses of Peripatetic in the Nineteenth Century* (Oxford: Clarendon Press, 1993).

Weiner, Annette, *Inalienable Possessions: The Paradox of Keeping while Giving* (Berkeley, CA: University of California Press, 1992).

Whalley, George, *Coleridge and Sara Hutchinson and the Asra Poems* (London: Routledge & Kegan Paul, 1955).

Willinksy, John (ed.), *The Educational Legacy of Romanticism* (Waterloo, ON: Wilfrid Laurier University Press for the Calgary Institute for the Humanities, 1990).

Willy, Margaret, *Three Woman Diarists: Celia Fiennes, Dorothy Wordsworth, Katherine Mansfield*, Writers and their Work Series, 173 (London: Longmans, Green for the British Council and the National Book League, 1964).

Wolfson, Susan J., *Romantic Interactions: Social Being & the Turns of Literary Action* (Baltimore, MD: Johns Hopkins University Press, 2010).

Woolf, Virginia, *The Common Reader: Second Series*, ed. Andrew McNeillie (London: Hogarth Press, 1986).

Wu, Duncan (ed.), *A Companion to Romanticism* (Oxford: Blackwell, 1998).

Zimmerman, Sarah M., *Romanticism, Lyricism, and History* (Albany, NY: State University of New York Press, 1999).

Zwierlein, Anne-Julia (ed.), *Gender and Creation: Surveying Gendered Myths of Creativity, Authority, and Authorship* (Heidelberg: Universitätsverlag Winter, 2010).

ESSAYS AND ARTICLES

Aldridge, D., 'Alzheimer's Disease: Rhythm, Timing and Music as Therapy', *Biomedicine and Pharmacotherapy*, 48:7 (1994), 275–81.

Alexander, Meena, 'Dorothy Wordsworth: The Grounds of Writing', *Women's Studies*, 14:3 (1988), 195–210.

Axcelson, John, '"The Dial's Moral Round": Charting Wordsworth's *Evening Walk*', *English Literary History*, 73:3 (Fall 2006), 651–71.

Bahar, Saba, 'Invention et Réinvention Britannique du Bonheur Suisse: *Descriptive Sketches* (1793) de William Wordsworth', in Bardazzi, Giovanni, and Grosrichard, Alain (eds), *Dénouement des Lumières et Invention Romantique*, Histoire des Idées et Critique Littéraire Series, 407 (Geneva: Droz, 2003), 263–76.

Barrell, John, 'The Uses of Dorothy: "The Language of Sense" in "Tintern Abbey"', *Poetry, Language and Politics* (Manchester: Manchester University Press, 1988) 137–67.

Bawer, Bruce, '"My Dear, Dear Sister": The Life of Dorothy Wordsworth', *The New Criterion*, 4:5 (January 1986), 26–34.

Bell, Susan Groag, 'Women Create Gardens in Male Landscapes: A Revisionist Approach to Eighteenth-Century English Garden History', *Feminist Studies*, 16:3 (Fall 1990), 471–91.

Birdsall, Eric, 'Nature and Society in *Descriptive Sketches*', *Modern Philology*, 84:1 (August 1986), 39–52.

Boden, Helen, 'Matrilineal Journalising: Mary and Dorothy Wordsworth's 1820 Continental Tours and the Female Sublime', *Women's Writing*, 5:3 (1998), 329–52.

Bond, Alec, 'Reconsidering Dorothy Wordsworth', *Charles Lamb Bulletin*, 47–8 (July-October 1984), 194–207.

Brownstein, Rachel Mayer, 'The Private Life: Dorothy Wordsworth's Journals', *Modern Language Quarterly*, 34:1 (March 1973), 48–63.

Butler, James A., 'Wordsworth's *Descriptive Sketches*: The Huntington and Cornell Copies', *Huntington Library Quarterly*, 46:2 (Spring 1983), 175–80.

——'Tourist or Native Son: Wordsworth's Homecomings in 1799–1800', *Nineteenth-Century Literature*, 51:1 (June 1996), 1–15.

Carroll, Robert, 'Finding the Words to Say it: The Healing Power of Poetry', *Evidence-based Complementary and Alternative Medicine*, 2:2 (2005), 161–72.

Chun, Sehjae, '"Tokens of a Mutual Bond": Sympathy in William Wordsworth's "Preface" and *Home at Grasmere*', *Nineteenth Century Literature in English*, 8:2 (2004), 151–72.

Comitini, Patricia, '"More than Half a Poet": Vocational Philanthropy and Dorothy Wordsworth's *Grasmere Journals*', *European Romantic Review*, 14:3 (September 2003), 307–22.

Cook, Kay K., 'Immersion', *a/b: Auto/Biography Studies*, 10:1 (Spring 1995), 66–80.

Coulehan, Jack, and Clary, Patrick, 'Healing the Healer: Poetry in Palliative Care', *Journal of Palliative Medicine*, 8:2 (April 2005), 382–9.

Crangle, Sara, '"Regularly Irregular... Dashing Waters": Navigating the Stream of Consciousness in Wordsworth's The Grasmere Journals', *Journal of Narrative Theory*, 34: 2 (Summer 2004), 146–72.

Crisafulli, Lilla Maria, 'Within or Without? Problems of Perspective in Charlotte Smith, Anna Laetitia Barbauld and Dorothy Wordsworth', in Crisafulli, Lilla Maria, and Pietropoli, Cecilia (eds), *Romantic Women Poets: Genre and Gender* (Amsterdam: Rodopi, 2007), 35–61.

Dangerfield, Anthony, '"The Faded Plain": Memory and Experience in Wordsworth's *An Evening Walk*', *The Wordsworth Circle*, 17:3 (Summer 1986), 164–8.

Dann, Joanne, 'Some Notes on the Relationship between the Wordsworth and the Lowther Families', *The Wordsworth Circle*, 11:2 (Spring 1980), 80–2.

Darlington, Beth, 'Reclaiming Dorothy Wordsworth's Legacy', in Johnston, Kenneth R. and Ruoff, Gene W. (eds), *The Age of William Wordsworth: Critical Essays on the Romantic Tradition* (New Brunswick, NJ: Rutgers University Press, 1987), 160–72.

Davidoff, Leonore, 'Kinship as a Categorical Concept: A Case Study of Nineteenth Century English Siblings', *Journal of Social History*, 39:2 (Winter 2005), 411–28.

Davis, Robert Con, 'The Structure of the Picturesque: Dorothy Wordsworth's Journals', *The Wordsworth Circle*, 9:1 (Winter 1978), 45–9.

Dugas, Kristine Ann, 'Literary Journals: Explorations in a Private Literary Form', *Dissertation Abstracts International*, 45:5 (November 1984), 1406A.

Easley, Alexis, 'Wandering Women: Dorothy Wordsworth's *Grasmere Journals* and the Discourse on Female Vagrancy', *Women's Writing*, 3:1 (1996), 63–77.

Edgecombe, Rodney Stenning, 'Regionalisms Ancient and Modern', *Classical and Modern Literature*, 14:1 (Fall 1993), 43–60.

Ehnenn, Jill, 'Writing Against, Writing Through: Subjectivity, Vocation, and Authorship in the Work of Dorothy Wordsworth', *South Atlantic Review*, 64:1 (Winter 1999), 72–90.

Essick, Robert N., 'Gender, Transgression, and the Two Wordsworths in "Tintern Abbey"', *Texas Studies in Literature and Language*, 36:3 (Fall 1994), 291–305.

Fadem, Richard, 'Dorothy Wordsworth: A View from "Tintern Abbey"', *The Wordsworth Circle*, 9:1 (Winter 1978), 17–32.

Ferguson, Frances, 'The Lucy Poems: Wordsworth's Quest for a Poetic Object', *English Literary History*, 40:4 (Winter 1973), 532–48.

Foca, Anna, '"Let Me Be the Calm You Seek": Imagination as (Safe) House in Wordsworth's "Tintern Abbey"', *Bucknell Review*, 42:2 (1998), 31–42.

Fosso, Kurt, 'A "World of Shades": Mourning, Poesis, and Community in William Wordsworth's *The Vale of Esthwaite*', *Modern Language Review*, 93:3 (July 1998), 629–41.

Freud, Sigmund, 'Mourning and Melancholia' (1917), in *The Standard Edition of the Complete Psychological Works of Sigmund Freud*, gen. ed. James Strachey, 24 vols (London: Hogarth Press and the Institute of Psycho-Analysis, 1953–74), vol. 14: *On the History of the Psycho-Analytic Movement, Papers on Metapsychology and Other Works*, 237–58.

Frosch, Thomas R., 'Wordsworth's "Beggars" and a Brief Instance of "Writer's Block"', *Studies in Romanticism*, 21:4 (Winter 1982), 619–36.

Gibson, Iris I. J. M., 'Illness of Dorothy Wordsworth', *British Medical Journal (Clinical Research Edition)*, 285:6357 (18–25 December 1982), 1813–15.

Gill, Stephen, 'Wordsworth and the River Duddon', *Essays in Criticism*, 57:1 (January 2007), 22–41.

Goodman, Kevis, 'Romantic Poetry and the Science of Nostalgia', in Chandler, James and McLane, Maureen N. (eds), *The Cambridge Companion to British Romantic Poetry* (Cambridge: Cambridge University Press, 2008), 195–216.

Grob, Alan, 'William and Dorothy: A Case Study in the Hermeneutics of Disparagement', *English Literary History*, 65:1 (Spring 1998), 187–221.

Hanley, Keith, 'Wordsworth's Grand Tour', in Gilroy, Amanda (ed.), *Romantic Geographies: Discourses of Travel, 1775–1844* (Manchester: Manchester University Press, 2000), 71–92.

——'"Things of which I need not speak": Between the Domestic and the Public in Wordsworth's Poetry', *The Wordsworth Circle*, 34:1 (Winter 2003), 39–43.

Harris, Morag, '"Some Small Distance in the Same Dark Room": Samuel Taylor Coleridge, Sara Hutchinson, Dorothy Wordsworth', *Questione Romantica*, 6 (Autumn 1998), 73–88.

Hartman, Geoffrey H., 'Wordsworth's *Descriptive Sketches* and the Growth of a Poet's Mind', *Publications of the Modern Language Association of America*, 76:5 (December 1961), 519–27.

Hayden, John O., 'The Dating of the "1794" Version of Wordsworth's *An Evening Walk*', *Studies in Bibliography*, 42 (1989), 265–71.

Heaney, Seamus, '"Apt Admonishment": Wordsworth as an Example', *The Hudson Review*, 61:1 (Spring 2008), 19–33.

Heffernan, James A. W., 'The Presence of the Absent Mother in Wordsworth's *Prelude*', *Studies in Romanticism*, 27:2 (Summer 1988), 253–72.

Heinzelman, Kurt, '"Household Laws": Dorothy Wordsworth's *Grasmere Journal*' *a/b:Auto/Biography Studies*, 2:4 (Winter 1986–7), 21–6.

——, 'The Cult of Domesticity: Dorothy and William Wordsworth at Grasmere', in Mellor, Anne K. (ed.), *Romanticism and Feminism* (Bloomington, IN: Indiana University Press, 1988), 52–78.

——'Roman Georgic in the Georgian Age: A Theory of Romantic Genre', *Texas Studies in Literature and Language*, 33:2 (Summer 1991), 182–214.

——'Poetry and Real Estate: Wordsworth as Developer', *Southwest Review*, 84:4 (Autumn 1999), 573–88.

Hill, A. G., 'Poetry and Ecumenism: The Legacy of the Wordsworths', *Lambeth Palace Library Annual Review* (1992), 49–64.

Hoerner, Fred, 'Nostalgia's Freight in Wordsworth's Intimations Ode', *English Literary History*, 62:3 (Fall 1995), 631–61.

Hubbell, Andrew, 'How Wordsworth Invented Picnicking and Saved British Culture', *Romanticism*, 12:1 (2006), 44–51.

Huftel, Sheila, 'Reflections on a Tour Made in Scotland: August 1803', *Contemporary Review*, 249:1447 (August 1986), 89–93.

Jacobus, Mary, '"Distressful Gift": Talking to the Dead', *South Atlantic Quarterly*, 106:2 (Spring 2007), 393–418.

Jarvis, Robin, 'The Wages of Travel: Wordsworth and the Memorial Tour of 1820' *Studies in Romanticism*, 40:3 (Fall 2001), 321–43.

——'Madoc in Scotland: A Transatlantic Perspective on "Stepping Westward"', *European Romantic Review*, 19:2 (April 2008), 149–56.

Johnson, Richard E., 'Wordsworth's Parenting Voice in the Two-Part *Prelude*', *Nineteenth-Century Contexts*, 12:2 (1988), 7–18.

Jump, Harriet, '"That Other Eye": Wordsworth's 1794 Revisions of *An Evening Walk*', *The Wordsworth Circle*, 17:3 (Summer 1986), 156–73.

Kahana, Anne Patricia, 'Illness, Health, and the Romantic Subject: An Intergeneric Study', *Dissertation Abstracts International*, 52:5 (November 1991), 1739A.

Kelley, Paul, 'Charlotte Smith and *An Evening Walk*', *Notes and Queries*, New Series 29:3 (June 1982), 220.

Khan, Jalal Uddin, '"To the Same [Lycoris]": Wordsworth's Uses of Dorothy and Coleridge in a Post-Napoleonic Dialogical Context', *Forum for Modern Language Studies*, 33:4 (October 1997), 315–27.

——'Publication and Reception of Wordsworth's *The River Duddon* Volume', *Modern Language Studies*, 32:2 (Fall 2002), 45–67.

Kim, Benjamin, 'Generating a National Sublime: Wordsworth's *The River Duddon* and *The Guide to the Lakes*', *Studies in Romanticism*, 45:1 (Spring 2006), 49–75.

Kroeber, Karl. 'Home at Grasmere: Ecological Holiness', in Gilpin, George H. (ed.), *Critical Essays on William Wordsworth* (Boston, MA: G. K. Hall, 1990), 179–96.

Larkin, Peter, 'The Secondary Wordsworth's First of Homes: *Home at Grasmere*', *The Wordsworth Circle*, 16:2 (Spring 1985), 106–13.

Laski, Marghanita, 'Dorothy Wordsworth's *Journals*', *Notes and Queries*, 9 (1962), 223–6, 271–2, 296–7.

Lerdahl, F., 'The Sounds of Poetry Viewed as Music', *Annals of the New York Academy of Sciences*, 930 (June 2001), 337–54.

Levy, Michelle, 'The Wordsworths, the Greens, and the Limits of Sympathy', *Studies in Romanticism*, 42:4 (Winter 2003), 541–63.

Liu, Alan, 'On the Autobiographical Present: Dorothy Wordsworth's *Grasmere Journals*', *Criticism*, 26:2 (Spring 1984), 115–37.

Lupini, Barbara, 'Dorothy Wordsworth's Place in English Literature', *English: The Journal of the English Association*, 9:50 (Summer 1952), 46–50.

McCarty, Mari, 'Possessing Female Space: "The Tender Shoot"', *Women's Studies*, 8:3 (1981), 367–74.

McCormick, Anita Hemphill, '"I Shall be Beloved—I Want no More": Dorothy Wordsworth's Rhetoric and the Appeal to Feeling in *The Grasmere Journals*', *Philological Quarterly*, 69: 4 (Fall 1990), 471–93.

McEathron, Scott, 'Stuck at Grasmere: Wordsworth and the Limits of Native Authority', in McDayter, Ghislaine, Batten, Guinn, and Milligan, Barry, *Romantic Generations: Essays in Honor of Robert F. Gleckner* (Lewisburg, PA: Bucknell University Press, 2001), 203–20.

McGavran, James Holt, Jr, '"Alone and Seeking the Visible World": The Wordsworths, Virginia Woolf, and *The Waves*', *Modern Language Quarterly*, 42:3 (September 1981), 265–91.

McKusick, James C., 'Stepping Westward', *The Wordsworth Circle*, 32:3 (Summer 2001), 122–6.

Manning, Peter J., 'Touring Scotland at the Time of the Reform Bill: William Wordsworth and William Cobbett', *The Wordsworth Circle*, 31:2 (Spring 2000), 80–3.

Matlak, Richard E., 'Wordsworth's Lucy Poems in a Psychobiographical Context', *Publications of the Modern Language Association of America*, 93:1 (January 1978), 46–65.

Meiners, Katherine T., 'Reading Pain and the Feminine Body in Romantic Writing: The Examples of Dorothy Wordsworth and Sara Coleridge', *The Centennial Review*, 37:3 (Fall 1993), 487–512.

Modiano, Raimonda, 'Blood sacrifice, Gift Economy and the Edenic World: Wordsworth's *Home at Grasmere*', *Studies in Romanticism*, 32:4 (Winter 1993), 481–521.

Moorman, Mary, 'William and Dorothy Wordsworth', *Essays by Diverse Hands*, 37 (1973), 75–94.

Newlyn, Lucy, 'Dorothy Wordsworth's Experimental Style', *Essays in Criticism*, 57:4 (October 2007), 325–49.

——'Confluence: William and Dorothy Wordsworth in 1798', *Journal for Eighteenth-Century Studies*, 14:2 (June, 2011), 227–45.

——'Wordsworth among the Glow-worms', *Essays in Criticism*, 61:3 (2011), 249–74.

Nichols, Ashton, 'Towards "Spots of Time": "Visionary Dreariness" in *An Evening Walk*', *The Wordsworth Circle*, 14:4 (Autumn 1983), 233–7.

Nussbaum, Felicity A., 'Toward Conceptualizing Diary' in Olney, James, *Studies in Autobiography* (New York: Oxford University Press, 1988), 128–40.

Ozarska, Magdalena, 'Some Observations on Dorothy Wordsworth's Status in English Romanticism', *Respectus Philologicus*, 11:16 (2007), 98–106.

Özdemir, Erinç, 'Two Poems by Dorothy Wordsworth in Dialogic Interaction with "Tintern Abbey"', *Studies in Romanticism*, 44:4 (Winter 2005), 551–79.

Page, Judith W., 'Neatly-Penned Memorials: Dora Wordsworth's Journal of 1828 and the Community of Authorship', *a/b: Auto/Biography Studies*, 17:1 (Summer 2002), 65–80.

——'Dorothy Wordsworth's "Gratitude to Insensate Things": Gardening in *The Grasmere Journals*', *The Wordsworth Circle*, 39:1–2 (Winter–Spring 2008), 19–23.

Palumbo, Linda J., 'Wordsworth's Coleridge in *The River Duddon*', *The Round Table of the South Central College English Association*, 27:2 (Summer 1986), 1–4.

Park, Chankil, '*An Evening Walk* and the Politics of the Picturesque', *Nineteenth Century Literature in English*, 2 (1999), 121–44.

Perry, Seamus, 'Coleridge and Wordsworth: Imagination, Accidence, and Inevitability' in Trott, Nicola and Perry, Seamus (eds), *1800: The New "Lyrical Ballads"*, Romanticism in Perspective: Texts, Cultures, Histories (Basingstoke: Palgrave, 2001).

Ponder, Melinda M., 'Echoing Poetry with History: Wordsworth's Duddon Sonnets and Their Notes', *Genre: Forms of Discourse and Culture*, 21:2 (Summer 1988), 157–78.

Pottle, Frederick A., 'The Eye and the Object in the Poetry of Wordsworth', *Yale Review*, 40 (1950), 27–42.

Powys, Llewelyn, *The Wordsworths in Docset*, ed. Malcolm Elwin (London: Covent Garden Press, 1972).

Randel, Fred V., 'Wordsworth's Homecoming', *Studies in English Literature 1500–1900*, 17:4 (Autumn 1977), 575–91.

Rapaport, Herman, 'Of National Poets and Their Female Companions', in Richter, Gerhard (ed.), *Literary Paternity, Literary Friendship: Essays in Honor of Stanley Corngold*, University of North Carolina Studies in the Germanic Languages and Literatures, 125 (Chapel Hill, NC: University of North Carolina Press, 2002), 197–214.

Reiman, Donald H., 'The Poetry of Familiarity: Wordsworth, Dorothy, and Mary Hutchinson.' In Reiman, Donald H., Jaye, Michael C., and Bennett, Betty T. (eds), *The Evidence of the Imagination: Studies of Interactions Between Life and Art in English Romantic Literature*, 142–77 (New York: New York University Press, 1978).

Reimer, Elizabeth, '"Her Favourite Playmate": Pleasure and Interdependence in Dorothy Wordsworth's "Mary Jones and Her Pet-Lamb"', *Children's Literature*, 37 (2009), 33–60.

Robinson, Daniel, '"Still Glides the Stream": Form and Function in Wordsworth's River Duddon Sonnets', *European Romantic Review*, 13:4 (December 2002), 449–64.

Roe, Nicholas, 'Authenticating Robert Burns', *Essays in Criticism*, 46:3 (July 1996), 195–218.

Rubenstein, Jill, 'Wordsworth and "Localised Romance": The Scottish Poems of 1831', *Studies in English Literature 1500–1900*, 16:4 (Autumn 1976), 579–90.

Ruddick, Bill, '"Clear as Glass, Reflecting all Things": Dorothy Wordsworth's Life and Letters Reconsidered', *Critical Quarterly*, 27:4 (December 1985), 45–9.

Rudy, John G., 'Wordsworth's 1820 Memorials: Emergent Unities in the Selfless Way', *Massachusetts Studies in English*, 10:4 (Fall 1986), 237–53.

Rzepka, Charles J., 'A Gift that Complicates Employ: Poetry and Poverty in "Resolution and Independence"', *Studies in Romanticism*, 28:2 (Summer 1989), 225–47.

Schleifer, Ronald, 'Wordsworth's Yarrow and the Poetics of Repetition', *Modern Language Quarterly*, 38:4 (December 1977), 348–66.

Schmid, Thomas H., 'Strained Tenderness: Wordsworth, Joanna Hutchinson, and the Anxiety of Sisterly Resistance in "To Joanna"', *Studies in Romanticism*, 40:3 (Fall 2001), 401–25.

Schwalm, Helga, 'The Lake Poets/Authors: Topography, Authorship, and Romantic Subjectivities', in Zwierlein, Anne-Julia (ed.), *Gender and Creation: Surveying Gendered Myths of Creativity, Authority, and Authorship* (Heidelberg: Universitätsverlag Winter, 2010), 131–48.

Shin, Kyung-sook, 'The Quest for Home: William and Dorothy Wordsworth's Discourse of Domesticity, 1795–1802', *Dissertation Abstracts International*, 54:4 (October 1993), 1379A.

Shklovsky, Victor, 'Art as Technique' in Lodge, David, *Modern Criticism and Theory: A Reader* (London: Longman 1988), 16–30.

Smith, J. Mark, '"Unrememberable" Sound in Wordsworth's 1799 *Prelude*', *Studies in Romanticism*, 42:4 (Winter 2003), 501–18.

Smith, Nowell, 'The Journals of Dorothy Wordsworth', *English: The Journal of the English Association*, 4:21 (1942), 84–5.

Snyder, William C., 'Mother Nature's Other Natures: Landscape in Women's Writing, 1770–1830', *Women's Studies*, 21:2 (1992), 143–62.

Soderholm, James, 'Dorothy Wordsworth's Return to Tintern Abbey', *New Literary History*, 26:2 (Spring 1995), 309–22.

Soeda, Toru 'On Wordsworth's Yarrow Poems', in Kamijima, Kenkishi (ed.), *Centre and Circumference: Essays in English Romanticism* (Tokyo: Kirihara for the Association of English Romanticism in Japan, 1995), 199–211.

Soule, George, '"The Solitary Reaper" and Other Poems "Written During a Tour of Scotland"', *Charles Lamb Bulletin*, 139 (July 2007), 134–44.

Spargo, R. Clifton, 'Begging the Question of Responsibility: The Vagrant Poor in Wordsworth's "Beggars" and "Resolution and Independence"', *Studies in Romanticism*, 39:1 (Spring 2000), 51–80.

Spencer, Jane, *Literary Relations: Kinship and the Canon, 1660–1830* (Oxford: Oxford University Press, 2005).

Stafford, Fiona, '"Inhabited Solitudes": Wordsworth in Scotland, 1803' in Duff, David, and Jones, Catherine (eds) *Scotland, Ireland, and the Romantic Aesthetic* (Lewisburg, PA: Bucknell University Press, 2007), 93–113.

——"'Plain Living and Ungarnish'd Stories": Wordsworth and the Survival of Pastoral', *Review of English Studies*, 59:238 (February 2008), 118–33.

Svoboda, Eva, McKinnon, Margaret C., and Levine, Brian, 'The Functional Neuroanatomy of Autobiographical Memory: A Meta-analysis', *Neuropsychologia*, 44:12 (2006), 2189–208.

Tappen, Ruth M., Williams, Christine, Fishman, Sarah, and Touhy, Theris, 'Persistence of Self in Advanced Alzheimer's Disease', *Journal of Nursing Scholarship*, 31:2 (1999), 121–5.

Thomson, Heidi, '"We Are Two": The Address to Dorothy in "Tintern Abbey"', *Studies in Romanticism*, 40:4 (Winter 2001), 531–46.

Tillmann, Barbara and Dowling, W. Jay, 'Memory Decreases for Prose, but not for Poetry', *Memory and Cognition*, 35:4 (June 2007), 628–39.

Tomlinson, Bernard, 'Editing Dorothy Wordsworth', *Contemporary Review*, 262:1524 (January 1993), 44–6.

Treadwell, James, 'Thinking of Burns's Place', *The Wordsworth Circle*, 31:2 (Spring 2000), 76–80.

Trickett, Rachel, 'The Language of Wordsworth's Later Poems', *The Wordsworth Circle*, 21:1 (Winter 1990), 46–51.

Trott, Nicola, 'Wordsworth Making Amends', *The Wordsworth Circle*, 21:1 (Winter 1990), 27–34.

Turner, John, '"Hauntings from the Infirmity of Love": Wordsworth and the Illusion of Pastoral', *Studies in Romanticism*, 43:4 (Winter 2004), 623–51.

Tyler, Lisa, 'Big Brother is Watching You: Dorothy Wordsworth's *Alfoxden* and *Grasmere Journals*', *University of Dayton Review*, 23:2 (Spring 1995), 87–98.

Ulmer, William A., 'The Society of Death in *Home at Grasmere*', *Philological Quarterly*, 75:1 (Winter 1996), 67–83.

Vincent, Patrick, 'Monuments and Memorials: Byron and Wordsworth in Post-Napoleonic Switzerland', in Lambert, Ladina Bezzola, and Ochsner, Andrea (eds), *Moment to Monument: The Making and Unmaking of Cultural Significance*, Cultural Studies Series, 32 (Beilefeld: Transcript, 2009), 71–82.

Vlasopolos, Anca, 'Texted Selves: Dorothy and William Wordsworth in *The Grasmere Journals*', *a/b: Auto/Biography Studies*, 14:1 (Summer 1999), 118–36.

Vogler, Thomas A., '"A Spirit, Yet a Woman Too!": Dorothy and William Wordsworth', in Perry, Ruth and Brownley, Martine Watson (eds), *Mothering the Mind: Twelve Studies of Writers and Their Silent Partners* (New York: Holmes and Meier, 1984), 238–58.

Walker, Eric C., 'Dorothy Wordsworth, William Wordsworth, and the Kirkstone Pass', *The Wordsworth Circle*, 19:3 (Summer 1988), 116–21.

Wilcox, Stewart C., 'Wordsworth's River Duddon Sonnets', *Publications of the Modern Language Association of America*, 69:1 (March 1954), 131–41.

Wildschut, Tim, Sedikides, Constantine, Arndt, James, and Routledge, Clay, 'Nostalgia: Content, Triggers, Functions', *Journal of Personality and Social Psychology*, 91:5 (2006), 975–93.

Willinsky, John, 'Lessons from the Wordsworths and the Domestic Scene of Writing', in
Willinksy, John (ed.), *The Educational Legacy of Romanticism* (Waterloo, ON: Wilfrid
Laurier University Press for the Calgary Institute for the Humanities, 1990), 33–53.

Wilner, Joshua, '"I Speak of One from Many Singled Out": Individuation, Singu-
larity, and Agrammaticality in Wordsworth', in Peer, Larry H. (ed.), *Inventing the
Individual: Romanticism and the Idea of Individualism* (Provo, UT: International
Conference on Romanticism, 2002), 193–203.

Wolfson, Susan J., 'Individual in Community: Dorothy Wordsworth in Conversation with William', in Mellor, Anne K. (ed.), *Romanticism and Feminism* (Bloomington, IN: Indiana University Press, 1988), 139–66.

Woodmansee, Martha, 'Collectivities in History', in *Collaboration and Ownership in
the Digital Economy* (London: Arts Council of England, 2002).

Woof, Pamela, 'Dorothy Wordsworth's *Grasmere Journals*: Readings in a Familiar
Text', *The Wordsworth Circle*, 20:1 (Winter 1989), 37–42.

——'Dorothy Wordsworth and the Pleasures of Recognition: An Approach to the
Travel Journals', *The Wordsworth Circle*, 22:3 (Summer 1991), 150–60.

——'Dorothy Wordsworth's Journals and the Engendering of Poetry', in Fletcher,
Pauline, and Murphy, John (eds), *Wordsworth in Context*, Bucknell Review Series,
36:1 (Lewisburg, PA: Bucknell University Press, 1992), 122–55.

——'Dorothy Wordsworth's *Grasmere Journals*: the Patterns and Pressures of
Composition', in Brinkley, Robert, and Hanley, Keith (eds), *Romantic Revisions*
(Cambridge: Cambridge University Press, 1992), 169–90.

——'The *Alfoxden Journal* and Its Mysteries', *The Wordsworth Circle*, 26:3 (Summer
1995), 125–33.

——'Dorothy Wordsworth in 1802', *Charles Lamb Bulletin*, 101 (January 1998), 2–17.

——'Dorothy Wordsworth, Journals', in Wu, Duncan (ed.), *A Companion to Romanticism* (Oxford: Blackwell, 1998), 157–68.

——'The "Lucy Poems": Poetry of Mourning', *The Wordsworth Circle*, 30:1 (Winter
1999), 28–36.

——'Dove Cottage in 1800', *The Wordsworth Circle*, 31:3 (Summer 2000), 133–42.

——'The Interesting in Dorothy Wordsworth's *Alfoxden Journal*', *The Wordsworth
Circle*, 31:1 (Winter 2000), 48–55.

——'Dorothy Wordsworth: Story-teller', *The Wordsworth Circle*, 34:2 (Spring 2003),
103–10.

——'The Solitary Poet at Home', *Charles Lamb Bulletin*, 130 (April 2005), 28–42.

——'Turner, Wordsworth and the Romantic Perception of Weather', in Harrison,
Margaret, *Earth, Air, Sky and Water* (Grasmere: Wordsworth Trust, 2006), 19–29.

——'Dorothy Wordsworth as a Young Woman', *The Wordsworth Circle*, 38:3 (Summer
2007), 130–8.

Woolsey, Linda Mills, 'Houseless Woman and Travelling Lass: Mobility in Dorothy
Wordsworth's *Grasmere Journals*', *Tennessee Philological Bulletin*, 27 (1990), 31–8.

Wu, Duncan, 'Wordsworth and Helvellyn's Womb', *Essays in Criticism*, 44:1 (January 1994), 6–25.

Yungblut, Laura H., 'Dorothy Wordsworth: A Natural Life', *University of Dayton Review*, 24:2 (Winter 1996–7), 31–8.

Zimmerman, Sarah MacKenzie, 'Romantic Lyricism and the Rhetoric of Actuality: Charlotte Smith, Dorothy Wordsworth, and John Clare', *Dissertation Abstracts International*, 53:7 (January 1993), 2386A.

ELECTRONIC RESOURCES

Bewick, Thomas, *Memorial Edition of Thomas Bewick's Works,* 5 vols (1885–7), Online. Available: <http://archive.org/stream/memorialedition02dobsgoog#page/n8/mode/2up> (accessed 06 June 2013).

Bushell, Sally, 'From Goslar to Grasmere: William Wordsworth—Electronic Manuscripts' Online. Available: <http://collections.wordsworth.org.uk/gtog/home.asp> (accessed 18 March 2013).

——'From Goslar to Grasmere: moving through and dwelling in Wordsworth's manuscript spaces' Online. Available: <http://www.landscape.ac.uk/landscape/research/smallergrants/fromgoslar-tograsmere.aspx> (accessed 18 March 2013).

Hess, Scott, 'Three "Natures": Teaching Romantic Ecology in the Poetry of William Wordsworth, Dorothy Wordsworth, and John Clare', *Romantic Pedagogy Commons* (December 2006), Online. Available: <http://www.rc.umd.edu/pedagogies/commons/ecology/hess/hess.html> (accessed 13 March 2011).

Steger, Sara, 'Paths to Identity: Dorothy and William Wordsworth and the Writing of Self in Nature', *Nineteenth-Century Gender Studies*, 5:1 (Spring 2009), Online. Available: <http://www.ncgsjournal.com/issue51/steger.htm> (accessed 13 March 2012).

Wallace, Anne, '"Inhabited Solitudes": Dorothy Wordsworth's Domesticating Walkers', *Nordlit* (Spring 1997), Online. Available: <http://www.hum.uit.no/nordlit/1/wallace.html> (accessed 13 March 2011).

Woods, Bob, Spector, Aimee E., Jones, Catherine A., Orrell, Martin, and Davies, Stephen P., 'Reminiscence Therapy for Dementia', *Cochrane Database of Systematic Reviews*, 2 (2005), Online. Available: <http://onlinelibrary.wiley.com/doi/10.1002/14651858.CD001120.pub2/full> (accessed 13 March 2011).

Wordsworth, Mary, *Mary Wordsworth's Journal of the Continental Tour* 1820 (DC MS 92): Transcript, online. Available: <http://www.day-books.com/diaries/wordsworth.pdf> (accessed 18 March 2013).

Index